# THE WORLD OF
# GOLD

# THE WORLD OF GOLD

**THE INSIDE STORY OF
WHO MINES, WHO MARKETS,
WHO BUYS GOLD**

# TIMOTHY GREEN

Rosendale Press
London

In memory of my father
Alan Leslie Green
1907–1991

First published in Great Britain in 1993 by
Rosendale Press Ltd
Premier House
10 Greycoat Place
London SW1P 1SB

Jacket and book designed by Pep Reiff
Maps and charts by Brian Milton
Production: Edward Allhusen, Old House Books

ISBN 1 872803 06 7

Typesetting: Ace Filmsetting Ltd, Frome, Somerset

Printed and bound in Italy by
G. Canale & Co., SpA, Turin

British Library Cataloguing in Publication Data
A catalogue record for this book is available
from The British Library.

# CONTENTS

# PREFACE

My interest in gold originally began in 1966 with an article for *Fortune* magazine on the London market and the private buying of gold. That article led, through the initiative of Michael Sissons at what was then A.D. Peters the literary agents, to the original *World of Gold*, which was published in March 1968 just as the modern gold market was born with the ending of a fixed gold price.

My long-term involvement with the gold business, however, came when David Lloyd-Jacob at Consolidated Gold Fields offered me a territory 'east of Venice up to and including Hong Kong' to investigate for the first of what became a series of annual gold market surveys. And I have been on that trail ever since, working with the successive editors Peter Fells, Christopher Glynn, David Potts, Louise du Boulay and George Milling Stanley. Fortunately, the demise of Consolidated Gold Fields in 1989 did not end the survey. Phoenix-like, it continued under Gold Fields Mineral Services, led by Stewart Murray and with the able team of Kevin Crisp, Philip Klapwijk and Tony Sutton-Pratt, journeying to the frontiers of the world of gold. I am very grateful to all of them who, over the years, have kept me and often accompanied me, on the road for what must be well over 1 million miles.

This edition of *The World of Gold*, twenty-five years on, is a new book; even the history chapters have been considerably expanded. While I have drawn on some of my previously published material, the gold business has changed so much that it was essentially necessary to start from scratch. My colleague Deborah Russell has helped greatly in assembling the research, especially for the extended section on mining. I must also pay special tribute to Jessica Jacks of RTZ, whose research into and papers on gold loans, hedging and options have been an education to us all.

Among many others in the gold business who have aided me, I am grateful to Irena Podleska who has worked with me over many years on European and North African research, to my great friend Madhusudan Daga in Bombay and to Shantilal Sonawala, now finally retired as president of the Bombay Bullion Association. In North America I have appreciated the assistance of Dr Paul Kavanagh of American Barrick, Paul Warrington at Noranda, Bob Calman and Paddy Broughton at Echo Bay Mines, Gordon Parker and his colleagues at Newmont Mining and Newmont Gold, Donna Redel at Comex and John Lutley and his colleagues at The Gold Institute. My knowledge of the history of gold and the London market was also greatly extended by the work I did for Dr Henry Jarecki at Mocatta Metals, New York, in the 1970s. In Tokyo, I have a special debt to Tanaka K.K., originally to their president, the late Jun-ichiro Tanaka, who was one of the most admired figures in the world of precious metals of the last generation, and now to Tadahiko Fukami, who succeeded him. In Australia, I always appreciate the cheerful thoughts of Ross Louthean at *Gold Gazette* and of Trevor Sykes at *Australian Business*, along with the guidance of Don Mackay Coghill and his colleagues at GoldCorp Australia, Peter Ellery and the staff of the Chamber of Mines and Energy of Western Australia, and Peter Walker at Dominion Mining. In South Africa, my way has been smoothed time and again by Tom Main, the chief executive of the Chamber of Mines, and Robin Plumbridge at Gold Fields of South Africa, along with Kelvin Williams at Anglo American, Gary Maude at Gencor, and Michael Brown at Frankel Pollak Vinderine. And in Rio de Janeiro, Peter Rich has been a consistent helper on Brazilian gold for many years.

At the World Gold Council, I am grateful not only to the chief executive, E.M. (Chick) Hood, but to his worldwide staff, including the 'bureau chiefs' Andre Bisang in Dubai, Jonie Lai in Hong Kong, Michael Barlerin in New York, Kerr Cruikshanks in Singapore and Jeff Toshima in Tokyo.

On the media front, both the *Financial Times* and *Mining Journal*'s International Gold Mining Newsletter, under the editorship of David Bird, are indispensable in alerting any observer of precious metals to what is going on around the globe.

The 'missing persons' here are, of course, the bullion bankers and central bankers in London, Zürich, Geneva, Basel, Frankfurt, Luxembourg, New York, Singapore, Hong Kong, Tokyo, Sydney and Pretoria who have made my research possible over many years. Often they have become good friends and I have followed their careers from 'rep' offices in Beirut or Singapore, to senior positions at home. Their friendship has been one of the things that kept me on the road for so long. They prefer the anonymous cloak of their business, but I am most grateful to them.

Finally, in our own office, I must pay tribute to my wife Maureen for her perceptive editing of the entire typescript, to Pamela Burden for cheerful encouragement, to Sarah Cahill for patient copy-editing and to Pep Reiff for an elegant cover design. My secretary Georgie Robins has done a wonderful job of typing up the book, often sorting out scrambled chapters received by fax, but always impeccably prepared within a few hours.

T.S.G.
London and Lauris
August 1993

# GOLDEN RULES

## Weight

The weight of gold is customarily measured in ounces troy or in metric units.

| | | | | |
|---|---|---|---|---|
| 1 oz troy | = | 31.1035 grams | | |
| 32.15 oz troy | = | 1 kilogram | | |
| 100 oz troy (Comex contract) | = | 3.11 kilograms | | |
| 32.150 oz troy | = | 1 tonne | | |
| 3.75 oz troy | = | 116.64 grams | = | 10 tolas (Indian sub-continent) |
| 1.2 oz troy | = | 37.32 grams | = | 1 tael (Hong Kong) |
| 0.47 oz troy | = | 14.62 grams | = | 1 baht (Thailand) |

## Purity

The purity of gold is described by its 'fineness' (parts per 1,000) or by the carat (karat in the United States) scale.

| Fine gold | | carat |
|---|---|---|
| 1,000 | = | 24 |
| 995 (London good delivery) | | |
| 916 | = | 22 |
| 750 | = | 18 (high quality jewellery) |
| 583.3 | = | 14 |
| 417.7 | = | 10 |
| 375 | = | 9 |
| 333.3 | = | 8 (normally lowest acceptable purity in jewellery in some European countries) |

# Introduction:
# The World of Gold

The world of gold has changed more in the last twenty-five or thirty years than in the preceding three or four thousand. One might argue that the story of the modern gold market began on 15 March 1968, when central banks gave up trying to defend a fixed price at $35 per troy ounce and left it free to float. Certainly that changed the perception of gold as a stable benchmark, which had long been one of its prime credentials; stability gave way to volatility. However, the signal that a fundamental change was due came a year or two earlier when the annual bullion review of Samuel Montagu, the London dealers, observed that in 1965, for the first time in history, the private buying of gold had exceeded mine supply, forcing central banks to sell into the market to hold the price. Until then gold had historically been in the domain of kings and princes, rulers of Egypt like Tutankhamun, and latterly of governments and their central banks; now it was no more the noble metal of the elite, but within the province of everybody.

Yet, what appealed, of course, was precisely its historic reputation. Au is not the chemical symbol for gold by chance, but derives from the Latin *aurum* or 'shining dawn'; Aurora was the Roman goddess of the dawn. The poet Pindar had another analogy in the fourth century BC: 'Gold is the child of Zeus, neither moth nor rust devoureth it.' Benjamin Disraeli had a slightly different view in a famous remark to the House of Commons that more men have been knocked off balance by gold than by love. For at least 6,000 years, men – and women – have fought for it, died for it, cheated for it, slaved for it. The civilizations of ancient Egypt and of Rome were nourished by gold wrested from mines in conditions of unbelievable misery. 'There is absolutely no consideration nor relaxation for sick or maimed, for aged man or weak women,' wrote the historian Diodorus in the first century BC. 'All are forced to labour at their tasks until they die, worn out by misery amid their toil.'

This is a scene not much different from the forced labour that accounted for gold production on many mines in the former Soviet Union at least until the 1960s. While perils to life and the environment have been seen all too clearly in gold rushes by hundreds of thousands of diggers in search of instant riches everywhere from Brazil and Bolivia to Indonesia and the Philippines in the last few years. The television and photographic images of gaunt, mud-covered diggers hauling pay-dirt out of the pit at Serra Pelada in the tropics of Brazil gave us an idea of the way it was. And amid the turmoil of the gold futures trading at Comex in New York, I once asked a floor trader what prompted him to join such a scrum. 'Greed', he said.

The fascination with gold has not been shaken off in the space age. Indeed, the umbilical cord that binds an astronaut to his spacecraft when he walks in space is gold-plated to reflect thermal radiation. When the Americans landed on the moon, gold foil shrouded both the lunar module and the moon buggies as they prowled its surface. The electronic circuitry of satellites and space stations relies on gold contacts and bonding wires. Back on earth, the worries of inflation, currency depreciation and political instability maintain gold as the anonymous lifebelt for all seasons – especially the tough ones. 'Gold takes no account of race, religion, culture or politics,' a dealer in Southeast Asia once remarked to me.

What John Maynard Keynes called 'this barbarous relic' is still the only universally accepted medium of exchange, the ultimate currency by which one nation settles its debts with another. The Soviet Union, on the brink of collapse, sold off or swapped virtually its entire gold reserves between 1989 and 1991 in an effort to sustain its credit. China was forced to liquidate some of its gold in the aftermath of the massacre in Tienanmen Square in 1989, when the world community cut off credit lines. Iraq and Libya have been trying to get around sanctions by selling gold held secretly at home and abroad. The unique advantage of gold is that it is no one else's liability; the dollar, sterling, the Deutschmark, and the yen are. Assets held in currency can be frozen; gold held in your vault cannot and there is always someone, somewhere who will buy it. Gold operates today as the means of exchange for many business transactions in Vietnam because the United States will not lift trade restrictions and allow dollar balances to be cleared through New York.

What governments find convenient, even necessary, so do millions of ordinary people the world over, who see gold as the sheet anchor against devaluations or the hazards of war. Go to Brazil, with its rampant inflation; investors, including large companies, buy gold for the traditional reason – insurance to avoid losing money. Go to Cambodia, struggling to emerge from a generation of merciless civil war, and find gold is payment for a rice crop or for a new motor scooter. Go to China, and see the crowds packing the gold shops that have sprung up in Beijing, Shanghai and Guanghzou, turning their paper yuan, which has depreciated almost daily in the last year or two, into ornaments of pure gold. Talk to Kuwaitis who bargained at check-points with gold bars or ornaments in the hours after Iraq's invasion. Travel on an aircraft from the frontiers of Siberia to Moscow and the man sitting next to you pulls out a little packet of gold nuggets for sale. Even in Italy the premium on the gold sovereign soared to 10 per cent during the currency turmoils of September 1992, when the European Exchange Rate Mechanism was under siege; gold coin gave not just protection but profit when the lira price of gold rose by 24 per cent in a week or two.

Moreover, in many countries gold remains an integral part of social and religious customs, besides being a basic form of savings. From Morocco eastwards to India and beyond, the status of a bride is still judged by the amount of gold in her dowry. An Indian farmer whose crop is good buys gold ornaments from his village goldsmith; if the monsoon fails next year or his wife is ill, he trades them in. As the gold analyst Robert Weinberg observed in a prize-winning essay, 'Gold fills many different roles simultaneously. It can be an adornment and an industrial metal, a means of displaying wealth and an anonymous form of saving, an insurance policy and a gambling chip; it is an international reserve asset yet officially it is not money. In short, it represents different things to different people and they will be driven by different motives at different times.'[1]

The charisma of gold permeates our language. We talk about a 'heart of gold', and a 'golden opportunity' and a 'golden wedding' celebrates fifty years of marriage. A pop star gets a gold record (actually, gold-plated) when a disc sells a million. Credit card companies and airlines reward us with 'gold' cards if our rating is good enough. In the Middle East a gold prize is all the rage in raffles or if you find a lucky voucher with your Lipton's Red Label teabag. Passengers at Sharjah Airport in the Gulf can even buy a raffle ticket for 1 kilo of gold (worth around $13,000).

What makes gold the noblest of metals? Its great strength is its indestructibility. Unlike silver, it does not tarnish and is not corroded by

---

1 Dr Robert Weinberg, 'What would happen to gold as an investment during a sustained period of deflation of the world economy?', Autograph Award, London, 1992.

acid, except by a mixture of nitric and hydrochloric acid (known as Aqua Regia), and dissolves only in cyanide. Gold coins have been recovered from sunken treasure ships after several centuries beneath the sea, looking as bright as new. An archaeologist who found a cache of coins that had been buried a thousand years ago in the Jordanian port of Aqaba said, 'They look as if they just came out of the mint.' The finest achievements of the goldsmith's art in ancient Egypt and in Mycenae have been uncovered, almost unscathed, by archaeologists. Heinrich Schliemann, the great German archaeologist who made most of his money in the California gold rush before going to excavate Troy and Mycenae, was able to telegraph the King of Greece, 'I have looked upon the face of Agamemnon,' after he had recovered a golden death mask at Mycenae.

To primitive man, the first appeal was obviously aesthetic. Gold glinted at him from the beds of streams and he found it easy to work; its beauty and versatility swiftly recommended it above all other metals. It was almost as soft as putty, so malleable that it could be hammered cold even by a primitive goldsmith until it was a thin translucent wafer only five-millionths of an inch thick. One ounce of gold can be beaten into a sheet covering nearly 100 square feet. It is also so ductile that an ounce can be drawn into 50 miles of thin gold wire. And as a superb conductor of electricity, gold has become indispensable for semi-conductors and connectors in computer technology.

Gold is so valuable that a single smuggler can carry $400,000 of it in his briefcase or beneath his shift, slotted into the pockets of a special canvas jacket. Gold refineries find it pays to shut down occasionally to spring-clean their chimneys and rooftops to extract from the soot and grime tiny particles wafted up from their furnaces. When the old Rand Refinery near Johannesburg was demolished in the late 1980s, 400 kilos of gold worth over $5 million was recovered from the floors, walls and ceilings. A London bullion firm used to take up the wooden floor of its vault once in twenty years and burn it, to melt out the specks of gold that had rubbed off the soft bullion bars. The high price of gold a few years ago prompted a California company to sign a contract with the city of Palo Alto to 'mine' its sewage to recover gold from the effluent of the many local microchip factories, which is contaminated with gold used to plate the chips.

Yet, in volume, gold is so dense that all the 120,000 tonnes mined throughout history could be contained in a cube measuring scarcely 24 yards on each side – no more than three or four family houses. The advertisements cultivating gold's image in the United States used to show such a cube dwarfed by the 555-foot high Washington Monument.

Gold's beauty, scarcity and almost mystical appeal as a symbol of power quickly won it divine attributes in antiquity, as a metal with which to adorn temples and offer appeasement to the gods: a custom which persists to this day in Thailand where statues of Buddha are daubed with gold leaf by worshippers, and in India where the Hindu temples hold one of the largest stocks of gold in a sub-continent that is a traditional sponge for precious metals. But the Golden Fleece that Jason and his Argonauts sought so assiduously was no more than a sheepskin which was commonly used then to trap the fine specks of metal in the fast-flowing waters of streams in Asia Minor; Jason's voyage seems to have been prompted by commercial expectations as much as anything.

The ancient science of alchemy, which was practised from well before the birth of Christ until the mid-seventeenth century, was directed in part towards finding or preparing the 'philosopher's stone', which could turn base metals into gold and silver. In its heydey, alchemy was practised by Kings Heraclius I of Byzantium, James IV of Scotland and the Emperor Rudolf II. Charles II of Britain had an alchemical laboratory built beneath the royal bedchamber with access by a private staircase. Charles, like so many of those early kings, was perennially short of cash for his treasury, and clearly dreamed of securing an unlimited source. Chaucer devoted one Canterbury Tale – the Canon's Yeoman's Tale – to the pursuit of the philosopher's stone. The Canon's Yeoman explained:

I seye, my lord can switch subtilitee
That all this ground on which we been ryding,
Til that we come to Caunterbury toun,
He could al clene turne it up-so-doun,
And pave it al of silver and of gold.

All alchemists started supremely confident that the magic formula was within their grasp, only to be finally disillusioned. Bernard of Trèves came up with my favourite recipe in 1450. He mixed 2,000 egg yolks with equal parts of olive oil and vitriol, then cooked this omelette on a slow fire for two weeks. All it did was poison his pigs.

Its aesthetic appeal aside, gold has no intrinsic value. It is hard to imagine being cast up on a desert island with anything more useless. Many primitive societies, particularly in the Pacific, managed very well with no gold at all. They simply adopted the sperm-whale-tooth standard, the boards-with-curved-tusks standard and the shell standard. The Solomon Islands favoured a standard by which 500 porpoise teeth bought one wife with good qualities. Lower down the scale, one shell ring equalled one human head, one very good pig or one male slave of medium qualities. Samoa was happier with the mat standard. 'No lover of money was ever fonder of gold than a Samoan was of his fine mats,' wrote an historian of the Pacific.[2]

It is all in the eye of the beholder. 'The production of shell money in the Pacific for the sake of being piled up in the house of a chief,' wrote the economist Paul Einzig, 'is neither more futile nor less futile than the labour spent on the mining of gold for the sake of being able to bury it once more in the vaults of Fort Knox.'[3]

In fact, for all the trumpetings about gold, it has been available in any real quantity just for the last 140 years. The true gold standard existed only in the fifty years preceding World War I. Before the California rush of 1848–9 ushered in an 'Age of Gold', the metal was in relatively short supply. There simply was not enough to implement a gold standard. It was used mainly as a commodity valuable for ornamental purposes and as a store of wealth of kings, princes, the Church and rich merchants. True, Croesus, King of Lydia (western Turkey), is credited with ordering the world's first gold coins to be struck as far back as 550 BC and the Greeks and Romans also made use of gold coins. However, silver and copper coins were used in harness with gold – and were much more widely accepted as a medium of exchange between ordinary individuals. Only the increasing supplies of gold, first from Brazil in the eighteenth century, then from Russia, California, Australia and South Africa in the nineteenth century, led to the demonetization of silver and enabled gold to become the sole standard of value. More gold was mined in the 100 years 1800 to 1900 than in the preceding 5,000.

The ground rules of the gold standard (more correctly a gold coin standard) were a fixed price for gold, with gold coin forming either the whole circulation of currency within a country or circulating with notes representing, and redeemable in, gold. Internationally, this meant completely free import and export of gold, with all balance-of-payments deficits settled in the metal. Thus, in theory at least, gold disciplined the economy of a country. If it was in deficit, gold flowed out, so there was less for internal circulation or backing of notes; these prices were controlled or came down, exports were more competitive and the balance of payments improved.

This was the standard which Britain adopted, virtually accidentally, in place of silver early in the eighteenth century. Even then the redemption of notes in gold was suspended during the Napoleonic wars; the gold was required instead to finance Wellington's armies against Napoleon. And it was suspended, too, at the outbreak of World War I, and never really came back completely. Politicians did not like the constraints it implied on the printing press. This strength of the gold standard was remarked on by a British Treasury official at a dinner given by Winston Churchill in March 1925 when he was Chancellor of the

2 George Turner, *Samoa a Hundred Years Ago*, London, 1884.
3 Paul Einzig, *Primitive Money*, Eyre & Spottiswoode, London, 1948.

Exchequer and canvassing views about Britain going back to gold. The gold standard, the Treasury man argued, was 'knave [i.e. politician] proof'. The Treasury won. Keynes, also at the dinner, did not agree, especially with the concept of going back on gold at the same price as before the war. But Churchill, overruling him, went for gold.[4] As did another great figure, Charles de Gaulle, one of the last statesmen really to go in to bat for it in a famous press conference in 1965 when he proclaimed, 'There can be no other criterion, no other standard than gold. Yes, gold which never changes, which can be shaped into ingots, bars, coins, which has no nationality and which is eternally and universally accepted as the unalterable fiduciary value par excellence.'

A splendid statement, but it came too late. The world of gold was already moving on; that was the year when private buying took up more than all newly mined gold. Three years later the fixed price was gone. Welcome to the modern world of gold, where it is traded round the world, round the clock, where the price can move more in an afternoon than it previously did over centuries, where jewellery demand alone outstrips mine supply and central banks are helping fill the gap, where it continues to make headlines and generate lively debate. When *The Economist* ran a leader early in 1993 headed, 'Fools' gold' on central bank sales (not before time, in their view), and concluded that for private investors, 'the conclusion is plain; sell', the outrage from gold bugs filled the letters page.[5] 'There is no point in history at which fiat currencies have not eventually become worthless,' snapped an American reader. 'You are quite right that gold will flow from the vaults of the feckless and improvident,' wrote a South African gold miner. 'As always it will flow to where the wealth is being generated. For the foreseeable future – to the East.' The gold standard is dead, long live the gold standard, as operated by perceptive individuals aware of the frailties of knaves. By curious chance the editor of *The Economist* was appointed as the deputy governor of the Bank of England shortly thereafter. A worried South African ambassador, lunching with the Bank's governor Eddie George, wondered what this foreshadowed? A shrewd Eddie George said he had no intention of selling Britain's gold. He is not the only one. I recall an official at the Bank of Thailand telling me that he was called in to see the Prime Minister at some moment of monetary crisis and ordered under no circumstances to sell a single ounce of the country's gold reserve. As for the leaders of most of the new republics in the former Soviet Union, if they have gold mines they want to hang on to the gold as if it were their birthright. The Swiss, of course, know where they stand. 'Forty per cent gold coverage of notes is anchored in legislation,' Jean Zwahlen, a member of the governing body of the Swiss National Bank recently

4 Robert Skidelsky, *John Maynard Keynes: The Economist as Saviour, 1920–1937*, Macmillan, London, 1992, p. 200
5 *The Economist*, 23 January 1993, p. 17; and 11 February 1993, p. 6.

confirmed at a gold miners' dinner. De Gaulle would be delighted.

Central banks though, are but one of the players in the complex and invigorating modern gold business, where the price is made from minute to minute by the interaction of many forces. In every respect the gold industry has matured since 1968 from a rather quixotic little club whose membership had not changed much in centuries (the London gold market had the same team as in 1853) to global traders. When I first made the rounds in 1966, prompted as it happens by that Samuel Montagu report about the scale of private buying, the oldest members of the London market, Mocatta & Goldsmid founded in 1671, consisted of two partners and a dealer working in a small room on an upper floor of Hambros Bank and a gold vault and packing room nearby, which they had been using since 1881 and was of quite Dickensian character. Mocatta today is an international trader in London, New York, Hong Kong and Singapore; as is N.M. Rothschild, which Nathan Mayer Rothschild set up in London in 1810, just in time to liaise with Mocatta in rounding up gold for the Rothschild's European network to spirit to the Duke of Wellington's armies. These old-timers, however, now face tough competition from heavyweight US banks like J.P. Morgan, Goldman Sachs and Republic National Bank of New York in all major markets.

Their presence underlines the biggest single change in gold since 1968 (save the floating price), namely the liberalization of the markets. In those days Americans were not permitted to hold gold privately; US banks could not trade it; Hong Kong did not exist as a market, nor did Japan (which was largely supplied by smuggling), nor did Singapore. The only true markets were London and Zurich. Elsewhere markets, such as they were, were fringe places like Beirut, Dubai, Macao and Vientiane in Laos, which were essentially springboards for smugglers. The barriers have come down virtually everywhere, not just in the United States and Japan but in Taiwan, Turkey and even India, long the largest and most profitable smuggling destination. A mere handful of nations have not yet agreed to open markets, of which the most significant is China, already a major consumer unofficially. Even China is studying how best to come to terms with its newly prospering population's appetite for gold. Thus gold has become legitimate, arriving by the front door, instead of the back.

Which is just as well, because the other revolution has been in gold mining. Higher prices coupled with new technology brought a mining boom in the 1980s that virtually doubled production. Although the initial boom has burned out, production will not decline because the gold miners, like the bullion banks, have gone global in their search.

Gold-mining twenty-five years ago was essentially the story of South Africa, with the Soviet Union as the only other serious contender. In the 1990s the sources of gold are becoming almost as diverse as the people who buy it. In Latin America, for instance, the long search for the legendary El Dorado is reaching its climax, as the origins of the gold of the Incas is tracked. The mining industry which, a generation ago, thought it produced for the ever-open vaults of central banks, has learned about marketing gold to its best customers – the jewellery manufacturers. The World Gold Council spends millions promoting the metal on the mining industry's behalf. The Gold Institute, in Washington DC, reminds senators and congressmen that the United States is now not just the world's second largest producer of gold, but is actually an exporter of gold, thus helping to reduce the deficit (shades of the gold standard).

Despite all this change, the gold business remains a club, at once confidential but loving its gossip. Genuine secrets are preserved, but occasionally a chance remark completes a jigsaw on who did what. My best clue in twenty-five years was revealed at a check-in line at Rome Airport. Everyone knows everyone else; perhaps between 300 and 500 miners and marketeers are the core of the business. When the phone rings in someone's office and he says 'Do you mind if I have a quick word with Freddie (or Martin or Neil)?' you know who it is. As a gold trader remarked to me, 'This market is a big, big family – sometimes we kill each other, but we are smiling at the same time.'

# PART I

# THE HISTORY

**CHAPTER I**

# In the Beginning

To appreciate, indeed to confront, the history of gold, there can be no more moving experience than to look upon the face of Tutankhamun, the boy king who ruled Egypt from about 1361 to 1352 BC. The great mask of solid gold, beaten and burnished, that was found over the head and shoulders of his mummy has an almost haunting presence that astonishes the thousands who have seen it in the Cairo museum or in the exhibition that toured Europe and the United States in the 1970s. Inlaid with semi-precious stones and coloured paste, the mask is a serene portrait in gold of a young man with rather narrow eyes, thin nose and full lips. And it lay in a coffin of solid gold sheet 2 millimetres thick, weighing over 90 kilos. The treasures of Tutankhamun are an unforgettable proof that 3,500 years ago, the techniques of mining, refining and working gold to the highest level of craftsmanship were already well advanced. To ancient civilizations the yellow blaze of gold was associated with the sun: to the Egyptians it was the symbol of the sun god Ra.

This was by no means the beginning. The earliest gold jewellery dates from the Sumer civilization that flourished between the Tigris and Euphrates rivers in southern Iraq around 3000 BC. The range astonished archaeologists who discovered the treasure in the Royal Tombs at Ur. Besides a king's gold helmet of great elegance, decorated in impeccable repoussé technique, and a queenly headdress of golden beech leaves, were earrings, bracelets and foxtail chains (a style still worn). Sumerian jewellery five thousand years ago was almost as sophisticated and varied as today. The goldsmith's skills progressed, so that the Egyptians understood fire assay to test the purity of gold, mastered the art of alloying it with other metals for hardness or colour variations, and casting, including the lost-wax technique which is the heart of much modern jewellery manufacture. Remarkably, similar knowledge was being acquired in parallel by goldsmiths of the Chavin civilization in Peru who, by 1200 BC, were making ornaments by hammering and embossing gold and soon after 500 BC had also learnt to cast gold.

The splendour of the ornaments should not overshadow the fact that gold was also coming to be used as a means of exchange. In China, gold was legalized as money as early as 1091 BC as an alternative to silk, circulating in the form of little squares and somewhat later in small cubes.[1] The first coins containing gold were struck in Asia Minor in the late eighth century BC. They were made from electrum, the natural alloy of gold and silver found in the rivers of the region, and had a design on one side and a seal on the other. The introduction of pure gold and silver coins is generally attributed to the Lydian king, Croesus (561–546 BC). Thereafter gold and silver coins, along with copper, came into increasing use as means of exchange both within states and along the expanding trade routes of the Mediterranean world. Silver, however, was usually pre-eminent, simply because most communities did not have enough gold for it to be commonly used as currency. Only in such civilizations as Mycenae was gold widely used. The Greek and early Roman Empires used gold coinage relatively rarely since it was in short supply.

Although there is no precise estimate of gold production in ancient times, it may have amounted to no more than a tonne or two annually, mainly from Africa in what are now Sudan, Ethiopia and perhaps Zaire, Zimbabwe and, rather later, Ghana. Gold was also found in Saudi Arabia and in rivers around the Black Sea (whither Jason went with his Argonauts, seeking the 'golden fleece' which was actually a reference to the sheep skins used to trap alluvial gold flakes in streams). And it was certainly mined in China before 1000 BC and also by the Pre-Columbian peoples of South America. The Roman Empire in its later years got gold from Spain and Portugal (where it was mined in conditions of unbelievable misery). This production probably increased output towards 5–10 tonnes annually. This supply enabled Rome from the days of Augustus to the third century AD to issue high quality gold coins up to 970 or 980 fine. But as the Roman Empire waned, the coins were increasingly debased (that is to say, they became worn and were clipped) and lost a lot of their value. Through much of the Dark Ages not enough gold reached Western Europe to sustain coinage, although Constantinople (Istanbul),

---

1 Eduard Kann, *The Currencies of China*, Kelly & Walsh, Shanghai, 1926.

as the hub of the Byzantine Empire, was the central market for gold that still circulated in limited amounts along trade routes through the Arab world and on towards the east.

### Venice: The Bullion Market on the Rialto

The roots of the modern gold market, however, can be traced back to the Italian city states of Florence, Genoa and, above all, Venice, that became not only the crossroads of medieval trade, but the birthplace of banking. 'In the later Middle Ages, Venice became the world's leading bullion market, probably handling more exchange of precious metals than any other city in the world,' wrote Frederic Lane and Reinhold Mueller in their seminal study of Venice's role.[2] Silver was coming south from new mines in the German states and from Hungary to be marketed in Venice by German merchants who had their own warehouse and lodgings, the Fondaco dei Tedeschi, just across the Grand Canal from the Rialto where the bankers and exchange dealers had their tables. Gold was arriving in increasing amounts, too, from Africa through caravan routes across the Sahara from West Africa (the Gold Coast), and from a revival of mining in western Sudan. By the mid-fourteenth century additional gold from new mines in Hungary was also flowing into Venice. Imports of gold and silver accounted for 20 per cent of the city's turnover. Venice secured its premier position because it was astride, and came to control, the trade routes to the east. 'Thus, after 1100, the main flow of precious metals moved from west to east,' observe Lane and Mueller. 'Much was hoarded within the Arab lands, but the flow continued eastward into India. The spices and drugs that came from India and the East Indies were to a large extent paid for with gold, silver and copper.'[3] Thus nine centuries ago the basic flows of today's gold market were already being established. Venice itself remained the pivot through the fifteenth century before being supplanted for a while by Amsterdam and then, by the late seventeenth century, by London.

The distinctive feature of the Venetian bullion market was that gold and silver could be freely exported, in strict contrast to most other European countries where export of gold or silver coin was usually prohibited as being a drain on the nation's natural wealth (and so were smuggled). The Rialto in Venice became such a cosmopolitan market place precisely because it was a free market for bullion. Strict regulation was imposed, however, on weighing and assaying all gold and silver, with sales recorded through official brokers. All transactions had to be recorded at the assay office on the Rialto, which was staffed by salaried officials. Assaying was done by touchstone, using needles graded from 1

2 Frederic Lane and Reinhold Mueller, *Money and Banking in Medieval and Renaissance Venice*, Vol. I, *Coins and Moneys of Account*, The Johns Hopkins Univesity Press, Baltimore and London, 1985, p. 134. This volume provides a unique insight into the bullion business from 1200 to 1500.
3 Ibid., p. 135.

to 24 carats; the word of two out of three assayers was final and all assays were recorded. Gold of low purity had to be refined and then re-assayed.

In the early years gold was usually refined up to 980 fine but by the fifteenth century Venetian refiners aimed for 990 fine. The Mint required gold to be at least 980 fine before it was accepted for coinage into ducats, which were first minted in March 1285. Venice even had a twice-daily 'fixing', held at the assay office at mid-morning and at vespers, which was heralded by the ringing of a bell. The Germans, who controlled much of the supply of precious metals, came across the Grand Canal from the Fondaco dei Tedeschi, and the Venetian bullion merchants assembled from their offices along the Rialto. The gold and silver on offer was then sold by auction. Bids might be on behalf of the government or local traders for coinage at the Mint, for merchants needing to dispatch it abroad or for local goldsmiths requiring it for jewellery or tableware. The gold market on the Rialto five or six hundred years ago bears a remarkable resemblance to that which evolved in London by the eighteenth century in terms of structure, regulation and customers.

### Plundering South America
In the intervening two hundred years, however, the dimensions of the bullion business expanded because of the sudden inflow of gold and silver from the Americas. The Portuguese and then the English were also voyaging to the Gold Coast of West Africa (Ghana) in search of gold, short-circuiting the caravans that had previously brought gold dust across the Sahara to the shores of the Mediterranean. Thus although Venice and, indeed, Italy, were at the high point of the Renaissance, trade flows were shifting and with them the markets for precious metals.

Across the Atlantic in South America, the growth of Venice as a great trading city state had been matched by the apogee of technical skills by the goldsmiths of the Chimu Empire in Peru between 1150 and 1450. They perfected lost-wax casting, alloys, welding and even gold plating (with an alloy of 30 per cent gold, 70 per cent copper, which was poured onto the ornament and then treated with acids extracted from plant juices, producing a copper oxide that could be cleaned off, leaving the surface covered with a thin film of pure gold). The Chimu were eventually conquered by the Incas, who were to suffer so grievously themselves at the hands of the Spanish invasion, culminating in Pizarro's capture and ransom of the Incas for golden ornaments, which went into the melting pot and off to Spain. An estimated 8 tonnes (over 250,000 ounces) of Pre-Columbian ornaments were taken and a tradition of craftsmanship built up over 2,500 years destroyed. 'Get gold,' wrote

King Ferdinand of Spain in 1511 to his invaders. 'Humanely if you can, but at all hazards get gold.' They obeyed.

For the next two centuries the Empires of Spain and, later, Portugal, were financed by the gold and, rather more, the silver their fleets brought back from the New World. Prior to these conquests, world gold production had probably been between 5 and at most 10 tonnes (160,000 to 320,000 ounces) annually. The new supplies from the Americas lifted this for a while to between 10 and 15 tonnes including the pillaging, although output slipped back again, to perhaps under 10 tonnes for much of the seventeenth century.

The market place for these precious metals was Amsterdam, which became the commercial emporium of Europe by the seventeenth century, at once the setting-off point for trade routes through Germany to Russia and for the Dutch East India Company embarking upon the establishment of a trading empire in India and Java (Indonesia). Where Venice had previously been the turntable, now Amsterdam waited for the annual arrival of the great Spanish 'plate' fleet laden with gold and silver (if it could escape the attentions of English privateers), then dispatched the metal to the east to pay for silks and cottons, spices and diamonds.

### The 'Accidental' Gold Standard

A challenge, however, was just over the horizon. In the aftermath of the Restoration of Charles II in England in 1660, London was bidding to become the capital of trade. The Royal Africa Company's ships went to Africa in search of gold, the East India Company's ships rivalled the Dutch in India and beyond. Two wars against the Dutch during Charles II's reign were fuelled primarily by commercial and colonial ambition. And the first seed of today's London gold market was established in 1671 when the young Moses Mocatta crossed the North Sea from Amsterdam (where he had been trading in sugar and diamonds) to set up business as a merchant, opening an account with Alderman Edward Backwell, one of the most famous of Restoration goldsmith-bankers. Initially his main business was in diamonds, but the ledgers of the East India Company for February 1676 record, 'By cash of Moses Mocatta for freight on 75 oz of gold on their ships "Nathaniel" and "Society" – £6.' The gold apparently was to pay for diamonds. Thereafter such shipments in gold and silver became regular events. Thus began nine generations of the Mocatta family in the precious metals business; they allied with the Goldsmids in 1779 to become the present Mocatta & Goldsmid, the oldest members of the London gold market. Soon after the Bank of England was founded in 1694, Moses Mocatta's son, Abraham, became its exclusive broker, first for silver, then for gold, while fulfilling the same function for the East India Company throughout its history and later for the India Office. Mocatta were exclusive brokers to the Bank of England until 1840. The story of the evolution of London as the world's foremost precious metals market through the eighteenth and early nineteenth centuries is very much that of Mocatta, the Bullion Office of the Bank of England, and the East India Company as principal customer for silver and sometimes as supplier of gold.[4]

Already the monetary framework of a sterling pound backed by gold that was to underpin the burgeoning British Empire for the next two hundred and fifty years was in place. In 1663, the guinea, made with gold from the Gold Coast of West Africa, had been launched with a nominal value of £1. At that time silver coinage circulated most widely in England, but was old and worn. The government, therefore, proposed a recoinage of silver in 1696, but in so doing slightly over-valued gold against it, so that people found it more profitable to take their gold to the Mint for coinage into guineas, while selling their silver (or old silver coin) to the market for export to India, where it commanded a higher price (the gold-silver ratio being 1:17 in Mexico and South America, 1:15 in Europe and 1:12 in India and China). For a while the guinea was valued at 22 shillings, instead of £1, or 20 shillings, then was written down to 21 shillings and sixpence in 1699. This accidental over-valuation swiftly increased the amount of gold, as opposed to silver, coins in circulation. England was on the way to a gold standard, while the rest of the world remained committed to silver as its basic standard of value and means of exchange. The trend to gold was confirmed in 1717 by Sir Isaac Newton, the mathematician and physicist, who was master of the Mint. A great debate in Parliament and the country had arisen about the over-valuing of the guinea at the expense of silver, which was all being exported to the east. Newton noted that the value of gold coin made at the Mint in recent years was thirty times that of silver coin. His answer was a further writing down of the value of the guinea to 21 shillings, confirming a gold price of £3.17s.10Hd per standard (i.e. 916 fine) troy ounces, which with a few interludes was to hold until 1931. Newton's recommendation was approved by Parliament in December 1717. It did not, however, have the desired effect because the Mint's buying price for silver had still not increased. The Mint's price for silver for coinage was 5s.2d. an ounce, the market's was 5s.7Hd. So it was still more profitable to make gold coin, while exporting silver to the east. The curious fact is that, although this action, recommended by Newton, is often taken as the benchmark setting the gold price for the next two hundred years, in essence creating the gold standard, no one thought of it in those terms and certainly did not intend it. Newton's clear intention had been to restore silver. As John Conduitt, Newton's successor at the Mint, observed, 'Gold is only looked on as a commodity, and so should rise or fall as occasion requires. An ounce of fine silver is, and always has been, and ought to be, the standing and invariable measure between nation and nation.'[5] As one economic historian wryly observed, 'England went over gradually to the gold standard by default.'[6] Luckily, mistakes which nevertheless yield such economic advantage are soon forgotten and often hailed as the mark of genius.

### Gold Rush to Brazil

Where did the gold for coins come from? Fortuitously the accidental transition from silver to gold as the main coinage circulating in Britain coincided with a gold rush in Brazil. Gold output had stagnated since the surge from the conquest of the Americas two hundred years earlier. But the discovery of alluvial gold around 1700, first in Minas Gerais province and then in Matto Grosso, touched off a gold rush that had all the characteristics of California over a century later. 'A swarm of adventurers and unemployed from all over Brazil and even Portugal quickly converged on the mines, following a few wilderness trails from Bahia, Rio de Janeiro and Sao Paolo,' noted one observer.[7] By 1720 Brazil was the largest producer with output in the best years estimated at over 15.5 tonnes (500,000 ounces), nearly two-thirds of world output. Ultimately, London got most of this gold. Initially, the Portuguese rulers of Brazil shipped it back to Lisbon where it was minted into *moedas de ouro*. This new-found wealth inevitably sucked in imports, especially woollen goods from England. The gold coins paid for them. Throughout the eighteenth century, *moydores* as they were known, or 'Portuguese gold' was widely accepted in England. Close to 200 tonnes (over 6 million ounces) of 'Portuguese gold' is estimated to have moved from Portugal to London in the first half of the eighteenth century. At the Bank of England, a special account for 'Foreign Gold Coin' was opened and the spate of gold prompted it to appoint Mocatta as its gold as well as silver broker in 1731.

The German scientist and explorer Baron Alexander von Humboldt, who spent five years studying the mines of the Americas in the late eighteenth century, and assembled the most comprehensive study of gold and silver output of the time, estimated that by 1750 world output had risen to about 25 tonnes (800,000 ounces). Thereafter as the richest

5 John Conduitt, 'Observations upon the present state of our gold and silver coins, 1730', reprinted in W.A. Shaw, *Select Tracts Illustrative of England Monetary History, 1626–1730*, Clement Wilson, London, 1896.
6 J. Sperling, 'The international payments mechanism in the seventeenth and eighteenth centuries', *EHR*, (2nd series), Vol. XIX, 1961.
7 C.R. Boxer, 'Brazilian gold and British traders in the first half of the eighteenth century', *Hispanic American Historical Review*, Vol. XLIX (1969), p. 457.

deposits in Brazil were worked out, it declined to around 18 tonnes (575,000 ounces) by 1800. The quantity is still very modest compared to what was to come in the nineteenth century and underlines that gold remained a relatively rare metal, little used for coin outside England. By comparison, annual silver output, according to Humboldt, rose from 11 million ounces in 1700, to 17 million ounces by 1750 and soared to 30 million ounces by 1800. Most of the silver also came through London on its way to become silver coinage in Europe or east towards India and China.

London's strength in gold was demonstrated by the recoinage of the guinea which took place between 1774 and 1777. The Mint used over 5 million ounces of gold (155 tonnes) in four years, much of it new 'foreign' gold bought in the market. In 1774 Mocatta, as the Bank of England's brokers, purchased 550,000 ounces on its behalf to be sent to the Mint; that amounted to perhaps 80–90 per cent of world output that year.

The recoinage, however, marked the high tide of gold in London for a generation. Supplies from Brazil were drying up, the War of Independence with America put pressure on the exchanges, but ultimately the Napoleonic Wars were to be the root of the trouble. Shortly after their outbreak in 1793, the drain on Britain's gold reserves began. It was not just the financing of armies abroad; allies came cap in hand for loans, while Napoleon's initial success in carving a victorious path across Europe strengthened the French currency causing (in true gold standard fashion) gold to cross the Channel to benefit from a higher price in Paris. The Bank of England, through Mocatta & Goldsmid, tried to buy more gold, but with production in Brazil down there was little to be had. Early in 1797, as rumour spread that the French were about to invade, there was a run on the Bank for gold coin. The governor of the Bank advised Prime Minister William Pitt that it could not for much longer honour its commitment to give out gold guineas against banknotes. Cash payments were suspended in February 1797; it was to be twenty-four years before Bank of England notes could again be freely redeemed for gold coin. This overnight creation of a paper currency was not just without precedent, but dangerous in time of war because of the temptation to print money.

### The 1810 Bullion Committee

The depreciation of the paper currency was not immediate. It was only in 1809 that a young stockbroker named David Ricardo, in a series of letters to the *Morning Chronicle*, wondered if the fact that the gold price, which had stood since 1717 at £3.17s.10Hd. per standard ounce, but had risen to £4.10s.0d. an ounce, was because the Bank of England was guilty of over-issuing notes. Ricardo's letter sparked off the great enquiry in 1810 by a Select Committee of the House of Commons on the High Price of Gold Bullion. The debate thus provoked was, as John Kenneth Galbraith once observed, 'the most famous in all history on money and its management.'[8] While looking at the relationship between gold and banknotes, the Bullion Committee unveiled a unique panorama of London as the centre of the international gold business at the beginning of the nineteenth century. The twenty-nine witnesses called before the Committee were the cast of the London bullion market. Their interrogation fills several hundred pages.[9] Here are a few 'nuggets'.

- John Humble, clerk to the Bullion Office of the Bank of England from the early 1770s until the 1830s, explained that the Office had two functions: it handled all the bullion for the Bank's own account and presided over all private transactions 'for the purpose of accommodation and safety between merchant and merchant, as a place of deposit'. The Bullion Office was open to all comers, but precious metal was generally deposited by ships' captains as soon as they put into port and remained there until the owners claimed it. The brokers then negotiated the sale, Humble explained, whereupon 'the parties come to the office and in their presence the packet is opened, the bullion weighed, we deliver the quantity sold to the buyer, and receive from him the price, which we deliver to the seller.' The Bullion Office was the 'umpire' (just like the assay office in Venice a few centuries earlier). As for the broker who negotiated it all, there was 'only one house . . . Mocatta & Goldsmid'.[10]
- Up stepped Aaron Goldsmid, partner in Mocatta & Goldsmid, to reply to the question, 'Are there any other dealers in Gold but yours?' that 'I apprehend none of considerable amount.' He explained that as exclusive brokers to the Bank they were the arbiters of the price, 'but not so to raise or depress it above or below its natural level. We endeavour to regulate the price so as to proportion the demand to the supply.'[11]
- Mocatta's price was the benchmark. 'Their price is what we sell at,' confirmed Samuel Binns of William & Jacob Wood, one of a quartet of refiners then operating in London.
- Back to Aaron Goldsmid, who agreed a great deal of gold was flowing out of the country because the sterling exchange rate was weak. The heart of his business was with perhaps twenty Dutch and French merchants trading on the continent, who bought up to 5,000 ounces through him at a time.
- Gold sales were 20,000 ounces a month, mostly bound for Amsterdam, which 'was the greatest mart for gold on the continent'. And he admitted that thence the gold might go to France where, in Paris, 'the course of the

8 J.K. Galbraith, *Money, Whence it Came, Where it Went*, André Deutsch, London, 1975, p. 36.
9 Select Committee of the House of Commons on the High Price of Gold Bullion, 1810.
10 Bullion Committee 1810, Evidence of John Humble, pp. 225–7.
11 Ibid., Evidence of A.A. Goldsmid, pp. 1–18, 41–7, 61.

exchange' had slipped from 24 livres to £1 in 1808 to 19.6 by 1810, a decline of nearly 18 per cent which made moving gold from London to Paris (or by circuitous routes) very profitable.

- But had sterling depreciated because the Bank issued too much paper money, since cash payments in gold were suspended? Certainly the Bank's note issue had more than doubled between 1797 and 1810, and the average amount of commercial bills discounted by the Bank had tripled. The Bank's governor, John Whitmore, told the Bullion Committee that the increases were in response to a genuine demand brought about by increased trade. The Bank, he insisted, 'had never forced a note into circulation'.[12]
- Distinguished bankers begged to differ. Sir Francis Baring, founder of the merchant banking house, saw the trouble as 'the increasing circulation in the Country of paper.'[13]
- Nathan Mayer Rothschild, founder of the London arm of the great banking family, who appeared before the Committee incognito as a 'continental merchant', had no illusions about the dangers of inconvert-ible paper. 'I value everything by Bullion,' he said. 'To the best of my recollection, a depreciation in the exchanges has always taken place whenever a paper currency has been put into circulation that was not convertible into cash.' He reeled off previous experiences in France in the early days after the Revolution, in Austria and in Denmark, 'where a forced paper currency exists'. The same problem now afflicted Britain, because the Bank of England was 'not allowing Bullion to perform those functions for which it seems to have been intended by nature.'[14]
- The Members of Parliament making up the Committee agreed with Rothschild. Francis Horner, their chairman, stated, 'there is at present an excess in the paper circulation of this country . . . this excess is to be ascribed to the want of sufficient check and control in the issue of paper from the Bank of England; and originally to the suspension of cash payments which removed the natural and true control.' The Bullion Committee recommended the resumption of cash payments in gold within two years.

That conclusion delighted David Ricardo, who had triggered the enquiry, but was not called to give evidence. The crux, he argued, was that 'a currency, to be perfect, should be absolutely invariable in value.' Precious metals provided the best base, even though their prices could fluctuate slightly. 'They are', Ricardo believed, 'the best with which we are acquainted'.[15]

For all that, it was not two, but eleven, years before full cash

12 Ibid., Evidence of John Whitmore, pp. 90–184.
13 Ibid., Evidence of Sir Francis Baring, pp. 194–9.
14 Ibid., Evidence of a continental merchant, pp. 77–90, 96–110.
15 David Ricardo, *The Works and Correspondence of David Ricardo*, ed. P. Sraffa, Cambridge University Press, Cambridge, Vol. IV, p. 58.

payments were resumed in 1821. In the meantime, the gold price did ease back somewhat, though in 1815 when the news came in that Napoleon had escaped from Elba, the gold price in London jumped briefly to £5.7s.0d. The big buyer was the 'continental merchant' Nathan Mayer Rothschild, under orders from the Treasury to dispatch gold quickly to the Duke of Wellington, who was marshalling his forces. Not until Wellington inflicted the final defeat on Napoleon at the Battle of Waterloo did the gold price simmer down. With peace, it slipped back to £3.18s.6d. an ounce, giving considerable ammunition to critics of the Bullion Committee who argued that the report over-simplified the matter in laying all blame at the door of the Bank of England. Sterling had depreciated in relation to gold, not just because of note issue but because of the inevitable inflationary pressures of a long war.

### The Sovereign Launched

Even so, as the Bank's gold reserves improved, the initial steps were taken towards resumption of cash payments. The first stage was to mint new coins because most guineas in circulation before had been melted for export. However, people had become accustomed to the £1 note, while the guinea had been worth £1.1s.0d. The solution was to relaunch cash payments with a new coin, the sovereign valued at £1, containing 123G grains (7.99 grams) of 916 gold.[16] The Coinage Act of 1816, authorizing the sovereign, gave the formal seal of approval to the gold standard. Coins of 22 carat (916) and of weights prescribed by the Mint were declared the sole standard of value and unlimited legal tender. The significance of this was summed up by Sir Alfred Feaveryear in his book *The Pound Sterling*. 'Thus a century . . . after the publication of Newton's famous report', wrote Sir Arthur, 'which resulted by accident rather than design, in the establishment of the guinea at 21 shillings, as the standard coin, that coin was superseded. The guinea upon which had been founded the great economic expansion and prosperity of the eighteenth century, gave way to the sovereign, of which the nineteenth century became so proud'.[17]

The first sovereigns were issued in July 1817, but the resumption of full cash payments had to wait until 1821 as the Bank of England gradually scaled down its note issue to be able to meet that fresh commitment. The Mint made ready by producing 35 million sovereigns that year, a level not reached again until 1853, when the full flow of the Australian gold rush reached London. Gold was already available, however, from fresh mines in Russia, east of the Ural mountains. Thus, even before the great discoveries of California and Australia in mid-

---

16 The original sovereigns were issued in 1489 by Henry VII and although issued by all Tudor monarchs had little circulation. James I suspended their minting.
17 A. Feaveryear, *The Pound Sterling*, Clarendon Press, Oxford, 1963, p. 213.

century, output was able to quadruple from around 19 tonnes (600,000 ounces) in 1800 to nearly 90 tonnes (2.8 million ounces) by 1847. The London market remained at the heart of the business, with an increasing cast of familiar names, not just the Rothschilds, but Sharp & Kirkup (forerunners of Sharps Pixley), who were acting as brokers, and Johnson Matthey as assayers and metallurgists. Their attention focused increasingly on Russian gold.

### A Russian Renaissance

Far back in the history of gold, the rivers and streams of the Ural mountains had yielded rich deposits of alluvial gold, which had passed down the ancient trade routes to the Black Sea and the Mediterranean. And it was on the eastern slopes of the Urals that the resurgence of Russian gold mining began in 1744 with the discovery of a quartz outcrop near Ekaterinburg. The new mine was soon being run by the Czar and, in its first forty years, it produced 2.6 tonnes (84,000 ounces). This relatively humble start in the eighteenth century stimulated the czars to greater exploration. In the first decades of the nineteenth century, there were extensive searches for alluvial deposits in the Berezovsk region. Czar Alexander I, encouraged by his finance minister Kankrin, established in 1823 a commission of the heads of districts to take charge of the hunt for gold and to draw up regulations for the exploitation of deposits discovered. During the next seven years, production in the Urals more than tripled from 1.5 tonnes a year to 5.4 tonnes (175,000 ounces), as many new alluvial gold fields were revealed in an area 60 kilometres to the north and south of Ekaterinburg. This city became the centre of administration for the gold fields, and all gold was hastened to the assay office there for analysis. Twice a year it was dispatched, under heavy guard, to St Petersburg.

The success of these gold fields led to expeditions farther east in the Altai mountains and along the upper tributaries of the Yenisei river. By 1842, at least fifty-eight alluvial deposits were being worked in these remote regions of Siberia; the yield was nearly 11 tonnes (350,000 ounces). The hunt for gold was through rough, marshy terrain. A traveller wrote, 'One must have the iron constitution of the inhabitants of Siberia to bear such fatigue and privations; but even of them many succumb.' Only a small minority really benefited from the riches of the gold fields. The deposits were worked either directly for the Crown, or by a handful of rich landlords who were supposed to pay tax on their gold to the czars. The labourers had to work every day, except Sunday, from 5 a.m. to 8 p.m. The only concession was that food was supposed to be available to them at fixed prices in the remote fields. Flogging was officially forbidden. The proprietors lived in great style. 'The Kalmyk in his felt cap brought me, on a plate of Japanese porcelain, oranges imported from Marseilles or Messina,' wrote one visitor to Siberia who was entertained in regal fashion, 'whilst after a meal in which the delicacies of all climates had been brought under contribution, not forgetting the grape of Malaga, the Rhine and Bordeaux, came the aromatic nectar of Arabia [coffee] along with excellent Havana cigars.' At the diggings, the proprietors regaled themselves with champagne while watching their men at work.

Under these opulent landlords, production soared until, by 1847, Russia was providing at least three-fifths of all the newly mined gold in the world, most of it from the new gold fields of eastern Siberia. Although Russian gold was virtually eclipsed by the dramatic finds of California and Australia, exploration of new areas on the Lena river east of Lake Baikal, and on the Amur river near the Mongolian border, increased production to 43.5 tonnes in 1880 and nearly 60 tonnes in 1914.

The champagne and Havana cigars of the Russian gentry would definitely have seemed out of place in the California of 1848, although there was, of course, plenty to celebrate. California was to be the gold rush of the ordinary man, the simple labourer who threw up everything, trekked west, and made his fortune. California, unlike Russia, was also to establish the gold fields as centres of rough-and-ready democracy where every miner, no matter what his origins, had his say and his vote.

# CHAPTER 2

# The Age of Gold
# 1848–1914

'The United States is on the brink of an Age of Gold,' reported the *New York Herald Tribune* in November 1848 when the full scale of the gold discoveries in California began to percolate to New York. The newspaper might more correctly have phrased it that the world was 'on the brink'. In the second half of the nineteenth century, the world of gold suddenly expanded beyond anything that seemed reasonable. The riches that Egypt had won nearly 5,000 years before from the mines of Africa, that the Roman Empire had wrested from Spain, and that Spain herself had shipped from South America in the sixteenth century, were dwarfed by an avalanche of gold. In the short span of a little over fifty years, more gold was mined than in the preceding 5,000. In the whole of the first century after Columbus discovered America the world's mined gold totalled roughly 750 tonnes (24 million ounces); in the last half of the nineteenth century it was a mighty 10,000 tonnes (320 million ounces). Annual production rose from 77 tonnes (2.5 million ounces) in 1847 to almost 280 tonnes (9 million ounces) in 1852.

During the winter of 1852, members of the Banking Institute in London, trooping in from the cold February evening for their monthly meeting at 52 Threadneedle Street, were greeted by the warming spectacle of a 100-pound nugget of solid gold from Ballarat, Australia, resting on the chairman's table. Setting aside their top hats, they sat back to listen to a lecture by a Mr Dalton on the impact of the gold discoveries. To their astonishment, they learned that while the average annual value of new gold coins minted in Britain, France and the United

States had been $8.4 million before the new discoveries, it was more than $75 million in 1851.

The changes were not, however, simply a matter of cold statistics. In human terms, the age of the individual prospector had arrived. Previously, gold mining had always been the exclusive privilege of, or had at least been heavily taxed by, the state. In the twentieth century, it was generally to fall within the franchise of great mining companies, at least until the gold boom in the 1980s gave the prospector his head again in Latin America, the Philippines, Indonesia and many parts of Africa. Now, for a short span of half a century, the prospector – the man in crumpled clothes and slouch hat, his ear constantly open at the diggings or in the saloon for the newest gossip of great finds – had his day. With his 'pan', he followed the latest rumours of gold: first to California, then to Australia, to New Zealand, back to Australia or Nevada, Colorado, Idaho or South Dakota, and finally – in a glorious finale – to the Klondike. 'The rush and struggle is awful,' wrote one Australian gold digger, 'and the only chance is to fly off at the first sound. The mischief is that you hear so many wonderful stories that prove false, that you will not listen to a first rumour, and by the time something authentic reaches you, it is too late.'

### California's Prize

It all began on a January afternoon in 1848, when a carpenter named James Marshall found what he thought were specks of gold in the tailrace of John Sutter's mill near the junction of the American and Sacramento rivers. One of Marshall's workmen recorded in his diary that night, 'This day some kind of mettle was found in the tail race that looks like gold, first discovered by James Martial, the Boss of the Mill.' In fact, Marshall was not at all sure that it was gold, so he hurried back to Sutter's house to consult the *Encyclopedia Americana*. The description of gold in its pages so convinced him that he went rushing back to the mill in pouring rain and missed his supper. At first, Marshall and Sutter tried to keep news of the discovery quiet, but rumours of gold were not easy to quench, and soon the word had spread to San Francisco – then a struggling port of about 2,000 people. By spring, half of California had deserted its farms and homesteads to rush to the gold fields. 'The whole country from San Francisco to Los Angeles and from the seashore to the base of the Sierra Nevada resounds with the sordid cry of gold, GOLD, GOLD!', reported the *San Francisco Californian* in May 1848. 'The field is left half planted, the house half built, and everything neglected but the manufacture of shovels and pickaxes.'

The gold seekers were hardly disappointed. They found not only the sandbars and banks of the rivers near Sutter's Mill rich in alluvial gold, but were also quickly able to trace deposits in other streams coming down from the western slopes of the High Sierras. Throughout that first summer, the Californians had their find almost exclusively to themselves, for in the days before the telephone or cable the news of the discoveries percolated slowly even to the eastern seaboard of the United States. The 5,000 men working painstakingly along the riverbanks and up mountain streams panned out about a quarter of a million dollars' worth of gold – a promising beginning, but only one-fortieth of the yield of the following year.

To most Americans on the eastern seaboard, California was still a remote, uncivilized strip of land that the United States was in the process of acquiring from Mexico, along with New Mexico, for $15 million. Indeed the ink seems barely to have dried on the agreement with the Mexican government before the gold rush began. By the autumn of 1848, the first rumours of the discoveries were flying around New York. Each day brought fresh news, and the excitement mounted. What happened during the next few months was unprecedented. Thousands of men suddenly saw a spark of opportunity to earn a fortune in a matter of days. Unlike previous gold discoveries, which had normally remained firmly under the control of governments, here was a chance for anyone to stake his claim and dig riches. Even before President Polk finally confirmed the extent of the finds in a speech to Congress in December 1848, the scramble to get to the West Coast was on.

'It is well and truly said', wrote a New York correspondent reporting to the *Banker's Magazine* in London, 'that the shoemaker is throwing away his last, the tailor his bodkin, the mason his trowel, the labourer his hod, the carpenter his chisel, the printer his stick, the painter his brush, the farmer his harrow, the quack his nostrums, the baker is leaving his dough, the butcher his stall, the clerk his desk and even the loafer his roost.'[1]

There were three routes to California: by ship around Cape Horn; by ship to Panama, then across the isthmus on a donkey and by ship on to San Francisco; or, finally, the long haul overland across the plains and through the mountains and deserts to the coast. Every transportation company, enjoying a heyday, pushed up its rates. First class by sea from New York to San Francisco cost $380; steerage was $200. A donkey across the Panama isthmus was $30. Casualties along all the routes were high. Many prospective gold diggers failed to get over the fever-infested Chagres river on the Panama isthmus. Cholera, Indians and accidents killed perhaps 5,000 of those taking the overland routes across the Great Plains in 1849.

---

1 *Banker's Magazine*, Vol. IX, 1849, p. 81.

For many of those who arrived early, the price was worth it. Although there was an inevitable tendency for miners to exaggerate their finds, those first on the scene could earn anything from $300 to $500 a week – a small fortune indeed when most industrial workers in the eastern United States were earning only about $10 a week. The average wage at the 'diggins' in California in 1848 was as high as $20 per day, but this fell to about $6 a day by 1852. Yet, assuming there were 100,000 men actually working in the gold fields in that year, the total yield of $81 million in 1852 would suggest a very rough average of $800 for each individual – much more than incomes back in the East. Clearly, not everyone did make that much, but many men who went to California made a small fortune.

The thousands who rushed to California from all over the United States found Englishmen, Frenchmen and even the Chinese hard on their heels. This was an international gold rush. By mid-1849, one Scotsman was writing home to his family in Edinburgh, 'This is the seventh week I have been here: we have averaged from 18 to 32 dollars every day till this week . . . as far as I can judge those who work steadily can make from 12 to 30 dollars per day. Cases are occurring of some getting from 100 to 200 dollars per day.'[2] By the end of 1849, there were at least 40,000 men actually working in the gold fields and they scoured out 10 million dollars' worth of gold.

Few of them knew the first thing about mining, but they quickly learned what telltale signs to look for amid the sand and gravel in the bed of a creek, and how to pan. It was essentially a simple process. The miner filled his pan with gravel and picked out the large stones by hand, then rotated the pan between his hands to keep the contents suspended in the water. One side of the pan was tilted slightly higher than the other so that the water carried away the light particles, while the heavier particles of gold were left as a residue. As the search for gold became more sophisticated, the primitive panning process was supplemented by a 'cradle' – a long wooden box on rockers – which enabled much larger quantities of gravel to be handled at a time.

From the original find at Sutter's Mill, the miners ranged out north and south along the Sacramento river and were soon tracing the gold back into the Sierras. There the prospectors soon located a belt of gold-bearing rock over 100 miles long and varying in width from a few hundred feet to 2 miles. They called it the Mother Lode, for it was from this quartz rock that the gold had been scoured over the centuries and washed down the rivers. The mining camps sprang up overnight wherever a promising new find was located. The prospectors lived in leaky tents, lean-tos or log cabins. It was a hard, often unrewarding, existence. They

2 *Banker's Magazine*, Vol. IX, 1849, p. 81.

toiled all day beneath the hot California sun, up to their waists in water. At night they went back to their huts to eat whatever food might be available and to soak up bad whisky. They got dysentery and scurvy. 'The miners of California never shave; never put on clean vests, clean dickeys or clean boots,' one traveller lamented. They were indeed a scruffy lot, far from the comforts of wives and families. The census of 1850 showed that 92.5 per cent of the population was male. Most of the females were girls working in the saloons amid long gilt mirrors and red calico curtains.

California was such a young country that it simply lacked the experience or the administrative machinery to cope with all the problems of the gold rush and a sudden population explosion of 100,000 newcomers in a year. The difficulties of maintaining law and order were hardly helped by the mingling of different nationalities. There were 25,000 Frenchmen in California by 1853 and nearly 20,000 Chinese. Many of them did not speak a word of English. There was one ugly incident in Placerville when two Frenchmen and a Chinaman, caught in the act of robbery, were flogged by the miners, then tried and hanged – all without being able to utter a word in their defence. There were forty-seven illegal executions in California in 1855, as opposed to nine lawful ones. The murder rate in the gold-mining counties was terrifying. Calaveras County topped the list with thirty-two; El Dorado County claimed second place with twenty-six; and Amador was third with twenty-one. The only real law was lynch law, which one Californian newspaper sadly admitted was better than no law at all. 'Lynch law is not the best law that might be, but it is better than none, and so far as benefit is derived from law, we have no other here.'

Throughout it all, the gold production increased year by year to 77 tonnes in 1851, then a peak of 93 tonnes (3 million ounces) in 1853. The US Mint began coining Californian gold in such profusion that silver coins became scarce almost overnight. Across the Atlantic, the gold reserves of the Bank of England rose from £12.8 million in 1848 to £20 million in 1852. 'As the creditor of the whole earth, London got the first of this gold,' notes Sir John Clapham in his *The Bank of England, A History*.[3] France fared even better; the Bank of France's gold stock soared from £3.5 million in 1848 to £23.5 million four years later. The City editor of *The Times* suggested, 'There will be considerable surplus of gold; in fact on the Continent, which is on a bimetallic system, more and more payments are likely to be made in gold.' But predictions that the price of gold must fall from its long-standing £3.17s.10Hd. per ounce standard (i.e. for 22-carat), proved false; rather, the flood of gold underwrote an immense expansion in world trade during the 1850s.

3 Vol. II, Cambridge University Press, Cambridge, 1944, p. 217.

### Australian Adventures

This bonanza was only the beginning. An Australian named Edward Hammond Hargraves, who had been to California, was certain that the same geological features were to be found in his own country. Returning on the boat from California late in 1850, he predicted that he would find gold within a week. 'There's no gold in the country you're going to and if there is, that darned Queen of yours won't let you touch it,' a fellow passenger told him. 'There's as much gold in the country I'm going to as there is in California,' snapped Hargraves, 'and Her Gracious Majesty the Queen, God bless her, will appoint me one of her Gold Commissioners.' Hargraves was right. Within one week of landing, he had found gold on a tributary of the Macquarie river not far from Bathurst in New South Wales. The gold rush was on. 'A complete mental madness appears to have seized almost every member of the community,' the Bathurst Free Press reported. 'There has been a universal rush to the diggings.' Hargraves was duly made a commissioner for lands, and received a reward of £10,000 plus a life pension. In 1854 he was presented at Court to Queen Victoria. For the rest of his life, he was regarded as a man with the Midas touch. He was sent to look for gold in Tasmania and in Western Australia, but failed in both places.

The first news of the fresh gold field reached England, along with the first £800 worth of gold, aboard the Thomas Arbuthnot. Her captain said, 'The colony is completely paralysed. Every man and boy who is able to lift a shovel is off, or going off, to the diggings. Nearly every article of food has gone up, in some cases two hundred per cent.' He had had to promise his crew double wages to get the boat away from Sydney; even then half a dozen had deserted. The impact of the Australian find on Britain was to be even more important than that of California. The bulk of Californian gold stayed in the United States; 80 per cent of Australia's gold was to come through the London market. It is no coincidence that two more members of the present London gold market were founded at this time. Pixley & Abell (later to merge into Sharps Pixley) was founded in 1852 by Stewart Pixley, formerly a senior clerk in the cashier's office at the Bank of England. Samuel Montagu, the merchant bankers and bullion dealers, opened their door for the first time in 1853.

The existing members of the market did record turnover. At Mocatta & Goldsmid, the oldest bullion house, brokerage earnings doubled between 1847 and 1849, while at Sharps & Wilkins (originally Sharp & Kirkup) profits shot up from £4,980 in 1847 to £14,523 by 1853. London's refiners were hard pressed to cope with the flood of metal. Rothschild's took over the old Royal Mint refinery in 1853 and in the first year put through over 9.3 tonnes (almost 300,000 ounces) of Australian gold and 14 tonnes from California. Meanwhile Henry Raphael, one of the partners in an old-established banking house, started a new refinery that was to handle much of the gold passing through London in the next seventy years. Raphael's bars were accepted as 'good delivery' by the Bank of England in 1856.

Even so, keeping pace was often difficult. Edward Matthey of Johnson Matthey later recalled in his *Memoirs*, 'These Australian gold workings . . . commenced a new era in the bullion business. As the sailing vessels arrived . . . the Bullion office at the Bank of England was sometimes flooded with gold. To meet the difficulty as to getting through the work, the Bank of England sent to Hatton Garden and Johnson & Matthey were at once made "Assayers to the Bank of England".'

In fact, Hargraves had touched only the fringe of Australian gold. New South Wales was yielding 26.4 tonnes (850,000 ounces) in 1852, but the neighbouring state of Victoria had joined the hunt. Victoria offered a reward of £200 for gold found within 200 miles of Melbourne. In the autumn of 1851, barely six months after the New South Wales discovery, gold was found at Ballarat, a mere 60 miles from Melbourne. Later in the same year came another find at Bendigo Creek, 30 miles farther north. Now the floodgates were really open; 370,000 immigrants arrived in Australia in 1852. The colony, which a few years before had been peopled only by convicts who had been transported, and a handful of farmers, had its economy transformed for ever. The Australian gold miners were never such a cosmopolitan bunch as their colleagues in California, but they insisted on the same democracy in the gold fields. There was, however, much more law and order in the Australian gold rush right from the start. Hard liquor was banned. Special gold commissioners were appointed to administer the diggings. They sold licences for 30 shillings a month, and normally parcelled out 15 to 24 feet along a creek to a party of three to six men. They were a wildly assorted crowd. G.L. Mundy, a visitor writing in 1852, reported, 'There were merchants, cabmen, magistrates and convicts, amateur gentlemen rocking the cradle merely to say they had done so, fashionable hair-dressers and tailors, cooks, coachmen, lawyers' clerks and their masters, colliers, cobblers, quarrymen, doctors of physic and music, aldermen, an ADC on leave, scavengers, sailors, shorthand writers, a real live lord on his travels – all levelled by community of pursuit and of costume.' 'Levelled' is just the right word. The miners lived in bark huts or tents. 'Our furniture', wrote one miner, James Bonwick, 'is of simple character. A box, a block of wood, or a bit of paling across a pail, serves as a table.'

Meals were primitive. 'The chops can be picked out of the frying pan, placed on a lump of bread, and cut with a clasp knife that has done good service in fossicking during the day.' Insects and flies added to the discomfort. 'The nuisance is the flies,' complained Bonwick. 'The little fly and the stinging monster March fly. O! The tortures these wretches give! In the hole, out of the hole, at meals or walking, it is all the same with these winged plagues. When washing at a waterhole, the March flies will settle upon the arms and face, and worry to that degree, that I have known men to pitch their dishes, and stamp and growl with agony. The fleas, too, are of the Tom Thumb order of creation, and they begin their bloody-thirsty work when the flies are tired of their recreation.'[4] For those who stuck it out, the rewards could be handsome. Almost 80 tonnes (2.6 million ounces) of gold were mined in Victoria alone in 1853; by 1856 it had risen to a peak of 90 tonnes (2.9 million ounces).

Yet the Australian rush, like that in California, had a relatively short life. In both countries, the alluvial gold that was easily available on the surface was quickly scooped up. Once it had gone, the search for gold called for more patience and better equipment. By the mid-1850s, the pattern of gold mining in both countries was changing. No longer was it the individual miner with his pan, but a group of men joining together and pooling their capital to build more elaborate crushing equipment and to dig deeper. As early as 1851 the San Francisco weekly *Alta California* noted, 'We have now the river bottoms and the quartz veins, but to get the gold from them we must employ gold.' Over $13.5 million was invested in California by 1859 in the building of deep mines, and over 5,000 miles of canals, ditches and flumes were dug to supply water. The lean years had soon arrived. Average wages in California, which had been $10 a day in 1850, had dropped to $3 ten years later.

Miners now dashed off at the least hint of gold, seeking new prosperity. There were many false rumours in San Francisco newspapers specifically designed to dispose of surplus labour. There was a rush to the Fraser river in British Columbia in 1858; Pike's Peak, Colorado in 1859; and Boise, Idaho in 1862. None of them produced gold on any scale comparable to California. The richest discovery was the Comstock Lode near Virginia City, Nevada in 1859. The Lode contained such high-grade deposits of gold and silver that, in the first twenty years in which it was mined, it yielded $306 million of the two metals, including 193 tonnes of gold worth $130 million. Among those in Virginia City at the height of the rush was Mark Twain, working for a spell as city editor of the *Enterprise*. He later wrote about the boom town in *Roughing It*: 'Money was as plentiful as dust: every individual considered himself

---

4 James Bonwick, *Notes of a Gold Digger*, 1852.

wealthy, and a melancholy countenance was nowhere to be seen. The "city" of Virginia . . . claimed a population of fifteen to eighteen thousand, and all day long half of this little army swarmed the streets like bees and the other half swarmed among the drifts and tunnels of the "Comstock", hundreds of feet down in the earth directly under those same streets. Often we felt our chairs jar, and heard the faint boom of a blast down in the bowels of the earth under the office.'[5]

Across the Pacific, Australia was also having its secondary rushes. One rumour of gold – on the Fitzroy river in Queensland in 1858 – sent 10,000 people trailing north. It was a completely false lead but, because of the lack of communications, there was no way of stemming the tide. Even New Zealand, which had jealously watched Australia's budding economy be nourished by gold, finally had its reward. Gold was found near Dunedin on the south island of New Zealand in 1861. More than 7,000 men were working the field by the following year, and a steady production of 15 tonnes a year was maintained until 1870.

### The South African Dimension

Such rushes took place essentially in fits and starts; for almost thirty years, from the mid–1850s until the late 1880s, the flood of gold slowed down (although far more was still being produced each year than before 1848), and the gold that had been mined was gradually assimilated. When the game resumed in South Africa, the character of the gold rush there was radically different. In the first place, the initial riches found in South Africa were diamonds, not gold. The first diamond was found near the Vaal river in northern Cape Province in 1867 and, within three years, the region around what later became the town of Kimberley was alive with diggers. Entrepreneurs, who had previously been lured by gold, arrived from all over the world to build up diamond fortunes that would later enable them to participate in the next scramble for gold. Among them were Cecil Rhodes and his partner, Charles Rudd; J.B. Robinson, Hans Sauer, Alfred Beit, Hermann Eckstein, Lionel Phillips, Barney Barnato and George Albu, who were to establish the mining finance houses to nurture the South African gold mines.[6]

During the early years of the Kimberley rush some gold was found in the Transvaal, primarily at Barberton in the east Transvaal in the shadow of the Drakensberg mountains. It was never enough to tempt the diamond men of Kimberley. Lionel Phillips was sent down from Kimberley to view the new gold field, but he reported back quickly that the field had little potential. With Kimberley unimpressed the boom quickly petered out, although a few small mines continued to produce gold for many years. Yet prospectors were not discouraged. The problem

5 Mark Twain, *Roughing It*, Vol. II, Chatto & Windus, London, 1885.
6 See the author's *The World of Diamonds*, William Morrow, New York, and Weidenfeld & Nicolson, London, 1981.

was that they were looking for gold as it had appeared in California and Australia. 'The prospectors of 1885 were slow, agonizingly slow, in their progress towards their unknown goal,' wrote A.P. Cartwright in *The Gold Miners*. 'They stumbled about as men do who are blindfolded, groping their way towards what they believed would be the "mother lode" from which had sprung the traces of gold they had found so far. They followed false trails, they panned in all the wrong places.'[7]

Yet, all this time, they were right on top of the richest gold field the world has ever known. They failed to understand the peculiar geology of the huge Witwatersrand basin in which the gold-bearing reefs, with gold flecks so fine that they could rarely be seen with the naked eye, outcropped only briefly on the surface near what is now Johannesburg, then plunged below the ground at an angle of 25 degrees or more, sloping inward towards the centre. The gold-bearing sides of the basin have never 'bottomed out'.

The credit for discovering the main reef of gold-bearing conglomerate – it looks like a sandwich of white pebbles packed tightly together – normally goes to a man named George Harrison who, so the story goes, found the reef outcropping on Langlaagte farm in February 1886 when he was digging up stone to help build a house for Widow Oosthuizen, who owned the farm. It was hardly so sensational a discovery as a find of alluvial gold. Harrison, who had had experience in the Australian gold fields, simply recognized the rock as a gold-bearing formation which, if crushed, might yield an ounce or two of gold from every tonne of ore. This is the essence of the South African gold mines. No one picks up nuggets. There is an unfathomable body of low-grade ore stretching in a wide arc from 40 miles east of Johannesburg to 90 miles west, then swinging down south west into the Orange Free State. The gold-bearing reefs, laid down perhaps 2,000 million years ago, vary in thickness from one-tenth of an inch to 100 feet but, on the average, are only 1 foot thick. Except in rare outcrops, they have been covered gradually with thousands of feet of hard rock. Tracking them this far below the ground calls for rare skill in geological detective work; mining them calls for capital and engineering skill.

Thus, although the news of gold on Langlaagte farm brought men rushing to the fledgling city of Johannesburg, it was only those with capital who could participate. The diamond men from Kimberley quickly established control. They came up quietly by coach, trying hard to avoid having their rivals know where they were bound. J.B. Robinson and Hans Sauer happened to be riding in the same coach, so at one stop each decided to leave the coach to try to prevent the other learning his real destination. There could, however, be no real secret. Within two years,

---

7 A.P. Cartwright, *The Gold Miners*, Purnell & Sons (SA) Pt Ltd, Cape Town, 1962, p. 39.

four of the present six mining finance houses had been established, all backed by men who had made their money in diamonds. The first was formed by Hermann Eckstein in 1887; it was soon nicknamed 'The Corner House', and eventually became Rand Mines. Immediately afterwards followed Cecil Rhodes and Charles Rudd with Gold Fields of South Africa, the Barnato brothers with Johannesburg Consolidated Investment Company, and George and Leopold Albu with General Mining and Finance Corporation. Adolf Goerz started a fifth group in 1893 after he went to look over the gold fields for a group of Berlin businessmen. It eventually became the Union Corporation (which is now merged with General Mining). But even the capital and mining experience of these men were not in themselves enough to get the South African gold-mining industry off to a flying start.

There were soon numerous claims staked out all along the south fringe of Johannesburg wherever the Main Reef and its associated reefs of the Main Reef Leader, the Bird Reef and the South Reef outcropped, but the real problem was getting a profitable amount of gold from the ore. The old methods of crushing ore to a powder which was carried by water over copper plates coated with mercury, which in turn amalgamated with the gold, might have been satisfactory for the gold in the quartz veins of California or Australia, but it was not subtle enough for the fine grains of gold sprinkled throughout the Rand. Such techniques extracted, at best, 70 per cent of the gold and, on the average, 65 per cent. Assuming that each tonne of ore contained 31.1 grams (i.e. 1 ounce) of gold, little more than 20 grams was being extracted. Gold mining on those terms did not make sense, and in 1890 the gold boom seemed finished. 'Grass will grow in the streets of Johannesburg within a year,' one miner predicted.

Indeed, it might have done so had not two doctors in Glasgow, Robert and William Forrest, and a chemist, John S. MacArthur, begun experimenting – quite independently – on the problem of gold extraction. In 1887, they patented the MacArthur-Forrest process for extracting the gold from ore with cyanide. Once the ore had been crushed to a fine powder, it was circulated through tanks containing a weak solution of cyanide, which has an affinity for gold. The solution dissolved the gold (and silver) but had no effect on the rock particles (in the same way that if sugar and sand were stirred together in tea the sugar would dissolve and the sand would remain as grains). The remaining rock pulp could then be filtered off. Zinc dust was added to the cyanide solution to replace the gold, causing fine specks of gold to be precipitated out. The precipitate was then refined. Properly developed and applied correctly, the MacArthur-Forrest process extracted 96 per cent of the gold from the ore. Without this invention the industry, as we know it today, would not exist. The MacArthur-Forrest technique is still the basis of much gold extraction, although increasingly replaced by carbon-in-pulp (CIP) technology.

While the MacArthur-Forrest process was being tentatively tried out, the Corner House was taking another major step forward. On the advice of an American mining engineer, J.S. Curtis, who had made a careful study of the angle at which the outcropping gold reefs plunged underground, The Corner House began to buy up, in great secrecy, large blocks of land to the south of the main outcrops. Boreholes soon revealed the gold reefs over 500 feet (150 metres) underground. The Corner House, backed by the Rothschilds, began the boom in the deep-level mines which have since become such an essential part of the South African gold-mining industry. Even at this early stage, the cost of establishing a new mine was considerable; at least £500,000 was needed. The yield of the mines quickly made such an investment worthwhile. In 1887, South Africa had contributed a mere 1.2 tonnes (38,580 ounces) of gold, a tiny 0.8 per cent of world production. Just five years later, her production topped the 30-tonne mark (almost 1 million ounces), worth £4.5 million, representing over 15 per cent of world production. By 1898, just before the Boer War shut down the gold industry for three years, output was up to 120 tonnes (3.8 million ounces), more than a quarter of the world's newly mined gold. In that year, she toppled the United States from first place in the world gold production league. Apart from the lull during the Boer War, South Africa has contributed more than a quarter of the new gold every year since 1898 and in many years, especially the 1950s–1980s, well over 50 per cent of world production. Her total output through 1993 will have been approaching 45,000 tonnes.

### Klondike Bonanza

Just as the South African industry was getting into its stride, the individual prospector, who had been king since 1848, had a final glorious fling to finish his century. Two prospectors, Robert Henderson and George Washington Carmack, were fishing for salmon on the Thron-diuck (which quickly became 'Klondike') tributary of the Yukon river in the far north of Canada, one August afternoon in 1896, when the gleam of gold caught their eye. For several decades there had been wild rumours of gold in these streams of the far north, but few of them had lived up to expectation. The best source of gold had been in the creeks lower down the Yukon in the United States territory of Alaska, where a bustling community called Circle City had grown up with a music hall, two theatres, eight dance halls and no fewer than twenty-eight saloons. It was gaily christened the 'Paris of Alaska'. Henderson's and Carmack's discovery on Thron-diuck made it a ghost town overnight. In that first autumn, as everyone from Circle City stampeded up the Yukon and the little community of Dawson City was born, the far north kept its discovery secret. Despite the desperate shortage of supplies (salt fetched its weight in gold), the prospectors held out against disease and starvation. A barber in Dawson City got a small slice of one claim, went out and dug up $40,000 in gold. In Harry Ash's Saloon in Dawson City, there was so much gold mingling with the sawdust on the floor that one enthusiast panned for gold right there. According to legend, he grubbed up $275 worth of gold dust that had filtered out of miners' pockets.

In the spring of 1897, the first packet steamers sailed south to Seattle and San Francisco, laden with gold stuffed into buckskin bags, glass fruit jars, tomato tins and blankets tied with string. It was a tonic for which the West Coast had long been waiting. The heady excitement of California was over and there had been little prosperity to follow it. Now, in one final insane rush, everyone was off to the Yukon. Fifteen hundred people sailed north from Seattle within ten days of the first news of gold. The mayor of that city, who was on a visit to San Francisco when the news came through, wired his resignation and raced north. Steamer offices were in a state of siege, and tickets were selling for $1,000. By February of 1898, forty-one ships were on the regular run from San Francisco to Skagway, the nearest port to the gold fields. From Skagway, the prospectors had to make the long haul up over the Chilkoot or the White Horse Pass, then down the Yukon to Dawson City. It was a harsh journey. Among the thousands who embarked on it, many failed. Pierre Berton, in his excellent book on the Klondike, reckons that of the 100,000 who set out for Dawson City, 30,000 to 40,000 actually arrived. Of these, perhaps 5,000 searched for gold; a few hundred got rich.[8]

Along the way, they fell victim to the weather and to men like Jefferson (Soapy) Smith, who ran the town of Skagway, cheating all comers and killing any who argued. One horrified traveller wrote, 'I have stumbled upon a few tough corners of the globe but I think the most outrageously lawless quarter I ever struck was Skagway. It seemed as if the scum of the earth had hastened here to fleece, rob or murder. There was no law whatsoever; might was right, the dead shot only was immune to danger'. Skagway, of course, was on US soil, but to reach Dawson City the prospectors, tramping in a never-ending line up the snow-clad mountainsides, had to cross the Canadian border at the top of the pass. Here a handful of men from the Canadian Northwest Mounted

8 Pierre Berton, *The Golden Trail*, Macmillan, Toronto, 1954.

Police sought to bring some sort of order to chaos. At gunpoint, they refused to let through prospectors who were not carrying a year's supply of food. Major J.M. Walsh of the Northwest Mounted Police reported, 'Such a scene of havoc and destruction can scarcely be imagined. Thousands of pack horses lie dead along the way, sometimes in bunches under cliffs, with pack saddles and packs where they have fallen from the rocks above.' Those who did get through swelled the population of Dawson City so fast that by the summer of 1898 it had become the largest Canadian city north of Winnipeg. It was a frenzied yet pathetic community, so short of supplies that the police would not bother to arrest a man unless he had his own provisions. Most boats that did come up the Yukon carried whisky instead of badly needed food. One year all the eggs were rotten when they arrived; hungry citizens had to wait a year for a fresh supply. When the governess of the local bishop's children married a missionary, the only thing he could find to give her for a present on her wedding day was a pot of marmalade.

It was all over as fast as it had begun. There was plenty of gold in the creeks around Dawson and it continued to be worked on a commercial basis until the winter of 1966, but the horde of prospectors had picked the cream off the field by 1900. The Klondike rush probably yielded about 75 tonnes of gold in the last three years of what was certainly the most exciting century in the history of gold.

### The Gold Standard Goes International

While the gold rushes of the nineteenth century had an immediate and profound effect in bringing vast hordes of people to virtually untouched territory and stimulating faster growth of cities and communications in one year than would otherwise have taken place in fifty, the impact was hardly less on the great financial centres of Europe. Not only was London to provide a major part of the capital to develop the South African gold-mining industry, but the gold itself flowed in. All of South Africa's gold was refined in London by Rothschild's, Johnson Matthey, and Raphael. The refiners sold the gold either directly to the Bank of England, which often offered a small premium of a halfpenny per ounce, or through Mocatta & Goldsmid and the other London brokers.

The impact of Californian and Australian gold had quickly been reflected in the gold reserves of Britain, France and other major European powers. Inevitably gold was used more and more in business transactions, although only Britain was truly on the gold standard, as it had been since its accidental adoption in 1717. In 1871, however, Germany – getting fat on the French indemnity after the Franco-Prussian war – issued a new currency unit, the mark, which was based on gold. The Germans bought £50 million worth of gold (about 466 tonnes or 12.8 million ounces) and coined it over two years. This demand for gold pushed up the price slightly and, in relation to it, the value of silver fell. More European countries were at once forced to switch to gold. Scandinavia demonetized silver in 1874; Holland followed a year later; France and Spain switched to gold in 1876. Before the end of the nineteenth century almost every country in the world had changed to a gold standard. Russia followed suit in 1893; India adopted a gold exchange standard (allied to sterling) in 1898; and the United States capped it all with the Gold Standard Act of 1900.

The silver lobby in the United States had fought a desperate rearguard action for almost half a century and had succeeded in keeping the country on a bimetallic system of gold and silver long after the flood of Californian gold had begun. They had pushed through the Sherman Silver Purchase Act of 1890, which decreed that the government must buy 140 tonnes (4.5 million ounces) of silver a month with Treasury notes redeemable in gold or silver, 'it being the established policy of the United States to maintain the two metals on a parity with each other upon the present ratio' (1:16). But not for long. The 1896 presidential election campaign, one of the fiercest ever fought, turned on the issue of silver. The Democrats, with the retention of bimetallism as the main plank of their platform, nominated William Jennings Bryan of Nebraska to fight the Republicans' William McKinley. In his speech to the Democratic National Convention, Bryan said, 'We will answer their demand for a gold standard by saying to them: "You shall not press down upon the brow of labor this crown of thorns, you shall not crucify mankind upon a cross of gold".' All stirring stuff, but Bryan was defeated in the popular vote by 7 million to 6.5 million. Four years later, the United States went quietly onto the gold standard. The dollar of twenty-five and four-fifths grains of gold 900 fine became the 'standard unit of value; and all other forms of money issued or coined by the United States shall be maintained at a parity of value with this standard'.

The shift to gold-backed currencies in Europe, North America, Australia and South Africa is clearly shown in statistics prepared for a British Royal Commission in 1913.[9] These reveal that in 1889 the value of gold held by central banks and note-issuing banks in twenty-nine leading nations amounted to £296 million (because the sterling price of gold was fixed, the amounts were always given in terms of money, not quantity, in those days); by 1899 the stock was up to £504 million in other US national and state banks, and the Bank of France and Bank of Russia, each had £130 million. The Bank of England, by comparison, got by with a modest £31 million because London, as the undisputed

9 Royal Commission on Indian Finance and Currency, ed. 7238, 1913, Appendix XXX.

financial capital of the world, was a substantial creditor on short-term capital account and by a slight upward adjustment of interest rates the Bank could always be sure gold would flow in from abroad to settle short-term debts.

When the world went to war in 1914, fifty-nine countries were on a gold or gold exchange standard; China was the sole major nation still wedded to silver. What was remarkable was that the price of gold in 1914 was effectively the same as it had been two centuries earlier in 1717, when Sir Isaac Newton, as master of the Mint, had set the Mint's buying price for 'standard' (22-carat gold or 916 fine) for transformation into coin at £3.17s.10Hd. per troy ounce (equivalent to £4.4s.11Hd. fine gold). The price quote was always for 'standard' gold; the present custom of quoting fine gold was not introduced until 1919. The only major price variations had occurred during the Napoleonic Wars, when, as we observed in the previous chapter, cash payment of banknotes in gold was suspended between 1797 and 1821. But for the remainder of the nineteenth century the price remained within very narrow margins. The Bank Charter Act of 1844 required the Bank of England to buy gold at not less than £3.17s.9d. an ounce, putting an effective floor to the price. But the market price was rarely much higher; between 1870 and 1914 the peak was £3.17s.11Gd. Such stability was helped, of course, during an era of expanding world trade, by the rapid rise in gold production. In the nineteenth century, more than 11,500 tonnes (over 350 million ounces) were mined, compared with around 2,000 tonnes (64 million ounces) in the previous century. In 1914 annual output was up to 622 tonnes (20 million ounces). World war, however, finally put the gold standard, or at least governments' faith in it, to the test (as had happened previously in Britain during the Napoleonic Wars). While in theory the gold standard survived, in practice it was never the same again.

**CHAPTER 3**

# Goodbye Gold Standard
# 1914–1971

The imminent shadow of war in 1914 led to a scramble for gold. 'There was considerably more continental demand for bar gold than during any one of the preceding three years,' commented a circular from one London broker.[1] Germany and France were topping up their war chests. Even the commercial banks in Britain took £12 million in gold from the Bank of England, in what John Maynard Keynes called 'a fit of hoarding'.[2] But Keynes, who was working as a special consultant to the Treasury, argued against a suspension of cash payments. He wrote to the Chancellor of the Exchequer, 'The future position of the City of London as a free gold market will be seriously injured if at the first sign of emergency specie payment is suspended.'[3] Not least in his thoughts was the fact that many other countries kept their gold stock in London and their continued confidence was essential. Although convertibility was not suspended, the circulation of £1 and 10-shilling paper notes was increased and notes were made legal tender for any amount, while sovereigns were quietly withdrawn from circulation when they came into the banks. At the outbreak of war £123 million in gold coin was in circulation in Britain; £100 million ended up at the Bank of England. The normal ebb and flow of gold in and out of the country also virtually ceased; export was permitted only on warships and then permission was rarely granted (not least because the German U-boat blockade made gold transport highly risky). Meanwhile, the Bank of England bought at source the output of South Africa and Australia, tripling its reserves in five months. 'There was magic in gold,' noted Sir John Clapham,

---

1 Mocatta & Goldsmid, Annual Circular, 1914.
2 *Collected Writings of J.M. Keynes*, Vol. VXI, Macmillan, London, 1972, p. 8.
3 Ibid., Memo of 3 August 1914, pp. 10–11.

'ignorance of the costs of twentieth-century war, a great and only half-mistaken faith in gold reserves, should war come.'[4] Elsewhere nations husbanded what gold they had, becoming increasingly reluctant to let it go, except for the most urgent settlements. In short, to all intents and purposes the gold standard was suspended. Even the United States stopped the export of gold when she entered the war in 1917, although Washington did resume full gold payments in 1919.

In the London gold market business virtually came to a halt, since production throughout the Empire was being taken up for the government abroad. 'There was no business in gold,' reflected Mocatta's 1917 review. Peace, however, brought much discussion of a swift return to gold. Few people realized how a world war had changed things, nor that it marked the watershed of Britain as a world power, with sterling being as good as gold. Henceforward, economic power shifted rapidly to the United States, and it was there that the future of gold and its price were to be determined over the next two decades. For the moment, though, the talk was of returning to a full gold standard with gold at its traditional price.

### The birth of the 'fix'

A crucial step was to restore London as the market place for gold. Initially the Bank of England agreed with South Africa's mining finance houses for them to ship all their gold to London for refining (the Rand Refinery not yet being open), after which it would be sold through N.M. Rothschild 'at best price obtainable, giving the London market and the Bullion Brokers an opportunity to bid'. Thus on 12 September 1919 the London gold 'fixing' was born. 'All fine gold available for sale on any day was delivered to Rothschilds,' noted a contemporary account. 'Rothschilds decided at 11 o'clock each morning, having regard to the various exchanges, what was the best sterling price of gold which could be obtained by realisation in any part of the world. The four bullion brokers, Mocatta & Goldsmid, Pixley & Abell, Sharps & Wilkins, and Samuel Montagu & Co., were given the opportunity of bidding and would obtain their requirements if the price they bid equalled or exceeded the realisation price fixed by Rothschild.'[5]

The bids were made by phone for the first few days, but it was then decided to hold a formal meeting at Rothschilds' offices. The first 'fix' was £4.18s.9d., reflecting an important change that henceforward the price was for 'good delivery' gold of 995 fine, compared to the historic 'standard gold' of 916 fine. This actually made the base price at which the Bank of England was required to buy all gold on offer £4.4s.11d. The higher price that day reflected the sterling–dollar exchange rate in

4 Sir John Clapham, *Bank of England*, Vol. II, Cambridge University Press, Cambridge, 1944, p. 415.
5 Internal paper, Archives of N.M. Rothschild & Sons.

New York. The New York gold price was $20.67 an ounce and from now on the sterling price of gold depended on the sterling–dollar rate. As sterling fell that winter, the price went as high as £6.7s.4d. an ounce. In fact, although the London fix continued to be in sterling for almost another fifty years, what really counted was the dollar price of gold, as the dollar gradually replaced sterling as the world's favourite reserve currency.

### The gold standard revisited – briefly

Reviving the gold standard was not so simple. In the aftermath of war, industries were ruined, inflation was rampant and there was talk of reparations by Germany that could not conceivably be paid. Governments everywhere had pressing domestic priorities, so that the discipline of the gold standard cutting in to restrict credit and cause deflation was not socially acceptable.

The future of the international monetary scene was thrashed out at a conference organized by the League of Nations at Genoa in 1922. The meeting agreed that while a return to the gold standard was desirable, prices had risen so much during the war that there was not enough gold around to finance world trade. So nations would 'economise in the monetary use of gold through the maintenance of reserves in the form of balances in foreign currencies'. In practice this meant a gold exchange standard, under which central banks in smaller countries kept all or part of their reserves in such key currencies as sterling or dollars, which were interchangeable for gold.

Britain, however, made a partial return to the gold standard in 1925, very much at the insistence of Winston Churchill, then Chancellor of the Exchequer. Actually it was a half-way house, a gold bullion standard, for notes were no longer convertible into gold coin, but could be exchanged for bullion in 400-ounce good delivery bars – a minimum purchase involving £1,700. The great mistake was to return to the old fixed price of £4.4s.11Hd. per fine ounce (equivalent to the historic £3.17s.10Hd. for standard gold) – regardless of the fact that prices had changed so much since 1914 that sterling was now trapped into an entirely unrealistic exchange rate. The British decision also took no account of a fundamental shift in the balance of gold reserves. Prior to World War I, Europe held 54 per cent of monetary gold stocks, Britain 9 per cent and North America (essentially the United States) 24 per cent; by 1925 the position was reversed with North America having 45 per cent, Europe 28 per cent and Britain a mere 7 per cent. 'The 1925 return to the gold standard', observes J.K. Galbraith, 'was perhaps the most decisively damaging action involving money in modern times.'[6]

6 J.K. Galbraith, *Money, Whence it Came, Where it Went*, André Deutsch, London, 1975, p. 168.

The new system was too fragile to last. In practice there was little free movement of gold; many nations still preferred to sit on what they had and Germany, Spain and Japan all refused to return to convertibility. France, having no faith in paper reserves, turned all surplus foreign exchange instantly into gold, bidding aggressively in the market. She even bought forward much South African production through the London brokers the moment it was on the boat to England. The Wall Street crash of 1929, with its immediate echoes throughout Europe in reducing trade, creating unemployment and causing general financial instability, was the death-knell. The collapse of Credit Anstalt in Austria in May 1931 brought fear of the fall of many financial institutions. Money fled the London market as loans were called in. The Bank of England's reserves fell to a dangerous level, and on 21 September 1931 the gold standard was suspended. Over two hundred years of a stable gold price, save for short interludes in the Napoleonic Wars and World War I, had ended. And the reputation of the pound sterling, backed by gold, as the international currency *par excellence*, was over. Sterling was devalued, creating a new gold price that fluctuated between £5.10s.0d. and £6.6s.10d. Several smaller European central banks, notably those of Belgium and Holland, were caught out holding a large part of their reserves in sterling, believing that under the gold exchange standard it was as good as gold. It was a bitter lesson not forgotten for many years and was one reason why, thirty years on, as their economies recovered from World War II, both these countries rebuilt a large part of their reserves in gold.

The knock-on effect of Britain leaving the gold standard caused several other nations, including Portugal, Sweden and India, to sever their links to gold. Only the United States and France, who had seen what was coming, sat on increasing gold stocks, but it was only a matter of time before they too had to relinquish a standard that many nations had forsaken.

### Enter the gold hoarder

The collapse of the gold standard, however, did not affect the position of London as the world's bullion market. 'The suspension of the gold standard only means that the Bank of England is no longer bound to part with gold at its statutory price,' *The Economist* pointed out. 'Gold may still be imported or exported freely, and foreign bankers and private individuals are free to lodge gold for safe custody in London.'[7] South African gold was still sold through the 'fixing', although with one important change that the Bank of England now became the principal for South Africa, instead of Rothschilds; and the Bank had a direct line

7 *The Economist*, 26 August 1933, p. 399.

to the fixing. The demand came from hoarders throughout Europe; commercial banks, businesses and individuals became distrustful of paper money and took refuge in gold. France's legendary private hoard of gold dates from this period, but in Germany and Austria, too, many people bought a little gold in case they had to flee the Nazis. The Bank for International Settlements once calculated that in the five years after Britain went off the gold standard, almost 3,110 tonnes (100 million ounces), or 70 per cent of all gold mined in the period, was hoarded, in undisclosed holdings by banks and private people.[8] Much of the gold, incidentally, came from India where the devaluation of the rupee in line with sterling made it profitable to dishoard gold and send it to London. India dishoarded nearly 1,250 tonnes (40 million ounces) during the 1930s, the only time it has been a significant seller.

Thus the immediate effect of the gold standard's suspension was to make the metal more attractive to millions, who started hoarding it and trading it as never before. The gold standard, one must remember, meant only that the gold price was fixed and paper notes could be cashed in for gold at that price. Banks and individuals could still buy and sell gold in the market, but at the prevailing price.

### Roosevelt decrees $35 dollar gold

While Indians sold gold and Europeans hoarded it, the United States stayed firmly on the gold standard with the price fixed at $20.67, so long as Herbert Hoover was in the White House. Franklin Roosevelt, however, took a different view. He knew he had to breathe fresh life into the US economy, to raise prices and increase the money supply. But the inflation that implied would weaken the dollar and lead to an outflow of gold. Within his first 100 days in office in 1933, Roosevelt not only banned the export of gold and halted the convertibility of dollar bills into gold, but also ordered US citizens to hand in all the gold they possessed (the prohibition on gold was to last until 31 December 1974). The next step was to tackle the gold price. Roosevelt's advisers, looking back over the previous century, observed that each of the great gold rushes to California, Australia and South Africa had led to a burst of economic activity. The trouble was there was no new gold rush (except by Europeans scrambling to buy); the alternative, the economists in Washington decided, was to raise the price of gold, enhancing the value of existing stocks and so the money supply. But by how much should the price go up? Roosevelt took to deciding the gold price himself over breakfast each day, with the help of Henry Morgenthau, his acting secretary of the Treasury, and Jesse Jones of the Reconstruction Finance Corporation. 'While Roosevelt ate his eggs and drank his coffee, the

8 Bank for International Settlements, 8th Annual Report, 1938, p. 45.

group discussed what the day's price should be,' wrote Arthur Schlesinger Jr. 'The precise figure each day was less important than the encouragement of a general upward trend. One day Morgenthau came in, more worried than usual, and suggested an increase from 19 to 22 cents. Roosevelt took one look at Morgenthau's anxious face and proposed 21 cents. "It's a lucky number," he said with a laugh, "because it's three times seven".'[9]

The daily game had little effect on other prices, because the revalued gold was not available to US banks to lend against. So on 31 January 1934 the price was given a final hoist to $35 an ounce (a total devaluation of the dollar of 40 per cent) but at the same time, to everyone's surprise, the United States announced it would go back on the gold standard. The US assay office stood ready to buy all gold on offer at the fixed price of $35 and would sell to foreign central banks still on the gold standard, such as France, Holland, Belgium and Italy. The effect was electric; a guaranteed price of $35 was irresistible. Everyone wanted gold for New York delivery. The Bank of France was furious and tried to obstruct shipments, yet it lost about 200 tonnes (over 6 million ounces) in the first month. The pattern of gold flows for a generation was set; Fort Knox was built in Kentucky in 1935 to store the great stock that was amassed. Ultimately, by 1949, the United States held 22,000 tonnes (707 million ounces), or 75 per cent of all official reserves, and half of all gold ever mined to that date.

### A gold-mining boom

Gold mining was galvanized too. It is ironic that, throughout the harsh years of the 1930s, mining boomed as never before, urged on by the new $35 price. World gold production doubled from 622 tonnes (20 million ounces) a year to a peak of over 1,200 tonnes (38.6 million ounces) in 1940. In California, thousands of the unemployed became gold prospectors, scouring the streams of the High Sierras for gold overlooked by the miners almost a hundred years earlier. The United States' gold production doubled, and in 1940 reached a record total of 155 tonnes (5 million ounces), which was not surpassed until 1988. Canada attained a peak of 171 tonnes in 1941 that has only been beaten in a single year, 1991. Indeed, throughout the 1930s South Africa found herself being challenged as the premier gold-producing nation for the first time in the twentieth century. Her share of world production, which had climbed to over 50 per cent in the 1920s, suddenly pitched down to 32.5 per cent in 1938. But it was the final effort for her rivals for forty years. Their most accessible ore reserves were spent, and it was not until higher prices and new technology in the 1980s made many low-grade deposits in Australia and North America viable that they

9 Arthur M. Schlesinger Jr, *The Coming of the New Deal, The Age of Roosevelt*, Vol. 2, Houghton Mifflin, Boston, 1960.

again contributed significant output. Meanwhile, in the intervening generation South Africa climbed into an increasingly commanding position in the world of gold.

### War and aftermath

While mining boomed, the situation in Europe deteriorated rapidly in the late 1930s. Hitler's invasion of the Rhineland in 1936 precipitated an even greater rush into gold by French private hoarders, despite the closure of both the London and Paris markets to coin sales. Unable to maintain the French franc at its old parity to gold, France devalued by 30 per cent in September 1936, and came off the gold standard. An embargo was placed on private gold dealing and the French were ordered to surrender their gold to the Bank of France (few did). Holland and Switzerland came off the gold standard shortly thereafter, leaving Belgium as the only nation in the world still flying the gold standard (although war eventually forced suspension there too).

Gold trading in London, where an increasing number of Europe's hoarders kept their gold in allocated and unallocated accounts, remained active, but actual movement of gold became more difficult. Insurers were demanding full war-rate premiums by the autumn of 1938. Forward deliveries were suspended early in 1939. The final fixing before World War II set a price of £8.1s.0d. an ounce, almost double that of 1931 (and 1717). When war was declared on 3 September 1939, the London gold market was closed and remained so for almost fifteen years.

The framework for revival after the war was set by the Bretton Woods Agreement in 1944, which created the International Monetary Fund to oversee a new monetary system based on fixed exchange rates. Fund members agreed to maintain their exchange rates, with only a 1 per cent margin either way, against a benchmark of their relationship to gold or the dollar, on 1 July 1944. The dollar and gold were interchangeable because the US Treasury stood ready to buy or sell at $35 an ounce to approved central banks. In effect, it was not a gold standard, but a dollar exchange standard. IMF members also agreed not to deal in gold at prices differing from its par value against currencies. This did not mean, however, that central banks were not active in gold. On the contrary, in the immediate post-war years they often sold what little gold they had left to the US Treasury for badly needed dollars to rebuild their shattered economies. The high water-mark of US gold reserves came in 1949, when its 22,000 tonnes represented 75 per cent of western world (that is, non-communist) stocks. Thereafter, a gradual decline set in, as European central banks began to trade in dollars for gold at the Federal Reserve, while also buying in the market. Central banks remained net buyers of gold every year until 1965, actually taking 40 per cent of all new supplies in that period. Thus gold was still perceived very much as a monetary metal well into the 1960s. The disappearance of the gold standard certainly did not mean the metal ceased to be a desirable asset.

Private hoarders found it equally attractive. Although the London gold market remained closed until 1954, in that the fixing was not resumed, the members developed a lively trade in 'manufactured' gold because the Bank of England would sell them gold to be manufactured into jewellery for export. Since markets abroad often offered a premium of $3 or more an ounce, a brisk business started in exporting not only 22-carat gold sheet, but pen nibs, ashtrays and even statues of Viking warriors to profit from the premium prices. Such jewellery was then melted back into bar gold. Switzerland initially took much of this metal as the three main banks, Crédit Suisse, Swiss Bank Corporation and Union Bank of Switzerland, began to build up their strong position as wholesalers. The Swiss had been active before the war, indeed Swiss Bank Corporation had even been a buyer in the first week of the 'fixing' in 1919, but in the decade immediately after World War II they established firm footholds in the Middle East and Southeast Asia. The greatest demand came from China in the final days before the communists took over; gold commanded $50 to $55 an ounce in Beijing or Shanghai, but could be had in Europe for only $38. Recalling those days, a Zürich dealer once told me, 'We made high profits, but the middlemen between us and China made whopping profits. I had a visitor once who knew the Far East well and sold him a lot of gold. Years later he came in again and asked me, "What did you make?" I said, "About forty cents an ounce". He admitted he'd made six dollars.' The links established in those years stood the Swiss in good stead. When I first went through the gold markets of Asia in the 1960s, the Swiss were well ensconced. Turn up in an exchange dealer's little booth in the main square of Beirut, and the chances were that Walter Frey of Swiss Bank Corporation was sitting there already sipping a Turkish coffee. Frey became something of a legendary figure: years later people in Asia would ask first what the gold price might do; then 'how is Walter Frey?'

### 'Fixing' reopens

The 'manufactured' gold trade lasted until 1954, when the London market was permitted to resume the fixing. The premium on the price had declined by then, helped by sales from the Soviet Union which began in the autumn of 1953 and brought the European market price back down to $35. The Soviet sales continued steadily for the next thirteen years, amounting in all to nearly 3,000 tonnes (96.4 million ounces) which mostly came through the London market. Thus London got back to business on 22 March 1954 with a fix of £12.8s.6d. an ounce; the increase from £8.1s.0d. at the last pre-war fix was due to the devaluation of sterling in 1949. The market's traditional strength was there because it had not only the South African production, which was up to 410 tonnes (13.2 million ounces) in 1954, rising to 665 tonnes (21.4 million ounces) by 1960, but also the Soviet gold. With other small producers also using London, the market was handling up to 80 per cent of the world's gold, most of it through the fixing (the Bank of England, as the selling agent for South Africa, would usually only sell on the fix). 'The Bank were the masters of the fixing,' a dealer once recalled. 'They were the only corner from which the gold came.'

Although the fix was still in sterling, the Bank's prime concern was to keep it in line with the equivalent of $35. That task became increasingly difficult during the 1960s, as the private market for gold grew and the United States itself became mired down in the Vietnam war, raising questions about the strength of the dollar and touching off a huge speculative demand for gold. As early as 1961 the Bank found it had to sell occasionally from reserves on the fix to hold the price at $35. This led to the creation of the gold pool, an alliance between the central banks of Britain, Belgium, France, Italy, the Netherlands, Switzerland, the United States and West Germany to maintain the $35 level. The Bank of England, operating for the pool, sold from its combined reserves if the price threatened to breach $35.20 and bought back for the pool account when it was weak.

The pool worked well until 1965, when for the first time, it was a net seller. Soviet gold sales had ceased and sterling was under pressure, causing many private buyers – and China – to switch into gold. Once sterling finally cracked in November 1967, the rush for gold by private speculators was really on. An attack on the dollar was not far behind. Could $35 gold be maintained? The members of the gold pool, except for France where General de Gaulle shrewdly opted out, thought it could. They had nearly 24,000 tonnes of gold at their disposal. William McChesney Martin of the US Federal Reserve Board rashly said he would defend the $35 price 'to the last ingot'. The Board's bluff was called. The Tet offensive in Vietnam in March 1968 touched off a tidal wave of gold buying. The pool lost 3,000 tonnes (94 million ounces), including nearly 1,000 tonnes between 8 March and 14 March 1968 trying to hold the price down. US Air Force planes rushed more and more gold from Fort Knox to London. So much piled up on the weighing room floor of the Bank of England that it collapsed. The pool had lost. Early on the morning of 15 March 1968, Roy Jenkins, the British Chancellor of the Exchequer, rose in a crowded House of Commons to announce a sudden Bank Holiday. The gold market was closed 'at the request of the United States'. The London market remained shut for two weeks.

It was the watershed in gold. So much changed at this point that the history of gold is really divided into before and after 1968. The price was no longer set; it was free to float. When the London market reopened it fixed the price in dollars, not sterling. And it had lost its historic ace, held since the 1660s, in being the market place for most gold production. The Swiss in a neat coup had secured the marketing of South African gold while London was closed. And the pace setters in determining what the price should do now that it was freed from the $35 straitjacket were private investors and speculators. Central banks were largely banished from the market for a while. For them the curtain came down in 1971 when the US Federal Reserve closed its 'gold window' at which so many of them, especially in Europe, had traded in dollars for gold for nearly two decades, once again changing the balance of gold power back across the Atlantic to the restored economies of Europe. With the Federal Reserve no longer standing ready to provide gold to central banks at $35 an ounce, the last vestige of the gold standard, albeit the watered-down dollar exchange version, had vanished. That was the way it was; the rest of this book is about the way it is.

# PART II

# THE MINERS

# CHAPTER 4

# The Global Miner

Gold rushes often seem the stuff of history; the stampede to California in 1848, the migration to Australia three years later, the new era ushered in by the South African discoveries of the 1880s and the scramble to Kalgoorlie and then the Klondike just before 1900. The twentieth century was rather short on prospecting drama, save the stimulant of the price jump from $20.67 to $35 in 1934 which triggered a seven-year mining frenzy, until the boom of the 1980s once again made the hunt for gold the only game in town. Production then virtually doubled in a decade. From a twenty-one-year low of 959 tonnes (30.8 million ounces) in 1980, western mine output rose relentlessly to around 1,850 tonnes (57.9 million ounces) by 1993, or worldwide to 2,200 tonnes when the former Soviet Union, China and North Korea are included.

The catalyst this time, as in the thirties, was the price; $850 in January 1980, with an average of $614 for that year and $460 in 1981 was a compulsive jolt to the gold-mining industry. Exploration budgets exploded; from 1969 to 1980 only $2.1 billion was spent on gold exploration; between 1981 and 1990 it was $14.9 billion, of which $7 billion was just in the three years 1987–9.[1] Not only was more money devoted to the search for gold in the 1980s than in its entire previous history, but so were more people. This gold rush was not just mining companies, including a host of new names, but hundreds of thousands of individual prospectors. Over 1 million diggers were probably involved in Latin America alone, while countless others took up pick and shovel everywhere from Ghana, the Ivory Coast and Zaire (indeed in most

1 B. Mackenzie and M.D. Doggett, *Worldwide Trends in Gold Exploration*, Centre for Resource Studies, Queen's University, Kingston, Ontario, 1992.

## WORLD: PRODUCTION

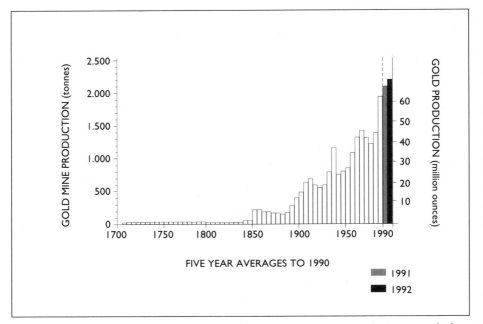

African countries) to Indonesia, Malaysia, Papua New Guinea and the Philippines. At the peak the prospectors alone were contributing in excess of 200 tonnes (6.4 million ounces) annually.

The transformation was not just in output; the world of gold mining altered radically in virtually every respect in the short space of a decade. New technology from heap-leaching to carbon-in-pulp recovery and computer control of mine planning, opened up the opportunity to go for low-grade gold; bullion banks came in with gold loans to provide cheap start-up capital and then followed through with innovative hedging programmes. A leading Swiss banker remarked to me that the only thing that made the gold business interesting for him in the late 1980s was the challenge of gold-mining finance and not, as one might expect of a Swiss, the handling of investors' portfolios.

Within a few short years the gold map of the world changed. South Africa produced 71 per cent of western mine gold in 1980 and 34.6 per cent in 1990; by 1993 this declined further to about 26 per cent of world output (including the republics of the former Soviet Union, China and North Korea, where some production estimates are available for the first time). South Africa remained number one in the world league, but her output fell, while elsewhere around the globe it was not just doubling or tripling, but in the United States soaring ten-fold and in

Australia rocketing fourteen-fold. The United States knocked the former Soviet Union from its long held second place in the league in 1991; Australia notched up third place in 1992. The cast of other serious producers in the 1990s embraces Brazil, Canada, Chile, China, Ghana (winning back its eighteenth century reputation as the 'Gold Coast'), Indonesia, Papua New Guinea, the Philippines and Zimbabwe. Which is not to ignore what is emerging from Bolivia, Ecuador, Guyana, Mexico, Peru, Saudi Arabia, Turkey, Venezuela, Uruguay, Vietnam and Zaire, to name but a few places where international mining companies are active. While the rapid growth phase is over (exploration budgets, a key signpost, were down over 50 per cent from 1987–1993), the prospect of gold output remaining on its new high plateau into the twenty-first century is a real one.

This revolution is without precedent. In the earlier history of gold the impact came from discoveries in a single country; Brazil in the early eighteenth century, California, Australia and South Africa in the nineteenth century. By contrast, gold mining, like the gold market, went global in the late twentieth century.

Previously, gold-mining companies had generally concentrated on home ground. Only mining finance houses such as Consolidated Gold Fields (which has since vanished after the 1989 takeover by Hanson), or RTZ Corporation (which came relatively late to gold anyway) or offshoots of the Anglo American/De Beers empire such as Charter Consolidated or Minorco really operated internationally and then not often in gold. Today it is hard to find someone who is not multinational. Even a Canadian company like Cambior, modestly still located in Val d'Or, Quebec, with a stable of little local mines, has hit the big time, going for the Omai deposit in Guyana backed by a 300,000-ounce gold loan. As for the major players, look at Placer Dome in Vancouver, which had spun a network not just through the Canadian provinces, but south to the United States and Chile and across the Pacific (via its Placer Pacific subsidiary) to Australia and Papua New Guinea (where it mines nearly as much gold as in Canada). Or take Newmont Mining in Denver; not content with a bonanza from Newmont Gold at the Carlin Trend in Nevada, it is branching out to Peru, Uzbekistan, Indonesia, and even has an office at Chiang Mai up country in Thailand. While Homestake Mining has augmented its historic mine at Lead, South Dakota with acquisitions in Australia, Canada and Chile. The South Africans' horizons have broadened too. Anglo American and Gencor have mines in Brazil, Gold Fields of South Africa is scouting Ghana, Ecuador, Venezuela and Zaire. As for the Australians, you meet them at every turn in Indonesia, Papua New Guinea and the Philippines. And it is that continued diversity, despite a disappointing gold price in the early nineties and the increasing constraint of environmental controls, that will keep gold output high. Australia, Canada and South Africa have peaked, but watch out for the Pacific Rim countries, China and eventually Russia and the other CIS republics. 'Russia', said a Canadian mining friend, just back from there, 'could be gold's final frontier.'

### Harnessing new technology

While the catalyst for the mining boom was the price, the new technology was also there to make it work. 'The 1980s have seen a revolution in gold extraction technology, paralleled only by the implementation of the cyanide leaching process in the late 1800s,' observed John Marsden, consulting metallurgist at Phelps Dodge Mining and author of a book on the chemistry of gold extraction.[2] 'This revolution', he went on, 'has been led by the widespread adoption of carbon adsorption processes for good recovery, heap-leaching of low-grade ores and the development of oxidation processes to treat refractory ores.'

The immediate advantages were the opportunity to recover gold profitably from ores with grades as low as 1 g/t (0.032 oz/t) – compared to a minimum of 5–6 g/t in many older mines – or from refractory ores, which may be higher grade but from which it is difficult to extract the metal. 'These ores must be treated by processes which break down the refractory component of the ore to liberate gold,' notes metallurgist Marsden. 'Most commonly, the refractory material must be oxidised to yield acceptable gold recovery by roasting, pressure oxidation (autoclaves), biological oxidation or chlorination.'[3] The ability to handle refractory ores is crucial in maintaining a high level of gold production going into the next century. In places as diverse as the Carlin Trend of Nevada, Chile and Papua New Guinea, output will depend more and more on liberating that gold. Another great question for the future is not just equipment, but the viability on a large commercial scale of bioleaching, in which bacterial cultures are introduced to oxidize those recalcitrant refractory ores (see Chapter 6). An important variation on this theme is bio-oxidation, pioneered by Gencor at the Fairview mine in South Africa and also in use in Australia, Brazil and Ghana, in which ore is crushed to a powdered concentrate, and mixed with water in tanks to which the bacteria is added.

The initial speed with which gold output grew, however, had more to do with heap-leaching and the new carbon-in-pulp recovery method. Heap-leaching, which we will look at in action in Chapter 6, enables low-grade oxidized orebodies to be mined economically by eliminating the costly milling of ore to a powder. Instead, ore direct

2 John Marsden and Iain House, *The Chemistry of Gold Extraction*, Simon & Schuster, New York and London, 1992.

3 John Marsden, *International Gold Mining Newsletter*, 'An overview of gold processing around the world', Vol. 19, No. 9, Sept. 1992, p. 138.

from open-pit operations is roughly crushed before being piled up on leach 'pads', which are sprayed with a solution of dilute cyanide which absorbs the gold as it percolates down through the pad. The technique, pioneered in Nevada and Montana in the United States, made possible the rapid development of open-pit mines. By the end of the eighties heap-leaching was accounting for half of all US production. Although this proportion will decline as more complex deeper ores have to be dealt with, it was the kick-start to the ten-fold increase in production there. The experience gained, however, is already enabling heap-leaching to be adapted to many other environments, such as Latin America, as a large-scale, cheap way of handling low-grade material. Newmont Mining, for example, one of the pioneers in the United States, is advising Uzbekistan (the second largest gold-producing republic in the former Soviet Union) on the heap-leaching of low-grade ore stockpiles at its huge Muruntau mine.

Heap-leaching also happens to work well in tandem with carbon adsorption recovery. The process known as carbon-in-pulp (CIP) or, slightly different, carbon-in-leach (CIL), is based on gold's natural affinity for carbon (a hard carbon made from coconut shells is preferred). A cyanide solution 'pregnant' with gold, either from heap-leaching or from normal milling, is passed through carbon adsorption tanks, where the carbon soaks up the gold like a sponge taking water. Carbon recovery has caught on so fast that it has become the predominant method, accounting for half (perhaps more) of world output; in Australia it is over 80 per cent. The Russians, incidentally, came up with their own variation of resin-in-pulp (presumably because they had more pine than coconut trees to hand).

The ability to find new gold mines and work them efficiently has been aided by everything from advances in geo-chemistry and geo-physics to computers. In the detection of new orebodies, the geo-chemist once identified three or four elements in a rock sample that might lead him towards gold; today he can pinpoint twenty elements in the same sample as pathfinders, using the ratio of these elements to track how the fluids bearing gold moved millions of years ago as they filtered up through the earth's crust. Geo-physics also enables airborne surveys to look for signals from radioactive emissions that may be linked to elements surrounding gold. That said, there is no substitute, as in any detective's job, for old-fashioned geological legwork in the field, chipping at rocks for clues. And then, as one geologist put it, 'in the end it's still a bunch of drilling.'

Computers, however, have given a new dimension to every aspect of mine planning from control of ore grades to marshalling trucks in a huge open pit. The ability to put up on a computer terminal a coloured three-dimensional mine plan, adapting it constantly to fresh information on faults, rock types, zones of mineralization, the metallurgy of ores or a thousand fresh assays, has wrought its own revolution. Geologists or mining engineers can journey mentally through the core of a deposit far underground. A mine plan, once devised by months of intense draughtsmanship, and so somewhat sacrosanct, can be revised in an afternoon, just by punching in the latest data. Even from my own standpoint, I came closer to an understanding of what was going on in the heart of Newmont Gold's vast open pit Gold Quarry on the Carlin Trend in Nevada by spending an hour at the screen with one of its computer planners, than descending to the bottom of the pit. On the screen I saw a coloured three-dimensional 'street map' of the whole place.

The catalogue of new technology is endless. Laser beams are replacing tight piano wires stretched between two points to detect any movement in mine walls. Radar probes through rock underground to alert miners to hazardous conditions ahead. Chemical explosives giving off dangerous fumes underground may be replaced by plasma blasting in which a fast discharge of electrical energy converts electrolyte into high pressure plasma which expands rapidly with explosive effect.

### Enviromental hurdles

In parallel with new technology, miners everywhere have to adjust to concern for the environment. They are frequently treated as an environmental pariah. As the chief executive of a North American company put it, 'We are tarred by the sins of our forefathers.' Whether it is the spraying of cyanide solution for heap-leaching or the high pressure cooking up of refractory ores in autoclaves, to the changing of water tables through pumping to keep open pits dry or the creation of vast waste dumps, the mining industry is in the spotlight of environmentalists' concerns. The awareness is in every annual report; right up front after 'operations' and 'exploration' is 'statement of environmental policy and principles'. Among a stack of annual reports before me, one starts this section with a Kenyan proverb, 'Treat the earth well. It was not given to you by your parents. It was loaned to you by your children.'[4] To show goodwill, an increasing number of companies, particularly in North America, are voluntarily making conservation areas through reclamation of waste dumps or the creation of pasture or wetlands with water pumped from mines. But they remain in the front line of criticism and the onus is on them to deliver. And standards have yet to be applied in much of Latin America, where

4 Battle Mountain Gold Company, 1991 Annual Report.

mercury from informal mining by thousands of individual prospectors has caused horrendous pollution in the rivers of the Amazon basin. Nor is anyone yet sure of the scale of ecological damage done by some gold mining in the former Soviet Union. Regulation will follow the miners as they diversify the search for gold into developing countries. 'Geologists and mining engineers from Latin America are educated here,' said the president of a Canadian company. 'They'll take our standards back home with them.'

Environmental protection is expensive. I visited one mine in California where meeting that state's very high standards added at least $10 an ounce to its costs; if the orebody had been just over the border in Nevada, construction would have been $50 million less. Such expenses could be absorbed more easily by the high gold prices in the 1980s; in the doldrums of the early nineties, when the price declined in real terms each year, the cost of meeting environmental standards, and the increasing time lost in getting the necessary permits became crucial in the decision whether or not to develop a new mine. 'A few years ago it took perhaps one year to go through the permitting,' John Lutley, president of The Gold Institute points out. 'Now it may take five years.' Indeed, in tandem with disappointment at the price (miners really did find it hard to believe that the price could go below $400 and stay there year after year), environmental pressures are exerting constraint on growth.

### Wooing investors

What a contrast this reveals to the golden days of the 1980s. The gold price averaged over $400, lots of new projects could be brought in with operating costs of $100 to $200 an ounce. Investors fell over themselves to get into real prospects and pipedreams ('blue sky' mining, the Australians aptly call it). In Canada wealthy individuals offset their taxes by investing in a 'flow-through' share scheme for mineral (i.e. gold) exploration, much of it channelled through the Vancouver Stock Exchange which became the free-wheeling emporium for bidding up the latest rumours. Gold mutual funds, investing in mining shares rather than the metal itself, became the rage in the United States; there were eight funds in 1982 and thirty-five a decade later. They remained, however, primarily the province of the small investor. Institutional investors in the United States still largely keep their distance from gold, either as shares or metal. The Australians had not had so much fun since the nickel boom. 'Man, it's out of control and there's tons of money being made,' was how I was greeted in the mining hub of Kalgoorlie in 1987. We were all drinking beer in a local grocery store, where local punters gathered, after it closed, to discuss the latest gossip from prospectors just in from the outback. It ended in tears, of course, when the Australian gold share index tumbled by two-thirds from its 1987 peak, but the game was rejuvenated by better prices in 1993.

A whole new generation of gold-mining analysts was born to track it. Previously there had not been much to analyse except South African stocks (which North Americans and Australians usually did not buy anyway) and a handful of rather parochial North American shares. Suddenly there was a host of new names to review, with mining companies laying on planes and lavish lunches to visit their latest crock of gold. The analysts became a very sharp breed, terrorizing mining chiefs with their pencils, notebooks, sharp questions and the ability to decree to expectant investors 'buy', 'hold', or (disaster) 'sell'. Certainly the fastest way to learn about a mine was to sit across the aisle on the company plane as one of these wizards probed some hapless executive on the mysteries of ore grades and head grades and mill throughputs. They have to know their stuff. *Institutional Investor* rates the top three analysts, plus a runner-up; to slip from, say, number one spot to mere runner-up could be to face career eclipse.

Their wisdom, however, is directed towards advising investors of the best bets in gold shares, not the right moment to go for the metal itself. Consequently, gold shares often have a life of their own, without the gold price itself responding; share value may imply gold at $500, when in fact the price is stuck at $350. Investors may wonder why the gold price itself did not go up. Very simple, they did not buy it. Yet, many people tell you they are 'in gold'. How? They reply, through a gold mutual fund or directly in American Barrick or Placer or Echo Bay. The point is that the new era in gold mining has given investors so many new shares to play with, they have forgotten gold itself. In the strong run in the gold price in early 1987, close to $2 billion went into US gold funds in a matter of weeks; yet only $50 million of that went into metal – 2.5 per cent. And then people wondered why gold itself did not perform.

## Gold loans and hedging
Miners naturally woo investors and worry over their share price, but they shifted increasingly in the 1980s from the traditional raising of capital through equity to gold loan finance instead. Gold could be borrowed much more cheaply than money, typically at 3 per cent. The miner (or often prospective miner) sold the gold spot to raise cash for the new mine, while simultaneously selling forward part of the future production to pay off loan and interest (usually also paid in gold). Gold loans became quite the rage. According to Jessica Jacks of RTZ

Corporation, who maintains one of the best databases, over 260 of them were negotiated, involving close to 400 tonnes (12.9 million ounces). In the peak year of 1988, 84 new loans amounting to over 150 tonnes (4.8 million ounces) were taken out. Gold loans first caught on in Australia, where they were pioneered by three banks, Mase-Westpac, Macquarie and Rothschilds Australia. Starting with the gold loan, it was but a short step for these banks to tailor more comprehensive packages embracing feasibility studies, the purchase or leasing of equipment, refining, marketing and hedging. A small mining company could virtually go into the bank for an 'off-the-shelf' package that would enable it to start producing gold within a matter of months. Indeed, the process became so streamlined that small open pits in Western Australia were sometimes in operation within six to nine months. North American mining companies, with notable exceptions, were in general slower to take the gold loan and the hedging route, and then were often guided by the Australian banks. In Denver, Colorado, which has become the gold capital of North America, Westpac, Macquarie and Rothschilds have all opened offices. 'The Australians were at least five years ahead of the North Americans on hedging,' the Denver manager of Westpac told me rather proudly.[5]

The fashion for gold loans was, however, relatively short-lived, partly because the gold-mining boom itself wound down after 1990, but more because the cost of borrowing money declined, largely eliminating the previous attractive gap between the two sources of capital. 'The gold loan experience', observed RTZ's Jessica Jacks, 'illustrates that what was yesterday's favoured product can become today's old hat.' Even so, the impact of the gold loans in putting 'accelerated supplies' onto the market for a few years was considerable. The process reversed, of course, in the early nineties as loans started to be paid back, with gold from the new mines going not to the market but to the original lenders. The net payback of gold loans by 1991 was 60 tonnes (1.9 million ounces), rising to over 100 tonnes (3.2 million ounces) in 1992.

The lasting importance is that loans got the mining companies accustomed to working closely with the bullion banks in hedging their output. Again, the Australians were first in the field, while the North Americans and the South Africans remain deeply divided on the question 'to hedge or not to hedge?' American Barrick or Anglo American see it as a necessary virtue, Homestake Mining or Gold Fields of South Africa are more inclined to view it as a vice that constantly caps the market. The added anti-hedging argument is that many investors choose gold companies precisely because they offer a different, often anti-cyclical, play to conventional base metal or industrial stocks; they do not want

5 A provisional agreement was reached in mid-1993 for Republic National Bank of New York to take over Mase-Westpac, the bullion banking arm of Westpac and the associated loan book.

the benefits of a sudden bull market in gold diluted by hedging (although a good hedging strategy will be more about protecting the downside risk in a bear market, leaving the upside as open as possible).

Without doubt, as hedging got into its stride the spate of forward sales, which either tended to curb rallies or precipitate declines (because of panic forward selling when the price showed weakness) did put considerable pressure on the market. I recall a trader in Hong Kong lamenting to me in 1990, 'What are these Australians up to? They sell us 10 tonnes in the morning because they are afraid of the price and naturally push it $10 lower.' As it happened that year, 'accelerated' hedging sales by mining companies were estimated at over 220 tonnes (a special factor being a new tax on gold mining in Australia from January 1991). The next year the net new business declined to 135 tonnes and with payback from gold loans at 60 tonnes, the actual impact was only 75 tonnes. In short, the pressure came initially while gold loans and then hedging programmes were getting up and running. Analyst Jessica Jacks calculates that the total amount of gold associated with outstanding loans and hedging remained almost constant between 1990 and 1991 at just over 1,130 tonnes, but rose to 1,215 tonnes by 1992.

The mining industry has become the single largest user of hedging products devised by the market over the last decade, as compared to the jewellery industry which does not use them widely. Many miners regard them as an integral part of their daily financial strategy. For a successful newcomer like American Barrick (see Chapters 6 and 7) hedging was one of the principles on which it was founded. Here's its treasurer talking to institutional investors in New York: 'We can be fully hedged until the middle of 1995, at a minimum average price of $420 per ounce should the spot price remain low,' he said. 'If the spot price of gold exceeds the contract prices, our coverage is extended and realised prices will be higher. Beyond that to the year 2000, we have begun establishing an increasing floor price for a small percentage of our production, taking advantage of higher, longer-term interest rates and the compounding effect of time.' Barrick, it is worth noting, got $422 for its gold in 1992 against the average price of $344.

The market's inventiveness in devising hedging strategies for miners knows few bounds. 'The range of products now available is nothing short of staggering,' wrote RTZ's Jessica Jacks after ploughing through the merits or otherwise of forwards, participating forwards, flat rate forwards, spot deferreds, to say nothing of options varying from forward starts, barriers, binary, compounds, lookbacks, Asian and exchange options (she cheerfully dreamed of her own look-back-through-time-to-happier-days-option which gets the holder back to $850 gold in January 1980).[6]

---

6 RTZ Corporation, Papers by staff, No. 12, *Bird in a Gilded Cage*, 1992.

Initially much of the hedging was in fixed forward contracts, an attractive proposition given that interest rates in the late 1980s were considerably higher than the cost of borrowing gold and many producers feared (quite rightly) that the price would decline. But declining interest rates later shifted attention to the more flexible spot deferred contracts. This is a long-term funding agreement, where the mine sells gold at the current spot price for cash, which is credited to a deferred account, on which both the interest rate and the gold borrowing cost float, while the date of maturity of the contract also is flexible and may be rolled over almost indefinitely. Identified spot deferred contracts by mines amounted to 232 tonnes (7.46 million ounces) by the end of 1992 compared with 245 tonnes (7.87 million ounces) of forwards.[7]

Options, the third element in hedging strategies, are much harder to quantify because they are largely invisible, being on a principal to principal basis in the over-the-counter options market on which there are no statistics (but which is infinitely larger than the market in exchange options). Mining companies do not always reveal their options positions. However, what has been pinpointed showed an expanded use of options in the early 1990s, as the contango on forward sales narrowed making them less attractive; no one was anxious to lock into a drifting gold price. Some mining companies simply gave up hedging for a while. But others, especially the Australians, began granting out-of-the-money call options (i.e. above the current price) to earn the premium.

Hedging needs, of course, are particular to each mine. Old, high-cost mines may find hedging in price rallies the crucial life-line to keep them going (this has applied particularly in South Africa). New mines with heavy expenses in their early years may elect to sell forward at a fixed interest rate for a year or two, so their cash flow is secured. Alternatively, they can opt for spot deferred contracts whose flexible delivery dates may give them breathing space if output is delayed. The package can be simple or complex. Mines may hedge in some years, with price rallies and high interest rates offering a good contango, and not in others, as in 1992 with a low contango and stagnant gold price. But for mines such as Gold Mines of Kalgoorlie or Sons of Gwalia in Australia, Anglo American in South Africa or Amax Gold and American Barrick in North America, hedging is a way of life. Indeed, such companies have pushed the hedging horizons out, first to five years and then to ten. American Barrick has part of its output hedged until 2002.

These strategies, coupled with the worldwide change in the pattern of gold mining, have changed not just gold flows, but the very nature of the gold market. A quarter of a century ago, most production, which was effectively from South Africa and the Soviet Union, went physically

---

7 Jessica Jacks, *New strategies in the derivatives business*, Financial Times World Gold Conference, Istanbul, June 1993

through the London gold market, as had most world output for nearly three centuries and then, after 1968, through the Swiss banks in Zürich. Today, regional markets like Tokyo, Hong Kong or Singapore, get much of their gold direct from Australia or Canada or the United States, which have all become substantial net exporters of the metal. London and Zürich are no longer the natural conduits, while dealers there have to compete with Australian, Japanese and North American banks for mining finance and marketing.

In the meantime, too, gold miners have started advertising their product. The World Gold Council (WGC), a non-profit association of forty-five gold-mining companies from nine countries, based in Geneva, promotes gold in jewellery, industry and investment. The mining members contribute up to $2.50 for every ounce they produce (that is to say, a company with 1 million-ounce output chips in $2.5 million), giving the WGC an annual budget of between $60 and $70 million, which it augments through co-operative programmes with jewellery manufacturers and retailers, who contribute a further $30 million. Thus nearly $100 million is now spent annually to back the message that 'nothing is as good as gold': a very practical and necessary admission by the miners that gold is no longer just a monetary metal, but that its future lies in the day-to-day demands of jewellery and industry. Actually, that was a hard bullet for the industry to bite. When I first looked at gold in the late 1960s most miners, especially in South Africa, saw gold's role as the basis of the monetary system; they mined it to be put in central bank vaults. No longer. The miner of the 1990s has to view gold, not as a commodity because the investment connotations remain strong, but as a metal for which jewellery is the fundamental cornerstone of the price. Hence the need to spend at least $2.50 an ounce on promotion. Some miners would go further; Peter Munk of American Barrick once told me he would give $10 an ounce on promotion – provided, of course, others joined him. He would also brook no nonsense from mining companies who do not contribute to the WGC and once publicly called on analysts to mark down the latter's shares for not doing their bit to help gold's fortunes.

The very existence of the World Gold Council, though, shows how gold mining has gone global. And as we turn now to look at mining in individual countries, none of them can be discussed in isolation. For that reason, the United States, Canadian and Latin American chapters run in sequence for they have become an integrated story with much the same cast; so, too, Australia is naturally followed by Papua New Guinea and the other Pacific Rim nations.

**CHAPTER 5**

# South Africa:
# at the Crossroads

At 4 p.m. on an October afternoon in 1992, Gary Maude, the soft-spoken managing director of Gengold, the gold division of Gencor, rose before a small audience of journalists and mining analysts assembled in a lecture theatre on the top floor of Union House in Johannesburg. 'I'm announcing the sale of West Rand Consolidated mine,' he said. The announcement took no one by surprise; West Rand Consolidated was by far the highest-cost mine in South Africa, producing gold at close to $600 an ounce on a gold price then $340, and with scarcely 2 tonnes (164,000 ounces) output annually was hardly a significant contributor to the 600 tonnes (19.3 million ounces) a year from the world's largest producer. And yet, sitting there, as the journalists asked questions about the specialist company purchasing the mine, to clean up and rehabilitate the old dumps and workings, I felt this was a real moment of change in the history of South African gold mining. For West Rand Consolidated itself started right back in 1887, just one year after the first declaration of gold on the Rand. Thus its lifetime had effectively spanned the entire history of the industry. Although the mine was never a large one, it had contributed with its neighbours in that great arc of mines swinging around Johannesburg and down into the Orange Free State to the 45,000 tonnes of gold (1,446.7 million ounces) – just under 40 per cent of all gold ever mined – produced by South Africa through 1993. And its death-knell encapsulated the dilemmas and the difficulties facing the gold miners in the mid-1990s. How does an industry based on very deep gold mines, plunging down almost to 4,000 metres, come to terms with a gold price declining in dollars and at best static in rands for a period of five or six years? How do you sanction the investment of new shafts in existing mines that still take several years to dig and cost millions of dollars, let alone pluck up the courage to start a brand new mine? Gary Maude had been discussing just that problem with me in his office before we went upstairs for his closure announcement. 'What is the financial reward', he had pondered, 'of a $2 billion investment to extend your business when you have to wait ten years for any return?'

The story in South Africa is that the great expectations built on the strong gold price of the 1980s have been dashed by the bursting of that bubble. The very nature of South Africa's gold mines means that swift expansion of output, as happened with open pits in the United States and Australia and even with relatively shallow new underground mines in Canada, cannot happen. In Australia it was only weeks till some open pits got going, here a new mine takes a decade. So while output everywhere else has soared, in South Africa it continued to fall from the record high of 1,000 tonnes in 1970 to a modest 600 tonnes annually in the early 1990s. And the replacement is not coming even to maintain that.

The catalogue of decline is depressing. Despite extensive cost-cutting and improved efficiency, South Africa has moved from being a low-cost producer in 1985 to being one of the highest cost with eleven of its thirty-one mines rated 'marginal'. In real terms the rand price received for gold in 1992 was the same as in 1975, when gold was $105 an ounce. Capital expenditure has halved since 1986 and over 160,000 jobs have been lost. 'Stilfontein, Harmony and Loraine are sick,' said an analyst in Johannesburg, ticking them off on his fingers. 'Deelkraal is a little sick, so is Western Deep Levels.' It sounded like a doctor's surgery. As Robin Plumbridge, chairman and chief executive of Gold Fields of South Africa, said, 'We have really had to batten down the hatches.'

The excited anticipation in the late 1980s that a whole wave of new mines would come in, particularly in what is known as the Potchefstroom Gap between the Far West Rand and Klerksdorp goldfields, was killed by the deteriorating gold price. 'A lot of mines are consigned to the filing cabinet,' said economist Michael Brown, who was once a protagonist for the 'third wave' of new mines. 'I know of fifteen potential mines, but they've not got over the hurdle of the rate of return.' The trouble is that at Potchefstroom the reefs are very deep, testing the technical limits of the industry, to say nothing of cost. 'The ultra-deep potential is there in the long run,' said Michael Brown, 'but it may be in two generations.'

This is just the basic mining problem; add to that the uncertainties

# SOUTH AFRICA: GOLD FIELDS

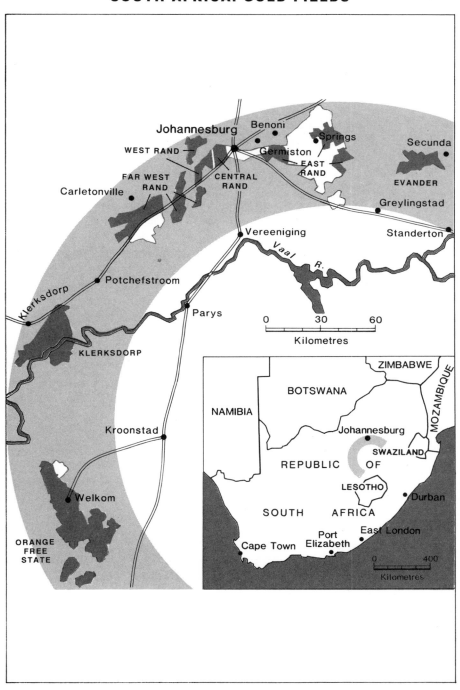

created by the immense pressures of political change as South Africa, at last, tries to find its way from an oppressive apartheid regime to a multi-racial democracy. The transition makes it an enormously stimulating moment to visit the republic as the debate swirls around you. I listened to Lee Kuan Yew, the former Prime Minister of Singapore, and Albie Sachs, a veteran member of the African National Congress, speaking to an investment and mining conference on the new challenges that lay ahead. Albie Sachs was calling for a better dialogue between the ANC and business, and had a little anecdote about how he realized the error of communist central planning not from the collapse of the Soviet Union, but from an attempt in Mozambique, where he was exiled, to provide everyone with the same hard-wearing shoes; it was a disaster; the citizens of Mozambique preferred stylish footwear of their own choice. Such experiences do not reassure the mining industry. Will they be nationalized? Or, perhaps 'unbundled', as the phrase goes, implying that the mining houses will be broken up? Unbundling of conglomerates like Anglo American, which reach into every sphere of South African business and industry, would meet the ANC's strong view that at present competition is restricted and that restructuring would enable more work to be sub-contracted to small businesses run by the black community. This might avoid nationalization and leave intact, for instance, the gold divisions of each house.

Such uncertainties do not help an industry that ought to be taking tough practical mining decisions in any event. Unprofitable mines ought to be closed, but the social implications of unemployment are grave. Decisions on new shafts ought to be made, but they are held over. 'The industry is focused on short-term problems,' admits Tom Main, chief executive of the Chamber of Mines. 'We need more strategic thinking – what does the future look like?' But he added, 'Don't give up on us. Every ten years or so people tend to write the industry off, but the most conservative projections suggest that at least 18,000 tonnes of gold can viably be recovered.'

### Trial run for Hades

To get to grips, initially, with the special circumstances of gold mining in South Africa, there is no substitute for going down a gold mine to see just what the miners are up against. On my first visit there in 1967, I journeyed towards the centre of the earth down what was then Free State's Geduld mine (now part of Free State Consolidated). The impression was a lasting one and at the time I wrote,

Going down a gold mine is rather like a trial run for Hades. You even leave all your clothes, including underwear, behind on the surface and, shrouded in white overalls, enter a steel cage which plummets through a mile of rock in two minutes. There below is a noisy, hot, wet world lit by the dancing fireflies of the lamps on miners' helmets. A 10-minute walk along a gallery cut through rock whose natural temperature is over 100 degrees Fahrenheit and any visitor is soaked by a combination of sweat and humidity. Then, above the constant hum of the air conditioning and the rumble of trucks along steel rails, comes the sound of compressed air drills biting into solid rock. On one side of the tunnel a narrow opening plunges down at an angle of nearly 25 degrees towards the bowels of the earth. It is barely 40 inches high and is delicately held open by props of blue gum. It is called, in mining parlance, a stope. Within the stope the rock seems to press in from all sides; tiny flakes fall from the roof into pools of warm water in which everyone is kneeling or lying. Almost hidden in a fine spray of water to subdue dust, the long needle nose of a drill chatters into a hole in the rock marked with a blob of red paint. All along the side of the stope a continuous line of red paint highlights a four-inch vein of rock that, even to the uneducated eye, looks markedly different from the rock above and below. It is a tightly packed bunch of white pebbles and between them, here and there, a minute speck of gold gleams in the beam of the miners' lamps. This vein is the meat in the sandwich . . . extracting this thin seam of gold, lying at a depth of two miles or more below the surface, is an agonizing and costly process. In human terms it costs over 500 lives a year in underground accidents; in economic terms it has meant that the entire South African gold-mining industry has grown up with a structure and character very much of its own. Because the gold is so finely dispersed among those pebbles (a rock formation geologists call conglomerate) not only the narrow strip of gold-bearing reef must be blasted and brought to the surface. Much of the rock on either side of this reef must also be hauled up and crushed, for it becomes inextricably mixed with the conglomerate each time the stope is blasted forward.[1]

Twenty-five years on the scene has changed remarkably little (nor has the casualty rate; there were 388 underground deaths in 1992). Refrigeration systems are better, so that miners can get down to 4,000 metres (13,000 feet). Small mechanized drilling machines, specially adapted to fit the confined space of the stopes, are used increasingly, while the traditional pneumatic and hydraulic drills have a new competitor in a fully water-powered rock drill. And in the working tunnels 'trackless' mining is common, as tyred vehicles replace the old-style trains running

---

1 Timothy Green, *The World of Gold*, Michael Joseph, London, Walker & Co., New York, 1968, pp. 45–46.

on rails. Yet extracting gold from inches-thin reefs up to two and a half miles deep remains labour intensive. The mines still employ about 370,000 workers (compared to the United States where mines employ just 79,000 workers to produce half as much gold), meaning wages on average account for more than 50 per cent of working costs.

In 1992 the thirty-six gold-mining companies belonging to the South African Chamber of Mines milled (that is to say, crushed) over 106 million tonnes of rock to win just 574 tonnes of gold (the balance of output coming from retreatment of dumps and small mines). The average grade was 5.37 g/t (0.17 oz/t), which is a radical change from my early visits to South Africa's mines in the late 1960s. The average grade then for seven successive years was over 13 g/t (0.46 oz/t), as the industry, still trapped in the straitjacket of the old $35 gold price, had to 'high-grade' to survive, even though it also got government subsidies in those days. The lower grade reflects the improved gold price (for all its inability to perform in the early 1990s), plus improved efficiency and technology in the mines and naturally declining grades as the gold reefs go deeper. However, high-grading is creeping back; the lowest annual grade ever was 4.99 g/t in 1989.

## 'Flywheel' of Expansion

Historically the gold mines in South Africa have been known as the 'flywheel' of the republic's expansion. As early as 1910 gold accounted for 60 per cent of export revenues; it was still over 50 per cent in 1980, in which year the mines also contributed nearly a third of the government's tax revenue. In the 1990s, however, the gold-mining industry is much less the central powerhouse of the South African economy. Although gold sales through the South African Reserve Bank, which still markets the gold, account for around 25 per cent of foreign exchange revenue, taxes paid by the gold mines accounted only for just over 1 per cent of government revenue. And the industry's contribution to gross national product was a modest 6 per cent. Simultaneously, South Africa's share of world markets is much less; down from 79 per cent of western production in 1970 to under 30 per cent and close to 26 per cent of world output when the former Soviet Union and China are included (in strong contrast to platinum, where South Africa has still over 70 per cent of production). The impact, therefore, to the market in general of any disruption to mining that might occur during the tense years of transition to a multi-racial government is less than it would have been even in the early 1980s when South Africa was still the dominant source of supply. That said, South Africa is still number one in gold and, excluding exceptional

## SOUTH AFRICA: PRODUCTION

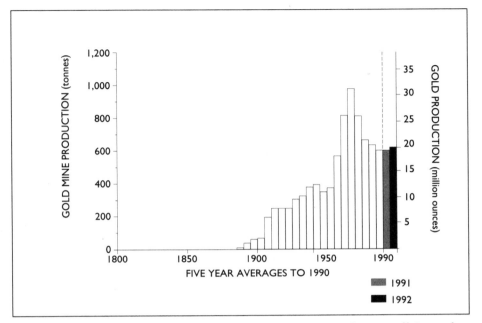

FIVE YEAR AVERAGES TO 1990

■ 1991
■ 1992

political upheaval and violence, is going to remain there well into the twenty-first century.

The sheer staying power since 1886 is due to the unique series of gold reefs, laid down between 3,000 and 2,700 million years ago, 'like layers of jam through a cake', as someone put it. These reefs, some of which outcrop on the surface (leading to the original discovery on Langlaagte farm near Johannesburg in 1886) form a crescent around the whole Witwatersrand Basin, sloping inwards towards the centre at an angle of 25 degrees to depths of at least 5,000 metres (3.1 miles). Many different 'layers of jam' are mined, including the Main Reef, Venterspost Contact, Kimberley, Carbon Leader and Basal, all averaging 20–30 centimetres in thickness. The gold-bearing conglomerates swing from the Evander field 80 miles southeast of Johannesburg to 90 miles west, then bend southwest to the Orange Free State 200 miles away. The constant detection and then development of new sectors of this arc have already kept the industry busy for over a century. First it was the Central Rand, where no less than sixteen gold mines were declared between 1886 and 1890, then West Rand (including West Rand Consolidated) and East Rand, so that for the first half century the industry was literally congregated in and around Johannesburg. Then in the 1930s the young German geologist Rudolf Krahmann, used a newly developed magnetometer, which would pick up the pattern of magnetic shales whose relation to the gold reefs was known, to pinpoint for Gold Fields of South Africa the Far West Rand field, where the first mine, Venterspost, was opened in 1939. It was the surge of output from the Far West Rand and then from the nearby Klerksdorp area, and finally from the Orange Free State and Evander by the 1950s, that pushed South Africa during the next two decades to reach its record production in 1970. Old mines were not just replaced by new, but the fresh ones came thick and fast with high grades and huge tonnages. Mines producing 20, 30, even 40 tonnes a year were the norm; mining houses have little interest in 5 tonnes.

The longevity and output of some individual mines have been remarkable. Crown Mines, born 1897, died 1977, output 1,412 tonnes (45.4 million ounces); Durban Roodepoort Deep, born 1898, still alive (just), output 702 tonnes; ERPM, born 1894, still alive, 1,400 tonnes. Whatever the mine, they all had one common factor; they were born and bred by the great mining houses that had the ability to raise capital and assemble a team of geologists and mining engineers capable of tackling the special problems of deep reefs. Even in the early 1890s it cost up to $2 million to start a new mine; that became $200 million to bring in Elandsrand in 1978, and today could reach $2 billion to start a mine that would not produce gold until after 2000.

### The Mining Houses

Thus, while the industry was still in its infancy, the mining finance houses were established; Rand Mines (otherwise known as The Corner House), Gold Fields of South Africa (GFSA), Johannesburg Consolidated Investment (JCI), General Mining and Finance Corporation and the Union Corporation, were all in business before 1900. Only two later challengers have come along. Anglo American, created in 1917 by Sir Ernest Oppenheimer (who, like the founders of the original houses, had first made his fortune in diamonds) and then Anglo-Transvaal Consolidated Investment (Anglo Vaal) was founded in 1933 by A.S. Hersov and S.G. (Slip) Menell. By 1980 these seven houses that shaped the South African industry had become six, through the merger of General Mining and Union Corporation into Gencor. However, under the umbrella of these houses each mine is floated as a separate company, with its own board, mine manager and shareholders (among whom the parent house will usually be the largest, although it may well be much less than 50 per cent). The mining houses provide the financial security, administrative experience and technical know-how that an individual mine could not hope to develop. Each house also operates a central buying service, charging its 'client' mines a nominal commission, but still achieving lower costs for them through bulk buying.

Although competition between the houses is intense in the initial exploration for and proving up of a new mine, there is remarkable cross-fertilization of holdings both among the main houses and on most mines. Anglo American, for instance, has a substantial holding in JCI, and lesser positions in both Gencor and GFSA, while also having a significant investment in GFSA's Driefontein and Kloof mines, with smaller holdings in the mines of all the other groups.

The knowledge that a new mine is backed by a finance house, often with support from the others, has always been crucial in persuading investors to risk their money in the capital-hungry South African industry. Geologists, after all, have been known to make mistakes and the initial investment in a mine, especially in the early days, was often staked on the evidence of a handful of cores from boreholes which, in themselves, would not yield enough gold to pay for a packet of cigarettes. Sir Ernest Oppenheimer's faith in the Orange Free State gold discoveries is a classic example. 'The Orange Free State was a gamble,' Adriaan Louw, the former chairman of GFSA, once remarked to me. 'No one would start a mine today on the information that was available on Free State in 1946.' But the backing of the Free State mines by Anglo American was enough to give both institutional and private investors confidence. Originally the South African mines looked to thousands of small investors in Britain and in Belgium, France and elsewhere in Europe, for much of their capital; a tradition long maintained. Looking through the brief provided by Gary Maude of Gencor when he announced the sale of West Rand Consolidated, I was intrigued to note that even in 1992 27 per cent of the shareholders of this old mine lived in France. And I know an investor from a small town in Germany who is as up-to-date on the latest quarterly earnings of every South African mine as the best analyst in London. When we had dinner early in 1993 I asked him what he rated as the best South African buys. He said he had been out of gold shares for a while, but looking at the low prices prevailing had recently started going back in. What did he like? He wrote down: 'Driefontein and Kloof', adding alongside, 'best mines in the world'. (In the United States he liked only Homestake and in Australia no mine really won his favour.) The serious money in the last few decades, however, has inevitably come from local institutional investors, especially once sanctions increasingly fenced South Africa off from the outside world. But gold loans, so much the vogue for financing new Australian and North American mines, have not caught on.

The industry has also become increasingly concentrated within the orbit of Anglo American, GFSA and, to a lesser extent, Gencor. Anglo and GFSA account for 65 per cent of South African production and this could rise to well over 70 per cent by the late 1990s. Anglo alone is already at over 45 per cent and, with the potential to produce over half of all output in the late nineties, is clearly in a league of its own, not just in South Africa, but worldwide. The group's gold production, at around 275 tonnes annually, is more than the entire output of any other country except the United States. Anglo is not only number one in gold. It is easily the largest mining company in the production of non-fuel minerals, contributing by value nearly 9 per cent of western world output.[2]

### The Oppenheimer Empire

Anglo American's headquarters is a solid-looking edifice at 44 Main Street, Johannesburg (with a duplicate block immediately across the street at number 45 to catch the overflow). 'I want something between a bank and a cathedral,' Sir Ernest Oppenheimer told his architect when it was put up in 1937. By then Sir Ernest already dominated both the gold and diamond businesses in South Africa (De Beers Consolidated Diamond Mines being also a part of his domain) and the decisions he took before his death in 1957 did much to shape the industry for the rest of the twentieth century.

On the gold front the real strength he bequeathed to Anglo American was the Orange Free State gold field, first located in 1946. At the time there were no roads, railways, power or water supplies in the area; the few farms were reached by unpaved roads. Sir Ernest was undeterred. He was convinced the new field 'is the most significant in South Africa since the finding of diamonds at Kimberley and gold on the Witwatersrand'. He was right. Four of the original mines there, Free State Geduld, President Brand, President Steyn and Western Holdings, which came on stream in the early 1950s, soon contributed half of Anglo's output (these mines now form Free State Consolidated north and south regions). By the early 1990s these Anglo mines had yielded in all over 6,000 tonnes of gold from an average grade of close to 10 g/t (0.32 oz/t); thus in forty years they contributed nearly 14 per cent of the entire output from South Africa in just over a century. At the same time, Sir Ernest also secured for Anglo a significant presence in the Klerksdorp area, where Vaal Reefs, now an immense complex of shafts, opened in 1956, since when it has produced close to 2,000 tonnes of gold.

Shortly before his death, Sir Ernest Oppenheimer took another crucial decision in giving the go-ahead for the Western Deep Levels mine in the Far West Rand field which, until then, had largely been pioneered by Gold Fields. Anglo American had agonized over Western

Deep since 1943 because the proposed mine presented major financial and technological hurdles. The best reef lay at 4,000 metres (13,500 feet), where rock temperatures were 130 degrees F (51°C). Just to complicate matters the mine lay in the Gatsrand hills, which contain vast quantities of underground water; each shaft would have to pump out 30 million gallons a day. Development costs were budgeted at $95 million – a formidable sum in the 1950s with gold pegged at $35. Sir Ernest was encouraged by two mines already sunk just to the north: Rand Mines' Blyvooruitzicht and Gold Fields' West Driefontein. Both had found very good grades. Boreholes showed that the rich Carbon Leader Reef, from which these two mines got most of their gold, plunged beneath the proposed Western Deep at between 3,000 and 4,000 metres. But on the way down, close to the surface, was the Venterspost Contact Reef, which could be mined to produce revenue long before the deeper shafts to the Carbon Leader were completed. In July 1957, just four months before he died, Sir Ernest watched the first shaft sinking drills commence work on what was then South Africa's most ambitious mine. His last gamble paid off. Western Deep Levels opened in 1962 and over the next thirty years produced over 1,300 tonnes at a handsome average grade of just under 12 g/t (0.38 oz/t) that compensated for the higher costs of mining at such depth.

Western Deep Levels confirmed the inheritance that Sir Ernest Oppenheimer left to Anglo American. The cornerstone of its output going into the twenty-first century remains the mines he originally authorized, which account for 90 per cent of the group's gold production in South Africa. The real task of his heirs has been to maintain and expand them.

Admittedly his son, Harry Oppenheimer, who was chairman of Anglo American from 1957 until 1983, and thereafter remained a formidable presence in the background for a decade, really never had such opportunities. The gold price did not encourage new mines in the sixties or early seventies. So Harry Oppenheimer diversified Anglo into everything from breweries to steel mills. Today, Anglo's list of 'interests of the corporation' under the heading of Industry and Commerce alone embraces such varied activity as agriculture and aluminium products, through food and wine, to textiles, travel and tourism, while on the mining front it is busy with coal, cobalt, platinum and potash, to mention but a few. 'You can't sit on your money waiting for a new gold field to turn up,' observed Harry Oppenheimer, when I first met him in 1967.

In the end, it was not a new gold field, but a sparkling gold price that cheered things up for a while. Encouraged by the upward kick given to the price by the first oil shock of the seventies, Anglo went ahead with a modest mine named Elandsrand right next to Western Deep Levels, essentially filling in a piece in the jigsaw of the Far West Rand field. Elandsrand opened in 1978 with a relatively low grade around 6 g/t (0.19 oz/t) reflecting the new hope that higher prices meant lower-grade mines were viable, as indeed they were for the next decade. Only the price crunch of the early nineties pushed Elandsrand towards higher grades.

But for Anglo, as for the other houses, the strong price was not so much a chance to open great new mines, as to exploit the best of mature ones and go for lower grades which had been neglected in earlier years (I recall Dr W.J. Busschau, former chairman of Gold Fields of South Africa, and a great authority on South African gold, lamenting to me in 1967, 'The Free State is being murdered, because it is producing too quickly.') A chance had come to repair some damage. Essentially what Anglo did in the Free State was not to bring in new mines in their own right, but to develop them as extensions of existing ones, thus writing off the capital costs against the profits. It also began the merger of some older mines, bringing together Free State Saiplass, Western Holdings and Welkom, with a new mine Erfdeel, into a jumbo called Western Holdings. Ultimately, Anglo's entire Free State operation was knitted together into Free State Consolidated Gold Mines Ltd (Freegold) to form the world's largest gold 'mine' with output around 110 tonnes annually. Freegold is actually an umbrella for seven mines.[3] At times that can be confusing when you see a picture in Anglo's annual report of Clem Sunter, head of the gold division, glad-handing people at the opening of 'Freddies' No. 1 shaft in 1991, because no such mine has been listed as a producer since 1976; actually it is that good old-timer Freddies Consolidated, which opened in 1954 and virtually forty years on is a part of the Freegold stable. The story was much the same in other areas. Apart from the new Elandsrand mine on the Far West Rand, Anglo's prime effort was to expand Western Deep Levels. It embarked on a major development scheme in the early 1980s, costing over $700 million, to increase Western Deep's output by over 70 per cent before the end of the century, from an already notable 40 tonnes (1.3 million ounces) annually to over 60 tonnes. Initially it put down a new 2,734-metre shaft to the Carbon Leader Reef, with a further sub-shaft, completed in the early 1990s, towards 4,000 metres, thus taking miners deeper into the earth than man had ever gone before. It proved no easy task. Western Deep Levels suffered a series of rock bursts that killed twenty-seven miners early in 1992, despite more concentrated computer control of seismic activity in the area to anticipate them.

---

3 Freddies Consolidated, Free State Geduld, Free State Saiplass, President Brand, President Steyn, Welkom and Western Holdings.

Meanwhile out at the Klerksdorp field, Vaal Reefs just grew and grew, expanding across the river into the South Vaal area until the complex eventually had ten shafts producing between them close to 75 tonnes annually. However, in 1992, Anglo broke with this new custom by announcing that what might otherwise have been No. 11 shaft for Vaal Reefs, was going to be a newly listed gold mine called Moab, developed by a new company, Eastvaal Gold Holdings. Moab, of course, is not a stand-alone project in the way that the original mines here or in the Orange Free State were a generation ago. It is really an extension of Vaal Reefs, pushing out to the southeast of the existing South Vaal area to tap deep extensions of the reef. The initial main shaft will plunge to 2,500 metres, with two sub-shafts eventually going on down to 3,700 metres. It will cost over $500 million to start up production by 1997 at 13 tonnes (418,000 ounces) a year, with an anticipated life span of twenty-five years.

Anglo's decision to go ahead with Moab, when much of the industry was putting new projects back into the filing cabinet, represented, however, a new approach by a South African mining house. As Clem Sunter, the chief of Anglo's gold division, put it, they applied 'Japanese logic'. Traditionally, the South African approach has been to work out the necessary capital expenditure and then simply allow the rate of return to be determined by the gold price; Sunter reversed this. He took the current gold price (hovering around $350), and established a desirable rate of return which told him how much his capital expenditure could be. This is quite against the grain in South Africa. As Tom Main, the chief executive of the Chamber of Mines, pointed out to me, 'The Moab shaft is being done cheaply, that's very unusual. The history of mining in South Africa is that in a new shaft money is no object, everything is the best.' The realities of the nineties, however, dictate, as a mining engineer noted, that you cannot always buy a Rolls Royce. For a start, Anglo shopped around for second-hand winding gear for Moab's shaft, and faced down the looks of horror from some old-school miners who felt mining engineering had given way to financial engineering. While Moab's output will be modest, it will provide Anglo with some crucial replacement for the late 1990s, at a time when most other houses are facing declining production.

But several other potential projects, extensively explored during the heady days of the late 1980s, remain in cold storage pending a sustained improvement in the gold price. And new initiatives have been of a simpler kind than the great expenditure of a new mine. Thus, East Rand Gold and Uranium Company (ERGO) was set up in 1977 to treat dumps and waste rock at old mining sites; a venture where the recovery grade is a minute 0.3 g/t (0.01 oz/t), which nevertheless yields 12 tonnes (386,000 ounces) a year from the wastelands of South Africa's mining history.

The trick is also to find new ways of getting at sections of reef a long way from existing shafts without going to the expense of putting down a new one. Anglo got around that at Western Deep Levels by signing up a 'tribute' deal with the neighbouring Blyvooruitzicht of Rand Mines, under which a corner of the Carbon Leader Reef in Western Deep's lease area will be tackled by Blyvooruitzicht, whose shaft and tunnels are close by. The costs are shared, 55 per cent to Western Deep and 45 per cent Blyvoor. Both mines benefit; Western Deep gets out some gold that is otherwise uneconomic at current prices, and Blyvooruitzicht, which was a marginal producer with low-grade reserves that might have kept it going for a year or two, gained at least five years' extra life. The mines hope that by buying such time, the gold price may eventually provide more permanent rescue.

Another life-line, of course, is hedging future production by forward sales; a policy on which the South African industry is deeply divided. 'It's set up quite a tension in the industry here,' admitted a marketing executive. Anglo American is firmly in the pro-hedging camp; its chief rival, Gold Fields of South Africa, is against. At Anglo, the gold division's Clem Sunter does not hesitate to point out that its price per ounce received has often been higher than that of other houses because of 'savvy hedging'. Anglo does not reveal precisely how much gold is hedged – and all the hedging is done on behalf of its individual client mines, not for the group itself – but it is easily the biggest hedger from South Africa and, just possibly, in the entire gold market. The dimension of its production at over 250 tonnes a year would not make this surprising; by comparison, famous North American hedgers like American Barrick have, until recently, had scarcely 30 tonnes a year output. So that even if Anglo hedged only 20 per cent of production, it would still amount to 50 tonnes a year.[4] The difference, however, is that although Anglo often rolls its hedges over, it is not, yet, hedging five to ten years ahead, as is American Barrick. But the quantities are growing. 'We secure a level of strategic cover,' confided a marketing executive. 'And it's seriously profitable. Of course, we lose money occasionally, but we've made more than we lost, so we do more and more.' The pressure on Anglo to hedge is considerable, because two of its major 'clients', Western Deep Levels and Freegold, are relatively high-cost producers, being eleventh and sixteenth respectively in the league table for operating costs for 1992. This is in sharp contrast with non-hedgers Gold Fields, whose two biggest operations, Kloof and Driefontein, ranked first and

4 Anglo American revealed in July 1993 they had been hedging up to 110 tonnes annually, of which 50 tonnes was to keep marginal mines in production, and 60 tonnes was to secure major capital expenditure projects. Total South African forward sales to June 1994 were estimated at 175 tonnes, but hedging slowed as the gold price rose in mid-1993.

second cheapest in the same period. As an Anglo executive generously conceded, 'GFSA has some rich mines, they are not vulnerable and investors often buy them [their shares] as a substitute for Krugerrand coins.'

### Gold Fields: West Wits Winners
The strength of Gold Fields' hand lies in the Far West Rand gold field, often known as the West Wits Line, about 80 miles due west of Johannesburg. This is its territory, just as much as Anglo's is the Orange Free State and Gencor's is Evander. The founders of what was originally The Gold Fields of South Africa in 1887, Cecil Rhodes and Charles Rudd, got their new mining and finance house well dug into such famous long haul mines on the Central Rand as Simmer and Jack (born 1888, died 1964, output 452 tonnes) and Robinson Deep (born 1898, died 1966, output 456 tonnes). The company, whose name was changed to The Consolidated Gold Fields of South Africa in 1892, and then to Consolidated Gold Fields in 1964, was always London based. The present Gold Fields of South Africa (GFSA) was at first a wholly-owned subsidiary, but that link was loosened in 1971 when Consolidated Gold Fields' holding was reduced to a minority 48 per cent and lapsed totally in 1989 when Consolidated Gold Fields in London was taken over by the Hanson group, after a year successfully fighting off another takeover bid from Minorco, the Luxembourg based arm of the ubiquitous Anglo American/De Beers empire. GFSA remains very much a gold group (in contrast to Anglo's diversity) with gold mines accounting for 65 per cent of its assets.

Despite the historic link with London, the real work was being done on the ground in South Africa. And if one asks who kept up the original initiative of Rhodes and Rudd to maintain Gold Fields as the second largest mining house for over a century, with output steady at 100-115 tonnes (3 million ounces plus) a year, then the first names that come to mind are Guy Carleton Jones and Rudolf Krahmann.

Guy Carleton Jones was a Canadian born mining engineer who moved to South Africa in 1913 to join Gold Fields. His promotion was rapid; he was managing the Sub-Nagel mine (another long survivor on the East Rand field) at the age of 33. By 1930 he had been appointed group consulting engineer. He found the Gold Fields board disillusioned with gold; costs were rising, the gold price was fixed (then $20.67 an ounce), and the best of the original Central Rand field worked out (sixteen mines in the Central Rand closed in the 1920s). The board was inclined to diversify into industry. But Carleton Jones knew that the full extent of the gold reefs, especially west from Johannesburg, had not been charted. Enter the German geologist Rudolf Krahmann with his magnetometer, suggesting that he could locate the reefs by tracking the underlying magnetic shales of the Witwatersrand system and plotting the relationship of the reefs to them. Carleton Jones offered him a fee of $850 plus $560 expenses for a three-month trial. Money well spent. The magnetometer traced the magnetic reefs; boreholes confirmed the gold reefs. In the depths of the depression, against much opposition, Carleton Jones persuaded Gold Fields to develop the new West Wits Line. The first mine, Venterspost, came into production in 1939, just one month after the outbreak of World War II. Over the next fifty-odd years the whole Far West Rand produced over 8,000 tonnes of gold (nearly 18 per cent of all South Africa's entire output) to become the richest of all fields. Gold Fields alone has mined almost 5,000 tonnes (160 million ounces) there from seven mines: Venterspost born 1939, Libanon 1949, West Driefontein 1952, Doornfontein 1953, Kloof 1968, East Driefontein 1972, Deelkraal 1980, plus the spin-off Kloof Leeudoorn division 1991. These mines all cluster around the town of Carletonville, honouring the man whose $1,410 investment in Rudolf Krahmann and his magnetometer gave South Africa's gold mining a new dimension.

The sheer regularity with which the new mines have been brought in every ten or fifteen years shows the scale of the West Wits Line, which even on low gold prices, has a future well into the next century. The bonus on the West Wits Line was that not only did the Main Reef series of gold-bearing conglomerate underlie the new field, but two hitherto unknown gold-bearing formations, the Ventersdorp Contact Reef and the high-grade Carbon Leader, were also buried there. The Carbon Leader regularly turns in grades between 20 and 30 g/t (0.96 oz/t), sometimes even better. At West Driefontein the average grade over the first forty years of the mine's life was an astonishing 21.49 g/t (0.7 oz/t), making it the richest in South African history (the grade is beaten only by the short-lived and well-named Bonanza in the Central Rand which averaged 29.65 g/t (0.95 oz/t) from 1896 to 1908). The catch on the West Wits Line is that the reef is deep, the rock often unstable and the potential for flooding horrendous. For that reason Gold Fields and other houses were able only to develop it slowly over decades, compared to the shallower deposits of the Orange Free State which were more accessible. (We have already seen that Anglo hesitated nearly fourteen years before going ahead with Western Deep Levels at Far West Rand.) The West Wits Line has always had mega-mines and mega-disasters.

The tale is told in the company profile for what is now Driefontein Consolidated (combining West and East Driefontein), half of which is devoted to crises. Once a surface crushing and sorting plant was swallowed up when ground subsided at West Driefontein. Then in 1968 when East Driefontein was being developed via the No. 4 shaft at West Driefontein, a sudden flood not only swamped the infant mine but threatened to engulf West Driefontein, drowning both forever. The threat was only overcome after almost a year by the sheer skill and determination of mining engineers who managed to seal off the inflow with enormous concrete plugs and pump out the maze of tunnels. Yet the complex has seemed remarkably resilient to both flood and fire. Between them, West and East Driefontein have yielded over 2,600 tonnes of gold (over 2 per cent of all gold ever mined worldwide) until 1993. Their long-term future was enhanced in 1981 when GFSA's chairman, Robin Plumbridge, announced the creation of what was then the world's biggest gold-producing complex through the merger of West and East Driefontein into Driefontein Consolidated, along with a neighbouring property, North Driefontein, that was to mine a rich section of the Ventersdorp Contact Reef. Driefontein is a long-life mine, set to last well into the twenty-first century. Some wits dubbed it 'Wonderfontein', but a senior executive of a rival mining house described it admiringly to me at the time as 'an imaginative and great scheme'. And it confirmed Robin Plumbridge, who took on the Gold Fields mantle when he was only 45 years old, as one of the real leaders in the South African industry. Indeed, it is hard to find anyone who has a broader understanding of the gold business worldwide and is more respected by bullion bankers (even though they despair of ever persuading him to hedge one ounce of gold). His ability was acknowledged in his appointment as chairman of the World Gold Council, the industry's promotional organization, for 1993–5.

While the Driefontein complex is the pride of the GFSA stable, providing close to 60 tonnes (1.9 million ounces) annually, it also has another high-grade, low-cost mine, Kloof, just to the northeast. Kloof, which opened in 1968, is really following the natural sequence down the Ventersdorp Contact Reef from the earlier Gold Fields mines at Venterspost and Libanon. Kloof gets grades of close to 16 g/t (0.5 oz/t) from the reef, handsome when you remember the industry average in South Africa is around 5 g/t (0.16 oz/t). And when drilling confirmed that the Ventersdorp Contact Reef kept on going to the south of the original mine, GFSA set up an entirely new division, Leeudoorn, to exploit it. The first serious production at Leeudoorn from 1991 turned in good grades around 13 g/t (0.4 oz/t), helping to push overall Kloof output to over 34 tonnes (1.1 million ounces) a year.

Life at Kloof, however, is not all that easy. It has had to take under its wing its marginal neighbours Libanon and Venterspost, both of whose financial position became precarious by 1992. 'Kloof has become their step-mother,' said a Gold Fields executive. Ideally Gold Fields might have closed both down, but flooding, the constant hazard on the West Wits Line, made that impractical. Left alone, Venterspost and Libanon would flood with the waters spilling swiftly into Kloof. Since Kloof still has a forty-year life, it cannot be allowed to drown, so Venterspost and Libanon are ticking over dry rather than invest in massive new pumps to keep water at bay in Kloof. There may even be an ultimate reward. As Mike Tagg of GFSA's gold division explained, 'If Venterspost is kept alive, we can always go back in quickly if the gold price improves. There's several accessible extensions of 4 grams [4 g/t] and in the Free State they are looking for new mines at 4–5 grams at a cost of billions.'

No such life-line was thrown to Doornfontein, Gold Fields' mine at the far end of the West Wits Line, whose assets were sold early in 1993. The mine opened in 1953 with the benefit of both the Main Reef and Carbon Leader Reef in its domain, but its later years were plagued by fire and violent strikes as grades slid to under 5 g/t and output to under 6 tonnes in its final full year. It has become the poor relation in the Gold Fields house; the closure caused little surprise (which is not to ignore the 560 tonnes of gold Doornfontein produced in its forty years).

The prospect for Gold Fields' youngest mine, Deelkraal, also on a southerly extension of the West Wits Line, is somewhat better. Deelkraal was Gold Fields' first 'non-$35-era' mine, born out of the initial rise in the gold price in the early 1970s; the decision to go was taken in 1974, and the mine opened in January 1980, to the birthday present of gold at $850 an ounce. From the start, Deelkraal was a modest operation, working the Ventersdorp Contact Reef and a parallel reef close by, known as the Deelkraal Reef. In its early years the grade was close to 4 g/t (0.13 oz/t), with 6 tonnes (192,000 ounces) output, shifting to over 6 g/t and 9 tonnes to contest low gold prices in the 1990s. Except in the days of high gold prices, it has never been a bonanza, but it still has a twenty-year life if the gold price is maintained in real terms. But it is Driefontein and Kloof that will keep Gold Fields in the big league.

Moreover, its prime exploration effort has shifted outside South Africa to such diverse places as Ghana, Venezuela and Ecuador. 'Who has the biggest cheque book in GFSA these days?' asked an analyst. 'Bernard van Rooyen, who is in charge of overseas new business.'

### Gengold: Going for Rationalization
Going through the list of Gengold's mines one might assume it was the

biggest South African group. It has eleven gold mines listed on the Johannesburg Stock Exchange (twelve before the closure of West Rand Consolidated reported at the beginning of this chapter) and its presence is in most major fields: Orange Free State, Klerksdorp and, exclusively, Evander. Yet the combined output is a modest 75 tonnes and two-thirds of that comes from just four mines: Beatrix, Buffelsfontein, Kinross and Winkelhaak. This rather curious assortment is explained by the mergers that have created the parent Genmin. In the beginning there was General Mining and Finance Corporation *and* Union Corporation, two of the original gold houses. During the 1970s General Mining, which had already merged with a newer mining group, Federale Mynbou of Afrikaaner origin, took 50 per cent of Union Corporation and secured the marriage with 100 per cent control in 1980. The new family tree has Gencor as parent, Genmin as the mining, minerals and metals arm within which Gengold looks after the gold mines. Gengold accounts for around 30 per cent of Genmin's assets (whose other holdings include the Impala platinum mine and coal mines).

General Mining's bid for Union Corporation, as the gold price gathered momentum during the 1970s, was designed to buy some winners. General Mining's own gold stable was rather weak, with just three mines on the Witwatersrand; Union Corporation had eight. The neatest package was the four mines of the Evander field, Bracken[5], Leslie, Kinross and Winkelhaak, which Union Corporation had pioneered on open veld from the late 1950s. The attraction of controlling an entire gold field, albeit a small one, was immense. Not that Evander has ever been an easy ride. The reef has only moderate grade (averaging about 7.5 g/t through its history) and although the reefs are less deep than the West Wits Line, the surrounding rock is riddled with fractures, which has often challenged the profitability of the mines (especially at Leslie). Nor have they been immune from accident; a disaster at Kinross in 1986 that killed 177 workers, most of them black, was the worst in the industry's entire history. But the Evander quartet have yielded over 1,300 tonnes (41.8 million ounces) in just over thirty years and continue to contribute just under 30 tonnes annually (mostly from Kinross and Winkelhaak).

Union Corporation also had two mines in the Orange Free State, St Helena and Unisel (which was only just opening at the time of the merger), where it was the only serious rival to Anglo American. And it is here that most of the subsequent development has taken place. At St Helena, which was actually the first mine to open in the Orange Free State in 1951, the best days are long over; production has halved since the late 1980s and its future is in doubt. But St Helena also controls

5 Bracken is in the process of closure.

Gengold's new Oryx mine, just to the south, one of the few new mines coming on in South Africa. Oryx is right next door to the unsuccessful Beisa gold/uranium mine which opened in 1981 and closed abruptly three years later (a rare example of a real failure in South African mines). Since 1988, as development on Oryx has gone ahead, it has nibbled at the neighbouring Beisa reef; the main new shafts are sunk to the Kalkoenkrans Reef which is its main target. Oryx came on stream in 1993 and once it is fully operational should produce close to 20 tonnes annually from a moderate grade of 7.5 g/t (0.24 oz/t). Meanwhile the Beatrix mine, sandwiched between Oryx and JCI's new H.J. Joel mine, has been a reliable, low-cost performer since it opened in 1988; grade and output (12 tonnes annually) are modest, but the reefs here are relatively shallow at 600–1,400 metres, making mining somewhat cheaper (Beatrix vies with Driefontein for the lowest costs). The test at Beatrix in the 1990s is whether to press ahead with a third shaft system giving access to higher-grade ores; Gengold was postponing the decision as long as possible. Beatrix, incidentally, is usually billed as Buffelsfontein, Beatrix division, because for tax reasons it has been for some years a division of Gengold's Buffelsfontein mine on the Klerksdorp field; an arrangement which no doubt saves tax, but can cause confusion in working out which mine is where, since they are several hundred miles apart. Just north of Beatrix, Unisel also ticks over; a small mine of 5 tonnes a year, moderate grades, moderate costs, just what a mining house needs for a quiet life.

Finally, there is the real Buffelsfontein up on the Klerksdorp field, started by General Mining in 1957, which has since produced almost a thousand tonnes of gold but, as a mining friend of mine once said, 'is in the evening of its life'. The trouble is that potential new ore reserves are deep and the rock very fractured; no one is going to chase the reefs at $350 gold. So Buffelsfontein works over what is left, and recycles its dumps (which is also happening nearby at Gengold's Stilfontein where all underground work has already ceased). Equally, the days are numbered at Grootvlei, once of the last mines of the East Rand fields, which is increasingly threatened by flooding from abandoned neighbouring mines. Gengold has no illusion about keeping unprofitable mines open. 'If one of our mines loses for three months in succession, we'll close it,' said Gary Maude bluntly. And Gengold has also halted in its tracks construction of a new mine at Weltevreden in the Viljoenskroon district of Western Transvaal. Time for some mines has been bought by hedging, a policy on which Gengold has been somewhat ambivalent. Sometimes it hedges, then lets it lapse, arguing that hedging is speculative. The argument was enlivened when a former chief consulting engineer to the group, Hugh

Monro, calculated that every tonne sold forward knocked 20 cents off the price; a suggestion that was greeted with considerable scepticism among mining houses who do hedge (like Anglo) and by the market in general. Anglo's Kelvin Williams quickly countered that there are too many dynamic factors impinging on the market to make such a basic calculation realistic.

Meanwhile, Gengold, like Anglo and GFSA, has set its sights abroad. Already it is well established in Brazil (see Chapter 8) and a small heap-leach operation may open in Turkey. The aim is modest projects, with short lead times and low costs.

### JCI; Anglo Vaal; Rand Mines

Johannesburg Consolidated Investments was the creation of Barney Barnato, the colourful entrepreneur from the East End of London, who made his first fortune in diamonds and went on to make another in gold. He waged a great rivalry in diamonds with Cecil Rhodes (founder of De Beers and Gold Fields), culminating in a famous series of lunches at the Kimberley Club (actually a corrugated iron hut) at which Rhodes wooed Barnato to sell him control of his Kimberley Central to augment his grip on diamonds at De Beers Consolidated Mines. In return, Barnato got a life governorship and a nice shareholding in De Beers. The diamond link remains; JCI's investments in De Beers still account for nearly 10 per cent of its assets.

Over the years this mining house, in which Anglo American has a 40 per cent holding, has become widely diversified, with its principal investments being, besides diamonds, in the Rustenberg platinum mine (the world's biggest), industry, property and coal. Gold accounts for scarcely 5 per cent of its assets and barely 3 per cent of its income. Its three mines, Randfontein, Western Areas and H.J. Joel, have been yielding around 50 tonnes (1.6 million ounces) annually, but this is likely to decline during the mid-1990s. Randfontein is the last survivor of the historic West Rand field. The original Randfontein Estates Gold Mining Company was floated in 1889 by J.B. Robinson, yet another Kimberley diamond man, who later sold it to JCI. Before the discoveries on the Far West Rand it rated as one of the world's largest mines, but eventually closed in 1967, squeezed by the static $35 an ounce price; revival came just seven years later when the price took off. In its second life, Randfontein, although low grade by South African standards at scarcely 3.5 g/t (0.11 oz/t), still produces a remarkable 30 tonnes annually as it embarks upon its second century.

The outlook is less promising at Western Areas on the West Wits Line, which lacks the sparkling high grades of much of that field. This mine, originally opened in 1961, is among the highest-cost South African mines and has been kept alive partly by some judicious hedging. Even the newcomer, H.J. Joel (named after another founding partner of JCI), which opened in the Orange Free State in 1988, and was regarded as one of the first of a new wave of South African mines, has proved a disappointment, with low grades and unexpected faulting, which has caused postponement of a second phase of the mine's expansion. Meanwhile, Joel produces around 5 tonnes annually. However, JCI has one long-term ace; it holds 41 per cent of a large orebody known as South Deep Exploration just to the south of Western Areas. The attraction is that several reefs all come together, making much more concentrated mining possible, with a good grade of 9 g/t (0.39 oz/t). JCI has calculated the deposit may contain 1,000 tonnes of gold, making it one of the largest unexploited anywhere. Already JCI is tentatively tunnelling into it from a shaft at Western Areas. The catch is cost. 'You need 3–4 million rand to develop it,' an analyst said, 'and that kind of money just isn't around.' The gold must await a better price.

Looking at Anglo Vaal's portfolio nowadays you might be excused for wondering where the gold was: earnings from base metals, rubber, fishing, frozen food, engineering, electronics all surpass it. Gold is 5 per cent of assets, and even less in earnings. Yet it has the fifth largest South African mine – the low-cost mine at Hartebeestfontein in the Klerksdorp field that has been clocking up a good average grade of over 11 g/t (0.35 oz/t) ever since 1955 to contribute over 1,000 tonnes. Although the grade slipped under 9 g/t in the early 1990s, the mine has pressed on with commissioning an eighth shaft and maintained production at just over 30 tonnes a year. The omens are less auspicious at Loraine in the Orange Free State (which opened the same year as Hartes), which has a history of geological hurdles and has finally resorted to mining some high-grade areas to stay alive, forsaking large low-grade deposits that would have maintained it with a better gold price. Its days seem numbered, although Anglo Vaal has run a very active hedging book in spot deferred and options in a real effort to carry the mines through difficult days.

Anglo Vaal also maintains a small corner in South African gold-mining history at Barbeton in the eastern Transvaal. A gold rush there in 1884 preceded the main Witwatersrand discoveries and for a short while the instant town of Barbeton boasted a stock exchange selling shares in companies on the 'Sheba' Reef on the assumption that the legendary King Solomon's mines had been found. Alas, there were only a few rich veins within a very fractured greenstone belt (quite different from the normal Witwatersrand conglomerate), but a few small mines lingered after everyone deserted for the serious gold on the Witwatersrand. And three survive under the umbrella of Anglo Vaal's Eastern Transvaal Consolidated Mines (Et Cons) — Sheba, New Consort and Agnes, chipping in together 3–4 tonnes a year.

Two other mines of those early days, ERPM and Durban Deep, also remain in the portfolio of Randgold, the gold division of the Barlow Rand group, which carries on the torch of Rand Mines, 'The Corner House', the very first South African mining house founded by the diamond magnate (as usual), Hermann Ekstein in 1887. ERPM, that is to say East Rand Proprietary Mines, is the great survivor; born in 1894 it was the very first mine in the East Rand field. Coming up to its centenary, it has produced over 1,400 tonnes (more than any other mine from the original fields) at an average grade of 7.5 g/t (0.24 oz/t). And by way of celebration ERPM is even putting down a new shaft to get at some fresh reserves, although this entailed securing huge loans and government support, so that the mine is winning longer life with a hefty debt hangover. Durban Roodeport Deep, also the last of the line on the original Central Rand field, is limping along toward its centenary in 1998, helped by a concentrated drive to go for higher-grade areas and cushioned by a government subsidy to help with pumping water from its ancient workings. The prospect is not so good for Randgold's main gold contributor, Harmony, in the Orange Free State, struggling along with grades of scarcely 3 g/t (0.096 oz/t) to maintain 20 tonnes a year output. Since Harmony's survival is crucial to the local economy, a major effort has been made with full union support to improve efficiency, even to the extent of accepting a seven-day week (most mines work five and a half days). Successful juggling has also kept alive Blyvooruitzicht, Anglo Vaal's stake on the West Wits Line, where, as we noted earlier, deals have been done with the neighbours, Driefontein Consolidated and Western Deep Levels, whereby more remote areas of their mines can be tackled from much closer shafts at Blyvoor. Without such alliances Blyvooruitzicht, the second mine to open on the West Wits Line back in 1942, faced demise from falling grades and reserves. This patchwork of mines in all is only giving Randgold around 35 tonnes a year and it may be hard to maintain that level if it takes casualties in the gold price war.

The question also has to be asked about the long-term role of the houses like JCI, Anglo Vaal and Barlow Rand in the development of the industry. Gold was their original springboard, but over the years they have used the profits to launch themselves into so many other activities. Is a group which gets less than 5 per cent of its earning from gold going to concentrate on the costly business of expanding existing mines or starting new ones? The board will most likely decide it can get a better (and certainly quicker) return for its money elsewhere.

Actually, the new initiatives of the last decade have come largely from small entrepreneurs outside the framework of the big houses reviving old mines and recycling tailings dumps. Among them is Loucas Pouroulis with Golden Dumps, which has taken under its wing the old South Roodepoort Main Reef and Consolidated Modderfontein mines, from which it recovers a few hundred kilos a year. Another newcomer, Steen Severin, got his hands on a dormant Anglo Vaal mine, Rand Leases, which he found he could bring into production for a modest $16 million (Anglo Vaal had estimated it would cost it $50 million) and win around a tonne a year. Although the enthusiasm of these small operators has been capped by the stagnant gold price, there is a niche for them. They avoid the overheads of the big mining houses, who tend to think in tonnes won rather than kilos.

### The Chamber of Mines

In the early days of the South African gold rush the Chamber of Mines of South Africa was set up as a central source of statistical information where all the latest borehole results were posted. Gradually, however, the Chamber took on a broad range of responsibilities not merely as spokesman for the industry, but as its refiner, recruiter and research centre. 'We're not just a lobby,' explained chief executive Tom Main. 'We provide services on a co-operative basis to our members, which keeps their costs down as they do not have to duplicate the Chamber's operations.' The Chamber even managed the worldwide marketing of the Krugerrand bullion coin launched in the early 1970s. Along with the six main mining houses, its members include over ninety other mining companies and independent mines. Its brief extends not just to gold (although the Gold Producers' Committee is a powerful voice), but to coal and uranium. The Chamber processes and markets all of South Africa's uranium, which is recovered as a by-product from many of the gold mines, through its Nuclear Fuels Corporation. Thus the Chamber of Mines is more actively engaged in the daily work of the industry than any similar association in other gold-producing countries.

### . . . As refiner

For a start, it has operated the Rand Refinery, the world's largest gold refinery, at Germiston, near Johannesburg, since 1921 (prior to that South Africa's gold had gone to London for refining). The refinery was completely rebuilt in 1989 to make it more streamlined and competitive (and when the old refinery was pulled down, over 400 kilos of fine gold dust was recovered from its chimneys, walls and floors). The first sign of its more modern image is a helicopter landing pad. Soon after dawn five mornings a week, a helicopter comes clattering back from an early round of gold mines to pick up the previous day's output. Each mine initially makes bars weighing 26–35 kilos (836–1,125 ounces) at roughly 850 fine; the Rand Refinery then upgrades them on a toll basis to either good delivery bars or to kilo bars.

The helicopter pick-up is part of a new determination to deliver gold quickly. 'Until the mid-1980s, we often kept gold in the safe for 14 days,' admitted refinery director Hermann van Heerden. 'Now, if a mine sends in gold this morning, it is assayed today, their account is credited tomorrow and the Reserve Bank pays the mine two days later.' All South African production, even if it is hedged, must ultimately be delivered to the Reserve Bank, which by law has the exclusive right to market it. The Bank pays for 995 good delivery bars. Increasingly, however, the Rand Refinery is making 995 or 999.9 kilo bars ordered by international bullion traders through the Reserve Bank for direct shipment to Middle East and Far East markets. This represents a significant shift of gold flows since sanctions on South Africa have been lifted and Rand Refinery bars can be marketed directly worldwide. Formerly, South African gold had gone to European refineries for manufacture into the smaller bars; they are now frequently by-passed. The Rand Refinery has also started making gold potassium cyanide (GPC) for gold plating, which is produced in little glass pots, like yoghurt containers, with a gold foil seal on top. Already its 'yoghurt' has established a niche in Hong Kong, previously a good market for European semi-fabricators' brands. 'South Africa is acceptable now in world markets,' said van Heerden, 'and we must be perceived as a threat because of our capacity.'

## . . . As recruiter

The Chamber of Mines' other traditional responsibility has been recruitment for the mines through The Employment Bureau of Africa (TEBA). Historically, this led to the migratory labour system, under which Africans came to work on the mines for six months or a year, lived without their families in hostels, usually within the mine compounds, and were poorly paid. Apart from a period immediately after the Boer War, when indentured Chinese labour was brought in from the Far East for five years, the mines have been a sponge for African labour. For many years, two-thirds of the workers came from outside South Africa, because the mines paid so little that local Africans could do better in other industries; the under-developed economies of Malawi, Botswana and Mozambique provided the workforce.

Radical changes, however, have taken place in the last few years not just in the handling of the recruitment by TEBA, but in stabilizing the workforce on the mines, in pay and conditions and, significantly, in the extensive teaching of English for the first time to many workers. Understanding English is essential in breaking down the previous barriers for advancement of black workers to responsible jobs, including the all-important 'blasting certificates', which they were finally permitted to obtain in 1988. The blacks' own National Union of Mineworkers has also been formally recognized for over a decade.

On the recruitment front, TEBA has moved from what its director, Roger Rowett, candidly admitted was once, 'the mass procurement of human flesh' to being the liaison between a more regular workforce on the mines, albeit still living in hostels, and their families and home communities. TEBA maintains over seventy offices in South Africa, Lesotho, Swaziland, Botswana and Mozambique through which workers sign on annually, payments are made, and messages to families are passed. TEBA also aims to work on rural development through training and agricultural projects.

To aid recruitment TEBA maintains a computer database in Johannesburg of 460,000 records of current workers, listing their skills and mine affiliations. This enables a mine to enquire by name whether a particular driller or machine operator is ready to return to work, whereas in the past they ordered up fifty or a hundred anonymous underground workers. The black workers are now usually employed for most of their careers at a single mine; in the past they often worked for a year on one mine, went home for a while and came back to another. Today, 90 per cent of the mine workforce is stabilized. A man works for a year, goes home on leave for a few months, but then returns to his old job, which also provides him with a pension. Frequently, if he works on a mine relatively near his home, even if it is in Lesotho or Mozambique, he goes home on Friday afternoon in a fleet of minicabs that makes a thriving business on weekend trips. Thus the migratory nature of the work continues, but that is largely by choice. A few years ago when the National Union of Mineworkers (NUM) was first gaining membership and muscle under its engaging secretary, Cyril Ramaphosa (now a leading figure in the African National Congress), the aim was to end the migratory system entirely. Miners, Ramaphosa argued, must live at the mines with their families for a more stable and dignified life. In practice, that is against the African tradition, as a survey for the NUM by the University of Capetown showed. For the African, wealth lies in cattle and land in his own community. If he leaves and takes his family to live at the mines, he loses that wealth. So he prefers his family to remain at home, taking care of cattle and land, while he lives in a hostel on the mine to which he is more or less permanently attached. For many families it is the tradition for sons to follow their fathers to the mines, especially in Lesotho and Mozambique where the local economies have little to offer. (Lesotho gets over 40 per cent of its GDP from the earnings of migratory miners; in Mozambique it accounts for close to 30 per cent.) Mozambique workers, incidentally, have the best reputation as underground miners and for the best work ethic.

The balance between workers from South Africa and other African states has shifted. Once two-thirds of the black workforce came from outside South Africa; now around 55 per cent are South African. A 'snapshot' cross-section of the country of origin of 372,733 workers in August 1992 showed 206,040 from South Africa, 87,144 from Lesotho, 50,065 from Mozambique, 15,731 from Swaziland, 13,005 from Botswana and 748 from other places. Notably missing is Malawi, once an important source for up to 17,000 workers, until a spot check one week for the AIDS virus showed that 125 new arrivals were HIV positive.

The creation of a permanent workforce has been matched by the mines themselves providing a more positive career structure and the teaching of English. The English lessons have replaced the traditional Esperanto of the mines, *fanakalo* (meaning 'like this'), a mixture of English, Afrikaans and African dialects that covered basic needs and instructions. But *fanakalo* was in itself restrictive; it covered phrases like, 'bring a shovel', but shut the African off from a true understanding of mining and the application of modern technology. 'Lots of able black people can take more responsibility,' remarked Gengold's Gary Maude, 'but they do not have the education. We want 80 per cent of our workers to read, write and talk English by the end of the decade.' Since the barrier against black workers holding 'blasting certificates' has also been removed, the opportunities for advancement are better. And the long rearguard action of the white miners' union, which held up the improvement for blacks for so long, has largely crumbled.

This is reflected in the elimination of the gap between the pay of whites and blacks; once 20:1, today it is almost irrelevant. By the spring of 1993 the average earnings of skilled surface workers was 3,632 rand ($1,100) per month and for skilled underground workers 4,553 rand ($1,400). Although by international standards this is low, by comparison with other African countries it is handsome; a semi-skilled worker on the mines in Ghana gets around $100 a month, and in Zaire a mere $40. A highly skilled technician in South Africa earns close to $2,000 a month. However, the priority, even for the National Union of Mineworkers, has shifted from pay to job security. As employment on the mines tumbled from around 520,000 to scarcely 370,000, saving jobs became urgent. An African who loses his job on the mines has little chance of finding another in the weak economies of South Africa and her neighbours; and a family of seven to ten people may depend on his income. The NUM has moderated wage claims, settled quickly and been ready to talk deals to keep mines afloat. 'The NUM has matured,' said the Chamber's chief executive, Tom Main. 'They are much more realistic.'

Although the job losses resulted in a small way from mine closures, most came from efficiency drives on the mines. 'We were overstaffed,' Tom Main admitted. 'We've lost 150,000 people − 25 per cent of the workforce − but the production of gold hasn't dropped.' The higher productivity also reflects technical advances, which are crucial for the industry to survive as a major producer. South Africa coasted for too long on the cushion of cheap black labour. While of necessity it pioneered the engineering skills needed in deep mines, there was little incentive to go for labour-saving equipment within the mines, although for years there were attempts to invent a rock-cutting machine to fillet out the narrow gold-bearing reef − like pulling the meat from a sandwich.

### . . . As technical researcher

The pressure for new technology embracing both improved mining methods and improved safety is increasing, because the industry has already been through massive cost-cutting exercises in everything from reducing the workforce to putting the squeeze on its suppliers. 'The obvious ways of reducing costs have been explored − so what next?' said Dr John Stewart, the general manager of COMRO (Chamber of Mines Research Organization), as he set out the challenges facing his team. Unless there is a sustained gold price increase, new mining methods using new technology offer the only route. Yet the problem is being compounded because the older, shallower mines are closing, putting the onus even more on deep mining. 'Three and a half to four kilometres down is an awfully deep hole,' said Dr Stewart. 'Look at the rock pressures; once beyond 2,500 metres, you are into high stress, so the problem is rock bursts.' To say nothing of the heat, for the temperature rises 9 degrees C every thousand metres. Thus the challenge is safety, 'coolth' (as the conditions at the workface are called), and then more efficient extraction of the gold reef itself. While tackling individual problems, John Stewart argues the real aim has to be to think about the total mining method, so that the sum of the benefits is greater than that achieved by any single one.

The priority has to start at the sharp end − in the stope, right up against the reef. Most accidents occur within 2 metres of this workface or in neighbouring access gullies; so the aim is to make this area safer, then provide better tools within it. Safety comes through new lightweight hydraulic props, with enough give in them to respond to sudden rock pressures and so hopefully prevent or contain a rock burst. They also eliminate the fire hazard of old-style timber props. Comfort is being sought through improved ice systems to cool the air; at Western Deep Levels, COMRO is investigating using a slurry of ice which can be pumped through the mine in steel and plastic pipes. This may be more effective than the 'ice jackets' worn by workers on some mines, which contain a series of water pockets that can be frozen. When the jacket thaws, the miner gets a fresh one from the deep freeze. Safety and comfort are also improved by 'backfilling' abandoned stopes and tunnels with waste rock. This not only provides support (rock burst accidents are reduced by up to 50 per cent) but by sealing off much of the rock face the heat flow is reduced.

Right up in the stope, two new gadgets are being tested on the reef itself: water-powered rock drills, replacing pneumatic ones, and an outsize water-powered chisel. The chisel chips into the reef with energetic blows five times a second, nibbling out just the thin seam of gold and automatically loading it onto a conveyor. The chisel could be a breakthrough in enabling just the gold seam to be extracted, not only eliminating the need to haul and crush much waste, but also the need for blasting. In short, it would make continuous mining possible without the daily stops for blasting and the clearing of the resultant mess. A variation on this theme, being studied by Anglo American, is a diamond-studded cutting wire which saws out the gold reef like a cheese wire cuts out a segment. At the moment it is expensive, but a mining executive told me that if the costs could be reduced by two-thirds it would 'look attractive'.

Confirming the richest areas of reef to be sliced out may also be helped by a gold analyser, which has come through tests on the Carbon Leader and Ventersdorp Contact Reefs, giving what scientists call 'unbiased' readings of grades. Normally the grade is assessed by chipping out samples to be sent for fire assay on the surface; the gold analyser in contrast scans the entire exposed reef within a stope providing an on-the-spot overall assessment. The next step is a lightweight backpack containing ground penetrating radar, which sees ahead up to 50 metres into the rock face detecting hazardous geological conditions.

Standing back for a broader look at the whole mining industry, the longer-term questions focus on the overall development of continuous mechanical mining, the extension of 'trackless' mining, which was first fully implemented at Western Areas, and the potential for digging yet deeper and wider shafts. A single deep shaft, by-passing the present main shaft to medium levels and then sub-shafts below, would cut out the time-consuming transfer level, which can mean each shift takes up to an hour each way to get from the surface to the working area at over 3,000 metres.

### *Into survival mode?*

Does all this spell salvation? The short answer is no. The timing is wrong. The mines are short of cash; often they are reluctant to make the capital investment on new equipment, let alone devise an entire new strategy for shaft systems. Even on a new mine like Moab the aim is to make it a Toyota rather than a Rolls Royce. The new technology will be used, it will help some mines to survive, but for the moment the industry is just not in the mood for the huge re-equipping that much of this implies. As one mining executive conceded, 'It would take a brave man to start a new gold mine right now.' And Harry Oppenheimer, stepping out of retirement to address a conference in London, observed that sustained prices of $500 or more would be needed to ensure the viability of new deep-level mines. What frustrates the mining executives, especially in the major groups like Anglo, GFSA and Gengold, is that they have vast reservoirs of knowledge, which they cannot use fully at home. They know the replacement is not coming in locally; the only answer is to use their expertise to secure it abroad. As Gold Fields' Robin Plumbridge observes, 'The change which has swept through Latin America regarding privatisation of mining activities and the encouragement given to foreign companies with a high level of professional skill, is extending itself throughout the developing nations of the Far East.' And he added pointedly, 'It is a sad commentary on the state of South Africa's economic policies that the country which once had some of the most far-sighted mining policies is now largely uncompetitive with the emerging nations'.[6]

No one has any illusions. As the Chamber's Tom Main conceded, 'The five-year flat gold price has left deep scars on the South African gold industry'. He told the Australian Gold Conference in Kalgoorlie in 1993, 'Production is expected to decrease from the current 600 tonnes a year to about 470 tonnes by the year 2000.' South Africa was last at that level in 1955, when the full benefit of the Orange Free State and Klerksdorp fields started to come in. Even so, South Africa will go into the twenty-first century as gold mining's number one, but no longer quite in a league of her own. As economist Michael Brown summed it up, 'We'll keep a solid core of fifteen mines; we'll still be the biggest,

6 Gold Fields, Chairman's Review, 1992.

we'll keep our hand in, but gold mining here is going into survival mode.'

# UNITED STATES: GOLD FIELDS

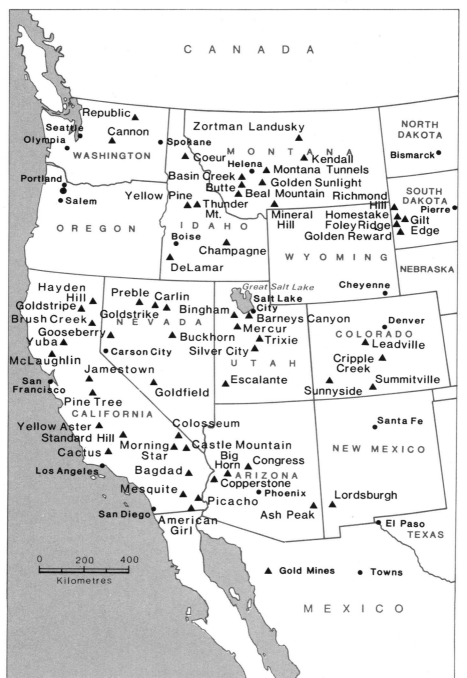

CANADA

**Republic** ▲

**Seattle** ●
**Olympia** ●
**WASHINGTON**

**Cannon** ▲
**Spokane** ●

**Zortman Landusky** ▲

**M O N T A N A**

**Coeur** ▲
**Helena** ●
**Kendall** ▲
**Montana Tunnels** ▲

**Basin Creek** ▲
**Golden Sunlight** ▲
**Butte** ▲
**Beal Mountain** ▲

**Richmond** ▲
**Hill**

**NORTH DAKOTA**

**Bismarck** ●

**Portland** ●

**Salem** ●

**O R E G O N**

**Yellow Pine** ▲
**Thunder** ▲
**Mt.**

**I D A H O**

**Boise** ●
**Champagne** ▲

**DeLamar** ▲

**Mineral** **Homestake** ▲
**Hill** **Foley Ridge** ▲
**Golden Reward** ▲

**Gilt** ▲
**Edge** ▲

**SOUTH DAKOTA**
**Pierre** ●

**W Y O M I N G**

**NEBRASKA**

**Hayden** ▲
**Hill**
**Goldstripe** ▲
**Brush Creek** ▲
**Gooseberry** ▲
**Yuba** ▲

**Preble** ▲ **Carlin** ▲
**Goldstrike** ▲
**N E V A D A**
**Bingham** ▲

**Buckhorn** ▲

**Carson City** ●
**Silver City** ▲

**Great Salt Lake**
**Salt Lake** ▲
**City** ●
**Barneys Canyon** ▲
**Mercur** ▲
**Trixie** ▲

**Cheyenne** ●

**Denver** ●

**C O L O R A D O**
**Leadville** ▲

**McLaughlin** ▲

**Jamestown** ▲

**San** ●
**Francisco**

**Goldfield** ▲

**U T A H**

**Escalante** ▲

**Cripple** ▲
**Creek**

**Sunnyside** ▲

**Summitville** ▲

**Pine Tree** ▲

**CALIFORNIA**

**Yellow Aster** ▲
**Standard Hill** ▲
**Cactus** ▲

**Morning** ▲
**Star**
**Bagdad** ▲

**Colosseum** ▲

**Castle Mountain** ▲
**Big** ▲
**Horn** ▲ **Congress** ▲
**A R I Z O N A**
**Copperstone** ▲

**Phoenix** ●

**Santa Fe** ●

**N E W   M E X I C O**

**Lordsburgh** ▲

**Los Angeles** ●

**Mesquite** ▲
**Picacho** ▲

**Ash Peak** ▲

**San Diego** ●
**American** ▲
**Girl**

**El Paso** ●
**TEXAS**

| 0 | 200 | 400 |
|---|-----|-----|

Kilometres

▲ **Gold Mines**      ● **Towns**

**M E X I C O**

**CHAPTER 6**

# The United States:
# Thank You, Carlin Trend

The signpost off Interstate Route 80 winding through the bleak hills of the high desert of northeast Nevada merely indicates 'Carlin Central'. It gives no clue as you turn off through a cluster of houses and trailer homes that you are approaching one of the richest gold fields ever discovered outside South Africa. Within the space of 30 miles going north along a narrow, twisting road fringed by sagebrush, where some scrawny cattle roam, are two open-pit gold mines each producing a million ounces or more (32.15 tonnes)[1] annually – world class by any standards, and well named Gold Quarry and Goldstrike. Around them cluster smaller open pits, Gold Bug, Genesis, Blue Star, Deep Star, Post/ Deep Post, Rodeo, Bootstrap; drilling rigs are burrowing into the hillsides nearby confirming the full scale of the Meikle mine, due in 1995, and the viability of an orebody initially christened Ren. While to the south, beyond the Interstate highway, is yet another successful open pit named Rain. Together they comprise the Carlin Trend, a strip of hills 50 miles long and 5 miles wide where over twenty epithermal deposits of disseminated gold – microscopic particles quite invisible to the naked eye – have been identified, with combined mineable reserves (that is, already proven) of close to 50 million ounces. 'The Carlin Trend', says Jonathan Price, director of the Nevada Bureau of Mines and Geology, 'has made the United States a major gold-producing country and net exporter of gold.'

Succinctly put, the United States has been transformed from trailing a poor sixth in the world league in 1980, at just under 1 million ounces

---

1 Since US mines normally quote their output and grades in ounces, in this chapter ounces are listed with the metric equivalent in brackets.

(30.2 tonnes) to number two position producing over 10 million ounces (over 300 tonnes) in 1993. In so doing, the United States overtook the former Soviet Union, long the second largest producer, in 1991. More significant, perhaps, the US industry now has a central role in world gold mining, with a range of unequalled expertise in the application of all aspects of modern technology for the efficient extraction of low-grade deposits. Indeed, what impressed me at mines like Gold Quarry and Goldstrike was the wide-ranging use of computer technology for everything from control of oregrades to the precise location and movement of every loader and truck in the giant pits. Three-dimensional displays on computer terminals now effectively enable geologists and mine engineers to 'walk through' ore deposits hidden far below ground, as if they were ghosts, to plan every step of production for a decade ahead. With this knowledge, it is no surprise to find US gold mining companies in the forefront of exploration, not just in Latin America, but in Africa, Southeast Asia, and in such CIS republics as Uzbekistan.

The industry's rapid growth has also enabled it to forge new links with bullion banks, who have attended to its every need in mining finance, marketing and hedging. While major US banks, such as J.P. Morgan, Chase Manhattan and Goldman Sachs, have all become closely involved, foreign banks, which won their gold-mining spurs initially in Australia, have arrived. Go to Denver, the capital of US gold mining, where groups like Amax Gold, Newmont Mining and Echo Bay are located and there, too, are N.M. Rothschilds, Macquarie and Mase Westpac with local banking offices explicitly established to service the gold miners, drawing on the expertise they gained revitalizing Australian gold (see Chapter 9).

Denver, Colorado may be the administrative and banking capital of gold; Nevada is where the real action is. Historically, Nevada has been known as The Silver State; it might be better renamed The Gold State, for it accounts for 60 per cent of US production. While the state is peppered with gold mines, the heart of the matter is the Carlin Trend. Already it contributes 50 per cent of the state's output; that share should rise to 60 per cent before the end of the century. By the year 2000 Carlin Trend operations could account for 40 per cent of all US gold production.

This is not to ignore what is being achieved at historic mines like Homestake at Lead, South Dakota or by new mines in other states from Alaska to South Carolina. One of the best bets is Battle Mountain's Crown Jewel open pit in Washington, due in 1994 with at least a ten-year life producing 175,000 ounces (5.4 tonnes) annually from a grade of 0.186 oz/t (5.8 g/t). In Idaho, FMC's small heap-leach operation,

## USA: PRODUCTION

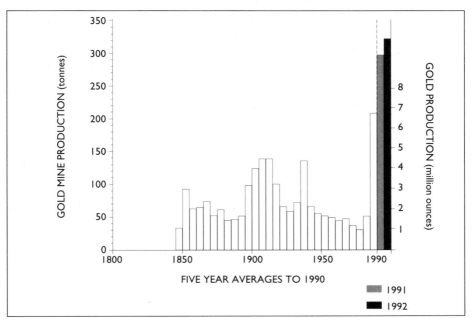

Beartrack, should expand to a fully-fledged mine at 100,000 ounces (3.1 tonnes) a year, and Hecla Mining's Grouse Creek is forecast to produce that amount too. While Montana, already home to Pegasus Gold's successful Zortman-Landusky property (which is still expanding), has Phelps Dodge/Canyon Resources shaping up with the Seven-Up Pete/ McDonald Meadows open pits scheduled for 400,000 ounces (12.4 tonnes), plus Hemlo Gold and Crown Butte Resources setting up New World, which has relatively high-grade open-pit and underground potential. And, although it is not a newcomer, one must not forget the long-running show at Bingham Canyon in Utah, where RTZ/Kennecott continues to mine its great copper-gold pit which yields, essentially as a by-product, upwards of 500,000 ounces (15.5 tonnes) of gold each year.

Across the United States sixty-five gold projects, completely excluding the Carlin Trend, are likely to be producing in 1995, with forty-five existing or new mines active in the year 2000 according to the Canadian geologist Dr Paul Kavanagh. None, however, approaches the scale of the Carlin Trend, for which Dr Kavanagh predicts a total of 4 million ounces (124.4 tonnes) in 2000. Carlin is in a class of its own.

### Introducing the Super Pit
Gold prospecting is not new to the Tuscarora hills of Nevada's Carlin

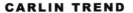

**CARLIN TREND**

△ Ivanhoe

ELKO

Dee▲ Bootstrap/Capstone
Goldstrike▲  Post

COUNTY

North Star▲△Deep Post
Bobcat△▲▲Genesis
Blue Star▲△▲Carlin
Lantern▲     △
          Pete

CARLIN TREND

Tusc
Mac △▲ Gold
          ▲▲ Quarry
Maggie Creek
          Carlin

To Elko

EUREKA    COUNTY

To Reno

Emigrant
Springs
Rain▲ △
Gnome △△
          SMZ

Map
Area
NEVADA

▲ Gold Mines  △ Gold Prospects
0        10        20
Kilometres

district. The Good Hope claim was pegged in the 1870s (but largely
produced silver and lead) and prospectors regularly worked the local
creeks right up to the 1960s, winning perhaps 10,000 ounces. They
even traced the original bedrock in some narrow quartz veins at Big Six
mine. But they had no way of knowing they were tramping over huge
epithermal deposits of invisible, finely disseminated gold, often on or
just below the surface.

The credit for the ultimate geological detective work goes to John
Livermore and Alan Coope of Newmont Mining, who started detailed
drilling exploration in 1961. Just 80 feet down they got assays of 0.20
oz/t (6.2 g/t). Soon after, Newmont's Robert Fulton took their
recommendation to acquire an initial eighty acres. Before long, assays
were as high as 0.74 oz/t (23 g/t). Yet no one could see the gold. The
largest specks were 0.0002 inches across (0.0005 centimetres) and had to
be magnified 1,800 times before they could be photographed. Eventually,
the geologists mapped out an orebody a mile long, and 600 feet deep
(183 metres), with an average grade of 0.3 oz/t (9.3 g/t). Even with
gold pegged at $35 in the early 1960s, that was viable. In April 1965
Newmont opened the Carlin pit, the first major new mine in the
United States for half a century.

Today you can stand on the rim of the giant artificial canyon from which Newmont filleted 3.2 million ounces (over 100 tonnes) during the next twenty-one years. 'This was the mother of disseminated gold pits,' Newmont geologist Joe Rota told me when I first went there. Operations were largely suspended in 1986, although new exploration is seeking the deep 'feeders' through which molten gold was forced 40 million years ago to create the Carlin mine. But today from this same vantage point above the canyon, swing round to look north; there is the future of the Carlin trend; the yellow, brown and red streaks of the heap-leach pads and waste dumps of Genesis, Blue Star and Post from which Newmont gets around 400,000 ounces (12.4 tonnes) a year. Almost hidden behind them are the top benches leading down into American Barrick's Goldstrike pit. In the distance beyond, a sharp eye can pick out the drilling rigs at Meikle, which will be the first underground mine on the Carlin Trend. Once Meikle starts in 1995, this northern area of the trend will be producing perhaps 2.5 million ounces or more annually. Turn around. Tucked away out of sight just a few miles south is Newmont's Gold Quarry, which started up in 1985 just as the best of the original Carlin pit was worked out. Gold Quarry underlines Newmont's real strength on the Carlin Trend; it owns much of it. 'We have the dominant land position,' admits John Parry, the senior vice-president in charge of exploration. Back in 1983 Newmont acquired the whole of the T-Lazy S Ranch, a wedge of hills and valleys around the present mines. 'Newmont Gold currently owns or controls the mineral rights on 58 square miles on the Carlin Trend,' added Parry. 'Furthermore, Newmont Mining [the parent company] owns or controls the mineral rights on 420 square miles surrounding our position.' And Newmont Gold also enjoys the right to claim any discoveries made by Newmont Mining on a much wider swathe of 2,300 square miles of surrounding terrain, in return for a 10 per cent royalty. Newmont Mining restructured the old Carlin Gold Mining Company as Newmont Gold in 1986, retaining 90.1 per cent of the shares, but going public on the balance. Newmont Gold's prime task is the development of the Carlin Trend, while Newmont Mining, also much more of a gold company than in the past, having got rid of coal mining and other interests, takes a broader worldwide view of gold- mining activities, with exploration going into Latin America and Southeast Asia. Moreover, in 1990 the Anglo-French entrepreneur Sir James Goldsmith, an advocate of the virtues of gold, became the largest shareholder of Newmont Mining. Initially, Sir James acquired 42 per cent of Newmont but in 1993, in a highly publicized and calculated play, he sold 10 per cent to the Hungarian-born money manager and speculator George Soros (Goldsmith himself used the proceeds to buy call options on gold). He then made further disposals, reducing his holding to 5 per cent.

Newmont Gold's initial mission in the late 1980s was rapid growth. When I first went to visit the company in 1986, it was aiming for an ambitious 1 million ounces (31.1 tonnes) a year from its combined pits on the trend. It reached that easily, going on to hit 1.7 million ounces (52.9 tonnes) in 1990. The next year Gold Quarry alone became the first mine in North America ever to produce over 1 million ounces inside twelve months (an achievement normally reserved for South African mines). Newmont Gold's task for the 1990s is not continued growth, but to maintain annual output on the Carlin Trend at 1.7 million ounces or better. It is no easy assignment. As T. Peter Philip, Newmont Gold's president and chief operating officer, likes to remind visitors, 'We must replace 2 million ounces [in reserves] each year just to stay even.'

Standing on the brink of Gold Quarry you get some idea of what Newmont Gold has done already. Before you is a great circular pit, over half a mile in diameter, that plunges down over 1,000 feet. There are rings of steps, or benches, each 25 feet deep, around the sides of this amphitheatre, narrowing in towards the base. A neat pattern of small holes, as if an army of moles had been at work, shows where charges have been laid for the next day's blast. Usually between 80 and 200 holes are drilled for each blast. Nearby, gigantic loaders are scooping up broken rock from yesterday's blast and dumping it onto trucks. From on high they look like children's toys.

Below, in the heart of the pit, the scale changes. The trucks each haul 190 tons of rock; they are so huge that their tyres alone are nearly 12 feet high (and cost $18,000 each) and the driver is almost hidden in a little cabin below his load, rather like the head of a tortoise tucked beneath its shell. Perched in this monster with the steering wheel on the left, the driver can only just see the side of the road immediately below him, so Gold Quarry, and a few similar pits, are the only places in the United States where driving is on the left. The trucks' routine is guided by a computer, which updates their location on the dispatcher's screen every twenty seconds. Their every move is monitored by small radio transmitters powered by solar panels, strategically placed along the pit approach ramps, which signal as each passes by. The composition of each load is not just known, but precisely determined and channelled.

### The Bonus of New Technology

Visually the action at Gold Quarry is in the pit. What counts equally, as with a play, is the unseen direction. The heart of that direction is the automated assay laboratory, which can process nearly 2,000 samples a day, both from the working pits and from exploration drilling. The samples arrive in little white bags, each tagged with its individual bar-code designating exactly which zone it comes from. Then the robots take over. A thimble-full of rock from each is sifted out and crushed. An endless choreography of delicate mechanical arms pops some of the powder into crucibles for fire assay. Another dose is dumped into a test tube which is topped up with cyanide, and whirled in a centrifuge. The resulting mixture is sprayed before a flame, enabling an atomic absorption spectrometer to analyse its gold content. The score flashes on a screen. One comes up at 0.035 (of an ounce). 'That's mill grade,' says the technician watching. The next is 0.00002. 'A bust – waste', he adds.

These assays are the raw data from which the geologists refining a new orebody or mining engineers planning their excavations can work. Programmed into a computer, the entire orebody comes up as a three-dimensional model on a screen like the coloured street map of a city. 'We can load up all the assays, all the boreholes and step down through the entire deposit, walking through each section,' explained Aaron Britt, the senior operations planning geologist, punching up a display of Gold Quarry. 'You can think inside the deposit.'

He pulls up an individual block of the southwest zone of Gold Quarry. The main outline of the mineralization is cross-hatched in yellow on his screen; individual boxes within are coloured blue for waste, green for heap-leach and red for mill feed. 'You can see,' said Britt, 'this is mostly leach.'

This ability to move figuratively within the deposit has transformed the understanding of and the ability to mine big pits efficiently. 'Before we got these computer graphics, it used to take weeks just to model a zone,' said Britt. 'Now I can do it in a couple of hours in the afternoon.'

The practical applications translate to the pit. When a fresh zone is blasted the gold content of each sector is known. Colour-coded flags indicate whether the material is waste, leach or mill material. The loader moving in has a computer console in his cab which also gives him the layout and tells him what to lift into each of the 190-ton trucks that pulls up alongside him. The dispatcher directs the truck to the appropriate destination. At Gold Quarry any rock that the robots in the laboratory have graded less than 0.006 oz/t (0.18 g/t) is waste. Above that rock up to 0.034 oz/t (1.05 g/t) is assigned to the heap-leach pads; at 0.035 oz/t or better, it goes to conventional milling.

Heap-leaching, in making the recovery of very low-grade gold viable, has been one of the prime factors in the success not just of the Carlin Trend and Nevada, but of much of the expansion in US gold mining since the early 1970s. Indeed, by the late 1980s, half of US output was leached. Heap-leaching of gold was first pioneered in the United States at Placer's Cortez open pit in Nevada in 1973, then at Pegasus Gold's Zortman-Landusky in Montana. Now it is commonplace. The prime advantage is the economic extraction of gold from low-grade deposits which would not be profitable if it had to go through the usual cycle of being crushed to fine powder in expensive milling plants. Milling still makes sense for higher grades and the recovery rate of gold is better. Heap-leaching, however, widens the range of ore in a mine that can be processed.

Ore for leaching is simply passed through a preliminary crusher before being heaped up on open-air leach 'pads' lined with a base of asphalt or impervious plastic sheeting. A network of hose is then laid across the top through which a solution of dilute cyanide is pumped. Originally the cyanide solution was sprayed over the top of a heap, as one might water a lawn, but it has been found more efficient (and environmentally friendly) to lay out a detailed patchwork of thin black irrigation 'dripper' hose with a pin-prick hole every 24 inches through which the solution drips into the pile. The drippers also enable leaching to continue at places like Gold Quarry right through the winter, even in sub-zero temperatures; previously the sprayed solution often froze.

The cyanide percolates down through the heap of ore for several weeks, leaching out the gold. This solution, rich in gold, drains from the bottom of the pad into the aptly named 'pregnant pond'. Heap-leaching usually enables about 70 per cent of the gold to be recovered relatively quickly. Thereafter an occasional additional dose of cyanide will eventually trickle out a little more gold.

At Gold Quarry on the original leach pad to which no more material had been added since 1989, as much as 100 ounces was filtering out daily, two years later. All told, Newmont Gold got 272,000 ounces (8.5 tonnes) from its leach pads at Gold Quarry in 1992 and 554,500 ounces (17.3 tonnes) from all its Carlin Trend pads, with an average grade of only 0.021 oz/t (0.065 g/t), clear evidence of the way in which heap-leaching has unlocked much gold that would otherwise never have been extracted.

The second new technical advance that has helped improve gold mining efficiency, not just on gold from leach pads, but also from conventional milling, then comes into play – carbon adsorption. The pregnant solution is pumped to the recovery plant, where it passes through a series of tanks containing carbon granules, usually made from coconut shells. Coconut is preferred because it turns into a hard carbon durable enough for repeated use. Gold has a natural affinity for carbon.

In six minutes 97 per cent of the gold transfers its allegiance from the cyanide solution to the coconut shell carbon as it passes through the adsorption tanks. The gold-laden carbon then passes through a strip circuit where, under pressure and heat, it expels the gold into a solution of sodium cyanide and caustic soda. Finally, this pregnant solution is passed through electrolytic or 'electro-winning' cells, whose cathodes are covered with steel wool. The gold is deposited on the wool, from which it is easily recovered by fire refining. Newmont Gold's refinery at Carlin turns out 800-ounce ore bars containing 94–96 per cent gold and the balance mostly in silver. As I left at the end of the day, so did a Wells Fargo security truck taking the bars for their final refining. Much of it goes to the Johnson Matthey refinery at Salt Lake City, Utah, 250 miles away.

### Unlocking Refractory Ores

The rapid growth in output Newmont Gold achieved at Carlin in the late 1980s was possible because it was mining oxide ores, from which gold extraction is relatively straightforward, at such open pits as Gold Quarry, Genesis, Blue Star and Rain, where the deposits were close to the surface. The catch comes when those orebodies are largely mined out and the next stage is deeper deposits of refractory sulphide ores, from which gold extraction is much more complex, even if they can still be mined in open pits. Newmont Gold faced this hurdle on the Carlin Trend by the early 1990s. It was not alone. Indeed, the future in the Carlin area going into the next century is not with easily accessible and amenable oxide ores, but with refractory ores that are devious both in metallurgy and in hiding themselves. So the mid-1990s is the moment of transition. The consolation is that the sulphide ores offer much higher grades – up to 1 ounce (31.15 g/t) in the best zones. That prize will keep the mining going.

To do battle with the refractory ores Newmont Gold will open a low temperature roasting plant in 1994 which will oxidize them, so they can proceed to conventional milling and carbon-in-leach extraction. The roaster will be costly, adding $8 per ounce to treatment costs, but the higher grades easily pay for it. And the roaster will not only give a new lease of life to Gold Quarry itself, where a new zone called Deep West is being probed, but enable Newmont to tackle much deeper deposits to the north, including Deep Star and Deep Post.

Deep Star epitomizes the new brand of Carlin discovery. It is a small, rich orebody tucked between 1,200 feet (366 metres) and 1,800 feet (549 metres) below ground with an elusive upper surface only 350 by 250 feet (107 × 76 metres). It will have to be extracted by underground mining. The cost is worth it. 'The grade', Eric Hamer, Newmont Gold's general manager at Carlin, said cheerfully, 'is approximately 1 oz/t [31.1 g/t].'

### Enter American Barrick

Deep Post, a mile beyond, will be an open pit, but launches another new Carlin tradition – joint venture. The deposit at Deep Post extends into territory owned by American Barrick, which is right next door with its huge Goldstrike pit. A deal has been struck for Barrick to mine the entire orebody on behalf of both companies; an alliance that has to make sense when you see the properties cheek by jowl. 'Co-operation is not optional – it's imperative,' said Newmont's Walter Lawrence. 'We could not be in an adversarial environment with Barrick.'

American Barrick and Newmont are intriguing bedfellows. Newmont is very much the old-established US mining group, dating from 1921 with wide historic experience in base metals and coal, and coming more recently to gold as its prime concern. American Barrick, based in Toronto, is a brash, professional newcomer founded in 1983 by Canadian entrepreneur Peter Munk, whose previous experience was in oil and natural gas (see Chapter 7). Barrick made its name by snapping up the Mercur gold mine in Utah in 1985 for a mere $40 million when the gold price was in the doldrums and swiftly doubling production. It paid for much of Mercur with a gold loan of 77,000 ounces (2.4 tonnes). It sold the borrowed gold spot for $25 million, paying back the loan from production over the next four years at 2 per cent interest. That set its style of financing. American Barrick has become a by-word for gold loans and hedging its production. Its track record in the bear market after 1988 made it look as if it might be on a special line to a gold market no one else knew about. In 1989 its hedging secured it $54 an ounce higher than the average Comex price for the year; in 1990 $53, in 1991 $76 and in 1992 a handsome $77 an ounce bonus. 'We need to hedge,' said Barrick's treasurer, Randall Oliphant, as we toured its latest prize, Goldstrike. 'This is too big an investment to be crap-shooting [on the gold price]. It makes the banks more comfortable with us.' And, one might add, shareholders. A review of the performance of twenty-three leading gold-mining companies carried out by *Mining Journal*'s International Gold Mining Newsletter revealed that between 1988 and 1992, the share prices of twenty-two of them fell; only one, American Barrick, showed an amazing 181 per cent increase.[2]

Actually, a couple of bankers were going round with us and they did not let Barrick off lightly, asking tough questions about the $40 million being spent on a battery of autoclaves, the high pressure, high temperature cookers, which loosen up that maverick gold in refractory ores. Were they safe? Hadn't someone on another Nevada mine had a fire in an autoclave? Pertinent questions, because much is riding on the ability of those autoclaves to crack sulphide ores at Goldstrike.

Although Goldstrike began as a conventional oxide pit, its true heart is the Betze deposit, located some 900 feet (275 metres) down, where the gold is locked up in iron sulphides. Although some test holes were first made at Goldstrike as far back as 1962, and several small mining companies took turns at heap-leaching from small pits on the surface in the late 1970s and 1980s, it was only after American Barrick purchased the property in 1986 that a full appreciation of what lay below began to emerge. Deep drilling eventually intersected with a long, narrow slug of high grade sulphides, whose gold content was estimated at 12 million ounces (373 tonnes). It was named Betze after the geologists Keith 'Bet-tles and Larry Korn-ze', who found it. 'With Betze, we are really into the second generation at Carlin with the sulphide ores,' said Barrick executive vice-president for operations, Alan Hill, as we drove up to the site. Geologist Keith Bettles himself was on hand to explain his discovery of this buried treasure. On the Carlin Trend, he said, the orebodies are contained within limestone; they outcrop on the surface and then dip to the north and are covered. On the surface the orebodies (as at Newmont's Gold Quarry) are oxides and the gold is easily recoverable. That has given Barrick its head start at Goldstrike; it recovered nearly 2 million ounces (60 tonnes) from oxide ores between 1987 and 1992 to help pay for excavating 350 million tons of waste material above Betze, the core of the deposit.

Actually, Betze is, as it were, a Siamese twin of Newmont's Deep Post deposit, for they are inextricably interlinked, justifying the plan for Barrick to mine it for Newmont Gold. Together the ore zones are a mile long, between 600 and 800 feet (183-244 metres) wide and usually up to 800 feet (244 metres) thick (although one drilled hole on Betze's southeast corner has nearly 1,200 feet (366 metres) of ore at a grade of 0.32 oz/t (9.95 g/t)). Pockets of Betze do even better. 'We've got one high grade zone of 300 feet of one ounce,' said Keith Bettles, 'and in general the grades once we get to production are higher than we predicted.'

Betze's full scope has yet to be determined. 'We're still looking for the southern end of this orebody,' Bettles went on. 'We're going deeper, getting down to 2,000 feet on the southern boundary.' He paused for a moment, then added, 'It's an elusive bugger.'

Mining it is expensive too. As Alan Hill put it, as we descended into the pit, 'it's a tremendous orebody – that's the good news. The bad news is that you have to mine it.' For a start, much of the rock below 1,000 feet is unstable and, because the best of the ore lies below the water table, over 50,000 gallons of very hot water has to be pumped out *every minute* to keep the Betze pit dry. That water has to be purified to drinking water standards before it can be discharged into a reservoir in the valley below, towards which it steams still at 128 degrees F.

Once recovered, the sulphide ores have to go through the extra processing step of the autoclaves to unlock the gold. The autoclaves cook the sulphide ores for fifty-five minutes at a temperature of 425 degrees F (220°C) under high pressure to oxidize them ready for conventional carbon-in-pulp gold extraction. The autoclaves which, as a Barrick press release observes, 'accomplish in minutes what nature takes millions of years to do', add between $40 and $50 to the cost of procuring every single ounce of gold. But they pay their way; without these pressure cookers, only 30 per cent of the gold in sulphides would be recovered, with them it is 90 per cent. Grades, however, must be good.

Pushing for productivity at every step, Barrick not only has computer control of its trucking and hauling operations at Goldstrike, but operates them in twelve-hour shifts from 7.00 a.m. until 7.00 p.m. seven days a week. Time is even saved with 'hot' shift changes, in which truck drivers for the new shift are whisked round in a small van and switched into their truck wherever it may be; it takes seconds for one driver to hop out and his relief to jump in (a remarkable contrast to deep South African mines, where the journey to the workface for shift changes may take one hour each way).

Barrick tapped into Betze in the autumn of 1992. 'We're in the goodies,' said Alan Hill, as we watched loaders scooping up the sulphide ore like hungry pelicans as they came into view at the bottom of the pit. 'Within a few months there will be no more oxide milling or heap-leaching; this is a sulphide mine.'

### Underground at Meikle

The next step, the Meikle mine, a mile to the north of Goldstrike, will bring another significant change, the Carlin Trend's first underground mine. Actually Meikle, named after Dr Brian Meikle, Barrick's senior vice-president for development, is a small deposit hidden deep in the Nevada hillside. The proven orebody is only 1,200 feet long, 600 feet wide and just over 1,000 feet deep (366 × 183 × 305 metres). 'A postage stamp', geologist Keith Bettles called it, adding cheerfully, 'but it contains 4.5 million ounces (140 tonnes) of gold.' Finding it was no mean achievement, as there were no strong surface clues. As Barrick's senior vice-president for exploration, Dr Paul Kavanagh had told me over breakfast in Toronto before I set off to Nevada, 'It's like finding it under our table in this restaurant.' Actually, Barrick struck gold with its tenth deep borehole, intersecting a wedge of ore 540 feet deep with an encouraging grade of 0.41 oz/t (12.7 g/t). Homing in, cores were soon turning up 1.12 oz/t, then 1.56 oz/t, and ultimately 1.84 oz/t (recall most of the oxide ores elsewhere on the Carlin Trend are mined profitably at 0.035 oz/t and the cut-off to heap-leaching is 0.006 oz/t). This 'postage stamp' is a collector's item. The average grade is 0.63 oz/t (19.6 g/t) with forecast operating costs of only $125 an ounce.

Meikle will be an underground mine because, unlike other Carlin deposits, there are no surface oxide ores to pay the bill for opening up a pit to reach an orebody starting 800 feet (244 metres) down. American Barrick will get at it directly by a conventional shaft, due to be open late in 1995. Annual production in full stride from 1996 will be at 400,000 ounces (12.4 tonnes), with reserves to keep it going for at least eleven years.

Meikle is the bonus that Barrick argues will push its Carlin output along towards 2 million ounces (60 tonnes) before the end of the century. Moreover, part of that is already sold. Maintaining its hedging momentum, Barrick has pushed out the time horizon to ten years for a 1 million-ounce package, securing revenue beyond the year 2000.

### The Newmont–Barrick Alliance

Meanwhile, the American Barrick–Newmont alliance for the joint development of the northern areas of the Carlin Trend harnesses a formidable combination. The orebodies here interlock so much from one property to another that it is the only rational way to proceed. Both companies hope for substantial savings. For example, Newmont had originally envisaged an underground mine for its Deep Post deposit next to Betze. Instead, Barrick is expanding the Betze pit eastwards to get directly at Deep Post's high-grade but refractory ores, which are calculated to contain 3.5 million ounces (108.9 tonnes).

Outlining the blossoming relationship, Bob Smith, the bluff Canadian miner who is Barrick's president and chief operating officer, explained, 'We've agreed to share exploration data for the northern section of the Carlin Trend. For example, joint exploration is underway at Deep Star [a Newmont mine on the southern fringe of Goldstrike] which, like Deep Post, straddles our boundary with Newmont.' The geologists reckon that Deep Star's ore zone extends under Barrick's terrain, giving it added reserves which Newmont would mine for it.

The alliance also enables Barrick to profit from Newmont's research into bioleaching, the revolutionary new technology which lets bacterial cultures loose into refractory sulphide ores. The bacteria, known as thiobacillus ferro-oxidans, feeding on the sulphides catalyse the oxidation of the ore (a kind of living autoclave), unlocking the gold for extraction by conventional means. The technique, originally pioneered by the South African group Gencor on its Fairview gold mine, has immense implications if it can be used commercially at Carlin (and elsewhere) on tricky sulphides. Successful bioleaching could make it viable to extract gold from huge tonnages of very low-grade Carlin ores. 'We've got 20 million tons of refractory sub-ore containing one million ounces of gold classified as waste,' said Bob Smith. 'If experiments are successful, Newmont will be able to tackle sulphides with grades as low as 0.065 oz/t [2 g/t]'.

Will it work? I drove by a huge black pyramid of 25,000 tons of Barrick's sulphide ores on which Newmont was conducting tests. The pyramid was laced around with a corset of thin irrigation dripper hoses through which the bacteria are drip-fed into the ores in solution (a variation on heap-leaching). Everyone was very tight-lipped about how the bugs were getting on. 'Proprietary information', people muttered. Actually, the basic process is proven, but how to make it work profitably on a grand scale here? The bacteria apparently are finicky about their working conditions; if it is too cold they go dormant, if it is too hot they die. Around 30 degrees C is ideal. 'You have to coddle the bugs to keep them alive,' confided Amy Gassman of Goldman Sachs, one of America's top gold analysts. 'They are sensitive to heat.' Nevada in high summer bothers them.

Newmont is persevering to create the right environment for the bugs. 'Bioleaching is a big step forward,' Newmont's Walter Lawrence told me. 'But it's very different from heap-leaching which just made it easy for people without a lot of resources to get in very quickly. The material for bioleaching is deeper and can only be got at by stripping a lot off the top.' The benefit is that the stripping will take place anyway to get at the high-grade cores of a Betze, Deep Post or Meikle deposit; around those cores is a halo of lower-grade material which will be ignored unless the bugs can be prevailed upon to do their stuff. Bioleaching thus offers a tempting bonus.

The real question, though, is how many more major deposits lie hidden in the Carlin Trend? It is one thing for Barrick and Newmont to extract 4 million ounces (124 tonnes) annually from the Carlin Trend, but they have to replace that amount in newly found reserves too, just to keep going (bioleaching promises only a useful supplement). So far the full extent not just of Meikle, Betze, Deep Post and Deep Star, but

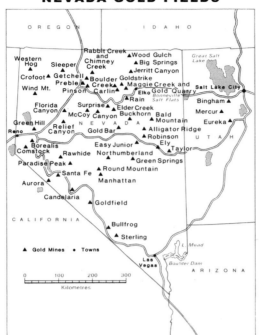

**NEVADA GOLD FIELDS**

of other smaller deposits to the north and west, has not been identified. There is active exploration around a small pit known as Ren, not far from Meikle, and older oxide pits such as Dee and Bootstrap may turn up something. Geologist Keith Bettles is confident (as a geologist needing an exploration budget must be). 'There are good targets at 2,000 feet,' he said, 'and even at 3,000 and 4,000 feet to the east. There will be more discoveries, but they will be deep; we and Newmont are going to make them.' Newmont's Walter Lawrence concurs. 'The Carlin Trend is the most significant area for exploration potential anywhere – it's elephant country and there are still some elephants to be found.' Their camouflage, however, is good. As Newmont's president T. Peter Philip remarked to the Society of Mining Engineers, 'It is not likely that there is another Gold Quarry sitting out there on the Trend crying for four hundred feet of drilling and a host of quick assays. The geologists are targeting deep ore which has no surface expression. Ore which is likely to be in discrete, compact zones'.[3]

### The Nevada Grand Gold Tour
The Carlin Trend may produce 40 per cent of the United States' gold by the end of the century, but there is plenty going on elsewhere.

3 Society of Mining Engineers, Salt Lake City, 1 March 1990.

Nevada alone is dotted with open-pit gold mines. A short helicopter ride across the hills to the northeast of Carlin is Jerritt Canyon, another early signpost to Nevada's potential. The mine, operated and 70 per cent owned by Independence Mining (a subsidiary of Minorco, the Luxembourg based arm of the Anglo American empire) with FMC Gold, opened in 1981 and was briefly the largest US producer. While overshadowed since by the Carlin bonanza, it has steadily built up output to 400,000 ounces (12.4 tonnes), persistently finding fresh reserves. The latest, the New Deep/Gracie deposit, which contains at least 1.5 million ounces of gold and may become an underground mine, secures production beyond the year 2000. And the transition from the easily accessible oxide ores of the early days to refractory sulphide ores has successfully been made. 'Jerritt Canyon,' observed the *Mining Journal*, 'goes from strength to strength.'[4]

Back on Interstate Highway 80 going west towards Reno, gold mines are more numerous than the towns, which are spaced out every 50 miles, because in the old days the steam engines of the Atchison, Topeka and Santa Fe Railroad had to take on water that often. The railroad company, which owns a nice land position along this new gold trail, has meanwhile branched out into gold mining, as we shall observe in a moment. But first, take a left for Battle Mountain's Fortitude to see what is left of a mountain 7,000 feet high, from which one side has been cut away in neat 20-foot high steps to get at a gold-silver-copper orebody that, at its best, produced 250,000 ounces (7.7 tonnes) annually in the late 1980s. Although the main Fortitude deposit is worked out, Battle Mountain Gold is continuing to heap-leach from satellite pits and is busy on joint exploration of neighbouring hills (it has also opened a mine in Bolivia).

Exit Interstate 80 again at Golconda, stop for coffee (coffee shops are rarer than gold mines hereabouts) before taking a dusty road north along the foot of the Osgood mountains towards a hamlet aptly named Midas. Along the way are Pinson (shared by American Barrick, Rayrock and Corona/Homestake), Getchell (First Mississippi Corporation) and then Chimney Creek and Rabbit Creek owned by Santa Fe Pacific Minerals. Santa Fe, a spin-off from the historic railroad group, is one of the largest private mineral landholders in the American west, but has only moved lately into gold mining, with two Nevada operations, Rabbit Creek and Lone Tree (just south of Golconda). It staked a more significant claim in 1993, however, by swapping its coal mines with the UK conglomerate Hanson for Gold Fields Mineral Corporation (GFMC) which Hanson had acquired in its 1989 takeover of Consolidated Gold Fields. The GFMC acquisition brought Santa Fe not only the small

Mesquite mine in California, but also the low-cost Chimney Creek right next door to its own Rabbit Creek. The two mines side-by-side have considerable potential for development as a single super pit. GFMC was also well advanced towards preparing two other gold mines, Mule Canyon south of Battle Mountain in Nevada and Elkhorn in Montana, with other exploration projects in North and South America. Already the swap has pushed Santa Fe's gold output from 295,000 ounces (9.2 tonnes) to over 750,000 (23.3 tonnes) annually, making the group the sixth largest North American producer.

Back on the main highway, press on westwards towards Reno and on your left look out for Florida Canyon, where Pegasus Gold, based in Spokane, Washington, has been successful in heap-leaching very low-grade ore on unique circular pads. Actually, Pegasus was one of the pioneers of heap-leaching at its Zortman-Landusky open pit on picturesque hillsides in Montana. When it started at Zortman-Landusky in 1979 there was still little practical experience in heap-leaching gold. As Philip Lindstrom, the consultant engineer who helped Pegasus in those days, once told me, 'We learned by trial and error, and we made a lot of mistakes. Now everyone follows our example.'[5] Zortman-Landusky still ticks over at 120,000 ounces (3.7 tonnes), while preparing to take the plunge in going for deeper refractory ores by 1995, which should lift output to 200,000 ounces annually for a while. Meanwhile, in Nevada, Florida Canyon also gives Pegasus 80,000 ounces a year.

The view from Interstate 80 alone catches much of Nevada's gold, but the venturesome can always press into the interior (although my Nevada map warns 'Inquire locally for current conditions before driving on unimproved roads'). The mines are now more widely scattered and the geology changes. In central Nevada the orebodies have a much higher silver content (a reminder of the state's original nickname). The Paradise Range, beyond the Walker River Indian Reservation, offers FMC Gold's Paradise Peak, once a high-grade/low-cost gold/silver operation (with as much as 5.6 oz/t of silver) that may not last beyond the mid-1990s unless some new reserves turn up. While due east by air, but a long detour by back road, is Round Mountain. Perhaps more correctly *was* Round Mountain, for Canada's Echo Bay Mines has been energetically removing it for nearly a decade on behalf of itself and its partner Homestake (of whom more in a moment) and Case, Pomeroy. What was a mountain, is now a pit. Although much of the highest-grade ore has been mined, a narrow but very high-grade vein of 2 ounces (62.2 g/t) of coarse gold was discovered in the pit in 1992, helping push output to 370,600 ounces (11.5 tonnes) and confirming Round Mountain as the lowest cost of Echo Bay's four mines. This rich vein, will

5 See Timothy Green, *The Prospect for Gold*, Rosendale Press, London, 1987, pp. 41–2 for details of this project.

supplement more conventional reserves for which additional milling facilities and new leach pads are being made to secure the mine at least to the year 2005. Echo Bay is also feeling happier about its twin gold-silver pits McCoy and Cove, a hundred miles to the north, in the Fish Creek mountains, where it pulled off record production of over 300,000 ounces (9.3 tonnes) of gold and 7.9 million ounces (246 tonnes) of silver in 1992. The original McCoy pit was mined out in 1991, but ramps have now been driven underground into high-grade sulphide ores below both pits, thus giving the project a fresh lease of life. Extensive exploration is also going on to locate other satellite deposits for it has been a struggle at McCoy/Cove to match output with fresh reserves; in 1992 gold replacement was only 78 per cent. But Echo Bay, which has also fought hard to cut operating costs here, still 'expects' to be operating into the next century.

The Nevada gold tour would not be complete without mentioning that the long desert road south (Nevada 95) to Las Vegas offers a bright prospect for gold. Drive through the town of Goldfield, detour right to Gold Point, and then 100 miles before Las Vegas is a serious mine: Bullfrog. This relatively low-grade open pit is the biggest producer for Canada's LAC Minerals, with output up to 300,000 ounces annually through the mid-1990s, but then declining. However, LAC has an interest in a possible new mine at Rosebud, a turn-off from Interstate 80 northeast of Reno.

### Amax Builds on Sleeper

As the best years pass for some of the Nevada mines, the intriguing question that remains is – what else is out there in the valleys? The Nevada boom at Carlin and elsewhere has been based on orebodies tucked into the hillside, either actually on the surface or lightly covered by topsoil. They are relatively easy to detect; natural erosion often reveals the tip. Geologists love to ponder what may be under the thick topsoil of the valleys with no surface clues. Their appetites were whetted by the appropriately named Sleeper mine. This was turned up by Amax in the Slumbering Quinn river valley due east of the Pinson, Getchell and Chimney mines. Was it a maverick?

In one sense, yes; some pre-production samples at Sleeper contained as much as 10,000 oz/t (311 kg/t). Sleeper was not quite a crock of pure gold; it settled down with more conventional grades in the late 1980s to produce close to 200,000 ounces (6.2 tonnes) annually, gradually declining, as the grades fell, to around 135,000 ounces (4.2 tonnes) for the mid-1990s. Sleeper's importance, as it turns out, was less that it broke the mould in Nevada in being under the topsoil of a valley, but that it gave a profitable launch to Amax Gold, one of the most innovative and aggressive of the new gold-mining companies bred in the United States by the gold boom of the 1980s.

Amax Gold Inc. was formed in 1987 as the precious metals subsidiary of the mining conglomerate Amax Inc. which has been operating, primarily in base metals, since 1887. Amax Inc. still owns 70 per cent of Amax Gold, but Allen Born, the chairman of both companies, gave Timothy Haddon, the president and chief operating officer of the gold company, free rein. Haddon, an energetic, fast-talking man in his early forties, wastes no time.

When I arrived at his office, strategically placed in Golden, just outside Denver, Colorado, he was busy on the phone. Waving me to a seat, he fished a white card out of the breast pocket of his shirt and handed it over. 'That's our mission,' he said. 'Amax Gold Inc. AGI's Mission is Quality,' I read, while he finished phoning. 'Quality at Amax Gold is a team of professionals dedicated to dynamic growth by increasing low-cost production and reserves, for maximum benefit of our shareholders, in harmony with the world around us.'

Thus briefed, we took it from there. 'We've got a very full plate,' said Haddon. 'We want to be a low-cost producer, but grow into a long-term mining company focusing on cash costs of $200 [an ounce] or less, and total costs of $300 or less.'

The initial course on Haddon's plate was Sleeper, but that is past its peak, although it can contribute gold for the rest of the century. Wind Mountain, a small, low-grade heap-leach operation in northwest Nevada, is also shutting down, but Haddon notes proudly that Amax took just three years to produce there what was projected for five.

So the menu has changed. Amax Gold's future lies in three other American states, Alaska, California and South Carolina, with cosmopolitan side dishes in Chile and New Zealand. In short, like other US mining companies, it is moving on from Nevada. The initial offering is Hayden Hill, just across the border in California, which came on stream in 1992 and will yield a steady 145,000 ounces (4.5 tonnes) annually well into the next century. Then in South Carolina, where gold mining started in the early 1800s long before the California gold rush, it is expanding the Haile mine, previously owned by Piedmont Gold, which could produce 60,000 ounces a year in the mid-1990s.

Amax Gold's fortunes are really riding on an outsider – Fort Knox, a huge, low-grade porphyry orebody (a deposit of volcanic origin with crystals finely disseminated) just 15 miles outside Fairbanks, Alaska. Haddon admits it is a risk. 'No one wanted 0.026 oz/t [0.8 g/t] grade in Alaska,' he said. 'It was thrown out of every office.' When the project landed on his desk, he realized that each short ton mined would contain only $8 to $10 of gold, but decided to approach it as if it were a porphyry *copper* project and mine it on that grand scale to make it profitable. So Amax aims by 1995 to start putting 36,000 short tons a day through a new mill at Fort Knox (ten times what it put through Hayden Hill), calculating that economy of scale will make it pay. Fort Knox has known reserves of 3.5 million ounces (109 tonnes); Amax's target is 350,000 ounces (10.9 tonnes) annually by 1996. That would push the group's total output towards 950,000 ounces (29.5 tonnes) annually, helped also by two projects, Guanaco and Refugio, in Chile (see Chapter 8) and a stake in New Zealand's Waihi mine; that is triple its 1993 output.

### To Hedge? Or not to Hedge?

However, Amax Gold is not just a gold miner, it is also a trader. Early in our conversation Tim Haddon said that when he moved from Amax Inc. to head up Amax Gold, 'I brought my gold trader to Denver.' That underlines Amax Gold's approach; of course, it has geologists and mining engineers, but Mark Lettes is its trading and hedging strategist. Just down the corridor from Haddon's office he runs a fully-fledged dealing room, not just hedging Amax's output, but actively trading gold and silver. 'We traded 20 million ounces of gold last year,' Mark told me later at dinner. 'Not bad on production of 300,000 ounces. We also traded 20 million ounces of silver.' The commitment to trading is serious; Mark and a dealing colleague left dinner early because they are always at their desks well before 5.00 a.m. each morning to catch European trading. That is akin to the life of a bullion bank, not the normal mining house. At the outset Haddon said to Lettes, 'Here's $100 million, protect our downside risk [by hedging], but leave us upside potential.' The strategy pays. Between 1989 and 1991 Amax got $42 an ounce above the average gold price for its output; in 1991 it achieved $427, $65 higher than the gold price, and held in at $402 for 1992 when the price averaged $344. Its future is protected, too. 'Amax Gold's sophisticated hedging strategy ensures [it] will exceed the market price by $30–$50,' notes Salomon Brothers analyst Leanne Baker. Mark Lettes is blunt on the virtues of hedging. 'It's no different from buying an insurance policy,' he told me. 'It's totally speculative if you don't hedge.'

A remark which encapsulates the great divide in the US and Canadian mining industry. To hedge? Or not to hedge? Lined up alongside Amax Gold as committed hedgers are American Barrick and LAC Minerals; pitched against them are Homestake Mining, FMC Gold and Newmont Mining (a change of policy in 1992), who do not hedge. A range of other North American mining houses, such as Battle Mountain, Echo Bay, Hemlo Gold, Pegasus, Placer Dome and Teck hedge part of their production, varying between 15 per cent and 50 per cent. No one comes close to American Barrick at well over 90 per cent hedged, much of it five to ten years out. Naturally attitudes to hedging change. High interest rates through 1991 made forward selling attractive, after which a sharp fall in rates made the contango less interesting. And the drifting gold price of a bear market offered few tempting rallies to sell into until mid-1993. Most mines sharply reduced their forward sales or spot deferred, although writing calls to benefit from a sudden spike. For a while only Barrick really kept going, persuading bullion banks to push the time horizon out into the next century. Ultimately, much depends on the history of the mining group and the attitude of its chief executive.

### Homestake in its Second Century

Thus Homestake Mining, the doyen of US mining companies, whose flagship mine at Lead, South Dakota has been going strong since 1877 producing over 37 million ounces (1,150 tonnes), has never hedged. Homestake's chairman and chief executive, Harry Conger, believes his shareholders have bought Homestake for over a century (Homestake Mining is the oldest continuously listed stock on the New York stock exchange) precisely because it is a gold company, providing a special insurance or anti-cyclical play not offered by any ordinary industrial (or base metal) stock. Homestake certainly has such admirers, whose loyalty helped keep up its share price even in the long bear market of the early 1990s. Indeed, among the leading twenty-three producers worldwide, listed by *Mining Journal*'s International Gold Mining Newsletter, Homestake rated fifth, when share prices between 1988 and late 1992 were compared, doing better than some well-known pro-hedgers like Amax Gold and LAC Minerals.[6]

Homestake's strength is its reserves; over 17 million ounces (530 tonnes) in the seventeen mines worldwide in which it has a stake. The original Homestake Mine at Lead alone still has close to 5 million ounces (155 tonnes) of proven reserves, enough to keep it going well into the twenty-first century. In nearly 120 years the miners at Lead have burrowed out over 200 miles of tunnels, taking them down to 7,400 feet (2,255 metres) beneath the Black Hills of South Dakota. More recently, an open pit has also been developed. It has not all been easy. As they have gone deeper, ore zones have become thinner, grades lower. By 1991 Homestake was faced with the need for a radical overhaul of its underground mining operations, with grades down 11

6 *Mining Journal* op. cit.

per cent and output down 17 per cent. Cash operating costs were up to $377 an ounce, when the company averaged only $361 for its gold sales. As the annual report that year candidly admitted, it 'was the most difficult year in Homestake's 115-year history'. For the first time since 1945, Homestake made a loss. But the reorganization brought benefits; output at Lead climbed back towards the normal 400,000 ounces (12.4 tonnes) annually. Deep exploration for new reserves to the north of the mine proceeded and cash costs were contained at $316 an ounce. The worst was over, although this historic mine remains the most expensive in the Homestake stable.

It has been more successful at keeping costs down at the McLaughlin open-pit mine, a golden bowl in the hills of northern California (named after Dr Donald H. McLaughlin, their former chairman and dean of US gold mining for a generation) which opened in 1985. McLaughlin was important for two reasons. It successfully pioneered autoclaves in the recovery of gold from refractory ores and it met extremely exacting environmental controls imposed by the California authorities, both of which added considerably to start-up costs. The environmental controls were more complicated because the mine straddles three California counties, each with its own authorities to be satisfied. Over 260 permits, filling sixteen volumes, had to be obtained. The processing plant had to be located nearly 5 miles from the pit; the water leaving the site had to be purer than the source stream from which it was drawn. Even the quality of the air around the mine had to contain lower dust levels than those of downtown San Francisco. It all cost Homestake $50 million more than a similar site in Nevada. But it has paid off. Helped by improving grades and productivity, McLaughlin has weathered the bear market in gold, achieving 291,000 ounces (9.0 tonnes) in 1992 on costs of $204.

Homestake Mining went international in 1974 with its subsidiary Homestake Gold of Australia, which owns the Fortnum mine and 50 per cent of Kalgoorlie Consolidated Gold Mines, which manages the Super Pit and other local pits at Kalgoorlie in Western Australia (see Chapter 9). It benefits from close to 250,000 ounces of Australian gold annually.

The future of Homestake Mining, however, took on an entirely new turn in July 1992 when it acquired International Corona, the Vancouver based Canadian producer. This merger overnight increased Homestake Mining's annual gold production from just over 1 million ounces (31.1 tonnes) to 1.8 million ounces (55 tonnes). The jewel in International Corona's crown was its strong stake in the Hemlo gold field of western Ontario, the most important new discovery in Canada this century (see Chapter 7). International Corona owned a 50 per cent share of Williams and David Bell, two of the three underground mines at Hemlo. The alliance, when you think of it, seems natural. Here are the owners of North America's oldest underground mine, Lead, taking under their wing mines at what may be the most important underground mining area (as opposed to open pit) discovered on the continent in the twentieth century. Hemlo, like Lead, is not an instant oxide pit to be mined out in a few years. This is long-term serious underground mining for which Homestake's credentials go back well over a century.

The Homestake-International Corona alliance is also part of the inevitable trend of mergers that follow gold booms. The 'junior' companies that start up and prosper on high gold prices, like in the 1980s, run out of steam. The long haul mining groups pick them up. The 1990s is certainly a period of consolidation in the US gold-mining industry. Newmont and American Barrick are working closely together at the Carlin Trend; there has even been talk of marriage if Newmont's Gordon Parker and Barrick's Peter Munk can agree.

The way ahead will also be dictated by tougher environmental controls, such as those which Homestake had to meet at McLaughlin. The prospect facing miners under President Clinton and his 'green' vice-president, Al Gore, may be difficult. Securing the necessary environmental permits can already set back the start-up of a new mine by several years. Amax Gold reckons its Hayden Hill project in California was delayed for two years by permitting. As one executive put it, 'Permitting time is the key – a rule of thumb nowadays is that it's seven to ten years from the first drill hole to the first gold.' The miners realize they have to respond to environmental concerns. 'Our sensitivity level on environmental matters must equal that of the whistle blowers,' T. Peter Philip of Newmont told the Society of Mining Engineers. 'We must be every bit as aware of the implications of our proposed projects as they are. My policy is to exceed what the letter of the law requires us to do. I do this not only because I believe it is right, but because I know that it eventually will lead to a competitive advantage'.[7] But it costs money and time. Already some North American projects (mainly in Canada) have been shelved partly because of the difficulties of meeting environmental rules.

The mining industry also perceives black clouds on the horizon from a fundamental rewrite of the Mining Law of 1872 under which they have long operated. If a revision of this law gets through Congress with President Clinton's approval, it could restrict prospecting on federal lands (which embrace much of the best terrain out west) and demand higher royalties from new (and perhaps even existing) mines there. 'The

7 Society of Mining Engineers, Salt Lake City, 1 March 1990.

new mining law would effectively stop new mining,' one senior executive in Nevada told me.

Initially the industry was anticipating an 8 per cent royalty, which might have added $30 an ounce to its costs. And a study for the Washington DC based Gold Institute reckoned that this 'would threaten the economic viability of at least 20 per cent of US gold mines' and might eventually jeopardize as much as 31 million ounces (942 tonnes) of output.[8] Then President Clinton came up with the suggestion, as part of his deficit reduction package, of a 12H per cent royalty on hard rock mining on public lands. That was seen as a body-blow. 'This would reduce the industry to one-third its present size over the next ten years,' snapped John Lutley, President of the Gold Institute.[9]

The gold miners will fight back, not least with the argument that the gold-mining boom of the last decade has boosted gold-mining-related employment from a mere 9,000 jobs to almost 80,000. They will also point to the transformation of a deficit of $1.7 billion for importing gold for jewellery and industry in 1980 to a surplus worth $1.5 billion in 1992 as the nation became more than self-sufficient in gold.

Playing safe, however, American mining companies are increasingly prospecting abroad. Homestake is well placed in Australia. Battle Mountain, based in Houston, Texas, is involved everywhere from Bolivia to Australia and Papua New Guinea. Amax is in Chile and New Zealand. Freeport McMoran Copper & Gold, based in Reno, Nevada, is not even in gold in the United States. Its nest-egg, the word is carefully chosen, is the Grasberg copper-gold orebody at West Irian, Indonesia, from which it is already getting over 500,000 ounces (15.5 tonnes) of gold a year, with the prospect of up to 1.5 million ounces (45 tonnes) annually by the late 1990s; its proven gold reserves already exceed 10 million ounces (311 tonnes) without mentioning all the copper and silver that go with it (see Chapter 10). Newmont Mining (the parent of Newmont Gold) also has its eye on Indonesia, while bringing in a mine in Peru and tying up links with the new republic of Uzbekistan to heap-leach tailings at the giant Muruntau mine. In short, US gold mining, having blossomed at home for a decade, is now flexing its muscles abroad. 'Why not?' said Newmont Mining's chairman Gordon Parker cheerfully. 'There are many more opportunities around the world.'

8 J.L. Dobra and P.R. Thomas, *The US Gold Industry 1992*, Mackay School of Mines, University of Nevada, Reno, 1993, p. 29.
9 John Lutley, *The United States Gold Mining Scene*, Australian Gold Conference, Kalgoorlie, Western Australia, March 1993.

# CANADA: GOLD FIELDS

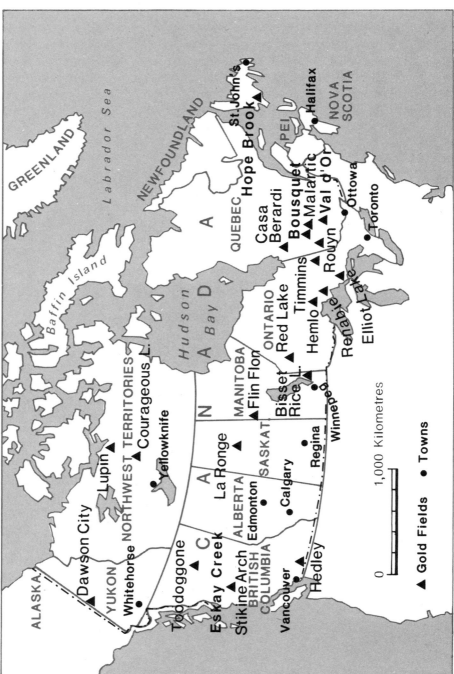

GREENLAND

Labrador Sea

NEWFOUNDLAND

St John's

Hope Brook

Halifax

NOVA SCOTIA

PEI

QUEBEC

Casa Berardi

Bousquet

Malartic

Val d'Or

Rouyn

Ottawa

Toronto

Baffin Island

Hudson Bay

C A N A D A

Timmins

ONTARIO

Red Lake

Hemlo

Renabie

Elliot Lake

Bisset

Rice L.

Flin Flon

MANITOBA

Winnipeg

NORTHWEST TERRITORIES

Courageous L.

Yellowknife

Lupin

La Ronge

SASKAT

Regina

Dawson City

YUKON

Whitehorse

Toodoggone

Eskay Creek

Stikine Arch

BRITISH COLUMBIA

Hedley

Vancouver

Edmonton

ALBERTA

Calgary

ALASKA

1,000 Kilometres

0

▲ Gold Fields    ● Towns

**CHAPTER 7**

# Canada:
# Going Multinational

A quarter of a century ago the Canadian mining industry was parochial. Small mining camps in the wilds of Ontario and Quebec struggled to survive on 'cost-aid' subsidy from the government; few geologists or mining engineers were schooled in the subtleties of finding or mining gold. Today, the industry is not only overflowing with professionals in gold (including some of the best hedgers) but is the most outward-looking and cosmopolitan in the world. You are just as likely to meet a Canadian gold miner in Chile as at home. The major mining houses based in Canada, American Barrick, Echo Bay, LAC Minerals and Placer Dome, actually win most of their production abroad, not just in the United States, but in Latin America, Australia and Papua New Guinea. Although the total annual output of these four houses is close to 5 million ounces (155 tonnes), scarcely 1.5 million ounces (46.6 tonnes) is from local mines. Only Hemlo Gold among the larger groups remains an almost exclusively Canadian producer, and even it has a foothold over the border in Montana; while, in a reverse play, America's Homestake Mining took over International Corona Corporation in 1992 thus securing a significant slice of Hemlo, the most important gold field found in Canada this century. The joke in Toronto's mining circles nowadays is to ask a young geologist fresh out of college, 'Have you got a passport and can you speak Spanish?' Russian might prove useful, too: mining executives love to regale visitors with hair-raising tales of forays to the frontiers of mining in Russia or other former Soviet republics, where both climate and geology are often akin to Canada.

## CANADA: PRODUCTION

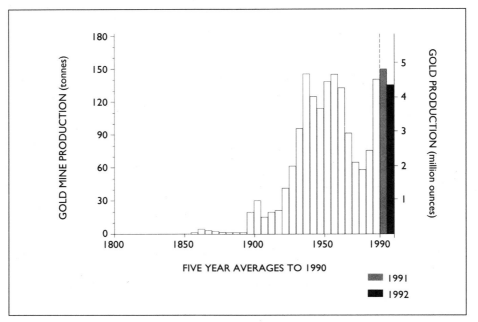

FIVE YEAR AVERAGES TO 1990

■ 1991
■ 1992

   This is not to diminish what has been achieved at home. Canada's output has more than tripled since 1980, from 1.7 million ounces (51.6 tonnes) to a record 5.7 million ounces (176.7 tonnes) in 1991 – thus just beating the previous high in 1941, when 146 mines produced 5.35 million ounces (166 tonnes); it then declined slightly to 157.4 tonnes in 1992. New mines opened everywhere; not just at Hemlo in Ontario, but from British Columbia to Newfoundland, while the world's most northerly gold mine, Lupin, flourishes on the Arctic Circle. In all, fifty-three mines were operational in Canada in 1992, plus a myriad of small placer workings in the Yukon, British Columbia and the North-West Territories, carrying on the tradition of the individual going for gold as he did in the Klondike rush a century ago. Placer production is still around 170,000 ounces (5.3 tonnes) at a moderate estimate, for much of it is not recorded.
   The boom of the 1980s transformed a rather diverse cast of small, conservative mining companies into a handful of new star performers, most of which simply were not around a few years ago. It was a colourful process. There were takeovers and scandals and lawsuits. Wealthy doctors and dentists were able to cut their tax bills by subscribing to what were known as 'flow-through shares' which enabled investors, private or corporate, to write off investment in mineral exploration

## ONTARIO AND QUEBEC: GOLD FIELDS

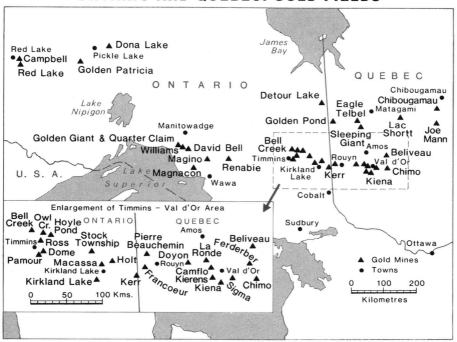

within Canada against other income; in three years $550 million 'flowed through', of which three-quarters went on gold exploration. While the scheme undoubtedly enabled much gold exploration to take place, it also financed many 'blue sky' (as the Australians like to say) projects that should never have been started. A Toronto mining executive reflected ruefully to me after the boom was over, 'Many of those cowboys would never have got inside the door of a bank if they had had to rely on them for money.' The action centred on the Vancouver Stock Exchange, which became the essential seed bed for many viable projects, including Hemlo, as well as many dreams. 'It is a source of madcap financing,' the chairman of a junior company told me happily then. 'It's a buyer beware market.' Few could resist it; turnover on the Vancouver exchange in the late 1980s was often second only to the New York Stock Exchange on the North American continent.

For all the false trails, the gold was there. The principal source has always been the Pre-Cambrian shield that covers much of the nation, notably in northern Ontario and Quebec. According to the geologist Dr Paul Kavanagh, who is not just one of the best forecasters of Canada's future gold output but keeper of its past achievements, 'Of Canada's all time production of 255 million ounces [7,931 tonnes] over 214 million ounces (85 per cent) have come from the Pre-Cambrian shield. The prolific Abitibi Belt in Ontario and Quebec has contributed 80 per cent of the shield's production and will continue to do so in future.'[1] The shield hosts most of the hard rock quartz vein underground mines that are the characteristic of Canadian mining. Unlike the United States, Australia or even Brazil, where the renaissance in gold output came primarily from easily exploitable open-pit operations, Canada remains all about underground mines, usually at 1,000–5,000 feet (300–1,500 metres). And they require capital and time to develop.

### Old camps never die

One advantage, as it turned out, was the system of 'cost-aid' by which mines, and thus mining communities, were kept alive in the long years of US$35 gold. Under the Emergency Gold Mining Assistance Act of 1948, over C$300 million was paid for a generation to ailing mines (the only major mine not subsidized was Campbell Red Lake). That kept going a hard core of mining camps, Kirkland Lake and Timmins in Ontario, Rouyn, Malartic and Val d'Or in Quebec, ready as the nucleus for revival. When you look at the map of Canadian gold mines in the 1990s they are still largely clustered around those towns. It is worth reporting the wording of a petition made by thirty-six mining communities to the government in Ottawa in 1966 for the continuation of cost-aid. Their petition argued, 'The central issue is a humanitarian and defensive one; to preserve and, if possible, expand the local economic basis of the gold towns. We believe that the federal government should not lose sight of this issue, nor confuse the development and employment of people with the preservation and operation of municipalities. It may help individuals to retrain them and move them to new opportunities. But it kills the towns they leave behind, loading them with economic burdens, ruining their standards of public service and creating as many problems as it solves.' Their eloquence won a reprieve. And the ultimate reward was that mines thus kept ticking over, eventually gained a new lease of life, (and the government much tax revenue).

Take the Dome mine at Porcupine camp near Timmins, Ontario, which has been in continuous production since 1910 yielding in all close to 12 million ounces (373 tonnes). Not only has it been completely modernized with a new shaft down to 5,000 feet (1,500 metres) that will ensure annual output of 140,000 ounces (4.3 tonnes) well into the next century, but its owner, Placer Dome, is considering a super pit to dig out at least 2 million ounces it has identified mostly under the existing mine buildings on the surface. Despite being rather high cost (US$298 total in 1992), Dome seems set to join the elite of hundred-year-old

1 Total output through 1992.

mines (club members being Mineracao Morro Velho in Brazil, Frontino in Colombia and Homestake at Lead, South Dakota, United States, with South Africa's ERPM due to join in 1994 and Durban Deep in 1998, if it can hang on).

The Campbell Red Lake mine in northwestern Ontario looks in even better shape, with its own half-century due before long. This mine has been the great Canadian performer since it opened in 1949 with a grade of 0.64 oz/t (20 g/t) that enabled it to brush aside any need for cost-aid subsidy. The grade has scarcely faltered, running a comfortable 0.615 oz/t (19 g/t) through 1992 as expanding milling facilities pushed output to a record level of 300,000 ounces (9.33 tonnes) that should be sustained well beyond the year 2000. The operating costs, by the way, were an enviable US$156 an ounce, with total costs contained at US$175.

Campbell Red Lake, like Dome, is in the Placer Dome stable, which was created in 1987 through the merger of Dome Mines, Campbell Red Lake Mines and the Vancouver based Placer Development. Its other Canadian properties are Detour Lake and Dona Lake in Ontario, both new but rather high-cost mines whose lives may be limited, and at Val d'Or in Quebec, Sigma which is approaching its sixtieth birthday, and the modern Kiena, which should both make the twenty-first century. Placer Dome's Canadian mines bring it around 750,000 ounces (23.3 tonnes) annually, but that was scarcely 45 per cent of the group's worldwide production in the mid-1990s. The rest came from Australia, Chile, the United States and, best of all, Papua New Guinea. The Papua New Guinea mines of Misima and Porgera gave Placer Dome over 500,000 ounces (15.6 tonnes) in 1992 via its subsidiary Placer Pacific in which it holds 75.7 per cent: a contribution that helped Placer Dome to bill itself, quite correctly that year, as 'the largest North American producer'. However, it is not the largest producer of North American gold, although it is the largest producer of Canadian gold. Indeed, in Canada, Placer Dome is comfortably number one and likely to remain so, backed by the longevity of Dome and Campbell Red Lake.

The battle really is for number two in the league, which is a contest between LAC Minerals, Hemlo Gold and the intruder Homestake Mining from the United States, now that the scalp of International Corona is on its belt.

### LAC's comeback
'LAC Minerals – in the BIG league now', said the headline of an assessment by Leanne Baker, Salomon Brothers' gold analyst. The headline did have a double meaning; LAC's output from eleven mines worldwide

had reached the 1 million ounce (31.1 tonnes) a year level, but BIG is also short for Bond International Gold, which LAC took over to achieve that total. Actually, LAC has been headed that way for more than a decade under its president Peter Allen who, in his early fifties, retains the boyish enthusiasm he had when I first met him in the 1970s before the gold boom got underway. He knows his target – 'We're hard rock miners whose main thrust is still in gold.' And over the years I have found him a weathervane on Canadian gold. Already by 1979, as the gold price went up into uncharted waters, he was telling me, 'I've really lit a fire under our exploration guys.' Until that moment Canadian gold mining, he admitted, had got along in 'a pre-historic way. Now we're using the best geological methods to get us out of that stone age.' Over the next decade it paid off, despite one horrendous setback for LAC, which we will come to in a minute. But reviewing what Peter Allen had said to me in 1979 before seeing him for this new book was very instructive. 'If I had to throw a dart at the map of Canada and mine gold where it landed', he had confided in 1979, 'the ideal would be northwest Quebec; it is accessible, has the best – conservative – government and the best unions.'

Guess where Peter Allen has LAC firmly placed in Canada in the mid-1990s? Bulls-eye! In northwest Quebec, first with the Doyon mine which opened in 1980 as an open pit and went underground in 1988, then with Bousquet No. 2 mine. There is also Bousquet No. 1, but that is much older, with low grades and rather high costs, contributing a steady 65,000 ounces (2 tonnes) annually. Bousquet No. 2 opened in 1990 to a comfortingly high grade of over 0.4 oz/t (12.4 g/t) that will keep it going nicely well into the twenty-first century at over 200,000 ounces (6.2 tonnes) a year, with costs contained at around US$220 to $230 an ounce. Doyon, operated by LAC but shared 50-50 with Cambior, cannot quite compete on grade or costs, but should see the century out at a steady 125,000 ounces annually. So will Macassa, a real old-timer just over the border in Ontario at Kirkland Lake, dated from 1933, which survived some serious rock bursts in the early nineties, to come back ticking up 90,000 ounces (2.7 tonnes) a year. LAC is also now looking after the Golden Patricia mine in the remote northwest of Ontario, not far from the famous Campbell Red Lake mine, which it acquired by taking over Bond International Gold (BIG) from the failed Australian entrepreneur Alan Bond. LAC first took 70 per cent of Bond's company in 1989 and the balance two years later. Golden Patricia is a narrow vein underground mine with a nice grade of 0.6 oz/t (18.7 g/t) that produces around 75,000 ounces (2.3 tonnes) a year. So that takes LAC's Canadian output, adding in a couple of small operations,

Lake Shore Tailings and Francouer, almost to 600,000 ounces (18.7 tonnes), easily making it the number two domestic producer.

The Bond buy-out brought LAC Minerals not only Golden Patricia, but also the prosperous Bullfrog open pit in Nevada (see Chapter 6) and an 83 per cent controlling share of the El Indio gold-silver-copper complex in Chile (see Chapter 8). They contribute another 450,000 ounces (14 tonnes) thus pushing LAC through the 1 million ounce a year barrier, the hallmark of a big player in North America.

The achievement was important for LAC, because it really put behind it the traumatic loss of the Williams mine at Hemlo in 1986 after a bitterly contested lawsuit. Which brings us to the story of the biggest gold field found in Canada in the twentieth century.

### Hemlo heartaches
As you drive along the Trans-Canada Highway north of Lake Superior, past the little towns of White Rock and Thunder Bay, the endless vision of rugged rocks, great stands of spruce and birch, interspersed by lonely lakes, is interrupted suddenly for just a mile or so by the headgear of three gold mines, each in distinctive livery. Driving west, first come the tan buildings of David Bell, then the blue of Golden Giant and finally the yellow of the Williams mine. Between them they produce around 1 million ounces a year, a fifth of Canada's output. The Williams mine is Canada's biggest producer; David Bell, with operating costs not much over US$100, is one of the world's lowest cost.

Prospectors had prowled over the Hemlo area for generations, but they had been looking for the conventional quartz veins that house most of Canada's gold. Hemlo was trickier to detect (as, in a different way, was the Carlin Trend in Nevada). Here the gold is finely disseminated in a thin strata, only 7–10 feet (2–3 metres) thick slanting sharply downwards at between 45 and 60 degrees from a few surface outcrops. And it sits, like the meat in a sandwich, between two different types of rock: sedimentary, composed of material found in a lake bed, and volcanic. A wonderful example, in fact, of how liquid gold from the earth's core originally flowed into fissures between different rock faces. At Hemlo, the gold zone is not only steeply angled, but weaves and curves as it goes, although, unlike many deposits, it is in a single horizon from the surface right down to 5,000 feet (1,500 metres) for a distance of about a mile and a half (2 kilometres). The grade is good, averaging 0.3 oz/t (9.5 g/t).

But this curvaceous ore horizon weaving its way ever deeper underground was a nightmare to divide among the companies competing to develop it. Logically, Hemlo should be one mine. It is three, plus a curious anomaly called the Quarter Claim which started as part of the David Bell mine, but was acquired by Golden Giant as the best place for their shaft. David Bell's owners, however, still get a nice royalty from Golden Giant's mining in this zone. This was just a start for the lawyers. Mining custom and law hold that a deposit pinpointed on the surface may be followed to its limits below ground. The trouble at Hemlo is that surface outcrops often dive below the claims of rivals. So on one level the gold horizon may belong to Golden Giant and on another to David Bell. Mine planning is a nightmare and each has to know what its neighbours are up to. They will even trade off small zones that are more convenient for one or the other to mine. As a geologist summed it up when I first went around Hemlo, 'It's one orebody and one mine really, but it's turned out as three mines with five shafts and made a mess of a nice orebody.'[2] And he added wryly, 'The lawyers get rich.'

Yet in the scramble to develop the Hemlo field in the early 1980s, when the gold price was usually averaging over US$400 an ounce with regular runs to US$500, the challenge was to be first into production. Hemlo is a real child of the 1980 record gold price; that year prospectors Don McKinnon and John Larche, working with the geologist David Bell, started doing detailed exploration. Then came Goliath Gold Mines and Golden Sceptre Resources controlled by entrepreneurs Richard Hughes and Frank Lang from Vancouver. As the potential unfolded, the big groups joined in. The race was on for the first mine. Noranda, the Toronto based natural resources group, teamed up with Goliath Gold and Golden Sceptre to start the Golden Giant mine. International Corona Resources and its partner Teck Corporation picked up David Bell's work and named their mine after him. And LAC Minerals went ahead with the largest mine, Williams, named after the late Dr Jack Kerr Williams an American doctor involved in the staking of 11 claims in 1945, which were later patented and became the Williams mine.

The actual race was won by Golden Giant, where the first bar of gold was poured in April 1985; David Bell came in just four weeks later. And LAC had Williams operational by December that year. But was Williams actually LAC's mine? Lawyers for International Corona argued otherwise. They claimed that in the very early days of the Hemlo gold rush, LAC's geologists had got a look at some work its rivals, Corona, had done on claims for what became the Williams mine. They did not just go for damages, but for the mine itself – and won. In 1986 the Williams mine was awarded to International Corona and its partner Teck. LAC Minerals appealed and lost. It was a devastating blow to develop what was set to become the largest gold mine in Canada, and lose it almost overnight. And it put Corona and Teck in the position of

2 Timothy Green, *The Prospect for Gold*, Rosendale Press, London, 1987, pp. 47–51, describes Hemlo's early development.

controlling two-thirds of the Hemlo output.

The Williams mine has since fully met expectations. Its output peaked at 594,128 ounces (18.5 tonnes) in 1990, the highest ever achieved by an individual Canadian mine. Although it has since declined slightly on lower grades (running 0.174 oz/t or 5.4 g/t), production is forecast to stay comfortably at 400,000 ounces ( 12.4 tonnes) annually at least until 2005. The David Bell mine has also got well into its stride producing close to 300,000 ounces (9.3 tonnes) annually at its peak in the early 1990s, with nice grades of 0.328 oz/t (10.2 g/t), and forecast to maintain over 200,000 ounces (6.2 tonnes) well into the next century. In short, a share in the Williams and David Bell mines made a very nice catch for Homestake Mining of San Francisco when it took over International Corona in 1992. It gets half of the output of each mine, the balance, of course, still going to Teck Corporation. And in the legal jungle of Hemlo, there is also a benefit of 15,000 ounces in royalty each year due from Golden Giant for the carve-up of the Quarter Claim.

Meanwhile, just down the road, things have been going very nicely at Golden Giant itself. The grade is excellent (at 0.43 oz/t or 13.3 g/t for much of 1992), the output has been humming along at close to 450,000 ounces (14 tonnes) a year, and the operating costs are not much over US$125 an ounce. While the grades probably peaked in the early 1990s, the mine is set to produce over 350,000 ounces a year well into the next century. The ownership of the mine has been concentrated since 1987 in Hemlo Gold Mines, which merged the interests of Golden Sceptre Resources, Goliath Gold Mines and Noranda. The latter holds 45.7 per cent of the new company. But since 1991 Hemlo Gold has largely divorced itself from Noranda, taking over full responsibility for management, finance and exploration. In fact, Hemlo Gold is shaping up as a mining group in its own right. While Golden Giant will remain its flagship, it already has a stake in the small Silidor mine in Quebec, taken over from Noranda, and in two prospective mines, Holloway near Timmins in Ontario and New World, across the border in Montana. If these mature in the mid-1990s, then Hemlo Gold will be benefiting from well over 500,000 ounces (15.5 tonnes) a year. As the Hemlo goldfield approaches its tenth anniversary with output already slipping marginally from the peak of 1.3 million ounces (40.4 tonnes) in 1990 to settle at around 1 million annually, the natural question is, what other secrets remain to be discovered there? The short answer, so far, is not much. 'Hemlo has been fine-tooth combed without finding anything,' geologist Dr Paul Kavanagh told me. That is not dismissing the field as a burnt-out case; the Hemlo mines will have delivered around 20 million ounces (just over 600 tonnes or the equivalent of a year's South African production) by the year 2005, which is not bad for starters.

### Lupin: Arctic Gold

While Hemlo grabbed the headlines of the 1980s gold boom, other reliable performers also turned up, notably Echo Bay's Lupin mine, 56 miles from the Arctic Circle in the Northwest Territories. Going there is an adventure in itself, taking off at dawn from Edmonton in the mining company's Boeing 727, eating a breakfast that puts regular airlines to shame, and circling in to land in the bright sunshine of high summer on the shores of Contwoyoto Lake which is still half-covered with ice floes. The front of the plane is loaded with supplies; seated in the rear is a fresh crew of miners. For the next fortnight they will work twelve hour shifts seven days a week and then fly back to their homes all over North America for a two-week break. 'It's wonderful,' said a miner who commutes from Texas. 'You bust your ass off for two weeks, and then have two weeks completely off.' The system pays; labour turnover is virtually nil and people get used to working with each other as teams for their two weeks on. (Administrators and other support staff have a different commuting schedule: four days at Lupin, three days at home every week.)

The story of Lupin (named after the wild flower that dots the tundra in summer) goes back to the early 1960s when two geologists prospecting for International Nickel (Inco) took a lunch break on a small hill. They chipped a few samples; not the nickel they wanted but gold, which no one then cared about at US$35 an ounce. Advance to 1979; enter Echo Bay which operated a small silver mine nearby at Port Radium which was shortly due to close. It needed something new; the gold price was at US$200 and rising; it took an option on INCO's property. Gold kept going up and, thanks to Bunker Hunt, so did silver. In mid-January 1980, Echo Bay took a snap decision. In two days it sold forward all the remaining 1.4 million ounces of silver coming from Port Radium at US$35 an ounce, netting a clear profit of C$29 million (perhaps the sanest decision anyone took that week, when the silver price went crazy). That was the money for Lupin; welcome to the gold business Echo Bay.

It built the mine in two short years, hauling in every single piece of equipment in an ageing Hercules aircraft that made 1,100 round trips to a gravel landing strip. Lupin opened in 1982; in its first decade it produced 1.7 million ounces (52.9 tonnes); it should have little difficulty matching that in its second decade with output steady around 200,000 ounces a year. The gold deposit itself is shaped like a giant compressed 'Z' with three main gold zones averaging 0.39 oz/t (12 g/t), which are known to plunge well below 3,000 feet (915 metres). Ten years on, and already mining at 2,100 feet (640 metres) the limits of the deposit have not yet been defined. 'We know the mineralization extends nearly twice as deep as that,' said Echo Bay's Ted Sheldon, 'with no indication of bottoming out.' A cheering thought in the special circumstances of Lupin, because the upper levels are very cold. And, because of permafrost, it actually gets colder as you first descend; at the surface the rock is −3 degrees C, at 250 feet it is −6 degrees, at 1,500 feet it actually warms up to zero, and not until 2,000 feet is it +1 degree. Thus, going even deeper can only be pleasurably warmer, although they may still get fog in the tunnels, which happens as very cold air is pumped down for ventilation.

Lupin's remoteness has constantly challenged Echo Bay's innovation. It built the mine entirely by air-lift. Fresh food and fresh crews still come by air, but bulk supplies are hauled in from Yellowknife 360 miles away, on a unique ice road created each winter along a succession of frozen lakes and rivers. For two months from late January to late March, snow ploughs keep open this ice road to gold, as trucks make 800 round trips with diesel fuel, explosives and equipment. The round trip, without a blizzard, takes two days. Truck drivers, running in convoy, have to learn such skills as slowing down as they approach land on the edge of a lake; if they are going too fast a surge of water from the ice bending under the weight of the trucks greets them at the beach.

Lupin was the foundation stone of Echo Bay as a major North American producer. But after first-footing in Canada, and retaining its head office in Edmonton, its subsequent successful expansion has been in the United States where its executive office is in Denver. This is not for want of trying in Canada, as an Echo Bay executive ruefully reminded me, when I enquired if they had 'deserted' Canada. 'We did grasp a number of opportunities,' he said, 'but unfortunately none of them happened to pan out nearly as well as the ones we grasped south of the Canadian border.' And he added, 'Ever since . . . the early 1980s . . . our growth policy has been to expand in North America. We have been truly binational.' So the next step, by 1985, was into the world's largest heap-leaching project at Round Mountain in Nevada, in which Echo has 50 per cent with partners Homestake Mining and Case, Pomeroy (see also Chapter 6). The following year it acquired the McCoy deposit in Nevada from Tenneco, capping that soon after by discovering a new oxide orebody, Cove, just a mile away. McCoy/Cove has since become its largest project. In 1990 Echo Bay also started output at a clutch of five deposits along the Kettle river in Washington State. This notched up the group's production at just over 700,000 ounces (21.8 tonnes) annually, making it then the sixth largest in North America. Its scorecard could rise to 1 million ounces by the mid-1990s, if it they can successfully bring in a large underground mine, Alaska–Juneau in Alaska, in 1995 with potential for 335,000 ounces (10.4 tonnes) annually. It also has 50 per cent of another Alaska venture, Kensington, due in 1996, of which its share would be 75,000 to 100,000 ounces a year.

Echo Bay sets its style as a new mining house with the original initiative of the forward silver sale to finance Lupin. Its chairman, an ebullient and charming man from Philadelphia named Bob Calman, has always seen the key as financial management, taking every advantage of gold loans, gold warrants (which were very successful with small European investors in the late 1980s) and hedging. His aim has been to look for proven deposits, like Lupin, and then put in strong management and innovative financing to develop them.

### American Barrick – the high flyer

This style has also been the hallmark of the most successful new gold mining group to emerge in North America – American Barrick – which, despite its name and its prominence on the Carlin Trend in Nevada (see Chapter 6) originated in Canada. Its president and chief operating officer, Robert Smith, learned the business with Camflo Mines, which merged with Barrick in 1984, and its senior vice president for exploration is Dr Paul Kavanagh, who was with the Kerr Addison mine when I first went to Toronto in the 1960s. The entrepreneur who made it work is Peter Munk, a tall, direct man, who always has an amused gleam in his eye, implying he knows what you are up to – or trying to get out of him. Peter Munk rode the oil and natural gas boom of the 1970s, then felt it was time to move on to precious metals. His tactic was to recruit a good team of professional miners, grafting to that bright, young managers to implement sophisticated financial strategies.

In Toronto, American Barrick's very location at once suggests this is an unusual company. It is not downtown in the skyscrapers of Bay Street along with the other mining companies and banks, but in the quieter atmosphere of Hazelton Lanes in Yorkville in a couple of town houses surrounded by boutiques and excellent coffee houses. As conversation develops, it becomes apparent that from its first day Barrick was set to take advantage of every new financial instrument the gold market could offer. 'The decision to minimize gold price risk through hedging was one of the principles on which the company was founded,' says treasurer Randall Oliphant. So Barrick actually got started by acquiring the old Camflo mine at Malartic in Quebec (yet another survivor of those years of 'cost-aid'). It paid for it by selling forward

US$40 million worth of the mine's future gold output. Then it went for the Renabie mine, another old-timer in northern Ontario with a chequered history of opening and closing and horrendous costs. In partnership with Royex Gold Mining, it cut costs from US$374 an ounce to $240, drilled some new reserves and tripled production. From that modest base, Barrick went on to develop its first new Canadian mine, Holt-McDermott at Kirkland Lake, which opened in 1989. The mine is a steady performer and, helped by the newer high-grade Mattawasaga zone, is set to deliver 70,000 ounces (2.2 tonnes) a year through the 1990s. Essentially, the Canadian operations were Barrick's learning curve for bigger and better things. 'Camflo gave us the technical background,' Bob Smith told me in the early days of Barrick. It was the springboard to the United States. Barrick soon jumped. When the gold price was in the doldrums in 1985, it snapped up for US$40 million the Mercur mine southwest of Salt Lake City in Utah, on which Getty Minerals had lavished US$105 million to start up before hitting teething troubles. As Bob Smith remarked then, 'The window was open and we got Mercur cheap.' Barrick paid for most of Mercur by borrowing 77,000 ounces (2.4 tonnes) of gold, selling it spot for US$25 million and then repaying the gold loan, at only 2 per cent interest, from Mercur production over the next four and a quarter years. It doubled Mercur output to 120,000 ounces (3.7 tonnes). By then mining analysts were really taking notice; 'the Midas touch', one applauded.

From those initiatives, American Barrick became in a decade the second largest producer of North American gold, although lately scarcely 5 per cent of that has been from Canada. The Camflo and Renabie mines, which got it going, closed in the early 1990s, so Holt-McDermott remains its sole Canadian mine. Barrick's future for the rest of this century is with the Goldstrike and Meikle mines on the Carlin Trend in Nevada, as we have seen in the preceding chapter. But the horizon from those quiet town houses in Hazelton Lanes in Toronto is broadening. 'We're beginning to do some careful research into possibilities beyond the North American borders,' Bob Smith confided in 1992 to New York institutional investors. 'We [are] in both Mexico and Chile.' The approach is softly-softly. In Mexico Barrick has cast an eye over three possible low-grade prospects. 'It's not another Carlin Trend,' said a geologist, 'but maybe a few hundred thousand ounces.' The difficulty is in persuading local Mexican partners to agree realistic terms. But Barrick knows what it is looking for. 'The mandate of our Chilean office is to source possible acquisitions,' said Bob Smith. 'The qualifying criteria are a minimum of 1 million ounces of reserves and 100,000 ounces of annual production potential.'

*Not only, but also*

Although the big names, American Barrick, Echo Bay, Hemlo Gold, Homestake Mining (now it has International Corona), LAC Minerals, Placer Dome and Teck Corporation (quietly enjoying its 50 per cent of Williams and David Bell mines at Hemlo), get most publicity, that is scarcely half the Canadian gold-mining industry. In fact, these seven between them account for scarcely half of Canada's 5 million ounces annual output. There remains a remarkable roll call of twenty-one small – and not so small – companies producing gold in Canada.

Take Cambior, based at Val d'Or in Quebec, where it operates a nice little clutch of mines with truly French, or rather Quebecois names, Chimo, Lucien Beliveau, Mouska and Pierre Beauchemin, each doing 30,000 ounces a year. And it has hopes of another at Sleeping Giant, just to the north, in the late 1990s. Cambior also has a 50 per cent share in LAC Minerals' Doyon mine nearby and 45 per cent of Hemlo Gold's Silidor. Stepping out from Quebec, Cambior has 75 per cent of the Valdez Creek place deposit in Alaska and, truly international, 60 per cent of the ambitious Omai project in Guyana in South America, which came on stream in 1993 at 255,000 ounces (7.9 tonnes) annually. Cambior raised much of the finance for Omai through a 330,000 ounce (10.3 tonne) gold loan.

The competition, just up the road from Val d'Or, is Agnico Eagle's LaRonde gold-silver-copper mine, which opened in 1988, contains over 1 million ounces of gold, and looks set at a steady 140,000 ounces (4.4 tonnes) a year for the rest of the twentieth century. The future of its Eagle/Tebel operations, however, is debatable; it escaped closure almost at the last second in 1992 with the dramatic discovery of a new ore zone with a handy grade of 0.35 oz/t (10.9 g/t) not far from the main shaft – a real Hollywood cliffhanger. Another Quebec outfit, Aur, has three tiny properties, Brador, Ferderber and Norlartic, that yield 50,000 ounces between them. At Casa Berardi, in the Abitibi region of northwest Quebec, which was billed as a real Quebec hotspot a few years ago, TVX Gold, in association with Golden Knight (of which Teck Corporation has a slice) is getting out just over 100,000 ounces a year at reasonable costs of just under US$200. TVX Gold, incidentally, is best known for its activities in Brazil and Chile (see Chapter 8), but it allied with the gold assets of Inco in 1991 to form this new company, which has 60 per cent of Casa Berardi.[3]

Over in Ontario a couple of famous old names survive. The Kerr Addison mine, which opened in 1938 and was once Canada's largest gold mine (its record was 592,245 ounces (18.4 tonnes) in 1960), is still

3 Inco sold its entire holding in TVX Gold in July 1993

good for 40,000 ounces a year. And Dickenson Mines has the Arthur W. White mine on the shores of Red Lake in northwest Ontario producing 70,000 ounces. 'Art' White was Dickenson's president back in the 1960s and a really colourful old-time gold miner. I first encountered him wearing a gold-coloured tie, gold cufflinks, gold wrist watch and lighting up his cigarette with a gold-plated lighter. 'I'm a gold bug,' he admitted unashamedly. 'There is a satisfaction in finding gold that you don't get with other metals.' A quarter century on, its nice to see a mine carrying his name still operating.

Speaking of old-timers, the Giant Yellowknife mine on the shores of the Great Slave Lake in the Northwest Territories is continuing a turbulent career that began in 1948. Originally the mine was owned by Falconbridge but later passed through three other owners in rapid succession, ending up with a new Vancouver company Royal Oak Mines, run by a no-nonsense woman named Margaret Witte, known to her friends as Peggy. Besides picking up Giant Yellowknife, she has acquired the old Pamour Porcupine Mine at Timmins, which is still good for 100,000 ounces (3.1 tonnes) a year, and the Hope Brook mine in Newfoundland. Hope Brook was opened in 1989 by BP Canada, closed two years later, but resurrected by Peggy Witte in 1992. In short, she is attempting the kiss of life on three difficult mines, challenging organized labour in an effort to drive down costs. If she is successful Royal Oak will be sitting on up to 400,000 ounces (12.4 tonnes) a year. 'Witte gathers rag-tag mines, builds major gold producer,' said a neat *Northern Miner* headline.

At Giant Yellowknife, she managed to bring operating costs down from US$400 to $305 an ounce, aiming eventually for below $290, which she believes could secure the mine for another decade. Union resistance was bitter. It called a strike. Peggy Witte flew in new workers and supplies by helicopter. The Royal Canadian Mounted Police dispatched fifty mounties to try to keep the peace. Then an underground explosion, which the RCMP decided was intentional, killed nine workers, including six union members who had crossed the picket line. Amazingly, the mine kept going. When I asked a Canadian mining friend if Mrs Witte would hang on at Giant Yellowknife, he responded, 'My absolutely-off-the-record gut feeling is yes.' Actually, her calibre had already been acknowledged. She was the first woman ever to be awarded the title 'Mining Man [sic] of the Year' in Canada.

### Betting on British Columbia
While Hope Brook has brought gold mining to Newfoundland for the first time, the real future of Canadian gold mining may lie to the west of

the continent in British Columbia. Actually the first serious Canadian gold rush took place there on the Fraser river in 1857, but in this century British Columbia has never been able to compete with the long-running underground mines of Ontario and Quebec. Even today, it is often an on-off business in a province ruled by a social-democratic government that is interventionist in imposing both high taxes and environmental controls. Indeed, that was one factor in Placer Dome's decision to write off nearly US$200 million on a low-grade copper-gold deposit at Mount Milligan. The Nickel Plate mine at Hedley, operated lately by International Corona, also has a chequered history as an underground mine before 1930 and from 1934 to 1955, and revised in the eighties as an open pit by Corona before fading out in 1993 due to high costs.

The positive story comes further north in British Columbia from the Snip mine, owned 60 per cent by Cominco with its partner Prime Resources Group (in which Corona has 49.8 per cent). The mine is what Canadians call a 'fly-in camp'; everything comes in either by plane or by hovercraft along the Stikine and Iskut rivers from the little town of Wrangell in Alaska. The mine itself is at Johnny Mountain, high above the junction of the Iskut river and Bronson Creek. It brings back memories of the early gold rushes to the nearby Yukon a century ago, but with the convenient access of modern transport. Snip produced a creditable 109,000 ounces in its very first year, 1991, with an excellent grade of 0.831oz/t (25.9 g/t) with direct operating costs of only US$167 an ounce. The catch is that reserves may last only until the late 1990s, but meanwhile Snip is a good bet. Greater hopes are riding on the nearby Eskay Creek gold-silver project which is scheduled for 1996. The lure of Eskay Creek, despite its remoteness, which requires the building of a 39-mile road from the nearest highway and the challenge of mammoth winter snowfalls, is high grades. Early estimates of reserves suggest 1.86 oz/t (58 g/t) of gold plus 74.8 oz/t (2,327 g/t) of silver, which could give 250,000 ounces (7.8 tonnes) of gold and 10 million ounces of silver annually for eight years. The controlling interest in Eskay Creek is held by International Corona (now Homestake Mining) through the original joint-venture partners Prime Resources and Stikine Resources, while Placer Dome has a direct 22 per cent share of the venture.

If all goes to plan, Eskay Creek will be the biggest new gold mine opening in Canada in the 1990s. That shows how things have changed.

### Mines die hard
The rest of the scorecard for potential new mines in the nineties is

limited. Actually British Columbia gets considerable attention. LAC Minerals is scouting at Red Mountain in northern BC not far from the Snip mine, Placer Dome has a copper-gold possibility at Kerr and various junior companies are looking at prospects in such scenic settings as Fish Lake and Williams Lake. While up in the Yukon a stronger gold price might give life to a 1 million ounce (31.1 tonne) heap-leach operation at Brewery Creek. Back east in the tried and tested camps of Ontario, Placer Dome may get the Musselwhite deposit going, and Hemlo Gold has hopes for Holloway. Otherwise on the home front the industry is marking time. For the 1990s it can ride on the back of the gold boom of the previous decade, with mines streamlining costs to live with a lower gold price. 'Mines die hard,' said Ted Reeve, the analyst at Sanwa, McCarthy Securities in Toronto. 'When a mine manager's back is to the wall, it is amazing what he can do to reduce costs and keep head grades. There was fat in the system; Placer's been cutting costs at Campbell Red Lake, but it's had no impact on production.'

Such tactics may well hold Canada's output close to 5 million ounces (156 tonnes) to the end of the century, but beyond is an open question. Paul Kavanagh reckons that on present form there will be only thirty-five mines still alive in Canada by 2000, compared with fifty-three in the early 1990s. 'The industry is not renewing itself,' he said. 'The gold is getting harder to find. There's Eskay Creek, some exploration in Newfoundland and LAC might find something more in Doyon or Bousquet, but the country with the significant fall-off early in the next century will be Canada.' This is a sentiment echoed by Ted Reeve, reciting the industry's woes: 'Exploration is halved, flow-through shares have ended, tax rates are high, and the environment is no longer friendly.'

The frustrations are plain, especially on getting permits. 'Eventually', said Reeve, 'mining companies get to the point where they say "how do I make a deal? You [the authorities] want so many things".' At Mt Milligan in British Columbia Placer Dome complains that if it had gone ahead, it would have been required to put out cleaner water into streams below the mine than was originally in the stream above. On another aborted project, streams that had never seen a boat were judged 'navigable', so that bridges would have been required where the torrents passed the mine, in the unlikely event someone might try sailing up them. As Claude Drouin of the Quebec Mining Association put it, 'We're not against the environment, but it's difficult to break a rock without creating dust and making a noise.' Even if projects are approved, the wait is long. Placer Dome reckons it takes more than two years in Canada, a year in Nevada and Papua New Guinea, six months in

Australia and no delay in Chile. Being based in Vancouver, with the Pacific on its doorstep, Placer looked west across that ocean long ago.

Taxation is also higher in the key provinces of British Columbia, Ontario and Quebec than in potential mining states in the United States, most of Latin America and the Pacific region. As Sandy Laird of Placer Dome lamented, 'From the point of view of tax, British Columbia must be counted as a high-risk region.' Frustrations were further increased when, in mid-1993, after four years of environmental wrangling, the BC government barred further development of the Windy Craggy copper and gold deposit in the northwest of the province, designating the area a wilderness park. In response, the chief executives of five BC based mining companies warned that investors would lose confidence in the province and employment opportunities would be lost.

And so, as Cominco's president, Robert Holbauer, observed in a speech, 'The exodus is now in full swing.' Chile is the favourite destination. 'Canadians have jumped into Chile with both feet,' said Ted Reeve. 'Forty companies are now active there, and Mexico has great opportunities too.' They also have warmer winters.

## CHAPTER 8

# Latin America
# Back in Fashion

The Museo del Oro in Bogota, Colombia houses perhaps the finest exhibition anywhere of craftsmanship in gold. The unique collection of Pre-Columbian jewellery and ornaments includes embossed burial masks, filigree necklaces and bracelets woven from fine gold wire, and wonderful replicas of animals, birds and plants (golden corn in a sheaf of silver leaves). The earliest were made by the first great Peruvian civilization of Chavin around 1200 BC. The show is a powerful reminder that South America has been a source of gold for at least three thousand years and, although the traditions of the goldsmiths and many treasures of the past were destroyed by the Spanish conquest (an estimated 8 tonnes of gold ornaments were melted down to pay Pizarro's ransom for the Inca), the search for El Dorado, the origin of the gold, has never abated.

A few years ago, it seemed to have been found in Brazil. Serra Pelada ('hill of gold' in Portuguese) was the name on everyone's lips as 40,000 diggers, *garimpeiros*, flocked into the jungle south of Belem on the Amazon delta to gouge out a great pit from which they won 13 tonnes (418,000 ounces) in a single year. The images of gaunt, mud-caked figures scrambling up rickety wooden ladders laden with pay-dirt haunted the pages of magazines and television screens. If one wondered what a true gold rush in the past had been like, here it was being played out before our eyes. And repeated endlessly across South America as *garimpeiros* or *barraqueros* (in Spanish-speaking countries) sought gold in Cumaru, Alta Floresta, Roiraima in Brazil, on the Rio Madeira on the Brazil-Bolivia border, at Kilometro 88 on the Caroni river in Venezuela, on the Saldana and Nechi rivers of Antioquia province in Colombia, and the Rio Madre de Dios in Peru. Their efforts more than doubled production in Latin America in the 1980s, alone accounting for close to 150 tonnes (4.8 million ounces) in the peak years, two-thirds of all production. Yet, like all gold rushes, they soon began to burn out as the best of the alluvial surface deposits were exhausted. 'This has been one of the world's greatest gold rushes, far outstripping the Klondike,' observed Peter Rich, an authority on alluvial mining in Latin America. 'But it is showing signs of wear.'

The *garimpeiros* and *barraqueros*, however, had proved the gold was there. The mining companies followed on their trail. The eighties was the era of the *garimpeiros*, the nineties is that of the mining company. The *Financial Times* headlined a survey of Latin American mining, 'The continent rolls out the carpet', reporting that nearly 200 Canadian and US mining companies were operating there.[1] The search is not only for gold; copper, nickel and zinc are also high on the list, but virtually every major gold miner I met in North America was involved down south; American Barrick, Battle Mountain, Cambior, Homestake, LAC Minerals, Newmont Mining, Placer Dome and TVX Gold are all there. It is the same story from Johannesburg; Anglo American, Gold Fields of South Africa and Gencor, the big three of South African gold, are already mining in or looking at various Latin American destinations (Anglo has been in Brazil for more than a decade). Although, as it happens, Brazil is the one country that is not rolling out the red carpet; its new constitution in 1988 decreed that foreign miners could not have a majority holding in local ventures: a ruling that instantly put Brazil on the international miners' blacklist; seven companies dropped all exploration there and departed forthwith.

The welcome elsewhere has compensated. The Metals Economic Group identified forty-two new gold property acquisitions in the region during 1990/1. Three factors tempt the foreigners. At home, especially in North America, they are feeling besieged by environmental controls, permitting delays and high taxes (especially in some Canadian provinces). By contrast, such countries as Bolivia, Chile and Venezuela have revised their mining laws to create a friendlier environment which not only gives security of tenure and tax breaks, but enables miners to bring in equipment, repatriate profits – and capital. While in Chile, which is the prime target for many companies, the return of democracy after the Pinochet regime made doing business there more acceptable (although analysts often argue that the best properties had already been snapped up by then).

The third attraction, of course, is confidence that large untapped

1 *Financial Times*, Latin American Mining, 17 September 1992.

# BRAZIL, GUYANA, VENEZUELA: GOLD FIELDS

Legend:
- Goias — Gold Producing Regions
- Crixás ▲ — Major Mines
- Natal ● — Towns

mineral reserves, including gold, await the explorer. The region offers the best of two geological worlds. 'South America is blessed with both the oldest and the newest geological environments favourable to gold,' says Peter Rich, who has been in the front line of exploration there for twenty years. 'Very rich epithermal gold occurs over the whole length of the Andes. . . . The remainder of the continent is predominantly Pre-Cambrian shield with widespread occurrences of auriferous greenstone.'[2] The significance of the greenstone, which runs in a broad belt 2,200 kilometres (1,370 miles) long and 750 kilometres (470 miles) wide from Colombia eastwards through Venezuela to Guyana and Surinam before swinging south into the Brazilian state of Amapa, is that similar rocks also happen to host the major gold deposits of Australia, Canada, Russia and South Africa. Geologists naturally hope South America's Pre-Cambrian shield will be as prolific. At the same time the volcanic epithermal deposits of the Andes are one end of the crescent of the Pacific 'rim of fire' which swings from Chile around the Pacific basin through Fiji, Papua New Guinea, Indonesia, the Philippines and up to Japan. These resources will not be developed overnight; rather they are the prospect for the next few decades, if not the whole twenty-first century. Latin America, however, is accustomed to a long time scale. After all, the two oldest underground mines in the western world (China has some more ancient workings) are here: the Mineracao Morro Velho mine in Brazil's Minas Gerais province opened in 1834 and the Frontino mine in Colombia in 1854. Geologist Peter Rich believes that if the full potential of the greenstone belt could be developed, Latin American output might one day be 300 tonnes (9.6 million ounces) rather than the present 200 tonnes plus.

For the moment, the main focus is in two countries of great contrast, Brazil and Chile, but well before 2000 rather more will be known about the potential for Bolivia, Guyana, Mexico, Peru and Venezuela, although as much will depend on the gold price as on the deposits.

### Brazil: Miners versus garimpeiros

For almost three centuries Brazil has been the foremost producer in Latin America (except for a short period when Colombia was number one); indeed, in the mid-eighteenth century it was the world's major supplier at 16 tonnes (over 500,000 ounces) annually. In all, over 2,500 tonnes (80 million ounces) has been produced since 1700.[3] Brazil will remain the leading producer in the region, at least into the next century. Despite the discouragement to foreign investment under the 1988 constitution, the twin track of garimpeiros working the alluvial deposits

2 Peter Rich, *South America's Giant Sleeping Gold Province*, Australian Gold Conference, Perth, March 1992.
3 *Worldwide Trends in Gold Exploration*, Centre for Resource Studies, Queen's University, Kingston, Ontario, 1992.

## BRAZIL: PRODUCTION

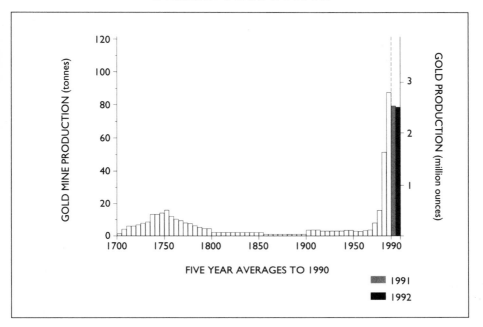

(*garimpos*) and mining companies, often still with heavyweight foreigners
as minority shareholders, will hold output around 70–80 tonnes (2.5
million ounces) annually. The balance of their contributions will also
shift; by 1995 *garimpeiros* and miners will each provide around half of the
output.

For the *garimpeiros* the game has become tougher and tougher. Not
only were the richest *garimpos* gutted very quickly – for all its reputation,
Serra Pelada had one incredible year before decline set in – but they
came into rapid confrontation with environmentalists for turning forest
into a wasteland of craters, for polluting the rivers with mercury and for
threatening the previously undisturbed life of remote Indian tribes in
the furthest regions of the Amazon basin. The hazard from mercury was
particularly critical. Peter Rich labelled it a 'time bomb' because of the
threat it poses, not just to the *garimpeiros* themselves, but to the fish in
the rivers, which may then be eaten by people miles away. It has
become a grim reminder of what happened at Minamata in Japan, where
a chemical company dumped mercury in a bay, poisoning fish and
thence the local people, of whom hundreds died.

The *garimpeiros* use mercury as their essential ingredient to separate
out the gold. While conventional panning removes nuggets and larger

grains of gold, the remaining concentrate is often poured into a bucket or old oil drum containing mercury. The gold amalgamates readily with the mercury to form a heavy alloy, while the debris is skimmed off. The alloy is then squeezed in a cloth, as one might make cream cheese, so that the loose mercury drains out. The residue is heated with a blow torch to burn off the mercury. The *garimpeiros* use as much as 1.3 kilos (45 ounces) of mercury for every kilo of gold produced, according to Brazil's National Mining Department. All told, they may have dumped over 1,200 tonnes of mercury during the 1980s. By 1986 the first cases of mercury poisoning were turning up on the Tapajos, a river running south from the Amazon. A doctor from Santarem who followed up the cases told a visiting journalist, Christina Lamb, that he was horrified by what he found in mining communities: 'Mercury in kitchens, on bar counters, dumped into the river, on people's hands, or escaping as vapour'.[4]

The free use of mercury has been banned since 1989 and *garimpeiros* are directed to use simple retorts which contain most of the mercury. Goldmine, one of the biggest buyers of gold in the *garimpos* has even set up its own foundation to research and develop an efficient retort. But abuse continues since it is impractical to police *garimpeiros* scattered through thousands of square miles of the Amazon region or the rivers of the Brazil/Bolivia border. The dilemma, too, is that prospecting for gold provides a living for up to half a million men, who might otherwise be unemployed in Brazil's cities. They are not there of choice, but of necessity.

Inevitably, too, as they have moved to more remote discoveries, the conflict with the local Indians has increased. The crunch came in Roiraima province, far to the north where Brazil squeezes up against Colombia, Venezuela and Guyana. A major gold rush developed by 1988 along the rivers Uraricoera, Mucajai, Couto Magalhaes and Catrimoni, about 500 kilometres north of Manaus. Forty thousand *garimpeiros*, using 400 small aircraft, operating out of the town of Boa Vista, set up scores of airstrips throughout the region (a friend of mine calculated how much gold was being produced in Roiraima by checking how much aviation fuel was sold in Boa Vista; there was a definite correlation). The gold, however, was in the homeland of the Ianomami Indians, a tribe previously little disturbed by the outside world. Following worldwide pressure on the Brazilian government, President Collor, as one of the first acts of his administration (and long before he was disgraced) declared the area a reserve for the Indians. The *garimpeiros* were driven out, and their airstrips dynamited. Across the borders, the Venezuelan and Colombian governments also initiated Indian reserves,

4 Christina Lamb, *Financial Times*, London, 9 October 1991.

pushing out their own *barraqueros* working the gold deposits along the rivers which extended into their territory as well. Since then the governments have been busy carefully re-marking their own boundaries, especially along the Serra Parima range, which divides Brazil and Venezuela and from which the gold-bearing streams flow north and south. The Serra Parima is right on that auspicious auriferous greenstone belt. Although the *garimpeiros* are officially kept at bay (actually thousands still sneak in), local miners believe that eventually mining companies will be allowed to have a look. Some twenty-five companies still hold exploration licences from the Brazilian government for the reserve area and they have not been revoked. The historic search for El Dorado used to lead explorers towards these little known regions of the Brazil/ Venezuela border. Will miners one day prove the Serra Parima is the home of the legend?

Meanwhile, back amid the reality of daily mining in Brazil the picture is of fitful growth. The mainstay of the mining sector is the Mineracao Morro Velho mine at Nova Lima in Minas Gerais where formal mining was started in 1834 by the English company St John d'el Rey, who took over the lease from a Father Freitas who had supervised some rudimentary diggings there since the eighteenth century (output was reported as 16 kilos (514 ounces) in 1814). The gold reef sloping gently down through the greenstone had yielded close to 400 tonnes (12.9 million ounces) of gold in 160 years and at 3,000 metres shows no sign of bottoming out. The controlling partner in the mine is the Brazilian company Bozano Simonsen, with Anglo American from South Africa holding 49 per cent. Nearby, Gencor from South Africa has a 49 per cent stake, with Brazil's Amira Trading, in the revival of another old property from the mid-nineteenth century, the Sao Bento mine, which produces around 2.5 tonnes annually. Anglo American's Brazilian hand is strengthened by its control, through Morro Velho, in the Jacobina open pit and underground mine in Bahia province, where output is just under 2 tonnes annually, and at Crixas in Goias province. The Crixas mine, developed by the Canadian group Inco from very old workings, came on stream in 1989 and is now jointly owned by Morro Velho (as operator) and TVX Gold from Toronto (which has taken over Inco's gold assets). Initially it is a shallow underground mine reached by a ramp, but three different layers of mineralization going down almost to 2,000 metres suggest that Crixas, like the Morro Velho mine, has a long life ahead. Output is around 4 tonnes (130,000 ounces) annually. The chairman of TVX Gold is the Brazilian entrepreneur (and some time world offshore power boat champion) Eike Batista, who has pulled off a series of coups in allying himself to major international mining groups in

Brazil and Chile, including setting up the successful La Coipa mine. When I asked a friend in Rio about Batista, he boldly painted him as 'the most colourful and successful mining entrepreneur since Cecil Rhodes'. Batista also secured for TVX Gold a slice of the large volume, low-grade (0.02 oz/t; 6 g/t) Brasilia open pit near Paracatu, which is operated by the Brazilian subsidiary of RTZ Corporation. The real outsider for TVX Gold, however, may be the Novo Astro mine located at Salamangone in the wilds 300 kilometres north of Macapa at the mouth of the Amazon in Amapa province. Novo Astro, which came into full production in 1991 at just over 2 tonnes a year, is right astride that Pre-Cambrian shield, which swings up through Amapa province into French Guiana and Surinam. The grade is a highly respectable 0.43 oz/t (13.4 g/t), with indications as the mine develops that a series of quartz veins which dip sharply from the surface might yield even better grades. Novo Astro is a small mine, but its significance is as an indicator that formal mining in Brazil is getting up and away from the historic areas of the last two centuries and into new territory of the Pre-Cambrian shield where long-term serious deposits may lie.

The other initiative in Brazil has come from CVRD, the giant state-owned iron ore company, which switched its sights to gold in the early 1980s. Already it has brought five mines into production, of which the largest is Fazenda Brasileira in Bahia which started as a heap-leach operation from an open pit, before going underground in 1989; with output at 3.6 tonnes annually, it is the second biggest in Brazil after Morro Velho. In all, CVRD's five mines should produce 12 tonnes (385,000 ounces) annually in the mid-1990s.

This modest output by Brazil's mines, where 1 to 3 tonnes is the norm, explains why it has taken so long for the formal mining sector to begin to match the *garimpeiros*. Original estimates that I made on a visit to Brazil in 1987 totted up mine output at 40 tonnes annually in the early 1990s. In fact it reached only 37 tonnes by 1992. True, the weak gold price has not helped, but more important, my calculation was prior to the 1988 constitutional revisions. When they prompted seven major international mining groups to pack up, it was a serious setback. Consequently, the genuine potential in Brazil will be explored and developed slowly. The action, meanwhile, has been across the continent in Chile.

### Chile: High Altitude Hazards
For the gold miner Chile is a radical contrast to Brazil or, indeed, much of Latin America. The gold deposits are epithermal, being of volcanic origin, usually very low grade at 1 to 2 g/t (0.6 oz/t), and often linked

# PERU, BOLIVIA, CHILE: GOLD FIELDS

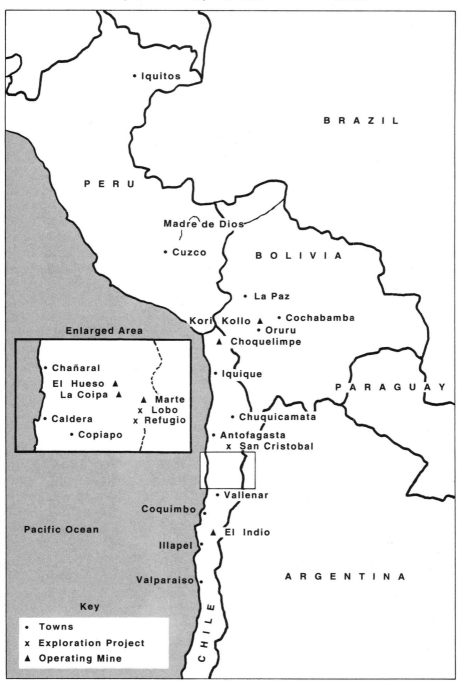

with copper (of which Chile is the world's biggest producer), but they have proved very amenable to heap-leaching, for which Chile has become a new proving ground. The best orebodies, however, are high in the Andes, often over 4,000 metres (13,000 feet) where the thin atmosphere adds altitude sickness (known locally as *puna*) to the normal hazards of mining. Yet since the late 1970s Chile has wooed international mining groups more successfully than any other Latin American nation. At least $600 million has been invested in new gold operations. One of the first acts of the regime of General Pinochet, who ousted President Allende, was to frame new foreign investment laws giving mining companies a firm legal framework in which to operate, with the right to remit profits immediately and capital after three years. Pinochet, despite the worldwide disapproval of his government, also offered a ruthless measure of political stability. The rising gold price in the late 1970s and the improved technology for dealing with low grades did the rest. The real catalyst, however, came in 1975 with the discovery by the St Joe Minerals Corporation, of El Indio, an astonishing cocktail of gold, silver and copper, high in the Andes of northern Chile. The immediate attraction of El Indio was several exceptionally high-grade zones with gold at 358 g/t (11.5 oz/t) and silver at over 1,000 g/t (32 oz/t). Plucked out separately when the mine first opened in 1980 at the moment of high precious metal prices, these nuggets helped pay for the start-up. The rich gold zones alone provided 6 tonnes (193,000 ounces) annually in the early days of El Indio, with a further 6 tonnes coming from more finely disseminated gold in the main orebody. The real goodies lasted only a few years, so that production slipped back gradually to 6 tonnes overall. But other neighbouring satellites have been found, so that the El Indio complex embraces six underground and six open-pit mines, plus the Tambo mine even higher in the mountains close to the Argentine border. Canada's LAC Minerals, which now controls 83 per cent of the properties (as a result of its takeover of Australian Alan Bond's international gold assets), implemented a substantial modernization programme in the early 1990s, and reduced operating costs to a respectable $150 an ounce, which should keep El Indio going into the next century at 5 to 6 tonnes annually.

The promise of El Indio naturally brought other mining houses in for a look. An alliance of Anglo American and Cominco (ANCOM) flew aerial reconnaissance of the entire high Andes chain from the Peruvian border south to Tierra del Fuego, following up any clues with helicopter and ground crews. This military style onslaught pinpointed no less than eleven orebodies at around 4000 metres in the Maricunga region about 600 kilometres north of Santiago. They could be spotted from the air in the barren mountain terrain, because they had a faint yellow ochre colouring easily visible in the clear mountain air (the geologists describe them as porphyry gold deposits with hydrothermal, epigenetic enrichments related to tertiary volcanism). The experienced geologist Merwin Bernstein, who helped find El Indio and supervised this reconnaissance, was convinced that here was the world's next great gold province. So it may be, but not at the gold price prevailing in the early 1990s. The price would have to return, as another geologist put it, 'to a more comfortable level'. Indeed, Marte, the one mine that did start up in 1989 on the back of the survey, as a heap-leach open pit, lasted scarcely two years as production fell way below target. The need for caution is evident from other operations that have started, but soon fallen on difficult days. The El Hueso mine, originally found by Codelco, the Chilean state mining company, and operated on a ten-year lease by Homestake Mining from San Francisco, started in 1987 as Chile's first heap-leach operation. But it has experienced high costs and disappointing grades for its 2 tonnes (64,000 ounces) a year, and unless Homestake can persuade Codelco to let it work some neighbouring claims, its life is limited.

A similar fate befell Choquilimpie, the world's highest gold mine poised right in the lip of a volcano at 4,825 metres (15,777 feet). It started as an open-pit, heap-leach operation in 1988, under a consortium of Billiton (the mining arm of Royal Dutch Shell), Northgate and Citibank. From the start it was plagued by high altitude problems. Like mountaineers, the miners had to live at a 'base camp' at 3,500 metres, journeying up to 4,800 metres and back for each shift. Once there, they had to operate a 'buddy' system, with everyone keeping an eye constantly on everyone else for the first signs of *puna*, whether lapse of memory, shortage of breath, cramps, indecisiveness, nausea, vomiting or loss of vision (to cite but a few of the potential afflictions). Since there was no pattern to indicate in advance who might be vulnerable, it was trial by ordeal on the spot. Labour turnover, not surprisingly, was 70 per cent. The gold was there, of course; enough to give over 3 tonnes (96,000 ounces) a year from surface oxide ores for a few years. Then came the crunch with the decision to go for deeper, more difficult sulphide ores. The gold price did not justify it, while environmental pressures, because Choquilimpie is in the middle of a nature reserve, prevented prospecting for other local surface deposits. So the mine closed at the end of 1992, pending at least a better gold price.

The real contender in Chile is undoubtedly La Coipa, jointly owned by Placer Dome and TVX Gold. The mine, at a slightly more comfortable 4,000 metres (13,000 feet) on the fringe of the Atacama

Desert, is a low-grade epithermal deposit with a grade of 1.2 g/t (0.038 oz/t), plus 71 g/t (2.28 oz/t) of silver. When the mine opened in 1989 it was initially treating a rather small amount of higher-grade (5 g/t) ore, but from 1991 the completion of a much larger milling plant really got La Coipa in its stride at 6 tonnes (193,000 ounces) annually with operating costs around $150. And its future, perhaps at slightly lower output, is set beyond the year 2000. The prospects are easier for the San Cristobal mine at a modest 1,800 metres, opened by Australia's Niugini Mining[5] in 1991. It is an open pit with heap-leaching on a passable grade of 1.19 g/t (0.4 oz/t) that provides nearly 2 tonnes a year. And coming along the pipeline for the mid-1990s are several other hopefuls. Among them is Refugio, which was pioneered by a small Canadian company, Bema Gold (after Anglo American let the property go) before it was joined in 1992 by Amax Gold from Denver in its first Latin American adventure. Refugio, located 1,100 kilometres north of Santiago, is actually two deposits, Verde and Pancho, which will be developed as an open-pit/heap-leach operation with potential production around 7 tonnes (225,000 ounces) annually. Amax Gold is also bringing the Guanaco project south of Antofagasta into production at 2 tonnes a year. Phelps Dodge is going ahead with the La Canderaria copper mine, which will have some useful gold by-product, while Anglo American and Cominco may start their joint Lobo project, very close to their ill-fated Marte venture.

Yet for all the big international names, it is not a great performance. The initial boom has faded. Since most new mines contribute at best a couple of tonnes, it is a haul to get Chile up from the present 39 tonnes to the 50 tonnes that some analysts forecast. Actually, the future may depend on new copper projects which, like Phelps Dodge's La Canderaria, chip in some by-product gold. A sustained rise in the gold price would be welcome too.

### B for Bolivia – and Battle Mountain

In the history of silver Bolivia has a place of its own; it is the home of the great Potosi mine, discovered by the Spanish in 1545 and worked constantly for centuries thereafter. And for that reason Bolivia is unique in the annals of mining for it has an unbroken tradition of very high altitude underground mining going back over 400 years. The *puna* that debilitates miners in the new high mines of Chile is almost unknown. Miners in Bolivia can live and work at 4,000 metres (13,000 feet) or above; no need for base camps, provided, as a geologist who lived there reminded me, 'an essential item in the company store is coca leaf to chew'. The leaf is the narcotic that keeps the numbing cold and sickness at bay.

5 Niugini Mining's majority shareholder is Battle Mountain Gold from the United States.

On the gold front Bolivia has not had much to offer up to now. A vintage dredge installed in the 1950s by Pato Consolidated still plies the headwaters of the river Beni in company with thousands of *barraqueros* working with pumps on small boats or burrowing into its banks. They also scour the Madre de Dios and other streams coming down from the high sierra to join the Rio Madeira near the Brazilian border. It can be a hazardous enterprise; several hundred miners were reported killed in December 1992 when a mudslide engulfed their camp. More organized mining had always been in silver and tin (of which Bolivia was a major producer until the tin market collapsed in 1986). Gold became more interesting only in the late 1980s when hyperinflation abated and new mining laws were passed to encourage foreign investment. Tempted by a modest royalty of only 3 per cent on gold production, plus a 10 per cent tax on dividends that can be repatriated, several foreign gold companies started exploration. RTZ Corporation and a local affiliate, Comsur, brooded over a gold deposit at Puquio Norte, while Cyprus Minerals set out with the state mining company Comibol to review the Los Pipez region.

The most advanced is Battle Mountain Gold from Houston, Texas, which initially got an open-pit, heap-leach operation going in 1990 at Kori Kollo through a Bolivian mining company Inti Raymi of which it acquired 85 per cent. The pit, located at 3,300 metres (11,000 feet) on a high flat plain half-way between La Paz and Potosi, where old workings for gold and silver go back several centuries, had a cap of oxide ore, which Battle Mountain could leach, while setting up large-scale milling facilities for the deeper sulphide ores below. The new mill came on stream early in 1993 lifting output to around 7.5 tonnes (240,000 ounces) a year (plus a bonus of around 45 tonnes of silver) at an operating cost of only around $180, an achievement which makes Kori Kollo one of the largest producers in Latin America. Battle Mountain hopes it is just the beginning. 'We went to Bolivia because we were fascinated by the opportunity to move into what is potentially a very productive area for precious metals before the rest of the world rushed in,' Karl Elers, Battle Mountain's chairman and chief executive told me. 'As people start looking there will be new discoveries.'

### G for Guyana – and Golden Star Resources
The rival for number one producer in Latin America, however, is the Omai project in Guyana backed by two Canadian companies, Cambior (60 per cent) and Golden Star Resources. Golden Star originally went to Guyana in 1985, when a new government relaxed foreign investment regulations (yet again demonstrating that a favourable investment

environment is essential for development). The real attraction was that greenstone belt sweeping from Colombia, through Venezuela into Guyana and on to Brazil. Golden Star got its hands on several projects, but the best bet was an open-pit operation at Omai on the banks of the Rio Essiquibo, Guyana's main river, which offers the best transport facilities in a country with little infrastructure inland from the coast. Initially it worked with Placer Dome, which withdrew in 1990, to be replaced immediately by Cambior as the major shareholder. Cambior generated the necessary start-up cash with a 10.3 tonne (330,000 ounce) gold loan to enable the initial low-grade (1.8 g/t; 0.058 oz/t), open pit to begin in 1993 with the potential for 7.8 tonnes (250,000 ounces) a year. Eventually, Omai may go underground if the higher grades (6.9 g/t; 0.22 oz/t) found so far prove extensive. Meanwhile, Golden Star, which has really been the entrepreneur if not the troubleshooter in Guyana (the company's chairman David Fennell is a former Canadian football star) has another clutch of properties up its sleeve, including a large alluvial gold field at Mahdia while, across the border in neighbouring Surinam, it is drilling Gros Rosabel (originally scouted by Placer in the 1970s) where some useful grades of 2.3 g/t (0.07 oz/t) have turned up. Golden Star's exploration team in both countries, incidentally, includes the Brazilian geologist Carlos Bertoli who is an expert on greenstone deposits in South America. Meanwhile, back in Guyana itself, another Canadian company, Sutton Resources from Vancouver, is scouting Marudi mountain, just across the border from Brazil's Roiraima province. Guyana is on the brink of becoming a producer of 10–20 tonnes (310,000– 620,000 ounces) a year by the end of the century. 'There is a large upside potential,' said mining expert Peter Rich. The work in Guyana confirms, too, the emerging pattern of exploration homing in on the greenstones in a territory framed by the river Orinoco to the north and the Amazon in the south that embraces the border areas not just of Brazil and Guyana, but Venezuela and Colombia too. And it explains why the respective governments are staking out their exact borders more precisely.

### *Venezuela – Finally Getting Serious?*
Each time I went to Venezuela during the 1980s there was high excitement on the mining front. It was not just that the alluvial activity by *barraqueros* in both gold and diamonds, which had long gone on around El Callao and towards the Guyanan and Brazilian borders, was expanding, but there were all kinds of new players to see. First it was the government mining group Minerven which was all set to formalize mining around El Callao where small-scale production has gone on for

more than a century. Those plans never amounted to much. Then it was a gold rush along the Caroni river to Kilometro 88 and Las Claritas, where a local Goldfinger, Emilio Grossi, held sway. A new entrepreneur, Courtney Brewer of Inversiones High-Tech Mining, was busy selling the Knelson Concentrator ('turn your golden dreams into golden realities') to improve the recovery rates from gravels in the rivers. And I could sit in the afternoons in the minuscule office of Jaime Tugues, an important dealer who runs the El Platino refinery, and meet an assorted cast of characters in from the gold fields with gold dust and nuggets – and the latest tall tales of output. One dredge – a small boat really with a pump – was getting 4 kilos (129 ounces) a day, another 5 kilos. Helicopters were coming in by night from Colombia to spirit away hundreds of kilos. How much was being produced? Twenty tonnes? Twenty-five? Thirty? One London analyst who went up country came back convinced it was 50 tonnes (1.6 million ounces) or more. Reality was more like 15 tonnes and perhaps 20 tonnes (640,000 ounces) in the best year of 1988. One gauge was the central bank, which set up its own gold-buying units in the field and usually managed to get its hands on 12–15 tonnes a year. A couple of foreign mining companies from London, Greenwich Resources and Monarch Resources, joined in but business did not amount to much at first. They were hamstrung by local mining laws. By 1990 not only were the best of the alluvial hotspots worked out, but the government was putting much tighter controls on the *barraqueros*, in particular trying to contain their indiscriminate use of mercury. Eventually all unofficial alluvial digging was banned around the headwaters of the Orinoco river in the state of Amazonas, leading to some bloody confrontations between *barraqueros*, who kept working anyway, and the national guard. But the government also eased the laws on foreign companies, notably reducing corporation tax from a prohibitive 60 per cent to 30 per cent. Thus encouraged, Monarch Resources, which was already on the ground, went ahead with developing La Camorra in the Eldorado region, as the first private underground gold mine in Venezuela for more than fifty years. It is due in 1994 at 2.7 tonnes (86,000 ounces) on very low costs of $115.

Meanwhile a splendid flurry was created early in 1993 when an analyst from the Toronto stockbrokers Burns Fry ventured up to that old hunting ground Kilometro 88 and returned with stories of gold gleaming from the rocks and proposed, 'The most important gold discovery in ten years.' That was good enough to double the value of stocks in several small Canadian companies which were dabbling in Venezuela as punters scrambled to get into 'the hottest exploration play' of the year. All this caused much annoyance to some large mining companies like Placer Dome which are already well established with exploration there. Placer has spent $2.4 million drilling at another former alluvial hotspot, Las Cristinas at Puerto Ordaz near Venezuela's border with Guyana, where it hopes to have an underground mine, while denying rumours it might contain as much as 310 tonnes (10 million ounces). Certainly something is up in Venezuela (even Gold Fields of South Africa is scouting two or three properties), but it takes more than a boom in gold shares and some fancy land prices to confirm a gold mine. The motto there is still wait and see.

The same applies next door in Ecuador, where both Gold Fields of South Africa and RTZ Corporation are nosing around, encouraged by yet another fresh welcome mat. Previously, Ecuador had the usual alluvial gold prospectors, known there as *petroleros*, in the Nambija, Penze, Enriquez and Zaruma Porto Velho areas, who did quite well, pushing up informal output to 10 tonnes. Most of the gold was sold to the central bank, which adopted the policy of its colleagues at the Brazilian, Colombian and Venezuelan central banks of laying their hands on as much of it as possible as a useful foreign exchange earner. The *petroleros* were often so aggressive that they held up prospecting by more serious mining companies, so the future of formal production in Ecuador remains uncertain.

### Colombia/Peru – Braving Guerillas

A quarter of a century ago when I was first looking at the gold business, Colombia was the second largest producer of gold in Latin America, marginally behind Brazil; in the 1990s it still vies for second place with Chile. What has also not changed is the violence that still threatens gold miners at every turn. I recall Patrick O'Neill, then manager for Pato Consolidated, which ran dredges and the Frontino mine, telling me, 'We have a bad problem with stealing; they've got laws in Colombia, but they don't seem to live up to them.' His dredges were constantly under armed attack. Danger is as prevalent today in the age of the drug cartel wars. International mining houses steer clear of Colombia, not because of mining laws (actually they are favourable) but through genuine fear of cartel battles and guerilla activity, which is noticeably high in Antioquia province which produces 70 per cent of the annual output of around 30 tonnes (1 million ounces). Only a couple of juniors from Canada, Greenstone Resources (an appropriate name) and Dual Resources have ventured in. On the formal front, the main mine is Frontino (once Pato Consolidated, but since nationalized), a legendary operation that began in 1854 and still produces just over 3 tonnes annually at an excellent grade of 15 g/t (0.48 oz/t). While Mineros de

Antioquia operates five huge bucket line dredges from a fleet of nine originally installed by Pato Consolidated fifty years ago on the Nechi river near El Bagere. The Nechi, the Saldana and other rivers in this corner of northeast Colombia from Zaragosa to El Bagere, also team with 200,000 or more *barraqueros* who use hydraulic monitors and bulldozers to turn over the riverbanks and small boats fitted with pumps to scour the river beds. Their diggings tripled Colombia's gold output during the 1980s and remain the main source of gold. Judging the precise level of output is difficult because the central bank, Banco de la Republica, often buys gold at a slight premium in local currency (which can be switched quickly into dollars, the preferred currency of all gold trading in Latin America's inflationary environment). Thus, it is sometimes profitable to smuggle gold kilo bars into Colombia through Panama, melt them down and refashion them as rough 'mine' gold to sell to the central bank. The bank's purchases, therefore, have occasionally been more than genuine local output. While the *barraqueros* are likely to remain the main source of Colombia's gold, their activity, to say nothing of the devastation and pollution, has depleted the most accessible reserves in Antioquia. By the early 1990s, the diggers were shifting to the Colombia, Venezuela, Brazil border area, which holds promise for all three countries. The state mining agency Ecominas was hard on their heels to look at the potential from the Pre-Cambrian greenstones there, which must offer the best chance for a serious development of Colombian mining in the twenty-first century.

Peru has also not offered international miners an hospitable environment in recent years, with the virtual collapse of its economy under President Garcia and the violent guerilla activities of the Shining Path. After 1991, however, President Fujimori sought to resuscitate the country and provide some stability. The new minister of mines started privatizing state mining companies, including the San Antonia de Poto gold field previously run by Minero Peru, and developed more liberal mining regulations for foreigners. While there has been no rush to take the bait, Newmont Mining has bravely acquired a 40 per cent stake to manage the new Yanacocha open-pit heap-leach project in northern Peru. Yanacocha has initial potential for up to 3 tonnes annually from oxide ores that respond very swiftly to leaching, giving 85 per cent recovery in just thirty days. If the operation is successful, it could provide the cash flow to mine several neighbouring orebodies on a much larger scale. Newmont's partners at Yanacocha are the Peruvian group Buenaventura and France's BRGM. On its own account, Buenaventura also operates Compania de Minas Orcopampa which extracts a tonne or so from gold concentrates. Meanwhile, up to 30,000 *barraqueros* have been working the Rio Madre de Dios in the jungles of the Amazon basin accounting for most of Peru's output of around 15 tonnes (480,000 ounces) annually.

### Mexico – The New Frontier?

My view of gold prospecting in Mexico is forever coloured by John Huston's wonderful film *Treasure of the Sierra Madre* with Humphrey Bogart, Walter Huston and assorted mules heading for the hills in search of gold. Nowadays one meets such prospectors, admittedly rather better shaven and dressed, at dinner parties in Toronto, Vancouver or Denver. Most likely they are just in from the high country around Hermosillo in Mexico's northwestern province of Sonora to the south of the American border. Two things tempt them: the liberalization of Mexico's property-owning laws since 1990 and the belief that Mexico must have gold deposits similar to those of the western United States. The background thinking, as one geologist put it, is that Nevada was a prolific silver producer before gold was discovered in quantity on the Carlin Trend, and Mexico has long been a prolific silver producer, too – so now how about gold? More than forty mining companies have set up exploration offices in Mexico to find out.

Already there are a few signposts. Phelps Dodge got going with the Santa Gertrudis heap-leach project in 1991; Santa Gertrudis has 'some characteristics of Nevada deposits', say the geologists. Hecla Mining has hopes for a small heap-leach pit at La Choya, which likewise has similarities to Gold Fields' Mesquite deposit[6] in southern California. But it is too early to get excited. One factor slowing up deals is the grandiose expectations of some local Mexican partners. Shrewd American and Canadian miners sit on their wallets waiting for better terms. Still, there is no smoke without fire. As Paul Kavanagh, the senior vice- president for exploration at American Barrick, told me, 'I've spent a lot of time in Mexico during the past year and whereas I'm not sure that a prolific Carlin Trend is going to be found, I'm certain that significant gold deposits will be developed and mined.' Patience and a stronger gold price may be called for.

A better price might also help in Costa Rica. Only one small mine operated by Canada's Ariel Resources is actually operating, but two or three other low-grade properties might look viable at $450; while it must not be overlooked that Newmont Mining has signed up to do a little quiet exploration of a gold/silver prospect on the Rio Chiquito.

Meanwhile, after all these small fry, we can conclude this survey of Latin America with a big serious mine, Pueblo Viejo in the Dominican Republic. This high-grade gold/silver operation opened in 1975 billed

---

6 Now controlled by Santa Fe Pacific Minerals.

as the world's largest open pit. In its prime it produced almost 12 tonnes (386,000 ounces) a year (making it the largest in Latin America), before slipping back to 4 tonnes in the early 1990s. Then along came plans to exploit over 100 million tonnes of refractory sulphide ores, with a grade of 3.7 g/t (0.12 oz/t). If it proves viable Pueblo Viejo could bounce right back to number one in Latin America at 12 tonnes annually.

# AUSTRALIA: GOLD FIELDS

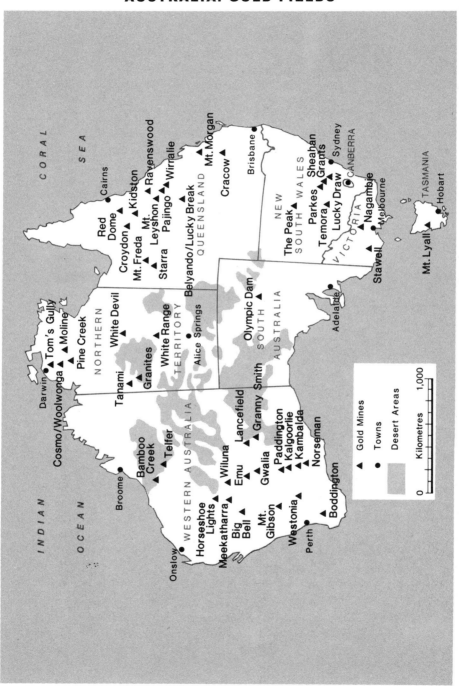

# CHAPTER 9

# Australia:
# Gold Day from WA

It is some time after midnight on Hannan Street, Kalgoorlie; a piano is thumping and drunks are braying in the bar of the Palace Hotel, while just down the road an eager crowd clusters round a game of two-up in Hannan's Club. There is standing room only in the Goldrush Tavern, while at 'Harry's The Night Club (10 p.m.–6 a.m.)', the night has scarcely begun. Business is brisk, too, in the 'traps' on Hay Street nearby, where the ladies of the night ply their trade. Back in the Palace Bar stockbroker David Reed orders up another round. 'My family opened an office in the gold fields in 1896 and I've lived here since 1963,' he says. 'Gold is our life blood; we talk it up and we talk it down.' Tonight he's talking up the latest hot tip – Bronzewing. 'We've got these new blind discoveries,' he confides. 'It's really re-kindled interest in gold stocks.'

Kalgoorlie was born because of gold, which Paddy Hannan discovered here in 1893. As the community celebrated its centenary in 1993 it retained the true spirit of a gold-mining frontier town, not merely thriving on the latest rumour, but genuinely booming again for the last decade. Just glance through the Yellow Pages directory. A is for Assay Offices (eight of them), D is for Drilling Contractors, G is for Geologist (eleven of these specialists), M is for Metal Detectors, Mining & Exploration Companies (take your pick of sixty-three names), and Mining Suppliers (thirty-nine), N is for Nugget Shop ('Natural Nuggets from the Australian Gold Fields') and, for refreshment, T is for Taverns (twenty-nine of them). The town itself has a Victorian air, with broad

## AUSTRALIA: PRODUCTION

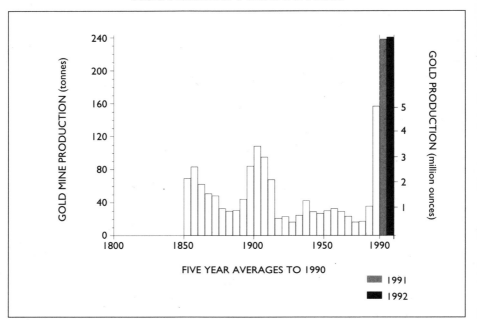

FIVE YEAR AVERAGES TO 1990

▨ 1991
■ 1992

streets and low buildings, many with railed balconies on the first floor where you could sit at ease in a rocking chair. Most bear plaques dating from the original gold boom: Grand Hotel 1895, Palace Hotel 1897, and a stately Town Hall finished in 1908. Right at the end of Hannan Street the headframe of the Mount Charlotte gold mine appears over single-storey bungalows and you can hear the rumble of machinery and see the ore from Australia's largest underground mine piling up in pyramid stockpiles from conveyor belts.

Beyond Hannan Street the town comes to an abrupt end, for this is the threshold of the Golden Mile, mined a century ago by a myriad of small operators, but today knitted together as Kalgoorlie Consolidated Gold Mines into the Super Pit that eventually will be 5 kilometres long, 2 kilometres wide and 500 metres deep. The Golden Mile has already yielded close to 1,400 tonnes (45 million ounces), while the burgeoning Super Pit is producing close to 20 tonnes (650,000 ounces) annually, as Australia's largest producer.

Although gold was discovered in Australia in 1851, first in New South Wales and then in Victoria, Western Australia has been the heart of the matter, not just in the gold boom of the 1890s, but in the remarkable comeback of the last decade. Originally the best Australian output, thanks to the first Kalgoorlie rush, was 119 tonnes (3.8 million ounces) in 1903; that record was not beaten until 1988. In 1980 Australian production was a mere 17 tonnes (546,000 ounces); by 1990 it was 243 tonnes (7.8 million ounces). It has remained close to that level since. As 90 per cent of the gold is exported, it has become the second largest mineral export (after coal), accounting for virtually 8 per cent of all Australian exports. The dormant gold share index was revived in 1985 and over fifty gold companies are listed on the main board of the Australian Stock Exchange. Major North American groups such as Placer Dome, Newmont Mining, Homestake Gold and Battle Mountain have all set up operations on the continent.

The credit for this remarkable fourteen-fold increase goes principally to Western Australia, which is responsible for over 70 per cent. Indeed, breaking down the 7,700 tonnes of gold produced in Australia between 1851 and 1993, precisely one-third was mined in the early gold rushes before 1893, and the remaining two-thirds has come since then, primarily from Western Australia. The Golden Mile alone has produced nearly 20 per cent of the entire historic production. But quite a new dimension has been given to Australian output by the gold rush of the late 1980s; over 1,400 tonnes, virtually 20 per cent of all gold ever mined there, has come just in the few years 1987–93 (it previously took from 1939 to 1986 to mine that same quantity). In short, Australia has become a major player in gold, climbing to number three in the league, a notch ahead of the former Soviet Union. Moreover, the momentum has been well maintained, despite the gold price (although this has done better in Australian dollars) and the introduction of a new 39 per cent corporation tax on gold-mining profits from 1991 (which the industry feared, or said it feared, would be its death-knell). When the world's gold bugs, or more correctly, bullion bankers, miners, refiners and analysts, gathered together in Kalgoorlie in March 1993 at the Australian Gold Conference to celebrate the centenary of Paddy Hannan's find, the word was that output might even rise further towards 295 tonnes (9.5 million ounces) by the late 1990s because so many new discoveries were being made.

They were needed. For the crucial difference between gold mines in Australia and their competitors in South Africa or Canada, is that for the most part they are short-life, open pits. As a South African mining man who had moved to Perth put it, 'A South African mine is like running a country, it's a huge investment with a 40–50 year life, so why rush it? Here it's a 4–5 year life, so you rush at it, sell forward and lock in profits.' Small 'resources companies', as Australians call them often, live just from project to project, with no long-term view. Although the renaissance in mining has led to takeover and larger groupings, especially

# WESTERN AUSTRALIA: GOLD FIELDS

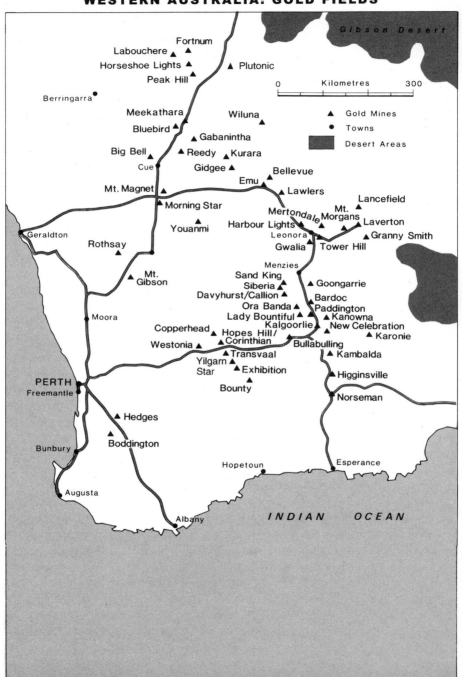

Gibson Desert

Fortnum
Labouchere
Horseshoe Lights
Peak Hill

Plutonic

Berringarra

0        Kilometres        300

Gold Mines
Towns
Desert Areas

Meekathara
Bluebird
Wiluna
Gabanintha
Big Bell
Reedy   Kurara
Cue   Gidgee
Bellevue
Mt. Magnet   Emu
Lawlers   Lancefield
Morning Star
Mertondale   Mt.
Youanmi   Harbour Lights   Morgans   Laverton
Geraldton   Leonora   Granny Smith
Rothsay   Gwalia   Tower Hill
Mt.   Menzies
Gibson   Sand King
Siberia   Goongarrie
Davyhurst/Callion   Bardoc
Moora   Ora Banda   Paddington
Lady Bountiful   Kanowna
Copperhead   Kalgoorlie   New Celebration
Hopes Hill/   Karonie
Westonia   Corinthian   Bullabulling
Transvaal   Kambalda
Yilgarn
Star   Exhibition   Higginsville
Bounty
PERTH   Norseman
Freemantle
Hedges
Bunbury   Boddington
Hopetoun   Esperance
Augusta
Albany   INDIAN   OCEAN

in the difficult days of the early 1990s, gold mining remains remarkably fragmented and 100,000 ounces (3 tonnes) output is billed as a 'big' mine. But this has led to immense energy and flexibility as small companies vie not just in exploration, but to get going. The time-frame here is not only unique in short-lives, but in quick start-up and payback. The Mount Percy mine on the edge of Kalgoorlie was up and running in a mere six months (a South African mine could take five to seven years), while the Plutonic mine, further north, paid back its capital costs within eight months of its start-up in 1990.

### Headframe geology

In one sense the Australians had it easy. The high gold price of the early 1980s suddenly made it attractive to scout round old workings, while low-grade 'haloes' could be mined very profitably with new technology. The immediate target was the flat weathered Pre-Cambrian shield that runs like a ribbon for 300 miles through Western Australia to the north and south of Kalgoorlie, while a second front, as it were, was opened up on the low-grade epithermal deposits of northern Queensland. In Western Australia there are four key belts of greenstone that play host to the gold: the Murchison field to the northwest of Kalgoorlie, home to such deposits as Horseshoe, Labouchere, Plutonic and Mount Magnet; the Eastern Goldfields, spanning from Harbour Lights, down through Paddington to Kalgoorlie and on to Kambalda and Central Norseman; the Southern Cross Belt with Marvel Loch and Yilgarn Star; finally the Boddington and Hedges region to the southeast of Perth.

Throughout these areas open-pit mines sprouted like mushrooms during the late 1980s in a classic example of what miners call 'headframe geology', meaning essentially you cast an eye round from the headframe of an existing property and drill a few more likely spots. 'Australian gold exploration was shallow and unsophisticated,' admitted Robin Widdup, the manager of mining research at stockbrokers J.B. Were, 'with the emphasis on picking a way around historic mines.'[1] Kalgoorlie stockbroker David Reed was more blunt: 'New discoveries in the early 1980s?' he responded, 'Bugger all!' Never mind, it got the gold miners back thinking gold, polishing their expertise, and bullion banks into the habit of financing them and marketing their gold. 'In the past, the classic bonanza gold camp was something like Norseman, with at least 10 grams per tonne,' a geologist at Western Mining told me, when I first went out to Kalgoorlie in 1987. 'Now technology is bringing home with a thunderclap the possibility of cut-off grades down to 1.5–2 grams, which no one had looked for. Suddenly what you'd call an orebody has changed and our exploration targets switched.'[2]

1 Robin Widdup, *The Australian Gold Review 1993*, J.B. Were & Sons, Melbourne.
2 Timothy Green, *The Prospect for Gold*, Rosendale Press, London, 1987, pp. 64–5.

That initial phase was more than enough to kick-start the industry. The old 1903 output level was finally surpassed with 157 tonnes (5 million ounces) production in 1988. But the scene then changed rapidly. The gold price was slipping, the gold share boom vanished like mist in hot morning sun and the easily accessible oxide surface deposits had finite lives. Exploration budgets, which had soared from a scant A$100 million in 1981 to almost A$600 million by 1987, slumped back towards A$300 million by the early 1990s. Despite tough efficiency drives, the challenge of deeper ores meant average cash costs in 1991 were US$264 and total costs $314.

A new approach was needed. On the production front a shift was starting from surface oxide deposits to more complex underground sulphide ores (just as is happening on the Carlin Trend in Nevada) which was often beyond the means of the smaller resources companies. That has favoured the consolidation of larger, more experienced groups which can raise the capital and have the know-how to treat tricky sulphides. New approaches applied equally on the exploration front. 'The scene is completely changed,' said Robin Widdup. 'A small group of well-financed gold producers are using remote techniques and advanced geological ideas to identify new orebodies buried below Australia's thin veneer of sand or soil . . . the 1990s appear as a golden age of virgin deposits.'

### Kalgoorlie – introducing the Super Pit

The way ahead, however, had already been signalled quite early by Alan Bond, that engaging Australian who sponsored the Americas Cup yacht race in Perth, bought fine art at Sotheby's and diversified from brewing, newspapers and TV stations into gold mining, before his entire empire collapsed. Mr Bond got the gold bug in 1986. The heart of his strategy was to pick up the small mines dotting the northern end of the Golden Mile and blend them into what he initially christened 'The Big Pit'. The logical next step was a joint venture with his immediate neighbours, Kalgoorlie Mining Associates, to develop the Super Pit to scoop out the entire Golden Mile to a depth of 500 metres (1,500 feet). The Super Pit plan, moreover, survived Bond's fall. 'While Bond is now vilified,' notes Ross Louthean, editor of the Gold Gazette, he must be credited as the captain behind the merger ... a consolidation that has transformed this phenomenal piece of geology into a long-term open cut mining exercise . . . [that is] once again Kalgoorlie's bread and butter and something for Australia's gold capital to crow about.'[3]

The Super Pit's fortunes are managed by Kalgoorlie Consolidated Gold Mines (KCGM) which is jointly owned by Homestake Gold of

3 Ross Louthean, 'Gold industry digs deep', Australian Business, March 1993, p. 68.

Australia (a daughter of Homestake Mining in San Francisco) and Gold Mines of Kalgoorlie (which is under the wing of Poseidon Gold, part of the Normandy Poseidon group). And it is Robert Champion de Crespigny of Normandy Poseidon who is seen as 'the shaker' in Australian gold mining in the 1990s, picking up failing mines, paring costs and boosting efficiency. Besides the Super Pit, Poseidon Gold's stable includes North Flinders, Mt Leyshon, Big Bell (taken on from Placer Pacific after a disastrous start), Gold Crown, and White Devil in the Northern Territory. This assortment brings Poseidon Gold around 700,000 ounces (21.8 tonnes) annually, making the group the third largest producer in Australia (behind Western Mining and Newcrest). Much faith, however, is riding on the ten-year project to create the Super Pit, gradually merging four individual pits into one great bowl. The hazards of the task become apparent when you weave down the ramps into any of the pits, passing monster dump trucks grinding uphill with their loads. The sides of each pit are riddled with tunnels from underground workings going back a hundred years; it is like trying to dig out an entire honeycomb without causing it to collapse. As the pit is burrowed deeper, so its steep walls creep ever closer to the edge of town. One casualty already has been the Boulder Block, the last pub on the Golden Mile. 'It's a sad loss,' said John Jones, its former owner and himself a mining entrepreneur. But then he cheered up, confiding, 'Robert de Crespigny [of Poseidon Gold] offered me $7 million for it and sent me home'. The good news is that the gold ores fortuitously peter out just across the road from the Kalgoorlie racetrack. 'They wouldn't dare touch that,' said my taxi driver, as we sped back to town from the fringes of the pit.

Actually, the real task for the Super Pit miners is to cut their costs. Although they are using large-scale mining equipment, including 200-tonne capacity haulage trucks, they are plagued by high energy costs because power comes from Perth, 600 kilometres distant and much of it just drains away *en route*. Salvation may come from a proposed 2,000-kilometre gas pipeline from the north of Western Australia, offering the prospect of cheap power. That would enable crushers to be used in the pit, and huge conveyor belts to be installed up its precipitous sides, greatly increasing efficiency and permitting much lower grades to be extracted profitably. The Super Pit has been operating on a cut-off grade of 1.5 g/t (0.48 oz/t), but there is 20 per cent more ore to be had at 1.2 g/t and even more at 0.9 g/t, which is at present stockpiled. Cheap power, therefore, will ultimately determine whether the pit can really be 'Super' (a man-made hole visible from the moon, they like to boast in Kalgoorlie). The initial programme is for ten years to 2001, but if successful the Super Pit is good at least to 2005 and beyond.

Such longevity is rare. 'Australia has one big problem,' argues *Gold Gazette*'s Ross Louthean. 'It has not revealed any world-class deposits – those with 20-year mine lives and upwards of 10 million contained ounces of gold.' This is in contrast, of course, to neighbouring Papua New Guinea, which has been engaging the interests of Australian miners for a decade, and turned up trumps with mines like Porgera yielding 30 tonnes a year.

### The top five players

At home the miners still have to be content with more modest finds. Only five Australian operations (including the Super Pit) produced more than 200,000 ounces (6.2 tonnes) in 1992. Among the top fifty gold-producing companies listed by the Australian Stock Exchange in its *Gold Producers' Handbook 1993* only 27 produced more than 100,000 ounces.[4] Even that list is deceptive: several leaders, such as Placer Pacific (which rates number one), Renison Goldfields, Highlands Gold and Battle Mountain Gold, actually get most of their output from Papua New Guinea or elsewhere abroad, while for other groups, like Poseidon, there is double, triple or even quadruple counting because each company it controls is also on the list.

The genuine top five groups producing from Australian mines only are: Western Mine Corporation, Newcrest Mining, Poseidon Gold, Dominion Mining, and Homestake Gold of Australia. Yet their combined output is only about 3 million ounces (93 tonnes) or less than 40 per cent of Australian production. Thus most Australian gold still comes from scores of modest operations scattered like star-dust across the continent. The *Gold Producers' Handbook* counts 86 'major' mines; the rival *Gold Gazette Annual 1993* tracks 151 'active' mines (96 of them in Western Australia).[5] And that is just for starters: *Gold Gazette* also bills a further 83 'projects' and no less than 404 'prospects'. Welcome to the home of 'Blue Sky Mines', a company created in the fertile imagination of columnist Trevor Sykes of *Australian Business*, whose absolute rule is never actually to mine a single ounce of gold. The spirit of adventure is alive and well in Australian gold mining; the rule for prospective shareholders is *caveat emptor*.

Scallywags aside, the leading five groups represent the growing trend of consolidation dictated not only by a static gold price, but by the needs for greater efficiency and more sophisticated exploration techniques to unveil the next generation of mines.

The largest producer until 1993 has been Western Mining Corporation (WMC), the diversified mining group based in Melbourne, whose activities span gold, nickel, aluminium, copper, uranium, phosphate

4 Australian Stock Exchange, *Gold Producers' Handbook 1993*, Sydney.
5 *Gold Gazette Annual 1993*, Resource Information Unit, Subiaco, Perth, WA.

and petroleum. On the gold front, WMC is primarily involved in Australia, although it also has interests in North America and Brazil (and in Fiji until 1992). The heartland of its gold mining is around Kambalda, 50 miles to the south of Kalgoorlie, where it got its first big break in nickel in 1966 and moved on to find an abundance of gold around Lake Lefroy. It had developed a clutch of open pits nearby, initially focusing on Defiance, Orchin and Victory (where operations are now underground), then shifting to Junction as the main provider to its centralized milling operations at St Ives (WMC gives only overall output figures for what it calls St Ives Gold Mines). The whole complex ticks up over 200,000 ounces (6.2 tonnes) a year. Junction itself, which began as an open pit, but is also shifting to underground working, is estimated to have half of all the Kambalda underground reserves with a respectable grade of 4.7 g/t which ought to keep it going comfortably beyond 2000. Drilling rigs are also busy proving up other neighbouring orebodies at East Playa, West Orchin, Thunderer and Sirius. WMC's other mainstay is another stable of open pits further north in the Murchison gold field at Mt Magnet, which also turns in close to 200,000 ounces annually. This, too, is a moveable feast with operations shifting to new pits as older ones become exhausted; WMC is also starting to go underground on two orebodies at Mars and Hill 50 (a famous old underground mine dating from 1934 that kept working even in the tough days of the 1960s). Underground mining is also the way ahead at WMC's Leinster operations north of Kalgoorlie, where a group of open pits that had been yielding around 100,000 ounces a year is exhausted and the future is with the underground Redeemer mine. WMC rounds up its Western Australia mines, which accounted for 86 per cent of group output in 1992, with Lancefield and Central Norseman Gold, where again mining is increasingly underground. This reflects the Australian trend; only 13 per cent of gold output was from underground operations in 1992, but it is forecast to be 25 per cent by 1995. Outside Western Australia, WMC's gold activities are vanishing. It closed the Goodall open pit in the Northern Territory and sold its stake in the Stawell mine in Victoria, leaving only a trickle of by-product gold from its joint venture in the copper–gold–uranium Olympic Dam in South Australia.

This left it vulnerable to be overtaken as leading producer by Newcrest Mining, which controls seven mines, six in Western Australia and one in New South Wales, worth just over 700,000 (21.8 tonnes) ounces a year. Newcrest was born in 1990 through the takeover of BHP Gold by Newmont Australia (originally a subsidiary of Newmont Mining in the United States but now almost entirely divorced). Newcrest's

strongest card is the well-established Telfer mine, the most northerly
major operation in Western Australia, that has been going strong
since 1977, yielding over 3 million ounces (almost 100 tonnes) by
1993. Telfer began as an open pit, but in tune with the times, has been
going underground since 1990. The grade was a respectable 4.91 g/t
(0.16 oz/t) for 11.8 tonnes (380,000 ounces) in 1992, making it Australia's
biggest producer after the Super Pit. Telfer may not be a mega-
mine, but it slightly belies Ross Louthean's comment that Australia
has no world-class operations; almost 12 tonnes a year after a sixteen-
year life means Telfer is no poor relation. Newcrest also enjoys a 20
per cent stake in Boddington (which it inherited with BHP Gold),
the low-grade (1.55 g/t) open pit southeast of Perth which was Australia's
biggest producer for a while in the early 1990s, notching up well
over 400,000 ounces (12.4 tonnes) a year. Although output has
since slipped, Boddington is gaining a fresh lease of life from
underground operations to tap rich veins grading as much as 22 g/t (0.7
oz/t). Going underground is also boosting output at New Celebration
(Newcrest 80 per cent) just south of Kalgoorlie, which should keep
the mine at 150,000 ounces annually for the rest of the century; and it's
the same story at Ora Banda a little further north, where output is
also helped by neighbouring small open pits. Newcrest's stable
is completed by Parkes, a string of small operations not far from
Bathurst, New South Wales, the site of the original Australian gold
rush in 1851. Robert de Crespigny's Poseidon Gold is, of course, hard
on Newcrest's heels in the championship stakes for the mid-1990s. The
ultimate winner will depend not just on the success of underground
schemes, but on new takeovers in the constant shuffle of good and
bad properties.

Meanwhile, keep an eye on Dominion Mining, the Perth based
group that only poured its first ounce of gold in 1987, but has five
gold mines under its belt (four in Western Australia, one in the
Northern Territory) producing comfortably over 400,000 ounces (12.4
tonnes) annually. All started as open pits, but will make the move
underground. Three of Dominion's operations, each yielding just over
100,000 ounces, are typical of the dispersed nature of Australian open
pits. Meekatharra in the Murchison field of Western Australia, for
example, embraces no less than fourteen pits with an average grade of
only 2 g/t. Mt Morgans, north of Kalgoorlie, is a scattering of five
pits over an area of 20 square kilometres, with the largest, Westralia,
already 1.2 kms long and 120 metres deep. While Cosmo Howley, up in
the Northern Territory just south of Darwin, is a chain of six pits.
Dominion's two smaller operations at Labouchere and Bannockburn

back in Western Australia, are also built around satellite pits, and are getting the group for the first time into underground operations.

Dominion hedges all its production. 'Hedging', says managing director Peter Walker, 'is a natural part of our business. Each time we look at a new pit we evaluate it by using the spot price plus an escalator, which is the contango, and if we decide to go ahead we'll lock that in.' The rewards are there; for its financial year 1991/2 Dominion sold all gold produced against forward sales for an average price of A$598 when the average Australian dollar price was only $457. Despite lower contango, Dominion has been pushing its forward sales out four or five years to secure a reasonable delivered price. Backed by that insurance it has actually increased exploration budgets, scouting around its existing mines and probing for virgin discoveries.

Australia's gold renaissance also owes much to Placer Pacific, created in 1986 as the spin-off of Canada's Placer Dome group, which still holds 75.7 per cent. Placer Pacific has been mining over 1 million ounces of gold annually; while 75 per cent of that comes from the Porgera and Misima mines in Papua New Guinea, the balance has been produced at its Kidston, Granny Smith and Big Bell mines in Australia. Kidston, which came onstream in 1985 and was then Australia's largest mine, was the first large low-grade epithermal mine to be developed in the region where the volcanic 'rim of fire' that girdles the South Pacific touches Australia. Kidston kicked off at 2 g/t, produced over 200,000 ounces (6.2 tonnes) annually and paid back its capital costs in less than one year. It was the first big new mine to ratchet up Australia's output. Although past its peak, with grades down to 1.4 g/t and tougher ore, it still ranks as the sixth largest mine and ought to survive the 1990s. Placer Pacific had a less happy encounter at Big Bell on the Murchison field in Western Australia, which it developed jointly with Australian Consolidated Minerals as an open pit to revive an old 1930s underground mine. Put bluntly, the orebody drove them crazy; not only was it erratic and unpredictable, but the surrounding waste material that had to be stripped was a real maverick, so hard that drills could scarcely penetrate it on occasions. Costs in 1990 soared to US$504 an ounce. Big Bell had inspired big hopes as a major producer; it has managed just over 100,000 ounces a year, but Placer Pacific had had enough. And in September 1992 it bowed out in favour of Poseidon Gold, leaving the aggressive newcomer, Robert de Crespigny, to sort things out. Placer has fared better at the Granny Smith mine northeast of Kalgoorlie, which it shares with Delta Gold (40 per cent), where output is a comfortable 150,000 ounces and fresh reserves are being unveiled nearby.

### The virgin deposits

Delta Gold itself has become a stockbroker's favourite as the Kanowna Belle mine, which it shares with Peko Gold, came onstream in 1993. Although Kanowna Belle is scarcely 20 kilometres from Kalgoorlie, the orebody was overlooked because there was no surface evidence and it was hidden beneath a 40-metre layer of clay from which any gold had leached out. Delta detected this concealed orebody in 1990 using geochemical techniques. Extensive drilling confirmed a shoot of ore 400 metres in length, and 80 metres thick that dips sharply to 600 metres; it contains at least 2.6 million ounces (80.8 tonnes) on a respectable grade of 5.33 g/t (0.17 oz/t), and will yield around 150,000 ounces (4.7 tonnes) a year, on cash costs of less than A$280. 'Kanowna Belle has given us an indication of what a virgin body can yield in spite of the flat gold price,' said stockbroker David Reed. 'Its discovery became the catalyst for a fresh focus on exploration to look for blind deposits, in places as obvious as Kanowna, which have been walked over by thousands of people with no hint of the riches lurking at depth.'[6]

Actually, proof of what can come from such fresh discoveries is already there in the Plutonic mine owned by Plutonic Resources in the remote northern tip of the Murchison gold field ('A long way from nowhere' ran a *Gold Gazette* headline). The deposit, which is 180 kilometres from the nearest town, Meekatharra, was first pinpointed in an overlooked greenstone belt in 1988 by Great Central Mines, but soon taken over by a young man named Ron Hawkes, then running an outfit called Pioneer Mineral Exploration. Hawkes circulated a memo to his board that he was 95 per cent sure of finding 250,000 ounces there, 60–70 per cent certain of 450,000 ounces and there was a 50 per cent chance of 2 million ounces within a 20-kilometre radius. The board backed him. Contracts for the mine and mill went out early in 1990, mining started in June 1990, the first gold was poured in August, by November Plutonic had produced 100,000 ounces, and by 9 January 1991 the entire A$49.7 million project debt had been repaid. In February 1993 Plutonic poured its 500,000th ounce, with reserves still at 2 million ounces. Along the way Pioneer Mineral changed its name to Plutonic Resources in which Malaysia Mining Corporation (MMC) from Kuala Lumpur shrewdly took a 30 per cent holding (MMC also has 45.5 per cent of Ashton Mining, which was initially in diamonds, but has moved more into gold in Australia and Indonesia). Such a success story made Plutonic Resources a blue chip stock in the early 1990s and even led to suggestions that its pit could end up as a rival to Kalgoorlie's Super Pit, spreading out to 2 kilometres long, 1.5 kilometres wide and up to 300 metres deep. Plutonic used some of the cash it

---

6 David Reed, *Sentiment and Outlook for Investing in Australian Gold Equities*, Australian Gold Conference, Kalgoorlie, March 1993.

generated to take over another small group, Forsayth NL, with five mines in Western Australia, lifting its overall production towards 400,000 ounces annually, which would enable it to overtake Homestake Gold as the fifth largest producer.

The catalogue of such newcomers, which provides a constant injection of fresh names in the shifting Australian gold scene, grows. In Western Australia alone, along with Plutonic and Kanowna Belle, there are Baxters, Bounty, Keringal (Placer Pacific's new find near Granny Smith), Yilgarn Star and, the latest favourite, Bronzewing. Bronzewing, found by Great Central Mines (which also initially identified Plutonic) north of Kalgoorlie in 1992, is another blind deposit covered by 30 metres of alluvium in an area trekked over for years. The initial grades were often spectacular; a central zone of 12 metres of 60 g/t (1.92 oz/t), 49 metres of 21.9 g/t, and more generally between 5 and 10 g/t. The word in Kalgoorlie (which must often be taken with a pinch of caution) is that Bronzewing is a major deposit suitable for both open-pit and underground mining. Elsewhere in Australia hopes are riding on Mt Todd and Callie in the Northern Territory. Callie, a high-grade deposit (10 g/t) in the lonely Tanami desert, is owned by North Flinders Mines which operates the Granites mine nearby. As luck would have it, for the ubiquitous Robert de Crespigny, his Poseidon Gold controls 49.9 per cent of North Flinders. Meanwhile, over in the interior of New South Wales, North Broken Hill Peko is proud of its detective work in finding a gold deposit with around 1.5 million ounces of gold at 1.5 g/t (0.048 oz/t) beneath the shallow portion of Lake Cowal. Despite the fact that the lake is on Australia's Natural Heritage list, North Broken Hill believes it can satisfy environmental concerns by building a barrier reef around the mining area, which will actually add to the nesting areas for migratory birds.

### Made-to-measure finance

The sustained momentum of the gold renaissance in Australia is due in no small measure to the back-up that mining companies, large and small, receive from the bullion banks. The sheer speed with which the boom got going owed much to innovative financing. Three local groups, Mase-Westpac (the bullion arm of Westpac Bank), Macquarie Bank and Rothschilds Australia were the pioneers. American, British and Swiss banks soon joined in this made-to-measure financing.

The initial step was gold loans. The banks lent a prospective mine, say, 30,000 ounces at around 3 per cent interest, which was promptly sold spot to raise the money to finance the mine; the loan was then paid back out of the first two or three years' output. The loans caught on fast.

Rothschilds Australia went from a standing start to 300,000 ounces of gold loans in eighteen months. 'The gold loan was an Australian phenomenon,' says RTZ analyst Jessica Jacks, who monitored it closely. She calculated that 107 gold loans involving 225.4 tonnes (7.2 million ounces) were taken out in Australia between 1984 and 1991, with 79 of the loans in just three years, 1988 to 1990. This compared with 65 gold loans in Canada and 69 in the United States. Full support, incidentally, came from the Reserve Bank of Australia, the central bank, which lent gold to the bullion banks to facilitate many of the loans. As another mining analyst summed it up, 'The gold loan was the locomotive of Australia's gold-mining resurgence.'

The banks then took the mining companies by the hand and, if they so wished, handled all arrangements for the hedging, refining and marketing of the gold. The alliances even went so far as 'off-the-shelf' mine packages for small companies, providing them with milling and carbon-in-leach recovery plants. The construction engineering group Minproc (Mining and Engineering Service) Pty could be called in by the banks to provide turnkey plants. Such teamwork meant that Minproc was responsible for the design and construction of more gold processing plants in the 1980s than any other company worldwide.

The refinery scene itself has been revitalized. The Perth Mint, now a part of Gold Corporation which also markets the nugget bullion coins, has a smart new refinery. The Golden West refinery, also set in Perth, has secured its London 'good delivery' status. And with Johnson Matthey refineries in Melbourne and Sydney, Australia has the capacity to handle not only its own output, but compete for Papua New Guinea and other Pacific Rim business.

Building on their home-grown experience, Minproc and the banks have exported their innovative hand-holding. Minproc has offices in most leading gold-producing countries, including Chile, Ghana, Indonesia, Kazakhstan and the United States. And Denver, the capital of US gold mining, has local offices of Mase-Westpac, Macquarie and Rothschilds offering to North American miners the all-round services they pioneered in Australia.

### Natural hedgers

For the gold market at large, it is the hedging programmes devised for the Australian mines that have had most impact. First, it was the gold loans providing 'accelerated supply', then as the mines got up and running so the hedging programmes built up, using forwards, spot deferred and options. And it could sometimes have a twin impact because the mines took advantage of any rally not just in the US dollar price, but any surge in Australian dollar terms too. And unlike major South African and North American producers, there is little debate for and against hedging; in Australia, with few exceptions, everyone hedges to the hilt. 'Compared to the North American industry, Australian companies not only have a greater proportion of their production hedged', observes Toronto analyst Ted Reeve, who produces a regular review of global hedging, 'but also hedging extends further into the future'. Reeve identified about 314 tonnes of hedged production at the end of 1992, which then represented an average of 14 months' production of the producers surveyed.

This is a natural response to a business that is still seen as somewhat transitory, flourishing on modest open pits with a short life and no guarantee that it will be profitable to extend them by going underground. Among fifty major gold producers listed by the *1993 Gold Producers' Handbook*, only sixteen had no declared hedging position. Some hedge virtually every last ounce. Sons of Gwalia, for example, produced 101,112 ounces in its financial year 1991/2, but had 405,000 ounces sold forward – equivalent to four years' production. While Aztec Mining, with only 75,000 ounces production from its new 'grassroots' Bounty mine, reported forward sales of 460,000 ounces, over six years' output. 'We find the banks are now comfortable to go out 5–6 years,' the managing director of a leading producer told me. 'In fact, they are all jostling each other to give us a better price. We're hedging with 12 dealers, because at any given moment one or other will be better tailored to our needs.'

Australian hedging has often been accused of killing rallies in the gold price. While the miners and their guiding-light banks have certainly taken advantage of several rallies, when the combination of a strong US dollar price was made to look even better in weaker Australian dollars, once the hedging programmes are up and running the net change from year to year is often very little. However, as interest rates and thus the contango came down in 1991/2, many Australian miners sought refuge in selling further out. 'Australian companies, in an effort to maintain high average gold prices, have been going to long dated forward contracts giving them several years of contangos,' noted analyst Ted Reeve.

Such tactics are undoubtedly keeping many mines alive, while they wait for something to turn up in the gold price. They provide, too, one reason why the Australian industry has maintained a high level of output, despite the introduction for the first time of corporation tax of 39 per cent on gold-mining profits from January 1991. The threat of that tax was opposed in a hard fought campaign by the gold miners, who sought to dig out every last ounce in 1990, prior to its introduction (and got a record 243 tonnes; 7.8 million ounces), while crying that taxation within a year or two would cut output to a mere 150 tonnes. One analyst who ventured to suggest that, actually, output might hold up rather well, was castigated in the worst terms by the managing director of one of the largest producers. But the analyst was right; output scarcely flagged, bouncing along the 230 to 240 tonnes level. The Australian Bureau of Agricultural and Resource Economics (ABARE) is even bullish enough to suggest that after pause for breath in the mid-1990s, the new mines now being discovered will help lift output towards 295 tonnes in 1997–8.[7] Some miners are sceptical, arguing that Western Australia alone could lose 30 tonnes a year as older open pits are depleted, while the trend to underground mining will inevitably cut throughput (although grades will be higher).

### The Mabo dilemma

The challenge facing the industry, however, is not just the shift to trickier underground sulphide ores, nor taxation, nor even the gold price, but the environment lobby. The test case is Coronation Hill, a proposed new mine on the South Alligator river in the Northern Territory 220 kilometres south of Darwin, from which Newcrest and Plutonic Resources hoped to get 70,000 ounces a year. The project got caught up in aboriginal religious objections about mining a sacred area and was banned by former Prime Minister Robert Hawke. Much bitterness was caused because the mining companies had been allowed to spend a great deal of money proving up the mine, only to have it blocked. Newcrest is appealing, but the outcome is uncertain. The debate was further clouded by an historic judgment by Australia's High Court in June 1992 in the case of an aboriginal, Eddie Mabo. The Court ruled that his aboriginal group owns a small offshore island between Australia and Papua New Guinea. The ruling implies that 'native title' may exist where ownership of lands in Australia has not been explicitly transferred to private hands. The Mabo judgment is historic because it means that Australia was not 'unoccupied' when European settlement began in the late eighteenth century, and will legitimize aboriginal claims that they were indigenous inhabitants who were dispossessed by the settlers. The implications are immense, not just for the mining industry, which prospects and mines on much land claimed by the aboriginals, but in many other areas (the aboriginals claim much of downtown Brisbane, the capital of Queensland). But it is the remoter areas of the Northern Territory and Western Australia, the heartland of mining, where the aboriginals have the largest claims. The new Mount Todd gold mine owned by Zapopan in the Northern Territory, initially

7 Tom Waring, *Outlook for Australian Gold Production*, ABARE paper, Australian Gold Conference, Kalgoorlie, March 1993.

facing environmental objections that it was close to the breeding grounds of the endangered Gouldian finch, had no sooner resolved that than it faced a 'Mabo' land claim from the nearby Jawoyn tribe. This, too, was settled, but the opening in April 1993 was delayed. Meanwhile, as the government sorts out the implications of Mabo, the mining industry fears to tread. 'The issue must be addressed with urgency,' said Dr Warren Atkinson of Western Australia's Chamber of Mines and Energy. 'The long-term maintenance and expansion . . . [of] the mining industry is in real jeopardy. Where land is granted to aboriginal people, the principle of Crown ownership of minerals should be preserved and reasonable terms and conditions of access put in place for exploration and mining.'[8]

The uncertainties created have started to worry bankers involved in mining finance. 'There is political risk in Australia now through government attitudes and environmental pressures,' a banker in Perth told me. 'Although our credit committees don't see it that way because Australia is "politically stable".' The ban on Coronation Hill, followed by the Mabo decision will encourage Australian miners to branch out increasingly overseas. Indeed, they are already heavily engaged in Papua New Guinea, Indonesia and New Zealand. Yet at home, there remains much to be done. For all the new hurdles, you have only to go to Perth and Kalgoorlie to experience a real spirit of enterprise that will keep Australia up in the forefront of gold production well into the twenty-first century. Gold got Australia going in the 1850s. It has now bounced back to revitalize many areas, especially in Western Australia and the Northern Territory. Some argue it will continue to be so for quite some time. 'Australia is still under-explored,' reflected Robin Widdup of J.B. Were. 'Large tracts of sand and soil-covered arid wilderness remain, largely untouched. Blind orebodies, deep deposits and remote areas of new geology thinly veiled with sand cover remain as treasures for the persistent.'

8 Warren Atkinson, 'Land rights for miners', *Australian Business*, March 1993.

**CHAPTER 10**

# The Pacific Rim:
# The Epithermal Challenge

A century ago South Africa presented a new challenge – deep reefs that could be mined only by mining houses calling upon large capital investment. Today, there is a new challenge, not in a single country, but through a broad arc of volcanic rocks swinging across the Pacific from Chile, through Fiji, New Zealand, the Solomon Islands, Papua New Guinea, and touching northeast Australia before continuing to Indonesia and then turning north through the Philippines to eastern China and Japan. This crescent is known as the 'rim of fire' and contains scores of epithermal gold deposits. 'Epithermal' means 'close to heat' and the orebodies are found on the surface near, or even inside, ancient vents and volcanoes. The gold has become concentrated as mineral-rich fluids pass through the heated rocks of a volcanic system, then, when the mineralization cools on the surface, it forms very rich gold deposits; often a gold cap sitting on top of a volcano. Although the cap will weather, spreading the gold over a larger area, grades are often spectacular. The Hishikari mine in Japan, operated by Sumitomo Metal Mining, has some zones of 150 g/t (4.8 oz/t) and regularly turns in 68 g/t (2.18 oz/t) for its entire annual output of around 7 tonnes (210,000 ounces), making it the world's highest-grade large mine. Stiff rivalry has come from Porgera in Papua New Guinea, which did 38 tonnes of 64.5 g/t (2.06 oz/t) in its first full year.

Epithermal gold mines are not entirely new. The Emperor mine on Fiji, a typical epithermal, has been worked since 1935. Many epithermals are actually huge porphyry copper deposits, with gold often as a cap

## PAPUA NEW GUINEA: GOLD FIELDS

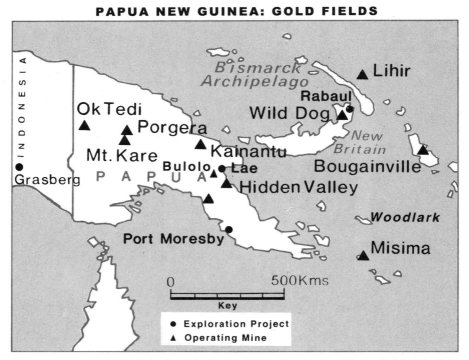

sitting on top or mingled with the copper. Bougainville and Ok Tedi in
Papua New Guinea, Grasberg in Indonesia, Dizon and Masbate in the
Philippines, have all been copper–gold operations, with the gold essentially
as a handsome by-product. Already no less than fourteen of the world's
top twenty mines outside South Africa, the United States, Canada and
Australia are located on the 'rim of fire'. Yet the rim remains the real
growth area in the years ahead, especially in Papua New Guinea,
Indonesia and the Philippines, where lack of infrastructure, tropical
climates and political uncertainty have slowed development, while
technical hazards in extracting gold from tricky refractory ores have also
made miners proceed with caution.

### Papua New Guinea: a volatile cocktail
Gold mining in Papua New Guinea has acquired a volatile image. It is
not just the local guerillas who forced the mothballing of the Bougainville
copper–gold mine in 1990, or the armed gangs of rival landowners that
prompted Australia's CRA mining group to abandon plans to produce
gold on Mount Kare in 1993. The mining itself is harsh and uncomfortable
in rugged terrain. 'Hot, wet, mosquitos, malaria', snapped a geologist
back from the hinterland. The proposed Lihir Island gold mine is inside

the crater of a collapsed volcano, with much of its ore simmering at over 100°C, so that it will have to be cooled in advance by injecting sea water. Tempers have also become heated by the PNG government suddenly deciding to up its stake in the highly successful Porgera mine. 'We were reluctant to cede a significant part of the profitable investment after having carried the risk, the exploration and the work,' sniffed one mining executive. Even a presentation on the future of gold mining in PNG at an Australian Gold Conference turned into a hostile battleground as the speaker accused Australia's mining press of being 'ill-informed and unprofessional', so 'isolated they have become inward-looking almost to the point of being in-bred'. Whereupon one editor jumped up to denounce the PNG spokesman as, among other things, 'a rat bag'.

At least everyone agrees on one thing: there is an awful lot of gold to be had. Papua New Guinea's output from only three mines and a little alluvial digging was just over 70 tonnes (2.25 million ounces) in 1992; the potential for the later 1990s is 100 tonnes. Moreover, the mines are world-class in size and longevity (in real contrast to most mines in neighbouring Australia).

Although Papua New Guinea discoveries have attracted much recent attention, there is a long track record of gold production. Gold was first reported near Port Moresby, the capital, in 1873 and thereafter alluvial mining, including several large dredge operations, produced at least 125 tonnes (4 million ounces) over the next hundred years. And in 1928 a small Canadian mining group, Placer Development from Vancouver, signed up extensive alluvial leases along the Bulolo river; between 1932 and 1938 five Placer dredges produced 683,217 ounces. This began a sixty-year association with Papua New Guinea, that has matured through the present Placer Pacific in which Placer Dome (the grown-up Canadian parent) holds 75.7 per cent. Today Placer Pacific has 25 per cent of the giant mine at Porgera, and 80 per cent of the Misima open pit.

The right perspective is essential in grasping the potential and the problems of gold mining in Papua New Guinea. The nation, which has been independent from Australia since 1975, is a mix of many culturally diverse people, living not just on the main island of New Guinea (which is split between PNG and Indonesia), but on islands out across the South Pacific almost as far as the Solomon Islands. So the inhabitants of Bougainville, Misima and Lihir Islands really have little in common with the tribes of the interior of New Guinea, who only relatively recently have come into contact with westerners, initially missionaries, with miners often not far behind. 'Papua New Guinea has all the complexity and interlocking issues of a country moving from the distant past into the modern world at break-neck speed,' said Placer Pacific's chairman, Alfred Paton. One thing the inhabitants do all have in common is the belief that land is part of a man and cannot be given away. 'Land and its ownership is entrenched in the cultures of the PNG people,' added Paton. 'This is fundamental and the alienation of the re-use of land releases strong emotions which, if not properly handled, have the potential for substantial conflict.'[1]

Conflict has indeed brewed up as mining has become one of the principal ways of opening up both the mainland and the islands. Often it is the mining companies, rather than the government, that are seen putting in the basic infrastructure of the country, from roads and airstrips, to power and water supplies. Local landowners and provincial governments want their share of the mining cake. And while the national government has always reserved the right to take up to 30 per cent of the equity in any projects requiring international investment, it has not always done so initially, thus being accused of changing the state of play once a mine is up and running, as in the instance of Porgera, where it started with 10 per cent, later demanded 30 per cent, but compromised on 25 per cent. One thing is clear. 'The government will not be pushed around,' declared Robert Needham, managing director of Mineral Resources Development Company, through which the PNG government makes its mining investments. 'And expects mutual respect. PNG is a young country and problems . . . [often] go back a long time.'

The case in point is the copper-gold mine that CRA opened on Bougainville Island in 1972, which successfully produced around 15 tonnes (500,000 ounces) of gold annually until 1989 when it came under sustained attack from local rebels who wanted the island to secede from Papua New Guinea. The rebels took to sitting in the dense jungle in the hills above the mine, constantly sniping at the workforce. Eventually, in May 1990, CRA, as the main shareholder, along with the PNG government, which had 20 per cent, decided it had had enough. The mine was mothballed, initially for three months, while a political solution was sought; three years on there was no sign of it reopening. The Ok Tedi mine at Mount Fubilan in western PNG, close to the border with Indonesia, has also had its share of troubles, not just with political friction, but huge mudslides and other natural disasters of the tropical rain forest. Ok Tedi, operated by Broken Hill Proprietary (BHP), with Amoco and the PNG government as the other main shareholders, is essentially a copper mine with a useful gold 'cap' that has yielded over 100 tonnes since the mine opened in 1984.

The new era for gold mining in PNG, however, really began when Misima opened in 1989. This is an open-pit operation at Mount Sisa on

1 Alfred Paton, 'Papua New Guinea – Future Directions', Australian Gold Conference, Perth, 1992.

a pint-sized island 190 kilometres west of the PNG mainland, in which Placer Pacific has an 80 per cent interest, with the balance shared with the PNG government. Although low grade, averaging around 1.8 g/t for its first few years, the deposit, which angles down through the mountain like a rich chocolate filling in a cake, contains at least 60 tonnes. Output rose steadily each year to hit 11.6 tonnes in 1992, rating it the fifth largest mine in the 'rest of the world' league outside South Africa, the United States, Canada and Australia.

Number one in this league, with no rival in sight, is Porgera at Mount Waruwari in Enga province in the western highlands of mainland PNG. The promise of Porgera was first detected as long ago as 1938 when alluvial gold was found in the area; Placer Development and other mining groups began serious exploration in the 1960s, but it was not until 1982 that a major high-grade zone was found by burrowing into the very heart of Mount Waruwari. Even then, it was not until September 1990 that the political and practical hurdles of putting a major mine in place were overcome and the first gold was poured. It was worth waiting for. The gold zone inside Mount Waruwari, which is being tapped by an open pit on top and underground mine below, demonstrates what happens in an epithermal deposit where gold has boiled up from the centre of the earth and then cools inside the walls of a volcano on the surface. Porgera kicked off with a grade of 64.5 g/t (2.06 oz/t) in its first year; compare that with an average grade of just over 5 g/t in South Africa or 2.8 g/t at Kalgoorlie's Super Pit. In the first full year of operation, 1991, Porgera delivered just under 38 tonnes (1.2 million ounces) and then really got into its stride the next year with 46.2 tonnes (1.5 million ounces), making it the world's sixth largest mine; only Freegold, Vaal Reefs and Driefontein in South Africa (and they are basically amalgamated mines), Newmont's Carlin operation in the United States and Muruntau in Uzbekistan, did better. The cash cost at Porgera, by the way, was a mere A$126 (US$98), with total costs at A$248 (US$172).

The original investors in Porgera were Placer Pacific, Renison Goldfields and Highlands Gold (the PNG based arm of MIM Holdings, the Australian resources group) each with a 30 per cent share, plus the PNG government with 10 per cent. However, after elections in 1992 the new Prime Minister, Paias Wingti, announced he wanted to increase the stake to 30 per cent. As the shares of the main partners took a nose-dive and there were many mutterings about driving investors away, a compromise was reached; all four partners now have 25 per cent.

The pitch for Porgera shares was soon followed by the PNG government's plans to increase its stake in Lihir, the volcanic island of gold out in the Pacific, 600 kilometres from the mainland. Lihir has been on the horizon for some time; this volcano is estimated to contain at least 1,300 tonnes (42 million ounces) of gold which would take thirty years to mine. Although the volcano is close to a deep-water harbour, making transport easier, the orebody is not just scalding, but complex. (For the technical, it consists of 0.01 micron particles of gold embedded in pyrite which is associated with arsenic, selenium, copper and nickel.)[2] Such tricky refractory ore has to be roasted or pressure-oxidized in autoclaves to free up the gold. This has given the partners pause on speedy development (as has the poor gold price). The main participant has been the British mining group RTZ Corporation (which got it when it took over BHP Gold) at 80 per cent, with Niugini Mining (in which the US group Battle Mountain has a 55 per cent holding) at 20 per cent. The risks at Lihir, however, have made RTZ proceed with caution and look for other partners. They were not queuing up. Canada's LAC Minerals pondered and said 'no thanks'. So the PNG government stepped in, asking for 30 per cent, then upped the bid to 50 per cent on the grounds that it did not want the project delayed, unless other partners were forthcoming. With luck, Lihir could start up by 1996, after a ten-year gestation, initially adding 20 tonnes a year to PNG's output, and later 40 tonnes (1.3 million ounces).

Other projects are ticking over too. Highlands Gold has a modest prospect at Woodlark Island and Placer Pacific is prospecting in the aptly named Hidden Valley. CRA has been exploring around Mount Kare, which has long been a successful alluvial area, but called a halt when its staff were threatened by armed landowners. The potential for conflict between local diggers, of whom there are at least 10,000 in PNG, and mining companies is considerable. Often there are very rich alluvial pickings to be had; around Mount Kare, so the stories go, you can often pull up handfuls of grass and find particles of gold clinging to the roots. 'You go up in a helicopter and see these guys almost hanging onto cliffs,' recalled one mining executive. 'They get wonderful nuggets.'

If the land disputes can be solved, if the government can offer mines security and ensure a framework in which they know their investment is safe, then those nuggets point to the fact that exploration in PNG has hardly started. As Norm Fussell, the chief executive of MIM, which controls Highlands Gold, stressed, much of PNG is barely explored. 'The geology is highly prospective,' he said, 'and indicative of much more to follow.' The prospect for the twenty-first century is that Papua New Guinea will be a big player. And for a country of scarcely 4 million people, gold could do for it what oil has done for such places as Brunei and the Gulf States.

---

2 *Mining Journal*, International Gold Mining Newsletter, London, February 1989.

### Indonesia: the decade of take-off

By one of those accidents of colonial history the island of New Guinea has been sliced neatly down the middle; to the east of this artificial boundary is Papua New Guinea, to the west the Indonesian province of Irian Jaya. Gold has no respect for such political borders and turns up in abundance on both sides. From the Porgera mine in Papua New Guinea it is but a short flight along the rugged mountains that form the backbone of the island to reach Ertsberg and Grasberg, twin peaks in Indonesia that host what Milt Ward, the president of Freeport McMoran, the US mining group, likes to call 'the greatest orebody in the world'. He has reason to be optimistic. By the late 1990s it will be producing 1 billion pounds of copper annually, with the pleasing bonus of 45 tonnes (1.45 million ounces) of gold and 100 tonnes (3.2 million ounces) of silver as by-products. Mr Ward even argues this is just the beginning; Freeport has a contract for up to fifty years to look around the neighbourhood. He believes he may find a dozen mines.

So a recent Indonesian mining conference in Jakarta had the justifiable theme of 'The decade of take-off'. Not that anyone is really surprised. Gold has been mined in Indonesia for over a thousand years. And under Dutch colonial rule in the late nineteenth and early twentieth century, there were small mines scattered through the ribbon of islands that make up Indonesia from Sumatra, through Java, Kalimantan (Borneo) and Sulawesi to the Lesser Sundra Islands. A serious dimension, however, only came into prospect in the 1980s with the gold-mining boom. International companies, especially from Australia, fell over themselves to get prospecting licences; by 1987 over 100 'contracts of work' had been issued and nearly $80 million was spent on exploration in 1988 alone. An Australian entrepreneur in Perth told me at the time he expected Indonesia to overtake South Africa as the world's largest producer. Then the gold price faded and with it many hopes; small companies packed their bags and went home.

The persistent professionals stayed. The proof of it is the Kelian mine, a classic epithermal, which came into production early in 1992 and in that same year jumped to number four position in the 'rest of the world' league with 14.5 tonnes (467,000 ounces). The mine, virtually astride the equator in the foothills of the mountains of central Kalimantan, is operated by Kelian Equatorial Mining in which Australia's CRA is the major shareholder along with the Indonesian government. Its location typifies the difficulties of access to many epithermal deposits. People fly in by helicopter from the oil town of Balikpapan 210 kilometres away, but all heavy supplies and equipment must come by sea from Singapore to the port of Samarinda, then by barge for 450 kilometres up the river

Mahakam and finally on a newly constructed road through thick tropical forest to the mine. Kelian is an open-pit operation consisting of two main orebodies within a large 'envelope' of low-grade gold. Although the average grade is 1.9 g/t, there are higher-grade pockets of over 3 g/t. The ore, in common with most deposits in Indonesia, is also rich in silver, balancing out at 50 per cent gold, 50 per cent silver. The mine got off to such a fast start because of a handy cap of oxide ore covering the main sulphide deposit from which the gold is trickier to extract. Once that is reached, output will settle back to a more modest 8 to 9 tonnes annually for the rest of the century.

Kelian is not the only primary gold mine in action in Indonesia. Lebong Tandai, an old Dutch mine in southwest Sumatra, was reopened by Billiton (the mining arm of Royal Dutch Shell), which also has a gold/silver mine at Lerokis on Wetar Island, just north of Timor. And several dredging operations have been initiated, with mixed success, on Kalimantan, where there is also extensive informal alluvial digging. The government's mining department, Aneka Tambang, is also bringing in the Gunung Pongkor epithermal mine near Bogor in west Java, a completely new discovery not known to earlier generations of miners, that is a very high-grade mix of gold and silver (17 g/t gold; 162 g/t silver). Ashton Mining (from Australia) starts another gold/silver mine at Mount Muro in central Kalimantan in 1994 at 4.7 tonnes annually for five years. All the doré from these operations, incidentally, is refined in Jakarta at Aneka Tambang's own Logam Mulia refinery, which transforms the gold into 999.9 kilo bars for export (the gold is not sold locally into Indonesia's own large domestic market because of tax complications).

All this, however, is modest when set against Freeport McMoran's growth in the mountains of Irian Jaya. Freeport initially went to Indonesia in 1967 in search of copper and soon found a huge remote deposit surrounded by glaciers at Ertsberg. It set up camp at 2,500 metres and built the longest single-span aerial tramway in the world to link it to the mine. It was getting copper by 1972, along with a modest couple of tonnes of gold as by-product each year. Twenty years on Ertsberg mountain has become a huge pit; much of the copper has been mined out, although operations are moving underground to obtain the rest. The action, however, is swinging to Grasberg mountain 3 kilometres away with its rich brew of copper, gold and silver that was detected using the latest aerial magnetic techniques. 'Grasberg – impressive, incredible, stupendous', said Goldman Sachs' analyst Amy Gassman, just back from a visit. 'You fly up by helicopter in fifteen minutes from tropical jungle to glaciers. Grasberg is on top of the world.' Already this complex is the third largest gold producer in the 'rest of the world' league, after PNG's Porgera and Ghana's Ashanti. Output is 20 tonnes (640,000 ounces) and rising. By the late 1990s gold production is scheduled at 45 tonnes a year, probably propelling the mine into the number one position. Already the proven gold reserves are 900 tonnes. That may only be the first chapter of the story. Freeport has a firm lease for thirty years, with potential extensions for another twenty, to explore a terrain of nearly 30,000 square kilometres. Already it has a new prospect named Big Gossen, just down the road from Grasberg, which is revealing some interesting copper and gold grades. 'They now know the "signatures" of what they are looking for,' said Amy Gassman, 'but it may be tomorrow or in seven years or twenty years that they find it.'

Mining is always a long-term business. Indonesia is on the threshold. Already it has the prospect of 50–60 tonnes a year and going into the twenty-first century perhaps rather more. 'Indonesia remains relatively unexplored compared with, say, Australia,' remarked Bill Davis of Kelian, 'and continues to be one of the most prospective areas of south-east Asia. Irian Jaya [has] the most potential.'[3] As a footnote in history, it is intriguing to imagine what might have happened without that colonial carve-up; if the island of New Guinea had remained a single nation, it would already be one of the world's largest gold producers.

## Philippines: promise unfulfilled

Geologically the Philippines has everything going for it; epithermal gold deposits, porphyry copper-gold deposits, and rich pickings for ordinary diggers on extensive alluvial areas. Regular gold mining dates back to 1907 and in the early 1970s the Philippines rated as the western world's sixth largest producer, ahead even of Australia. Well-established mining companies like Benguet Consolidated, Atlas Consolidated, Philex Mining and Lapanto Consolidated were experienced in underground mining of primary gold and in copper-gold concentrates (over half the gold was by-product). Yet the gold-mining boom of the 1980s virtually passed them by (although thousands of alluvial diggers did well, especially around Mount Diwata in southern Mindanao). In the latter years of President Marcos and then the uncertain times of President Corazon Aquino, the Philippines represented high political risk; no international mining company was going to make a serious investment there. And the earnest exploration which has proved up deposits in Papua New Guinea and Indonesia just has not taken place. As Joel Muyco, director of the Bureau of Mines, laments, 'Because we have not developed any new orebodies in the past decade, there is nothing to work on.'

As if investment famine was not enough, the industry also suffered severely from an earthquake and typhoon in 1990, followed by the

3 Bill Davis and T.M. van Leeuwen, 'Indonesia – Gold Production and Potential', Australian Gold Conference, Perth, 1992.

eruption of Mount Pinatubo the following year. Production actually slipped from a peak of 39.5 tonnes in 1987 to 27.2 tonnes in 1992. Even so, three Philippine mines rate in the top twenty 'rest of the world' league; Philex's Santo Tomas, just notching up 3 tonnes, Benguet's Dizon copper-gold mine that started in 1980 but was hard hit by the Mount Pinatubo explosions, and Atlas Consolidated's Masbate, the biggest single deposit being mined. Benguet remains the largest gold-mining group, however, with seven operations centred near the Philippines summer capital of Baguio, 200 kilometres north of Manila. They bring the group around 8 tonnes a year. Originally, Benguet mainly worked underground deposits in the area, but has now also developed a clutch of open pits, notably Grand Antamok, at 2.6 tonnes a year, while installing more efficient carbon-in-leach milling. Baguio region remains the centre of attraction, not just with Philex's Santo Tomas, but a potential newcomer Far East Gold Resources, a joint venture between Lepanto and Australia's CRA for an open pit producing over 7 tonnes a year.

The real test in the Philippines, however, will be a new mining code, which for the first time will permit foreign mining companies to have 100 per cent control of their operations at least for the first eighteen to twenty years, provided they invest at least $50 million. Previously they could hold only 40 per cent of any Philippine mine and few wanted to take all the risks for such small participation. Already a couple of Australian companies have signed up under the new deal, but there remains a long haul to pull the country back up as a serious contender in the gold stakes.

### New Zealand: Trying for a new record?

Gold was first discovered near Dunedin on the south island of New Zealand in 1861; the resulting gold rush turned up 15 tonnes a year for a while. Although more than 830 tonnes (27 million ounces) have since been produced, that annual record for the 1860s has yet to be beaten. It may be soon. Some large epithermal deposits on the north island look tempting to geologists and already things are stirring. The trouble is that the best bets are on the Coromandel Peninsula. 'This is both the playground of Aucklanders and home to many environmentalists due to its temperate climate, wonderful beaches and pristine beauty,' admits Miles Kennedy of Macraes Mining, which has wisely restricted itself to activities in less sensitive areas of the south island. Still there are now three hard rock mines on the go. Macraes itself has an open pit at Otago, south of Dunedin, which came onstream in 1990 and is producing about 3 tonnes a year at a grade of 1.85 g/t. It ranks twelfth in the 'rest of the world' table. Macraes is also exploring the extensive Reefton gold field on the west coast of the south island. Up on the contested Coromandel Peninsula, the Martha Hill mine, which was originally worked from 1879 to 1952, was reopened in 1988 by a consortium of Poseidon Gold from Australia (as manager), Amax Gold from Denver, Colorado, and Mineral Resources. The mine has 2.3 tonnes of gold annually, with an added silver dividend of nearly 12 tonnes. And a newcomer, Golden Cross, also on the north island and near Waihi, opened up in 1992 giving its joint owners Cyprus Minerals (80 per cent) and Todd Corporation an initial 3 tonnes of gold and 10 tonnes of silver. One thing all three mines have in common, after the trials of most Pacific Rim mines, is a nice location. 'None is more than 30 minutes drive to the beach,' reports Miles Kennedy, 'and at Macraes we are two hours from the snowfields.' No wonder they cannot beat the mining output of the 1860s; everyone is too busy swimming and skiing.

## A pattern of islands

The beach is also a feature of the gold miner's life in Fiji, at least according to a miner from those parts, who is a great raconteur of dinner parties by the ocean. Gold was discovered in Fiji in gravels on the Navua river in 1868, but serious mining did not begin until the Emperor Mines opened in the epithermal Tavua gold field on the largest island, Vitu Levu, in 1935. Today Emperor Mines has open-pit and underground operations centred on Vatukoula in the Tavua gold field. With an improving underground grade of 8.5 g/t and 1.9 g/t in the open pits, Emperor is still securing close to 4 tonnes annually after almost sixty years' mining (London stockbrokers James Capel call Emperor a 'Lazarus' stock, because it keeps coming back to life). Meanwhile, Placer Pacific is pressing on with exploration of a porphyry copper-gold prospect at Namosi and there is a chance of a small gold mine at Mount Kasi.

Placer Pacific is also scouting Vanuatu in the Coral Sea between Fiji and the Solomon Islands, where it senses the chance of Porgera-style gold or copper-gold deposits. Vanuatu, which fortuitously is a tax haven, has been a natural exploration target for some years as its little nest of islands (formerly the New Hebrides) lies directly in the arc from Papua New Guinea to Fiji. Over 100 exploration licences were granted in the late 1980s and several epithermal gold/silver deposits were located on Malekula and Espiritu Santo Islands, although no one has yet proved up a viable mine. An equal exploration flurry has been going on in the Solomon Islands, where the best bet is at Gold Ridge on Guadalcanal, which should produce a modest 1 tonne a year, while freeland diggers scour the nearby Chovohio river.[4]

4 This section draws on *Gold Potential of the South-west Pacific*, East-West Center, Honolulu, Hawaii 96848, 1991.

The time scale for development on these islands will be drawn out. The initial enthusiasm prompted by high gold prices has waned. The reluctance of island people to have their land, regarded as a common heritage, taken over by miners has been demonstrated in Papua New Guinea. Yet these volcanic outcrops scattered through the southwest Pacific represent another new frontier for gold that will gradually be expanded through the twenty-first century.

# CHAPTER 11

# The Commonwealth of Independent States: After the Fall

Russia was the world's largest gold producer before 1848 and the Soviet Union was the second largest for much of the twentieth century. Today, the Commonwealth of Independent States (CIS) that has replaced the disintegrated Soviet empire ranks fourth, while the Russian Federation alone rates fifth in the league. As the veil has gradually been lifted on the former Soviet Union, so one of the enigmas of the gold business has been resolved. The great debate for over half a century was about how much gold the Soviet Union produced. How much was consumed at home? How much was exported? And how large were the remaining reserves?

Fitting together the jigsaw puzzle was a nice pastime for western analysts, whether for mining companies or intelligence agencies. The Soviets were amused by that. In the early days of *glasnost* under Mikhail Gorbachev, I once asked Evgeni Ulyanov, the gold man at the Bank for Foreign Economic Affairs in Moscow, was it not time they came clean on the numbers? He laughed and replied, 'No, it would put people like you out of business.' When the statistics, albeit often slightly inconsistent ones, were finally revealed in 1991, it became apparent at once that we could have used a little more help from our friends. While the broad assessment of Soviet production and exports over the last generation has been largely correct (very precise numbers on exports could be obtained for many years), the catch was two-fold. Production had been slightly over-estimated, while domestic consumption, mainly in the military-industrial complex, had been under-estimated with the inevitable result that the Soviet Union's gold reserves were reckoned to be considerably higher than they were. The received wisdom was that Soviet reserves might be 1,500 to 2,500 tonnes; in the event, in 1988, as the Soviet Union entered its crisis period, they were only 850 tonnes (27.3 million ounces), according to the Ministry of Finance. In short, the emperor had few clothes.

Since then, not only have the reserves largely been swapped and sold, but production itself has slipped. Shortages of spare parts, raw materials and energy, declining infrastructure and the general turmoil, especially in Russia itself, have caused output in the entire CIS to decline from a peak of 285 tonnes (9.2 million ounces) in 1989 to under 240 tonnes (7.7 million ounces) in 1992. Meanwhile, the gold industry is being reorganized from a centrally planned structure to an uneasy mix of state, private and foreign enterprise. Despite the unsettled economic environment, no one doubts Russia, which produces nearly two-thirds of the gold, and the other CIS republics have great mineral wealth. 'I've seen some very attractive projects,' said a Canadian miner, just back in Toronto after a visit. 'They would be mines already here, but in Russia they will be a long time coming.' It will require economic and political stability, together with clarification of who really has the authority in granting mining rights, before western mining companies, whose capital and technology is needed, will invest. Add to that the Russians' natural pride, which makes them somewhat reluctant to accept foreign help. As Leyla Boulton of the *Financial Times* reported from Moscow, 'Another problem in opening the door to Russia's mineral wealth has been innate Russian reluctance to let go of rich resources to foreigners and a tendency to move the goal posts in the name of reform.'[1]

Such resistance to foreign investment is less evident in Uzbekistan and Kazakhstan, the other main gold-producing republics, which are still run on more centralized lines. Free enterprise hardly has a toe-hold and deals can be done directly with the government. Yet, in all three republics, there is an almost obsessive concern to hold on to newly mined gold rather than sell it for much needed foreign exchange. As a Russian banker told me, 'It is part of our national heritage'. When an IMF team visiting Alma Ata, the capital of Kazakhstan, asked about the gold reserve, no one would reveal it in an open meeting and it was finally whispered in the corridor outside. Kazakhstan and Uzbekistan stopped delivering their gold output to Moscow as the centre crumbled, and began to build their own reserves.

The result is that the former Soviet Union's influence on the gold market is less than it has been for a generation. Production and marketing is no longer centralized, but divided among the republics. Even the

---

1 Leyla Boulton, 'Delays on mining deals', *Financial Times*, 27 May 1993, Survey on Russia, p. X.

# THE COMMONWEALTH OF INDEPENDENT STATES: GOLD FIELDS

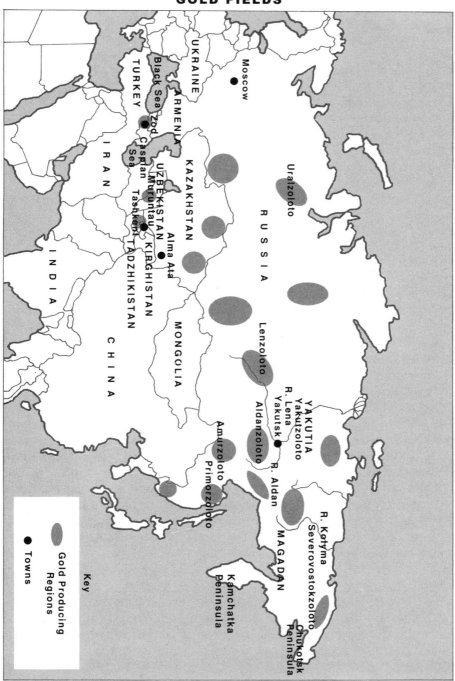

Moscow

UKRAINE

TURKEY

Black Sea

ARMENIA

Zod

Caspian Sea

IRAN

UZBEKISTAN

Muruntau

Tashkent

INDIA

KAZAKHSTAN

Alma Ata

KIRGHISTAN

TADZHIKISTAN

CHINA

MONGOLIA

RUSSIA

Uralzoloto

Lenzoloto

YAKUTIA

Yakutzoloto

R. Lena

Yakutsk

Aldanzoloto

R. Aldan

Amurzoloto

Primorzoloto

MAGADAN

R. Kolyma

Severovostokzoloto

Kamchatka Peninsula

Chukotsk Peninsula

Key

Gold Producing Regions

Towns

combined production is less than before. The Soviet reserves have been emasculated; while a few swaps from the old regime still remained in place as late as 1993, most of the historic stock has been sold. Russia itself admitted to reserves of only 240 tonnes in late 1991, which were slightly revised upwards to 320 tonnes (10.3 million ounces) early in 1993, reflecting some stockpiling of new production. Uzbekistan holds between 100 and 150 tonnes, which it is trying hard not to sell, and Kazakhstan has rather less. The overhanging threat to the market of Soviet reserves, perceived as the Empire began to fall apart, has vanished. Gone, too, is the Bank for Foreign Economic Affairs of the USSR, which not only marketed all production but was an active trader in the international gold market, often providing support for a weak gold price. The Bank adhered to that famous line of Lenin's that, although in the ultimate socialist society gold might be used only to cover the walls and floors of public lavatories, while capitalism survived the Soviet Union must conserve its gold. 'Sell it at the highest price, buy goods with it at the lowest price,' wrote Lenin; 'when living among wolves, howl like the wolves.'[2]

Its successor, Russia's own Bank for Foreign Economic Affairs, may be market-orientated but it has much less experience and clout. Indeed, one problem is that the team of aggressive and intelligent young gold traders who grew up in the Soviet Bank for Foreign Economic Affairs in the 1980s have all moved on to other banks or become 'consultants' as the spirit of private enterprise invaded Russia.

Yet the gold market's fascination with the former Soviet Union remains, or rather there is new business to be done, not just by western mining companies scouting investment potential, but by bullion banks and refiners. The planes to Tashkent in Uzbekistan and Alma Ata in Kazakhstan are crowded with bankers offering to refine and market the gold, which was once delivered direct to Moscow, where the only refineries in the CIS with London 'good delivery' status are located. Potential travellers, by the way, may like to know that the best route to both cities is via Istanbul, from where Turkish Airlines offers non-stop flights; a facility which is helping to make Turkey a more important regional gold market for all the Central Asian republics along the traditional 'Silk Road'.

### The way it was

Before considering the way ahead, however, a little history may be useful just to see how Soviet gold-mining evolved in the twentieth century (see Chapter 1 for the earlier origins). The driving force was Joseph Stalin, inspired by the writings of Bret Harte, the chronicler of

---

2 Lenin, *'The importance of gold now and after the complete victory of gold'*, Essay, 1921.

the American West. Stalin's own preoccupation was the stimulation of the economy in the far wastes of Siberia, where he feared Japan might try to establish a foothold. Through Bret Harte, Stalin became fascinated with the California gold rush and its influence in opening up the West. That was the answer. He told A. P. Serebrovsky, the head of Glavzoloto or Gold Trust, set up in 1927 to foster gold mining, 'This process must be applied to our outlying regions . . . at the beginning we will mine gold, then gradually change over to other minerals such as coal and iron.' Serebrovsky promptly set off under the guise of a professor from the Moscow School of Mines to study US gold mining and ended up recruiting an American mining engineer, John D. Littlepage, to mastermind a Russian gold rush. Littlepage worked in the Soviet Union from 1928 until 1937 supervising the creation of a fleet of ninety steam and electric dredges in the alluvial gold fields which account for the major part of production, and powerhouses, mechanical hoists, crushers and cyanide plants in lode mines. With Stalin's approval, prospectors who found new gold deposits were richly rewarded, while special stores well supplied with food, clothing and luxury goods were established on the gold fields – with all payment in gold. Stalin's purges also provided plenty of cheap labour for the new gold fields; political prisoners were sent to the gold mines, as well as the salt mines of Siberia. Soviet production surged ahead; by the mid-1930s it was 155 tonnes (5 million ounces) annually, pushing the Soviet Union back into second place in the world league. John Littlepage himself, in a book written on his return to the United States, suggested that the Soviet Union had the potential to beat South African output.[3]

That was never achieved. However, from the mid-1930s precise details of production ceased to be issued; the secrecy lasted almost sixty years. Yet there was no question that the Soviet Union was number two (except probably in 1940/1 when Canada and the United States achieved short-lasting peaks). Soviet reserves also benefited in 1937 when Stalin accepted around 500 tonnes of Spain's gold reserves as security for payment for arms and aircraft during the Spanish civil war and neglected to give it back.

Once secrecy was imposed, the guessing game of output and reserves was on. In fact, we know now that reserves were rather healthy in those days. The reserve in 1952 was a respectable 2,050 tonnes (almost 66 million ounces), according to Ministry of Finance figures issued in 1991, which meant the Soviet Union's stock was second only to that of the United States. Then the rot set in; the reserves have never looked so good since. Stalin died in 1953; his successor, Nikita Khruschev, being more liberal on imports, began to sell the gold. Over the next

3 J.D. Littlepage and D. Bess, *In Search of Soviet Gold*, Harcourt Brace, New York, 1938.

twelve years the Soviet Union sold at least 2,900 tonnes (93 million ounces) of gold through the London and Paris gold markets, including 1,244 tonnes between 1963 and 1965 alone. This seriously depleted the reserves, which were certainly under 1,000 tonnes by the end of 1965 and probably as low as 500–600 tonnes. In any event, the Soviet Union then disappeared from the gold market for six years and did not return with serious sales until 1972.

The more recent history of Soviet gold has to be seen in that context. The reserves had almost been wiped out; a major programme was begun to develop new mines, which began to bear fruit with the opening of the huge open-pit development at Muruntau in Uzbekistan, which poured its first bar on 25 July 1969. Throughout the next twenty years the industry grew to peak production of 285 tonnes (9.2 million ounces) in 1988. But the fragility of the economy, beset by bad harvests which meant that the nation could not feed itself, often led to large gold sales, occasionally of 400 tonnes in a single year. Thus, the reserve was never really rebuilt, even though gold was regarded strictly as a bottom line foreign exchange earner when the balance of payments was in deficit. The regular export earners were oil, natural gas and arms exports; gold was the last resort. But because sales were determined by bad harvests rather than the price of gold, they did not necessarily coincide with a high price. Although in a given year sales were well handled to maximize the price by selling into rallies, and often completed in advance of the news of a poor harvest, sales were low in 1980 when the price averaged over $600. I recall a European bullion banker telling me he had pleaded with Moscow to profit from the exceptional price; to no avail because the oil price was also high and the balance of payments secure.

### Russia's inheritance

While the export flow could be monitored quite precisely, the true state of the mining industry was harder to gauge; information on domestic demand was also vague. My own view had been that the internal requirements annually were 70–90 tonnes, most of it for use in electronics in military and space programmes. Statistics released in 1993 reveal, however, that even by 1977 the annual domestic allocation was sometimes as high as 110 tones, rising to a peak of 131 tonnes (4.2 million ounces) in 1990 (when much more jewellery was being made to try to satisfy public demand for consumer goods).[4] This gold may not all have been used, giving some grounds for stories that the military-industrial complex held considerable amounts of gold. Here is the key, however, to the low reserves. Domestic demand was taking up one-third or more of mine

4 Gary O'Callaghan, The structure and operation of the World Gold Market, IMF Occasional Paper No. 105, Washington D.C. 1993

output; the mines themselves were inefficient and under-capitalized and thus did not produce as much as western analysts calculated (reflecting, of course, the general picture of business and industry that has emerged in Eastern Europe and the Soviet Union as the barriers have come down).

The inheritance for Russia itself is a gold-mining industry that is widely dispersed, with scores of small co-operatives, *artels*, working alluvial deposits and relatively few large mines operating with obsolete equipment. Originally, Stalin had been correct to target Siberia. The output for the last sixty years has been focused primarily on placer deposits in Siberia, in an area embracing the Lena and Aldan rivers, on the Kolyma river in the province of Magadan, and on the Kamchatka and Chukotsk peninsulas which jut out in the Bering Sea opposite Alaska (the deposits naturally being very similar to those found in the American state). Large nuggets abound, sometimes weighing a kilo or more. A colleague of mine on a Siberian flight recently was offered 3 kilos of nuggets by a young man who chanced to sit beside him on the plane.

This is harsh, remote terrain. The placer deposits are often far from towns or paved roads and severe winters mean that work can go forward for only five or six months of each year. Permafrost makes the ground rock hard. Sometimes the top soil is stripped and the site left open for two years in an attempt to thaw the permafrost in lower layers, or holes are drilled into the permafrost and filled with heated water. At the most northerly gold field on the Karal'veyem river, huge boulders are dug out of the permafrost and crushed to recover the gold. Gigantic electric dredges wallow up the rivers of Siberia in summer, scooping up gold-bearing sands from depths of 50 metres. One monster on a tributary of the Lena river is almost 250 metres long, 40 metres high and weighs over 10,000 tonnes. A special road over 100 kilometres long was built to get this behemoth to the river.

Under the old Soviet regime the mining was presided over by Glavzoloto in Moscow, which directed fifteen regional *zolotos*. Thus, Uralzoloto looked after gold fields by the Ural mountains which have been mined for two centuries. The most important *zolotos*, however, were Lenzoloto on the upper reaches of the Lena river, Yakutzoloto in central Siberia near the junction of the Lena and Aldan rivers and Severovostokzoloto on the Magadan peninsula.

This basic framework remains, although it is becoming much looser. Glavzoloto has been renamed Almazzoloto, which is a voluntary organization to which the regional *zolotos* belong. They are asserting their independence. Lenzoloto has become a joint-stock company, taking on foreign investors, while managing the same deposits for which it was responsible as a state-controlled enterprise. Considerable friction with Moscow developed when it tried to do its own deals. The heart of the system, however, is the *artel*, or co-operative. Under the umbrella of the *zolotos*, well over half of Russia's production comes from more than 200 *artels*, which employ 80,000 people, with staffing varying from 30 to 1,000. Each *artel* manages its own affairs and pays its own workforce, although they may obtain supplies and equipment from central amalgamations. 'They are a tough, self-reliant and disciplined workforce,' reported Stewart Murray of Gold Fields Mineral Services, after a visit to the Siberian front. 'They work in harsh conditions, often on inferior deposits and with limited availability of equipment.'[5] Their extraction methods, he noted, were more akin to the California gold rush than the late twentieth century. '[They] use almost exclusively gravitational jigs, they use no mercury, though one [*artel*] operates a carbon-in-pulp plant.' The real problem facing the *artels* in the new Russia has been the price they receive for the gold. Under the old system the local *zoloto* never paid them such a high price as it did to gold mines. Although this has improved somewhat as the official price paid by the Russian state has been adjusted to take account of the international price and the falling rouble exchange rate, it does not always filter down to the *artel* level. Payment also may be delayed and it is not in hard currency. Although by law gold should still be sold to the Ministry of Finance's Committee on Precious Metals, an increasing amount has been sold outside the system, either for local hoarding or unofficial export. Unrefined gold is regularly turning up everywhere from Poland to Turkey and Dubai to be bartered for electrical and other consumer goods. Even in Beijing I heard of Russian gold coming south into China from Amurzoloto and Primorzoloto just over the border.

Output in the *artels*, however, has held up better than in Russia's mines, where chronic shortages and under-capitalization have led to falling output. The officially declared output in Russia for 1992 was 146 tonnes (4.7 million ounces), down from around 190 tonnes (6.1 million ounces) a few years earlier. The way ahead is for western investment, but that is not as easy as it first appeared. Consider the experience of a small Australian company, Star Technology Systems, which took a 31 per cent stake in the new joint-stock Lenzoloto, with the express intent of investing up to $250 million to develop Sukhoi Log (meaning Dry Gulch), perhaps the largest hard rock deposit in Russia. The State Geology Committee thought otherwise; although Lenzoloto owns the Sukhoi Log deposit, the Committee argued that a foreigner should not have access to such a find without it being put out to competitive tender

5 Dr Stewart Murray, *New Perspectives in Gold Production in the Former Soviet Union*, Financial Times World Gold Conference, Montreux, June 1992.

among home-bred Russian companies. At least one new Russian entrepreneur, Andrei Chuguyevsky, who has already tied up a deal on a huge Siberian copper deposit, has his eye on Sukhoi Log and does not want to be short-circuited by Lenzoloto's Australian alliance. While this is livening up the gold-mining scene, it is no encouragement to western mining companies. 'There is an enormous conflict between the bureaucracy at the centre and in the regions,' the chairman of a South African mining house remarked to me. 'Each has their vested interest, but who has the authority in granting the mining rights?' Until that is resolved, western investment may be on hold. Eventually, however, there is much to go for. As Stewart Murray observed after his Siberian foray, 'There has been a perception that the rich alluvial deposits . . . are running out, but I believe this is an over-simplification. There are plenty of unexploited alluvial deposits, but there is a desperate shortage of finance to find, develop and operate them'.[6]

### Uzbekistan banks on Muruntau

A hard day's drive southwest across the Kyzyl-Kum desert from Tashkent brings you to the town of Zarafshan (literally 'golden'), built to accommodate the 40,000 miners and their families who work one of the world's largest gold mines, Muruntau. Once the pride of the Soviet Union when it opened in 1969, today it is the pride of the republic of Uzbekistan, whose other main asset besides gold is cotton. Muruntau (meaning 'hilly place') produces around 55 tonnes (1.8 million ounces) annually, or close to a quarter of all output in the CIS which, along with a handful of *artels* and some by-product gold from nearby copper mines, ensures that Uzbekistan is easily the second most important republic in gold. Overall its annual output is about 70 tonnes.

Muruntau is a gold mine on a grand scale. The very shape is unique; it resembles a tree with branches spreading out near the surface and the trunk plunging deep into the earth (in that sense it is remarkably similar to the kimberlite pipes in which diamonds are found). One can almost visualize how, millions of years ago, the molten gold came boiling up a pipe and spread out to cool. Originally, three distinct orebodies were located, each several hundred metres thick, containing an estimated 1,000 tonnes of recoverable gold. The initial programme, spread over more than twenty years, was effectively to lop off the 'branches' of the tree. Already those excavations have created a huge pit 3.5 kilometres long, 2.5 kilometres wide and 300 metres deep, that often reminds western visitors of the Grand Canyon. The gold, scattered in tiny specks (only 0.001 millimetres in diameter) through the quartz veins of the Muruntau tree, is of exceptional purity, being up to 990 fine without any preliminary refining. In the early years the grade was reported to be 3 to 4 g/t (0.13 oz/t), but by the 1990s had declined to 2.6 g/t (0.08 oz/t).

Controversy long surrounded the output. Estimates made by Consolidated Gold Fields, the former London mining finance house, in the late 1970s by analysis of satellite information made available by NASA and studying technical journals, indicated production at 80 tonnes (2.6 million ounces) annually.[7] This was later contradicted by a Soviet mining consultant living in the United States who declared that Muruntau had a design capacity of 22 tonnes a year, but rarely managed 20 tonnes.[8] The truth, now ascertained by western visitors, is in between; Muruntau is producing between 52 and 57 tonnes annually. However, the mine is beset by practical and financial problems. The prime hazard as the open pit gets deeper is ventilation; temperatures may soar to 50 degrees C at the bottom in high summer. The 180-tonne capacity trucks that shift the ore out of the pit have air-conditioned cabs, but the temperature inside the cab is often 25 degrees C lower than outside, causing the drivers frequent colds and 'flu (they work only six-hour shifts). Since Muruntau is scheduled eventually to go down to 700 metres, the mine's managers talk of resolving this by moving back one whole wall of the pit to allow air to circulate more freely. However, this would require huge capital investment. Meanwhile, lack of spare parts, especially tyres, means that the fleet of 126 trucks is not fully utilized, while in the milling plant lack of parts and shortage of chemicals has resulted in 40 per cent of the units being idle part of the time. This scene led a western mining executive on a tour of inspection to observe that although Muruntau may once have been a 'robust' pit, 'I wouldn't take it if they gave it to me.'

The issue turns on modernization and fresh capital. Reserves at Muruntau remain extensive. Exploratory drilling has gone down to 4,000 metres, and two preliminary 2,000-metre shafts have been sunk at the side of the open pit. The plan is for Muruntau to go underground by 1997 to tap the 'trunk' of the tree. 'That must be a moveable feast,' said a banker, looking at financing. 'They've run out of capital to go underground.'

Salvation in the shorter term, however, undoubtedly comes from a deal struck between Newmont Mining from the United States and the Uzbekistan government, still run with a firm hand by President Islam Karimov, to heap-leach low-grade ore stockpiles at Muruntau, which are not worth putting through the mill. In a 50–50 deal with the government, Newmont has initially raised a $90 million loan with Barclays Bank in co-operation with the European Bank for

7 *Gold 1978*, Consolidated Gold Fields, London, pp. 207–9
8 V.V. Strishkov, 'The Muruntau gold complex', *Mining Magazine*, September 1986, pp. 207–9.

Reconstruction and Development. Newmont will import crushing equipment and then heap-leach the gold, aiming for 1 g/t from stockpiles, that should provide 6 to 7 tonnes (around 200,000 ounces) in the first year and 5 to 6 tonnes annually thereafter. Newmont hopes that the joint venture will be a model for future projects.

President Karimov, meanwhile, is intent on husbanding the gold. He stopped sending Muruntau's gold to Moscow for refining and export in 1991, even before the attempted coup against Mikhail Gorbachev, preferring to build Uzbekistan's own gold reserves. Despite a pressing need for foreign exchange, he refused to sell, so that by mid-1993 Uzbekistan had accumulated an initial reserve of around 150 tonnes (4.8 million ounces). How long this can continue in such a hard-pressed economy is another matter. Already the Uzbekistan central bank has close links with European bullion banks, with whom it must eventually swap, if not sell some gold. As the bankers are pointing out to it, Uzbekistan is a gold-producing nation and it is natural to sell. In Uzbekistan, however, the gold is regarded as part of the birthright of the new republic and, like family silver, will be disposed of only as a last resort.

### Kazakhstan, the next contender?
Kazakhstan, that immense wild sweep of a country from the Caspian Sea to the borders of China, has the biggest mineral reserves of any of the Central Asian republics; it is a major producer of oil, natural gas, lead, zinc and, increasingly, gold. So far the gold output is nothing dramatic, only 15–20 tonnes annually, putting it in a lowly third place in the CIS league a long way behind Russia and Uzbekistan. In the past, the gold has come primarily as the by-product of lead and zinc mining and from a scatter of *artels*. Kazakhstan has thirty-one of these co-operative ventures, far more than any other republic except Russia itself (by comparison, Uzbekistan has only three *artels*, Kirghistan, squeezed between Kazakhstan and China, has two, and Tadzhikistan and the Ukraine have one each). This relative proliferation of *artels*, mainly spread through northeast Kazakhstan, is one reason why the prospect for gold may be good. 'There's a lot of alluvial gold worked by the *artels*,' explained a mining executive, 'so there must be hard rock sources.' In that pursuit foreign mining companies are already lining up at the government's door in Alma Ata. And since Kazakhstan is still presided over by the former communist leader, President Nursultan Nazarbayev, it is easier, as in Uzbekistan, to verify deals, since it is clear where the authority lies.

First into the breach is Goldbelt Resources, a Canadian based company, with a gold and silver tailings project on the leftovers of an old polymetallic mining operation that lasted for seventy years with no attempt at that point to recover the gold and silver. Goldbelt has already forecast it can recover almost 19 tonnes of gold (plus almost 80 tonnes of silver) in the first five years of a project ultimately expected to last fourteen years. A rather grander scheme is evolving in a joint venture between Australia's ubiquitous mine engineering group Minproc with a private American company Chilewich and the Kazakhstan government to develop a major deposit at Bakyrchik in northeast Kazakhstan. A small mine, without its own processing plant, has operated there since 1965, but the new Bakyrchik Gold (BK Gold) group has negotiated a 40 per cent interest in the deposit and proposes a ten-fold expansion. The deposit is reported to contain up to 250 tonnes of gold, grading at over 9 g/t. BK Gold has boldly floated the mine on the London Stock Exchange, initially to raise money for heap-leaching pads, a recovery plant (using a new Minproc process of nitric acid oxidation) and refinery. The ultimate target is 7 tonnes output annually, which will be offered first to the Kazakhstan central bank, who must pay for it in dollars; if they cannot do that, then BK Gold can export the gold.

Casting quickly around the remainder of the CIS, there is not much to report, save a small, high-grade mine at Zod Pass, over 2,000 metres up in the mountains of Armenia, not far from Mount Ararat. Alluvial gold has been worked there since neolithic times and Alexander the Great conquered Armenia in 33 BC to secure gold for his Empire. The alluvial deposits were largely exhausted centuries ago, but Zod proved to be a serious quartz vein deposit which was estimated to produce 10 tonnes annually in the late 1970s, although output has declined considerably to a mere 2 tonnes. Given the civil war in the region, the precise fate of the mine and its gold is by no means clear.

Any assessment, therefore, of the prospect for gold mining in the CIS over the next ten to twenty years must focus on Russia, Uzbekistan and Kazakhstan, which today account for at least 95 per cent of output. The potential, taking a long view, is enormous, for the more the curtain comes up on what was the Soviet Union, the more it is apparent how its mining industry has been starved of exploration, new technology and, above all, capital investment. The test will be political stability and the readiness to work with the west.

# CHAPTER 12

# China:
# Going for *kam*

'We have a good tomorrow for China's gold mining industry,' says Mr Yang from the Chinese National Gold Corporation as he welcomes us to his office in Beijing. Outside, the skies are clear blue, but an icy wind is blowing down from Mongolia and there is no apparent heating, so we sit around a bare table for the next two hours warming our hands on mugs of tea that are, mercifully, constantly replenished from thermos-like teapots. Our hosts are full of a journey they have recently made to South Africa to learn about the deep mines there, and bubbling with plans for joint ventures with international mining groups to help China achieve its own target of doubling gold production under the current five-year plan running from 1991–6. But doubling output from a starting point of how many tonnes? Ah, that is a state secret.

The avalanche of information put out nowadays on ore grades, mill throughputs, recovery rates, costs, output and reserves at every western mine is just not available here. In China, it's back to pure detective work. 'Gold mining glitters with rapid growth,' says a five-column headline in the *China Daily*, noting that output is up 19.7 per cent (over what?) on the same period last year despite disastrous floods. 'Silver and gold strike in Hunan,' reads another story on a potential mine of lead, zinc, gold, silver and sulphur, which might yield one tonne of gold (at least a firm number). Piecing together the jigsaw, a broad picture of gold mining does gradually emerge.

China ranks sixth in the world league, a short way behind Canada. There are about 450 mines in the official sector, employing around

300,000 people, which produced (according to western estimates) 130–140 tonnes annually by 1993. There is also a thriving unofficial alluvial sector which probably contributes another 25–30 tonnes. This alluvial gold is sold on the black market and not to the People's Bank of China, the central bank, which legally should be the recipient of all output. The People's Bank, however, has been paying around $278 an ounce; since the street price for pure gold jewellery in China is close to $600, the incentive to ignore the People's Bank is considerable; the private channels are more lucrative. Even then, it must be added immediately, this diversion in no way meets the domestic demand for gold in China. 'The Chinese people got rich,' said a friend in Beijing with great satisfaction, reflecting that after a decade of growth at 10 per cent annually, the economy surged by over 12 per cent in 1992. Gold demand in China responded by rising to at least 400 tonnes, mostly in jewellery. And although China's own gold production may be doubling, demand is far out in front. There is actually no prospect of gold-mine output in China catching up with domestic jewellery demand in the present economic environment, particularly while the ordinary Chinese still have relatively few options of what to do with their savings, beyond buying a television set, washing machine, perhaps a new bicycle and then more gold jewellery. The Chinese have an historic affinity for gold, *kam*, which was first legalized as a medium of exchange during the Han Dynasty in 1091 BC (long before King Croesus is said to have issued gold coin in Lydia).[1] Today, their new-found prosperity is drawing them back to gold as a basic form of saving, as we shall observe shortly in Chapters 20 and 21).

On the mining front, meanwhile, the industry is not only modernizing rapidly, buying in the latest western technology (which, unlike the former Soviet Union, it can afford), but edging towards the concept that new mines must make a profit, while existing mines may be semi-privatised and required to stand on their own feet, instead of all their needs being met by central planning. In short, they are set to become profit-oriented gold companies in the western sense. This is a radical change. The hierarchy of gold mining in China still begins with the State Gold Bureau, directly responsible to the government, which plans mining and decreed, for example, that $1,400 million be spent on doubling gold output in the current five-year plan. The implementation is then in the hands of the China National Gold Corporation which directly controls the larger mines. A 'large' mine in China means 1 tonne (32,150 ounces) or above, while other benchmarks are 10,000 taels (12,000 ounces) and 20,000 taels (24,000 ounces). China National Gold also has provincial offices overseeing smaller local operations.

1 Eduard Kann, *The Currencies of China*, Kelly & Walsh, Shanghai, 1926.

# CHINA: GOLD FIELDS

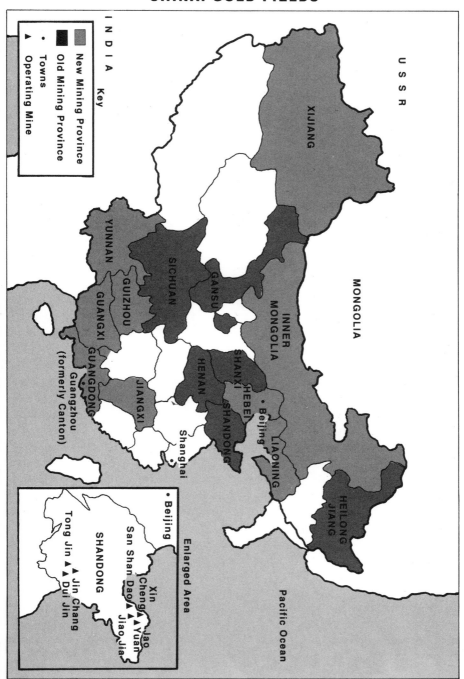

However, the centralized authority of the State Gold Bureau and China National Gold is clearly waning as power shifts to provincial authorities and to the main mines themselves. Within the next few years, we sensed in Beijing in 1993, major mines will become integrated businesses, responsible for their own future and probably quoted on the blossoming local stock exchanges.

Indeed, the historic Jao-Yuan mine in Shandong province which has been worked, on and off, for over a thousand years, is already earmarked to become a separate gold company, with initial responsibility for buying its own machinery and explosives. Shandong province on China's east coast north of Shanghai is just touched by the epithermal deposits of the Pacific Rim (see Chapter 10) and has long been the centre of mining. Other small mines there, near the town of Yiman, date back to the seventeenth century. The mines were very primitive until the late 1970s, when a determined attempt was made to modernize them. The first step was a new mine, Xin-Cheng, close to the Jao-Yuan workings, which opened in 1979 with a modest output of 1.4 tonnes from a grade of 9 g/t.[2] Later came two other mines in the neighbourhood, Jiao Jia with an even better grade of 13 g/t that probably yielded 3 tonnes annually, and Hiaojiashi, which was heralded as China's largest mine. The output was not revealed, but the mine was planned to treat 1,500 tonnes a day, which could provide over 4 tonnes if the grade was 10 g/t.

Assessing grade, however, does seem to be the Achilles heel of Chinese geologists. An experienced western mining executive who toured several Shandong mines told me that they had often experienced difficulty in accurately determining the run of the grade through an entire orebody. He found one of the tricks they were most eager to learn from foreign visitors was how to 'see' the grade of the entire orebody so that they could make their mine plan accordingly. The clear implication is that some projects have started on the basis of a few good drill holes, only to have the ore peter out because its shape had not been properly delineated. The problem, my friend said, was that the geologists were thinking textbook geology, perhaps not surprising in a centrally planned economy, and lacked the field experience to comprehend what wily mavericks some orebodies can be; defining them is an imaginative battle of wits.

The mines are also labour intensive. A well-travelled official from China National Gold admitted that, although its labour costs were one-tenth those of the United States or Australia, it employed ten times as many workers. Even so, it talks of operating costs averaging between $180 and $200 an ounce, although its definition of operating costs may

2 Timothy Green, *The Prospect for Gold*, Rosendale Press, London 1987, p. 98.

well differ from that of a western mine – and it depends on the exchange rate used.

### Expansion in Hebei

The Chinese do not stint, however, on new technology. International companies specializing in mining engineering, such as Davy McKee and Australia's Minproc have installed the latest carbon-in-pulp and carbon-in-leach plants. Heap-leaching is being widely tried, especially on big new open pits in Shandong province. The benefits are admitted candidly. A booklet in delightful English on gold mining in Hebei, the second largest gold-producing province that almost encircles Beijing, lists improvements. At the Zhangjiakou mine, just to the north of the Great Wall, which originally opened in the 1970s, the installation of CIP technology in 1984 improved the rate of gold recovery from 75 per cent to 93 per cent. 'The production reaches international level,' says the text, 'and obtains excellent profits in this gold line.'

The booklet on Hebei province reveals the extent to which gold mining has been expanded. It is controlled by a local office of China National Gold Corporation, which presides over no less than seventy-six local gold enterprises, ranging from full-scale mines to dredges and village co-operatives. Hebei, says the book, has been a centre of gold mining for 3,000 years. A chart plots output from 1949 to 1990, revealing not only that it has risen twenty-seven-fold in that time (without stating, of course, how much it actually is), but that after the communist takeover in the late 1940s, output fell for more than a decade. Most of the growth has been since 1976. Assuming Hebei's output in the late forties was small (China's output historically was never significant) at perhaps 1–2 tonnes, then output in the 1990s must be at least 27 tonnes, and perhaps as much as 54 tonnes. The mining is primarily in the Yanshan and Taihong mountains, but remains remarkably diverse. Just take the account of Qinglong county. 'There are over 280 lodes of varying sizes,' says the Hebei report. 'There are 6 locally-administered state-run mines [and] 175 mines run by collectively-owned townships or villages.' Judging from the accompanying pictures, at least one large dredge is in operation. Combined output in the county is said to be over 20,000 taels (24,000 ounces or 750 kilos). Further north in the Chengde area of the Yanshan mountains there are more than ten gold mines. And the booklet even lets slip that in Kuancheng county alone output is '800,000 ounces' (25 tonnes), although this looks like an error, because it is so much out of line with any other statistics.

This account of a major producing region suggests that one reason why China is reluctant to reveal its total gold output is that, quite simply, no one knows what it is. The output of the 'large' mines under the wing of China National Gold Corporation can be controlled, but what about the 175 'mines' run by the towns and villages of Qinglong county alone? What happens to their gold? Does it filter up the bureaucratic chain to get less than $300 an ounce from the People's Bank? Since provincial governments are wielding increasing influence, are they not tapping directly into the output of many smaller mines? For example, what is happening to the gold being produced in another new mining area ranging over 20,000 square kilometres at the junction of Sichuan, Shaanxi and Cansu provinces in central China? When I enquired in Beijing, no one was quite sure, and said they thought it was mostly alluvial. And what about the announcement by the provincial government of Guizhou, in southern China, that a gold refinery is to be built in the city of Xingyi to handle the output from five large orebodies discovered locally that will increase the province's output six-fold? Beijing officials were not certain on that one either. In fact, after a few toasts over an excellent dinner, they conceded privately that gauging China's true gold production is increasingly difficult.

The problem actually dates back to the beginnings of economic reform in China in the late 1970s, when the long march back to the market, instigated by Deng Xiaoping, began. The government ordered local authorities to encourage collectives and even individuals to run small gold operations in places where large-scale mining was unsuitable or uneconomic. They worked not only on the fringe of state mining areas, but on low-grade quartz veins in state mines. New alluvial gold camps opened. Soon, at least 200,000 prospectors were busy throughout China and for a while they accounted for up to half of production. Not that they sold all gold to the government; a steady flow of alluvial gold dust started turning up over the border in Hong Kong. In the mid-1980s, it was sometimes as much as 20 tonnes in a single year. The authorities countered after 1988 by trying to restrict individual diggers, on the grounds that it caused conflicts on land use and spoiled the environment. Yet alluvial gold mining continues. China National Gold Corporation admits it still amounts to 20 per cent of all output. However, not much of it turns up in Hong Kong nowadays. The local market within China easily digests it, refining it and making it up into the bangles and chains that fill the new shops.

The alluvial mining is principally located in the northeast, in the provinces of Heilongjiang, Jilin and Neimongol (Inner Mongolia), up against the borders with Mongolia and Russia, where the placer deposits continue. Indeed, two of Russia's autonomous gold *zolotos*, Amurzoloto and Primorzoloto, nestle right next to Heilongjiang and Neimongol.

Cross-border gold smuggling has developed since the collapse of the Soviet Union. Russian gold is bartered for consumer goods that are increasingly plentiful in China. The gold, of course, is easily swallowed up in China's black market.

The proximity to some of the best gold fields in the former Soviet Union applies also in the vast semi-autonomous region of Xinjiang, which borders on Uzbekistan, the second largest of the CIS republics. A considerable flurry was caused in the late 1980s when China signed up a joint venture with Galactic Resources, the junior Canadian mining company, to prospect the gold fields of Xinjiang, where China's Geological Institute claimed to have located 4,000 orebodies. Some grades were said to be up to 30 g/t. Galactic's chairman even forecast that the region might eventually produce 300–400 tonnes a year. It has yet to appear.

### Privatization drive

In fact, the Chinese gold-mining industry, while seeking its target to double output by 1996, is in the midst of immense structural changes as it shifts from central planning to semi-privatized or at least provincialized mines that will soon raise their own capital on local stock exchanges. Western mining companies will be cautious to embark on large joint ventures until they see how this process evolves. After all, with whom will they make the deal? Meanwhile, China does have the capital to buy in equipment, but what it really needs to import is experience. A signal of the change is that since mid-1992 the authorities have been much quieter in boasting of advances in mine output. They admitted to only 10 per cent in 1991, and a modest (by previous announcements) 7.4 per cent growth in 1992. That implies not only that they need professional help to make the next leap forward, but that the centre is losing its grip on mining as more gold is diverted into the hands of provincial governments or the black market.

To counter that the People's Bank of China has to start paying the price of the day for the gold it buys from the mines. Central banks everywhere from Brazil and Venezuela to the Philippines have found this is the only way to secure production, especially when much of it is from elusive alluvial diggers. The bank also has to work out what it really wants to do with the gold. When I first called on the People's Bank in 1987, it told me gold mining in China was being encouraged because it saw gold 'as foreign exchange' and it would use it to help repay large loans falling due in the early 1990s. As it turned out, the economy grew so fast that the country now has a good surplus. So the People's Bank stockpiles most of the gold production, which is refined to 'good delivery' status at the state-run Refinery of China whose bars are acceptable on the London market. The bank makes a small allocation, probably 20–30 tonnes (the amount is secret) to the local jewellery industry, for which it charges $435 an ounce – a good profit because it is paying around $278. The Panda bullion coin, launched in 1982, is also made from locally mined gold, but an equivalent amount of gold is bought and held on China's account in the London market to match the gold used in the coins. The rest of production goes into reserves, but the amount is not revealed. China does declare official gold holdings of 394 tonnes (12.7 million ounces), but they have stood at that level for more than a decade, even though most mine production has been retained. The true level must be towards 1,000 tonnes. China sells rarely on the international market, usually only in moments of crisis, as after a severe earthquake in 1976 and in the aftermath of the Tienamen Square massacre in 1989, when its credit rating slipped. Such selling is done through the Bank of China, which acts as the commercial arm of the People's Bank. The Bank of China and its sister bank Po Seng in Hong Kong are, however, active traders in the international gold market, which means that genuine sales could be cloaked by day-to-day trading activities. But China 'buying' or 'selling' usually means Bank of China's trading book. Bank of China is quite a shrewd player; it bought heavily early in 1993 on the seven-year low in the market below $330.

The People's Bank, however, has to evolve a new policy in the face of the huge domestic demand in China. Production, including unofficial, is somewhere over 150 tonnes, of which perhaps 50-60 tonnes is fabricated for jewellery from the combination of People's Bank sales and unofficial output. Yet demand was at least 400 tonnes in 1992, and although it slowed down considerably in 1993 on higher gold prices, Hong Kong traders suggest it could reach 600 to 900 tonnes annually by the end of the decade. There is no prospect of local mining meeting that. Even so, does the People's Bank at least make available more local production? Does it buy also on the international market directly or via the Bank of China and sell to jewellery makers? Or does it liberalize the gold market and let the business go through commercial dealers, essentially recognizing officially what is already happening discreetly? The role of China is one of the most intriguing in the gold market of the 1990s and the way both the gold-mining industry there and the People's Bank respond will be worth watching closely.

# CHAPTER 13

# Africa:
# Building on History

Throughout history, Africa has been a constant source of gold. Where were the mines that provided Egypt with the gold for the treasures of Tutankhamun? Where were King Solomon's mines? Was the gold of the Pharaohs brought down the Nile from the heartland of Africa in Zaire or Zimbabwe? African alluvial deposits have been worked for at least four thousand years. The Phoenicians and Carthaginians sailed their ships to the Gold Coast, today's Ghana, in the fifth and sixth centuries BC, in search of gold. In later generations came the Portuguese, who pioneered the European gold trade, and after them came the English (in 1553 Captain Thomas Wyndham came back from the Gold Coast with 150 pounds weight of gold dust). The English guinea, first minted under Charles II in the 1660s, was made with gold from the 'Guinea Coast of the Gold Coast'.[1] And William Merle, of the London refiners Cox & Merle, told the famous 1810 Bullion Committee of the House of Commons that they got '4,000 ounces of gold dust from West Africa' every few months. The great Ashanti mine in Ghana opened in 1897 and will shortly celebrate its centenary. And in the 1930s no less than thirteen Ghanaian gold-mining companies were listed on the London Stock Exchange.[2]

Sadly in modern times this track record has almost been ignored. For most of the 1980s, sub-Saharan Africa (excluding South Africa) produced scarcely 50 tonnes (1.6 million ounces) annually and although this has improved towards 90 tonnes, the real potential has yet to be explored. Until very recently, political instability, civil wars and

1 T.E. Anin, *Gold in Ghana*, Selwyn Publishers, Accra, Ghana, 1987.
2 Mark Keatley, *Africa's Gold Potential*, Financial Times World Gold Conference, Montreux, 1992. This paper is the best single assessment of the sub-Saharan Africa gold scene.

ideological opposition to foreign investment hampered development. More auspicious signs, however, are appearing. The ideological clashes of the Cold War are over, governments are becoming more pragmatic and, significantly, the easing of tensions with South Africa means that the gold-mining industry there can turn its expertise north. 'Africa is a gold-rich continent,' claims Mark Keatley of the International Finance Corporation (IFC), who has worked closely on setting up new projects. 'Sub-Saharan Africa . . . offers some of the greatest growth potential in gold mining.'[3]

### Ghana: the Gold Coast reborn

The comeback is strongest in Ghana, where the geological formations are auspicious, and much of the country is overlaid with a variety of Pre-Cambrian greenstones known as Birimian. When the country first gained its independence from Britain in 1961, it already ranked fifth in western world output at 34 tonnes annually. But a generation of neglect brought the industry to the brink of disaster. Ashanti Goldfields Corporation, the main producer, was starved of foreign exchange to modernize. By the early 1980s, Ashanti's output was scarcely 8 tonnes; the mine was literally dying. No foreign exchange was available to buy vital spares abroad and at best they could be bartered from other local mines. The cages in which the miners went underground were home-made from scrap metal. The ultimate rescue recipe was a new Minerals Code in 1986 that welcomed foreign investors and a new president (former Flt Lt Jerry Rawlings), whose economic recovery programme won the support of the World Bank. The World Bank realized that a revival in gold offered the most serious export benefit to an economy otherwise adrift on the whims of the cocoa market. The International Finance Corporation – the World Bank affiliate which invests in private sector projects in the developing world – organized a long-term financing package of $160 million to get Ashanti back on its feet.

The Ashanti Gold Fields Corporation, which is 55 per cent owned by the government[4] and 45 per cent by Lonrho, the UK conglomerate that has interests throughout Africa, has a large concession covering 250 square kilometres in the Obuasi gold field 200 kilometres northwest of Accra. A new team under managing director Sam Jonah has completely modernized the operations to treat surface oxide ores, quartz veins and tailings. The old underground mine, now down to 2,000 metres, is getting quartz with a handsome grade of 16 g/t; a new open pit is turning in oxides at 3 g/t and will later go for sulphides at 7 g/t. The operating costs in 1992 were just $160 an ounce, giving high cash flow to reinvest in more new technology. And output? It has bounced from

3 Ibid.
4 In June 1993, the Ghanaian government offered a 20 per cent stake for sale and invited bids from mining companies. The sale emphasizes Ghana's commitment to privatization, rare in Africa, and is being handled by the IFC.

# AFRICA: GOLD FIELDS

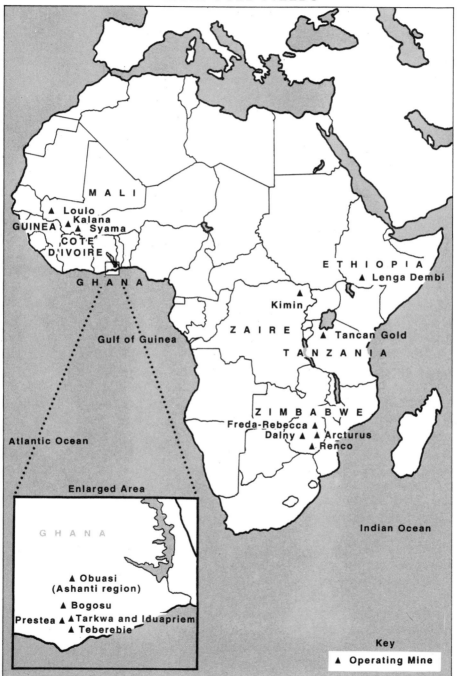

the meagre 8 tonnes of the early 1980s, to just over 20 tonnes (650,000 ounces) in 1992. Already Ashanti is the second largest mine in the 'rest of the world' table, beaten only by Porgera in Papua New Guinea. This is just the first step. The IFC has lined up another $305 million loan package that will enable Ashanti to lift output to 33 tonnes (over a million ounces) by 1996. The investment has also been protected by hedging between 30 and 50 per cent of the annual output through the IFC. A key stage in the new expansion is a $140 million project that will make Ashanti the leading user of bioleaching technology to unlock gold in sulphide ore. It is adopting the process developed by Gencor in South Africa in which ore is first ground to powder and then mixed with water; bacteria (thiobacillus ferro-oxidans) is added to this solution and dines on the ore, thus releasing gold (this is a variation on the menu that Newmont Gold and American Barrick are trying on the Carlin Trend in Nevada, where the bacteria are introduced to sulphide ore stockpiles). Incidentally, the engineering work for the Ashanti bioleaching is being handled by Australia's Minproc, a good example of how the reborn Australian gold industry is marketing its expertise around the world. Bioleaching is both cheaper and more environmentally friendly than roasting or pressure oxidization of refractory ores. Ashanti hopes the process will give it at least 10 tonnes of extra gold annually. And with total reserves close to 700 tonnes, it takes great pride in having re-established the gold industry on the Gold Coast. As managing director Sam Jonah said, 'We are at the cutting edge of both gold production and financial engineering.'

Ashanti's ascent to record output has been matched by a batch of other new mines in the Tarkwa basin, Ghana's other main gold field, which has conglomerate reefs similar to those of South Africa's Witwatersrand basin. The first two opened in 1991: Billiton International Metals at Bogosu and Pioneer Resources (a small US company) at Teberebie, both being open pits, producing 2–3 tonnes annually. Then, early in 1993, President Jerry Rawlings himself opened the Iduapriem mine, which is set to produce 3–4 tonnes a year. Iduapriem is owned by Ghanaian Australian Goldfields, in which Australia's Golden Shamrock Mines holds nearly 70 per cent, with the IFC having 20 per cent and the government 10 per cent. As at Ashanti, the IFC's backing was crucial in persuading a consortium of European banks to put up a $55 million loan to start the mine. Such new-found access to foreign investment has been crucial in Ghana's gold renaissance and will prove the real test of development elsewhere in Africa. Meanwhile, the initial success in Ghana is a magnet for other mining groups. Cluff Resources, another African specialist house, is looking at an open pit at Ayanfuri in central

Ghana. Gold Fields of South Africa has already acquired a controlling stake of the state-owned Tarkwa underground mine and is considering the purchase of the neighbouring Prestea mine (also government – owned). Both mines are in desperate need of modernization. All told, Ghana's output was back to 34 tonnes (1.1 million ounces) by 1992 and could rise to 60 tonnes in the late 1990s. Gold is once again the number one foreign exchange earner for the first time in over twenty years.

### Competition for galampsey and pailleurs?

Throughout the rest of West Africa, indeed through much of the continent, most other gold comes from local diggers known as *galampsey* where the British once ruled, or pailleurs (from the French word *paillette* for a grain of gold dust in a stream) in francophone Africa. They are busy in Ivory Coast, Guinea, Burkino Faso, Mali and Togo producing gold dust, which is spirited away on flights bound for Europe, mostly from Bamako in Mali, and sold quickly for cash to local refiners in Switzerland and Antwerp (where the carriers also go with illicitly mined diamonds from Sierra Leone). It has become a substantial trade involving upwards of 15 tonnes annually, from all of West Africa. Serious miners are now on their heels, tracking the greenstone belts into Ivory Coast, Burkino Faso and Mali.

Actually, the former Soviet Union was first to open a new mine at Kalana in Mali in 1984, which was theoretically to produce about 2 tonnes annually, a target apparently not reached because much of the gold just disappeared. But Australia's BHP Minerals has had better luck with a large open pit at Syama, which initially produced 3 tonnes at 3.1 g/t and is now being expanded (with the help of the ubiquitous IFC) to 6 tonnes by 1994. France's BRGM[5] also has a modest joint venture with the Mali government at Loulo and a slice of the action at the small Ity heap-leach operation which opened in Ivory Coast in 1991. While Australia's Golden Shamrock Mines, building on its experience at Iduapriem in Ghana, is exploring the Siguiri prospect in Guinea, a country where the *galampsey* already scour at least 3 tonnes a year from alluvial deposits.

To get back into serious mine production, however, it is necessary to head south to Zimbabwe, which has a long history of gold mining. Indeed, when the government opened its own refinery, Fidelity Printers and Refiners, in Harare in 1988, one European bullion banker hazarded in a speech of congratulations that Zimbabwe may have been the home of King Solomon's mines. Certainly there is a host of small mines tapping into greenstones that cover much of the country, and producing

5 Bureau de Recherche Géologique et Minéral.

20 tonnes annually. The mining industry here benefits not only from better infrastructure than most African countries, but also from the local stock exchange, which it can use for raising money. Nothing, however, is on a grand scale. The biggest producer is Lonrho, which amasses around 5 tonnes a year from holdings in Corsyn Consolidated and Independence Mining.[6] RTZ gets a couple of tonnes from three small operations, Renco, Patchway and Brompton, as does Cluff Resources from Royal Family, Freda and Rebecca, while Falcon Gold has the modest Dalny mine. But the industry has been hemmed in by government controls since independence and the ultimate test for expansion in the 1990s is the extent to which these will be relaxed (under World Bank pressure), allowing more exploration and investment by foreign mining companies.

The question for Zaire is more complex. A source of gold for centuries, it had a well-established mining industry when under Belgian colonial rule. Since then, President Mobutu has reduced the country to the brink of disaster and, although some foreign mining houses have been exploring known deposits, there is no real way to proceed until political stability is restored. The best gold deposits are in the northeast in Haut Zaire and Kivu province, close to the borders with Uganda, Rwanda and Burundi. A thriving *pailleurs* business in the region has produced up to 10 tonnes annually, much of which has been smuggled into Burundi and thence to Europe. The state gold-mining company, Okimo, has done little and the only serious attempt has been to get a South African/Belgian consortium going at Kimin, with help, once again, from the IFC, with a start-up potential of 2.5 tonnes a year and perhaps 14 tonnes eventually. The logistics, however, are frightening. 'The difficulties of operating . . . are not trivial,' noted the IFC's Mark Keatley with wonderful understatement. 'Supplies need to be trucked in for about 2-6 weeks through East Africa. Zaire is in the throes of a political and economic crisis unparalleled in its history. All central institutions have practically collapsed.'[7]

By contrast, the news from Tanzania is more encouraging. The country is emerging from a cocoon of more than twenty years of socialist experiment to give a cautious welcome to foreign mining groups. The government no longer insists on majority ownership in mines and mining groups can retain 70 per cent of earnings in offshore bank accounts. Tanzania already has a modest history of gold (and diamond) mining, mostly in greenstone belts around Lake Victoria. Informal alluvial mining has actually thrived since the early 1980s, with much of the 3–5 tonnes a year produced being spirited out via Nairobi to London or Dubai. When the central bank experimented with offering

6 Lonrho also controls a small alluvial operation in Mozambique.
7 Keatley, op. cit.

a competitive price for the gold dust they acquired 1.6 tonnes in a matter of months. Three small semi-mechanized mines were working in 1991, including Tancan Gold close to Lake Victoria. The relaxation of mining regulations has brought a rush of applications for exploration licences from international companies.

The tour of Africa ends finally in Ethiopia, another nation with a history of gold mining stretching back at least four thousand years as one original source for the Pharaohs. I once visited Addis Ababa, the capital, in the last years of the reign of Emperor Haile Selassie, to call on the central bank. I was invited to the vaults to see 'our gold reserve'. At first all I saw was twenty-four 'good delivery bars' (amounting only to less than 300 kilos) neatly stacked on a table. Around in the gloom, however, were piles and piles of stout wooden ammunition boxes filled with gold dust from local mines. They may have been there for years. I asked why they did not get this treasure refined. The bank official said they feared they would be cheated unless they accompanied the gold to the refinery. I reassured him that international refiners' credentials were trustworthy. A year or two later this Ethiopian gold was dispatched to Johnson Matthey, the UK refiners, but a couple of bank officials went along for the ride. In the calamity that befell Ethiopia after Haile Selassie was deposed, this gold was eventually sold. There was little to encourage exploration and new mining again until the early 1990s, when a new era of stability brought the opening of one small new mine at Lenga Dembi in the Adola gold field of southern Ethiopia, with the potential of three tonnes a year and fresh activity in traditional alluvial areas. Once again the central bank is back in the act, stacking up the gold dust in its vaults and sporadically shipping it to Europe for refining.

Yet, in Ethiopia, as in so much of Africa, although the broad brush of geological structures is known, few have come under the eagle eye of modern aerial techniques for locating deposits, let alone drilling to prove them up. The proper realization of Africa's gold potential will still take time. The IFC's Mark Keatley, who has the best overview of anyone I have encountered, argues that production could eventually virtually double from around 80–90 tonnes annually to 165 tonnes. But he admits there are critical factors in achieving that target. Not only must political and business climates be favourable, but much depends on how far the South African industry is ready to turn its energy, expertise and capital to help its northern neighbours. Will exploration budgets be switched? The whole of sub-Saharan Africa attracts about one-sixth of the annual budgets for mineral exploration devoted to Australia or Canada and scarcely half that spent in South Africa. And then where does the equity capital come from to develop the mines? Much of what has been achieved so far is due to the IFC putting together finance packages. Little local money is available, and only Zimbabwe has a stock market. No one doubts the gold is there (that was proved at least four thousand years ago). The question is, how to tap it.

# PART III

# THE MARKETS

## CHAPTER 14

# The Global Menu:
# Spot, Futures and Options

In December 1850 the London bullion brokers, Mocatta & Goldsmid, made a payment of £1.19s.6d. to the 'Electric Telegraph', for a cable which must have sealed one of the first electronic deals in bullion history, signalling the beginning of a communications revolution in precious metals. Today you have only to step up to the Reuters Monitor in your hotel lobby anywhere from Riyadh to Tokyo and key in GLDA for World Gold Prices to come spilling out in a neat list on the screen; or you may prefer GLDX for the London Gold Price, HKGG for the Chinese Gold and Silver Exchange Society in Hong Kong, or GLDP to get US Composite Gold Prices. While to get the news behind the price, try GDJB-C for the Tokyo Gold Report or CDLW-X for the Zürich Gold Report. If you are a real Scrabble enthusiast, the Reuters Monitor Dealing Service actually offers a choice of twenty-five codes for the latest worldwide Gold and Precious Metals Information. And that's without the option of punching up the individual page for each and every bullion bank, be it MGTNGL for J. P. Morgan, New York, MNGL for Mocatta and Goldsmid, London, or SBCBGL for Swiss Bank Corporation, Zürich to learn the latest price they are making. While at those banking houses each dealer sits before his own battery of screens talking to and trading with the world.

In understanding the gold market of the 1990s, it is debatable whether the decision to end the fixed price of gold in 1968 or the subsequent radical transformation in communications had the most influence. Both opened up entirely new horizons. A floating price for gold, $35 in 1970, $850 in 1980, $350 in 1990, meant that, for many new players in the market, volatility, not stability, was the chief attraction; to them it did not matter whether the price went up or down, as long as it moved. The communications network brought everyone together, round the world, round the clock, and made the gold price a moveable feast. Previously it had largely been the London fixing (or two fixes after 1968) which had been the anchor for the day, and in countries like Saudi Arabia the price was often learned a day late by cable from Beirut. By the early 1970s, direct dial telephone and telex links were binding the gold community together like an extended family. The sudden ability to trade minute by minute with Hong Kong, London, Zürich or New York totally changed the approach to gold, for it was no longer something physical to be bought and hoarded in the vault or under the bed, but a vehicle that could be traded in pursuit of money. Dinner became difficult; in the Middle East traders said they could not eat until 'the market', that is, New York, closed at 9.30 p.m. their time, while in Hong Kong, they excused themselves about the same local time to dash off to catch New York's opening.

The market itself became like a chef who finds his customers have tired of fixed *table d'hôte* fare and suddenly serves an *à la carte* menu, including *nouvelle cuisine* in which the art is as much presentation as substance. The gold market dished up futures, options, warrants, in ever more exotic combinations to woo a new clientele whose prime concern was often a piece of the action without the acute embarrassment of having to take delivery of a single ounce. Such derivatives, of course, have become staple fare in financial and commodity markets. As the *Financial Times* observed, 'In the past ten years, the most creative engineering in the world of international finance has been concentrated in the huge and rapidly growing market for derivatives products. Futures, options, swaps and related instruments today make up an estimated $10,000 billion in investments traded both over the counter (OTC) and on regulated exchanges.'[1] The gold market is only a side-show in this revolution much of the time, but mobile money can be switched into in an afternoon if the mood is there, as happened in 1993 when high profile players like Sir James Goldsmith and George Soros kick-started a rally that ran from $340 to $400 triggering not only a scramble for cover, but luring the weight of serious money from managed futures funds who saw gold as play-of-the-day. Such a wave can easily swamp momentarily the rather modest physical market in gold, in which the total value of newly mined gold each year is worth less than $30 billion a year at $400 an ounce. This is petty cash when one considers that $1,130 billion is traded every day in currency markets. The impact is

1 Survey on 'Derivatives', *Financial Times*, 8 December 1992.

even greater because the derivatives offer immense leverage, with an original margin of only 5–20 per cent being required on futures and only the premium at risk on an option.

While devising this growing menu of derivatives, gold dealers have also come to offer a much wider choice to the miners, central bankers, refiners and fabricators who are hands-on the metal itself. The bullion banks provide the miners with every financing, marketing and hedging facility, as we observed earlier (Chapter 4). They arrange gold loans to pay for start-up, while for hedging take your pick of fixed forwards, floating gold rate forwards, floating forwards, spot deferred and an infinite array of options. Undoubtedly the latest favourite is spot deferred, because that is flexible on just about everything – interest rate earned, gold borrowing cost and maturity date. On a spot deferred contract, a mine sells gold for cash at the current spot price. This cash is credited to a deferred account, which can run almost indefinitely, and to which the interest earned on floating rates is credited, while the gold borrowing cost, almost at the floating rate, is deducted.

The gold borrowing rate highlights another new facet of the modern market: lending or leasing gold into the market by central banks or, on occasion, by speculators to make some money on large positions, and borrowing from the market by just about anyone. The point is that it is usually cheaper to borrow gold than money. So miners borrow for gold loans, central banks borrow to mask forward sales, while refiners and fabricators in jewellery or electronics borrow for their working inventory. The daily liquidity of the market is substantially supplemented by the gold lent to it, which amounts to between 1,500 and 1,800 tonnes (38.6 million ounces). The interest earned by the lender can fluctuate quite widely; typically it is between 0.5 and 1 per cent, but on occasion has shot up briefly to over 2.5 per cent. The borrower can normally expect to pay 3 to 3.5 per cent.

One of the telltale signs to watch for is the rise and fall of leasing rates (available on Reuters by tapping in GOFO). Rising leasing rates, for instance, could mean that central banks are withdrawing deposits from the market for some reason (as they did after the collapse of Drexel Burnham, in which several banks lost gold on deposit) or equally that a large central bank sale is underway with delivery due some months ahead and meanwhile gold must be borrowed to cover (as happened during the Netherlands central bank sale late in 1992). Leasing rates may also be a weathervane of fresh loans or hedging programmes for gold miners. Or they may simply show that physical demand is exceptionally strong, so that refiners need gold to keep their pipeline full to make kilo or 10 tola bars or jewellery manufacturers require larger inventory.

After all, the arrival of paper gold has not diminished the appetite for the real stuff; an ever wider range of designer small bars and bullion coins is on offer to suit every fashion and pocket. Indeed, in the doldrum years from 1987 to 1992, while the gold price declined to the great disillusionment of most paper traders, the physical market boomed as never before, opening up an increasing gap between mine production and demand. At the grass-roots level physical metal often remains the preferred form of savings and security, even if purchased in the form of jewellery. In Saudi Arabia, India, Thailand, Vietnam and, most recently, China, gold remains an integral part of the investment scene. Demand in India varies with the whim of the monsoon, in Thailand with the price of rice, in Vietnam with lack of faith in the dong and in China with the size of newly introduced bonuses. Women in Saudi Arabia are constantly on the phone to or popping in to see their jeweller to check the latest prices and trade in old ornaments for new. They are also the shrewdest judges of price. As canny shoppers, they know a cheap gold price (like $329 early in 1993) and will buy, while their husbands hunched over Reuters screens are selling short, gambling the price must fall. This leads to what may be called 'the view from New York', which is that the action on futures and options is thin, so 'no one is buying gold.' On the contrary, in the souks of the Middle East, the villages of India and on Wangfujing Street in the heart of Beijing they are scrambling for the metal.

This diversity provides not only much of the fascination of the gold market, but means it runs on a twin track. Sophisticated products on exchanges or over-the-counter, must go hand in hand with a complex network of physical distribution to regional markets such as Istanbul, Dubai, Singapore, Hong Kong, Taiwan and Tokyo. After all, it was the depth of demand in these markets which underpinned the gold price much closer to $350 an ounce in the early 1990s than many pundits predicted. Together, Dubai, Hong Kong, Singapore, and Taiwan imported 1,200 tonnes (38.6 million ounces) in 1992, which amounts to almost 55 per cent of world mine output.

London is the centre of the network. While this market has seen many changes in fortune in recent years, it is the clearing house for most round-the-world dealing and its twice daily gold 'fix' remains the most widely accepted benchmark of the price (not least through the BBC World Service, to which countless small gold dealers everywhere listen eagerly). Many banks and bullion dealers elsewhere automatically quote a *loco* London price, meaning gold for delivery there. This term is not exclusive to London; gold may be quoted *loco* Zürich, New York or Tokyo, but in the absence of such specification it normally means

London. Time is also on the side of London and its rivals in Zürich and Frankfurt in that their working days can start conveniently picking up Tokyo and Hong Kong just before they close and end by passing on any unfinished business to be wrapped up by their New York offices.

The presence of European, US and Japanese traders in most key markets has done much to internationalize the business. The way ahead was shown by London dealers, who successfully grafted themselves on to the Hong Kong market in the mid-1970s. They established a parallel market in *loco* London gold during Hong Kong's trading hours, with all the opportunities for arbitrage between a Hong Kong price quoted in Hong Kong dollars per tael and a London price quoted in dollars per ounce. Their German, Swiss and American colleagues soon followed. So the interlocking network evolved. Crédit Suisse, Deutsche Bank and Sumitomo Corporation (among many others) are active traders in New York; J. P. Morgan, Goldman Sachs, Chase Manhattan and Bank of Nova Scotia are at home in London; Republic National Bank of New York is in London and Singapore, along with Crédit Suisse, Rothschilds and Mocatta; and Swiss Bank Corporation is firmly established in Tokyo.

These dealers have also orchestrated the most significant change in the pattern of physical gold flows in the history of the market. For three centuries London and latterly Zürich have been the prime turntables through which gold passed *en route* to its eventual destination. The output of South Africa and the former Soviet Union, which dominated supply until the mid-1980s, moved essentially through one or other of these centres. Suddenly, in a few short years, the rapid rise in output in North America, Australia and other countries of the Pacific Rim, has meant that much more metal can be dispatched direct to hungry Asian markets from these producers. All Australian gold, for instance, can easily be taken up in Singapore, Hong Kong and Tokyo. And as sanctions on South Africa have been eased, while the new Rand Refinery there has the facility to make more 999.9 kilo bars, so more of that gold is air-freighted direct to Southeast Asian markets and even to Dubai. These dispatches may well, of course, be on behalf of bullion dealers in London and Zürich, but the gold no longer passes physically through those cities.

The creation of this global market came about step-by-step in the wake of deregulation. In that watershed year of 1968, the only real markets were London, Zürich and, to a lesser extent, Toronto, while Beirut, Dubai, Macao (actually a front for Hong Kong) and Vientiane, a tiny town on the Mekong river in Laos, were the distribution points. Gold trading was either forbidden or hedged with restrictions in Hong Kong, New York and Tokyo. Although Singapore kicked off by opening its gold market in 1969, the hurdles elsewhere fell slowly; Hong Kong in 1974, the United States on 31 December 1974, Tokyo in 1982. Since then the pattern of deregulation has spread; Taiwan in 1986, Turkey in 1989 and India in 1992. Good news for integrating a global market, bad news for the smugglers who lost some of their best outlets. Liberalization, especially in Hong Kong and the United States, irrevocably changed the nature of the gold market, for it made way for twin newcomers – futures and options.

### The Futures Revolution
The credit for initiating the first gold futures contract actually goes to the Winnipeg Commodity Exchange in Canada, which began trading a 400-ounce contract, denominated in US dollars, in November 1972 when Americans over the border were still expressly forbidden to hold or trade gold. The inspiration came from a tall, engaging Canadian, Bob Purvis, of Inter-Ocean Grain, who felt that if Winnipeg could trade grain, why not gold? He made the circuit of European dealers and won their slightly sceptical support. The first trade on Winnipeg was $62.50 an ounce. Delivery, if desired, was effected by gold certificates issued by the Bank of Nova Scotia and the Canadian Imperial Bank of Commerce. Winnipeg's timing was perfect; it slid aboard gold's first run up towards $200 an ounce in 1974, trading close to 100,000 contracts that year. It was a grand flourish, cut short by the gold liberalization of the United States. Once the heavyweight US exchanges in New York and Chicago weighed in, Winnipeg's *raison d'être* really vanished, although remarkably it kept the gold contract going until 1988.

The concept of futures trading, involving a legally binding contract for the delivery of a commodity at a specified date in the future at an agreed price, originated in Chicago in the 1830s. The idea was to provide farmers with the means of hedging their forthcoming harvest of wheat or soy beans. Futures trading became formalized at the Chicago Board of Trade, after the American civil war, and later in New York. As long as the gold price remained fixed, the futures exchanges had nothing to offer. The moment gold was free to float, however, it was a different story. The New York Commodity Exchange (Comex) had already started a silver contract in 1963; the removal of the ban on gold trading at the end of 1974 was too good to miss. The Comex 100 ounce gold contract was up and running at midnight on the last day of the year. It was another landmark in the history of gold, ushering in a new dimension in trading volume even though it took a couple of years to take off. Other US exchanges, notably the Chicago Board of Trade and the Chicago International Monetary Market, joined in, but over the long haul of nearly twenty years it has been Comex which has made the running (see Chapter 16). Comex's ace was the banks and financial institutions on its doorstep in New York which gave it access to a worldwide clientele. And that is the real impact of the futures revolution. The world of gold stays awake for Comex.

Gold futures became a tantalizing attraction for a disparate cast of players in every corner of the globe. I recall late one night in Jakarta, in the early 1980s, being hustled on a late night car ride to a back-street garage, where an illegal 'bucket shop' was in operation with assorted Indonesians barking buy and sell orders down direct phone lines to the floor of Comex. Futures offer, of course, the miner, the refiner or fabricator the chance to hedge production or inventory, but they also provide speculators with a cheap and highly efficient way of getting into gold. In one sense the action on a futures exchange is the interplay between the professionals who need to hedge and the speculators. Speculators like futures since most contracts are liquidated ahead of maturity, thus eliminating the headaches of delivery, storage, insurance and re-assay upon sale that go with physical gold (fewer than 5 per cent of contracts are fully paid up and delivered).

The added temptation for speculators, who have a great deal of money at their disposal but no desire to own gold, is that they can buy on margin which at the most will be 20 per cent, but is often much less. So, assuming gold at $400 and 10 per cent margin, they can buy a 100-ounce contract for $4,000; they will be required to put up variation margin if the price moves against them (i.e. if it goes to $420, they will have to post an extra $200), but they still have tremendous leverage. For $1 million margin, they can secure a claim on $10 million in gold, which is 25,000 ounces. Managed futures funds, which have over $20 billion at their disposal, think nothing of zipping in and out for 100,000 ounces or more at a clip. Annual trading volume on futures thus dwarfs conventional physical markets. Since 1978 when futures trading in the United States really got into its stride, as the dollar weakened and inflation soared, the volume on US exchanges has rarely fallen below 10 million contracts annually, involving over 30,000 tonnes (which is nearly as much as total central bank holdings). Volume faltered seriously only in the early 1990s, when gold was stuck in a narrow trading range for months on end, and the high rollers drifted away to more volatile arenas like currencies. Comex managed scarcely 6 million contracts in 1992, the lowest level since 1978. A freshly rising market, however, lures speculators like salmon leaping for the fisherman's fly. When gold rose nicely off $326 early in 1993, Comex volume bounced back to more traditional levels, hitting over 1 million contracts in May 1993, the best month since early 1990.

The success of US futures naturally led other markets to follow suit, with mixed results. The Tokyo Commodity Exchange (Tocom), which launched a 1-kilo contract in 1982, has been the only one to notch up significant volume, peaking at nearly 7 million contracts in 1990 and thereafter settling back to just over 4 million (see Chapter 17). Elsewhere there has been a succession of casualties. The London Gold Futures market, unwisely starting with a sterling contract in a business that thinks in dollars, lasted three brief years in the early 1980s. The Sydney Futures Exchange in Australia tried a 50-ounce contract from 1978 to 1989, including a flirtation with Comex allowing participants to open positions on one exchange and liquidate them on the other, but it faded away from lack of volume. And the Singapore International Monetary Exchange (Simex) was established in 1983 from an alliance between the Gold Exchange of Singapore and the International Monetary Market (IMM) in Chicago to trade a 100-ounce contract, but it has never really flourished. The lesson from these experiments is that a successful futures market needs a natural team of local players to give it liquidity and it then attracts an international clientele. Americans have long loved to trade everything from pork bellies to soya beans and orange juice; gold could easily be grafted on. But the British, the Australians and the Singaporeans have much less feel for futures trading (and the British and Australians little interest in gold) and so were not ready to play; they sat back and waited for the foreigners, who did not turn up. By contrast in Japan the trading houses and the brokerage firms provided energetic local participation, giving Tocom the liquidity that made it attractive to foreign players (the only trouble being that initially they found it hard to get exchange membership and the entry costs were high). In Hong Kong, of course, the old-established Chinese Gold and Silver Exchange Society, which is essentially an undated futures market, has plenty of local punters who will gamble on almost anything, unless it is Saturday afternoon when they will be at the horse races (see Chapter 17).

### Options Come of Age

The growth of futures was increasingly challenged in the 1980s by options. They have become the third dimension of the gold market, along with physical gold and futures; but a dimension that is hard to measure because most are over-the-counter (OTC) options offered through international bullion banks in London, Frankfurt, New York and Zürich for which there is no published record. By contrast, exchange options, mainly on Comex, Brazil's Bolsa Mercantile et Futuros in São Paulo and the European Options Exchange in Amsterdam, are the tip of the iceberg. Ask a dealer how large the OTC options volume is compared to exchange volumes, and he will shrug – perhaps four, five, six times? No one opens their books, so no one is sure. What is certain is that options set the pace in the gold business in the last decade. Miners, central bankers, investors and speculators have all grappled with their initial complexity and learned to use them.

For a while a few years ago, almost every dealer's or mining executive's office you visited had a prominent blackboard on which a litany of options terminology and tactics had been chalked up. 'Butterfly', 'Delta', 'Naked', 'Out-of-the-money', 'Straddle', 'Strangle'; what could this exotica mean? Once understood, however, the message was clear. Not only could OTC options be tailored precisely to the needs of each client, but for the buyer any loss is limited to the initial premium agreed when the option is written. One day when I was in Zurich and had that gut feeling that the gold price ought to rise, I was almost tempted into an option contract myself by a charming lady dealer. She punched a few numbers into her computer and proposed to me a premium of $17 an ounce on a 100-ounce contract. 'You understand,' she said, 'that all you stand to lose is $1,700?' I took her out to lunch instead.

Since the language of options is a mystery to many (and can actually be an initial deterrent in using them) a little explanation may be useful.[2] An option gives the holder the right, but not the obligation, to buy or sell gold at a predetermined price by an agreed date, for which privilege he pays a premium. This premium, or cost of the option, is the compensation the writer or grantor of the option receives from the buyer. Thus a central bank writing an option to sell some of its reserves at an agreed price is guaranteed the premium income, even if the option is never exercised, and thus gets some income from its gold holdings. The right to buy is known as a call option, the right to sell is a put option; normally abbreviated to 'call' and 'put'. The predetermined price is known as the strike or exercise price.

The premium is calculated using a mathematical formula originally devised by Dr Fischer Black and Dr Myron Scholes from data at the Chicago Board Options Exchange on sixteen commodities and securities, and later applied to gold. The Black and Scholes model embraces a combination of the current gold price, the strike price, current interest rates, the time before expiry and the anticipated volatility of the gold price. In fact, the only unknown in this equation is price volatility, so the premium ultimately depends on how the dealer views that evolution. Premiums fluctuate considerably though they usually range between $15 and $25 an ounce. That is the appeal. For a small known outlay the buyer of a call or a put can build up a large position at little capital cost and risk. He stands only to lose the premium. The writer of the option,

2 For a fuller explanation of the techniques and language of options see: Timothy Green, *The Gold Companion*, Rosendale Press, London, 1991 for cross-referenced definitions of terminology. Also Terry Mayer, *Commodity Options, A User's Guide to Speculating and Hedging*, New York Institute of Finance, 1983.

on the other side of the transaction, benefits from the premium, but is exposed if the price moves against him, and should hedge.

Within this framework of calls and puts a myriad of options strategies evolve. For example, gold is $375 and a call option is bought at a strike price of $400; if the price subsequently rises to $400 during the life of the option, it is described as 'at market' and could be exercised to buy gold at that price, or held; if gold pressed on to $410, it would be 'in-the-money' and could be exercised to buy gold at $400, giving an immediate profit of $10. Similarly, a put option may be purchased with gold at $400 and a strike price of $375; if gold falls below $375 before the expiry date, the holder can exercise the right to sell at $375. This tactic has been used increasingly by mining companies to protect themselves in a bear market; even if gold slips overnight to $360, they can still dispose of their put at $375. If the strike price is not reached by the expiry date, the option is 'out-of-the-money' and only the premium paid by the buyer is lost.

The impact of the unseen 'iceberg' of options can be felt in two ways. First, coming up to an options expiry date, especially on Comex, there can be efforts by parties with large positions to manipulate the market to get their options 'in-the-money'. Secondly, almost daily pressure can come on the market through what is known as the 'delta hedging' of an option position by the writer or grantor of options to protect his exposure. He may need to buy or sell depending on how close the spot price is getting to the strike price. The amount of the 'delta' is worked out by a variation of the ubiquitous Black and Scholes model, but the constant covering of large positions of 100,000 ounces or more can precipitate a much sharper rally or decline than might be expected. When the market is in turmoil, watch for the comment 'options-related activity' as a sure sign that this may not be genuine new business, but delta juggling.

Options were originally pioneered in the 1970s by Mocatta Metals Corporation in New York and Valeurs White Weld (later Crédit Suisse First Boston Futures Trading) in Geneva. They set the initial pattern of OTC options (sometimes known as European options), which are now widely offered by the bullion banks, acting as grantors, who craft an OTC package to meet the precise needs of each buyer. The latter actually specifies strike price, date of expiry (although this usually matches Comex expiry dates) and quantity (which may be 100,000 ounces or more if a central bank or mining house is involved); the grantor responds by quoting a premium for that package. Thus an OTC option is an agreement between two principals and not a tradable instrument. By contrast a 100 ounce exchange option on Comex, which is in effect an option on a futures contract, is tradable (see Chapter 16).

Tactics in both options and futures have become increasingly dictated by technical charting and computer trading, which are all about 'buy' and 'sell' signals and give short shrift to the fundamentals of who mines and who buys gold. 'The computer can be a deadly weapon to those who don't see it coming,' observed John Powers, the publisher of *Intermarket*, a Chicago based magazine on global trading and risk management.[3] Acting on a computer signal is an act of faith for the managed futures funds, with no regard at all for the supply-demand balance. A colleague of mine who ventured to tackle a fund manager, after a New York seminar on the growth of managed money, with the suggestion that the mine production numbers might mean something, had his head snapped off. 'I don't care if South Africa produces one ounce or one million,' the manager said, turning on his heel and leaving. His fund looks after a modest $650 million, some of which may shift into gold from time to time, when the computer says so.

Detecting when those signals may be triggered is a part of a dealer's life. Every bullion bank has its in-house chartist, plotting support points, moving averages and momentum indicators (oscillators in the United States), in the knowledge that at least in the short term key chart points, usually based on the London p.m. fix or, in the United States, on a high-low-close bar chart of daily prices, dictate price. A dealer ignores at his peril a downside support point of, say, $365.75, because the second it is broken computers will initiate stop-loss selling which may drive the price much lower. The dedication to such homework is often surprising. I stopped by to see a Swiss trader early in 1993, as gold looked as if it might lift off, and found him pouring over the latest 'technical' advice on 'the long-term indicator', 'intermediate momentum' and Elliott Wave prognosis, like a brain surgeon studying scans. By the way, the Elliott Wave Theory is that gold prices make three major upward price movements, interrupted by two minor downward moves and then reverse to make a major two-wave decline, interrupted by two minor rising waves. On this occasion, the Elliott forecast was that 'the wave structure since the breakout bears impulsive characteristics . . . it is just the first part of a larger upward primary wave formation.' Actually, since gold was then $338, anyone bold enough to grab their surfboard could have taken a nice ride to $369 in just three weeks.

Technical analysts argue that price is everything; that a scrutiny of the current price and its history will provide the answers. In short, the technician believes that history repeats itself.[4] The only thing is that with gold, the price as a moving target has rather a short history of scarcely twenty-five years; although that is several lifetimes to traders on

3 *Intermarket*, Vol. 3, No. 11, November 1986, p. 1.
4 For a more detailed explanation of technical analysis, see the author's reference book, *The Gold Companion*, op. cit., pp. 137–9, and associated cross-references.

a gold desk, for whom the next few minutes or hours is all. 'A week is a long time in politics,' the former British Prime Minister Harold Wilson, once said; so it is in the global gold market.

# CHAPTER 15

# Europe

## *London: Still the Crossroads*

Watch those ubiquitous Reuters Monitors in any bullion trader's office worldwide at 10.30 a.m. and 3.00 p.m. London time on working days and for a few minutes prices go into suspense. Instead of a firm quote from market-makers, the screen announces 'trying 375.50' or some similar price; the moments slide by, then up pops 'trying 376.00' or 'trying 375.00' according to the mood of the market. Finally, it reads 'fixed 375.25'. What captures the attention of the gold community twice daily is a sober gathering of five traders hunched over little desks in the offices of N. M. Rothschild & Sons in St. Swithin's Lane in the City of London 'fixing' the price of gold. This is no rampaging open-outcry market, but a dignified balancing up of buy and sell orders through five members of the London market, linked only by a telephone line to their own trading rooms in what has been a regular ritual since September 1919 (save for the years 1939–54 when the market was closed by war). Normally it is all over in a few minutes; the longest was 2 hours 36 minutes on 23 May 1990 when a Middle East syndicate came in offering about 15 tonnes (480,000 ounces). The very scale of that disposal illustrates the fixing's long-running appeal; it is the only place where real volume can be sold, or bought, at one clearly posted price. And it remains the most widely accepted international benchmark for deals, even if they do not go through the fixing.

Much prestige and no little mystery has long been attached to the 'famous five' with seats at the fix; actually, four of the original cast of this long-running show remain: Mocatta & Goldsmid, N. M. Rothschild (which acts as chairman), Sharps Pixley, and Samuel Montagu. But the fifth, Johnson Matthey Bankers, fell by the wayside of insolvency (though not through gold trading) in 1984 and its seat was taken by Mase Westpac, the bullion bank owned by Australia's Westpac Bank.[1] Although these houses hold the exclusive seats, they are today but five of thirteen market-making members and about fifty other wholesale traders in the London Bullion Market Association (LBMA) which was formed in 1987, under the watchful eye of the Bank of England, to provide the formal framework to the market.

### London: Mark II

The much wider membership evolved from the late 1970s as Canadian, Japanese, Swiss and US bullion banks and traders opened up in London, in recognition of its special role as the crossroads of gold. The London gold market Mark II, as it were, has its origins in the crunch year of 1968 when, as we saw earlier (Chapter 3), the international gold pool failed in its attempt to hold gold at $35 an ounce by selling extravagant amounts through the Bank of England on the fix, which ended in the abrupt closure of the market for two weeks. When it reopened the gold business had a new structure. A meeting of central bankers in Washington had devised a 'two-tier' market. On the top tier, central banks and monetary institutions, such as the IMF, would continue to deal with each other at the 'official' price of $35 an ounce, while on the second tier was a free market for everyone else on which the price would find its own level. Central banks were forbidden, as part of the Washington Agreement, to have anything to do with the free market, a divorce of monetary from non-monetary gold that lasted for the next seven years.

The change was a severe blow to London. 'The UK gold market was seriously damaged by the collapse of the gold pool,' a senior Bank of England official admitted much later. 'The loss of the daily central bank business, as central banks effectively withdrew from the market . . . hit London as the main wholesale market, particularly hard.'[2] That was only half the story. During the enforced two weeks' closure, not only did London's great rivals, the Swiss, open as usual, but they snatched the marketing of South African gold. The three major Swiss banks, Crédit Suisse, Swiss Bank Corporation, and Union Bank of Switzerland, hastily formed their own gold pool and, presenting a united front, persuaded South Africa they could market most of her production. They argued they had been the biggest buyers in London for several years and since,

1 Westpac entered into an agreement in July 1993 for the sale of Mase Westpac to Republic National Bank of New York, part of the banking empire of Edmond Safra. Republic was expected to take over Mase Westpac's seat at the fixing. Sharps Pixley was bought by Deutsche Bank in 1993, but the name is retained.

2 T.R. Smeeton, Chief Foreign Exchange Manager, Bank of England, *Gold in the UK Market*, The 5th Nikkei Gold Conference, Tokyo, September 1992.

under the Washington Agreement, South Africa was expressly forbidden to sell to central banks, they could distribute most of the gold to the growing markets of Italy and the Middle East. It was an offer South Africa, then coming up to the peak years of her production at 1,000 tonnes annually, could not refuse.

So when London reopened after brushing up its own image by deciding to fix henceforth in dollars, instead of sterling, and to introduce a second fix at 3 p.m. to woo American business, the rug had been pulled from beneath its feet. London had been the premier market since the eighteenth century, because it distributed most of the world's gold. Suddenly it had lost South Africa, which was then producing virtually 80 per cent of western mine output, quite apart from central banks' business, which was then still a cornerstone of the market. This loss was further underlined in 1972 when the Soviet Union returned as a substantial seller for the first time since 1965. Previously it had sold through Moscow Narodny Bank in London, which used Samuel Montagu as its outlet; when the Soviets came back, the business went through Wozchod Handelsbank in Zürich, principally to the Swiss banks.

The whole character of today's London gold market stems from those events. However, far from destroying London, in the long run they actually strengthened it. The bullion houses were free to move with the wind of change blowing through the gold trade. And that trade, as we noted in the previous chapter, was less about shifting the metal itself to all corners of the world, and more concerned with non-stop international trading on metal accounts, or futures and then options. So while the Swiss diligently went about cornering physical markets, London had a free hand to serve a growing assortment of rival market-makers and speculators, who were attracted like moths to a flame by the aura of gold's freshly floating price. By good fortune, too, the London houses also took in an influx of young traders, who had cut their teeth on foreign exchange dealing and immediately applied that expertise to gold. 'We got a whole new cast,' recalled one leading dealer some years later. 'London had not got a trading mentality before – we weren't really making a two-way price; we were just a distributor of South African and pool gold.'[3] Denied those supplies, London became a trading forum, making prices, developing forward books, competing for customers and setting up shop in any new market that came along. London houses led the way in Hong Kong and hurried to New York once gold trading started there.

### Bank of England Support
In these adventures, London had a unique asset and ally – the Bank of

3 See Timothy Green, *The New World of Gold*, Weidenfeld & Nicolson, London, 1985, pp. 132–3.

England. For three centuries the Bank has been intimately involved with the bullion business in London, with its own Bullion Office providing the main warehouse for much of that time (see Chapters 1 to 3). The Bank was also the agent for South African sales up to 1968 and, being a major IMF gold depository, stores gold for many other central banks, for whom it sometimes buys and sells. Indeed, there is no other central bank today with such close links to the gold market, except for the special situation of the South African Reserve Bank which markets that country's gold. As a Swiss dealer put it to me rather enviously, 'The Old Lady [of Threadneedle Street] is doing a beautiful job for the London market.'

The Bank is not just there in a regulatory role, although it does provide a code of conduct for members of the London Bullion Market Association (LBMA), but is the repository of much of the gold in the London market. All of the market-making members of the LBMA and many of the ordinary members keep all or part of their stocks at the Bank. Since many of the market's customers nowadays are central banks (that two-tier divorce being long over) who also keep their gold at the Bank, the metal is all under one roof, or rather in one vault. Incidentally, pictures of the vault (visitors never being allowed) show the bars are not stacked from floor to ceiling for the simple reason that the Bank is built on clay, which might subside if subjected to too much weight; the gold loading has to be very evenly distributed. But since so much gold from so many participants is located there, settlement of transactions can take place within the Bank's own computer system; the metal does not have to be shifted around the City.

The Bank itself, although no longer agent for South African sales, is also a regular participant in the market, not just as manager of the United Kingdom's gold reserves, but for many other central banks. 'With very few exceptions, all of the world's major holders of gold keep some part of their reserves with the Bank of England and a number of them ask us to conduct operations on their behalf,' said Terry Smeeton, the chief manager of foreign exchange, whose department also presides over gold. 'Conducting their business through the Bank of England, which is in the market more or less on a daily basis, provides for anonymity.'[4] These operations include leasing gold into the market, which the Bank of England does in a small way with the United Kingdom's own reserves, while also leasing on behalf of other central banks. The availability of so much gold in hand at the Bank has enabled London to become a leading, if not the leading, centre of leasing.

4 Smeeton, op. cit.

### Good delivery status

From this focus on the Bank, three unique pillars of the London market stem: the 'good delivery' system, *loco* London gold and central clearing for market-makers worldwide. The tradition of bars being accepted as 'good delivery' in London is almost as old as the market itself. The Bank of England was always most particular about the bars that it would accept; originally these were 200-ounce 'standard' bars (that is, 916 fine), but this gradually gave way after 1871 to the 400-ounce bar (still 916 fine). In those days the Bank approved the bars of only four refiners and insisted on triple assays, accepting the approval of only five assayers.[5] The present 400-ounce good delivery bar at 995 fine dates from 1919 when the market switched from making a price from 'standard' to fine gold. The accredited list, now drawn up by the LBMA, is longer, but just as exacting. A good delivery bar must have a minimum gold content of 350 fine ounces and a maximum of 430 fine ounces, the fineness being minimum 995. The bar must be marked with a serial number, stamps of an acceptable melter and assayer and the fineness. 'Gold said to be 1000 fine will be marked down to 999.9 fine,' the specifications note sternly, adding, 'Bars should be of good appearance, free from surface cavities or other irregularities, layering and excessive shrinkage, and must be easy to handle and convenient to stack.' The seal of approval is accorded to fifty-five melters and assayers in twenty-three countries, ranging from Australia (4 recognized) through Brazil (3) and China (1) to Switzerland (6), the USA (7) and Zimbabwe (1). At home in the United Kingdom only Engelhard and Johnson Matthey are approved, but they own other accredited refineries elsewhere; Engelhard has four approved refineries and the Johnson Matthey group leads the entire field with six. Johnson Matthey has the oldest pedigree of all metallurgical companies specializing in precious metals; it officially dates its foundation from 1817, although the Johnson family were assayers of precious metals as far back as 1750. Johnson Matthey was made assayer to the Bank of England in 1852, to help cope with the flood of gold from the Australian gold rush and has been a pioneer of many technical advances in the uses of gold and, above all, platinum.[6]

The good delivery bar is the unit of dealing in the London market including the fixings. And although no one can be required to deliver bars of any particular brand, delivery must be of one or more bars on the good delivery list. Moreover, the price quoted is precisely for a good delivery bar *loco* London. Naturally the market members can provide the full range of bars from kilo bars through 10-tola bars to 1 ounce or 1

5 George Forbes, *The Bullion Business of the Bank of England*, privately circulated by the Bank of England, 1867.
6 It was only Johnson Matthey Bankers, the banking and bullion trading arm of Johnson Matthey plc, which collapsed in 1984. The largest shareholders in Johnson Matthey plc are Johannesburg Consolidated Investments (JCI) and Minorco, both part of the Anglo American empire of the Oppenheimer family. Minorco, Anglo's Luxembourg based arm, also owns 30 per cent of Engelhard.

gram, but they will always be at a premium. The bars are made for them by Engelhard and Johnson Matthey, and despite changes in flows in recent years, these brands can be found everywhere from Dubai to Singapore and Istanbul to Taiwan. Johnson Matthey's 'chop' or stamp is still perhaps the best known universally. The Bank of England, incidentally, only holds good delivery bars and will not take in kilo bars.

### The Benefits of Loco London

The concept of *loco* London (meaning simply gold in London) really grows out of the good delivery system, for a trader anywhere is confident to accept gold on his account *loco* London, knowing that it is part of a stock under the eye of the Bank of England. Thus much trading is accomplished *loco* London, with no movement of metal at all, not just on behalf of market-makers, but for many other central and commercial banks and financial institutions. Indeed, as one dealer put it, 'The simple spot quotation for gold in the international sense means London and nowhere else.' Banks in Singapore, for example, offering gold savings accounts to their customers, which must truly be backed by gold, keep part of it *loco* London. The introduction of a sales tax in Japan resulted in some institutional buyers there preferring *loco* London gold. Confidence in the system is crucial. When Drexel Burnham collapsed in 1990 and several central banks lost gold with its unregulated US parent, the Bank of England made certain that all gold contracts entered into by its UK subsidiary (which was solvent) were honoured.

Building on this reputation, London is the centre through which most market-makers clear their worldwide transactions and sort out their balances on a *loco* London basis. 'The facilities we offer for handling metal accounts and exchange metal accounts are unequalled,' a dealer claimed. 'All of us have exchange accounts with each other.' The creation of the LBMA, providing a single code of market practices for clearing and settlement, has enhanced this role.

Not that London always gets it right. The London Gold Futures Market, launched in the early 1980s, had only a brief life, since there was not enough natural local business to give it the initial liquidity to attract international players; while the contraction in gold-trading volumes in the bear market from 1987 cut seriously into the turnover of all the market-makers. And the original London houses have faced serious competition from the cream of US banks, which got into gold after 1975. Although they have been taken under the wing of banks themselves – Mocatta & Goldsmid by Standard Chartered, Sharps Pixley by Kleinwort Benson, and Samuel Montagu by Midland – being a division of a bank that may have other priorities is not always an ideal environment. Above all, the presence of J. P. Morgan, a Triple A bank with strong links to central banks and other financial institutions, which has been in London for over a century and added gold dealing to its activities in the early 1980s, has provided tough competition.

Just glance down the list of market-makers in London to see the challenge that has emerged. Besides Morgan, there are AIG Trading, J. Aron, Chase Manhattan, Phibro Energy Bullion and Shearson Lehman from New York, and Crédit Suisse and Union Bank of Switzerland from Zurich. That is without the LBMA's other fifty-odd members who may not be market-makers, but can be lively traders. They include Bank of China, Bank of Nova Scotia, Canadian Imperial Bank of Commerce, Crédit Lyonnais, Deutsche Bank, Dresdner Bank, Mitsubishi Corporation, Mitsui, Morgan Stanley, Sumitomo Corporation, and Swiss Bank Corporation. No other gold market can line up such a list of players on its home turf.

### In at the fix

The original London houses, of course, still have an ace up their sleeve – the fix. This quiet ceremony at N. M. Rothschilds at 10.30 a.m. and 3 p.m. has changed very little since its inception in 1919, except to quote in dollars, instead of sterling. The special room set aside for it is like any ordinary committee room, fitted with an olive-green carpet, green chairs and an ancient pendulum clock. On the walls are portraits of Nathan Mayer Rothschild, who founded the London branch of the banking house in 1810, his daughter Charlotte and an assortment of European monarchs for whom the Rothschilds negotiated loans in the nineteenth century. The head of the Rothschild bullion department, or one of his colleagues, sits at one end of a long table with an electronic calculator in front of him, and a telephone linked to the Rothschild dealing room down the corridor. The representative from each of the other four members sits at a desk, each with an open line to his own trading room and a small Union Jack flag beside him. The flag enables the dealer to stop the session at any moment with a cry of 'Flag up!', while he confers with his own trading room, where fellow dealers are in direct contact by phone and telex with bullion banks around the globe who may, in their turn, have clients on the line. 'They're in at the fix,' the word goes out, as if the horses were in the gate under starter's orders.

The fix begins with the chairman suggesting an opening price, based on where the market has just been trading. Each dealer relays this to his trading room, which will hold instructions to buy or sell at certain prices for some clients and have others on the line for instant decisions.

What actually comes on the fix is any surplus between each member's sell and buy orders. If one has 2 tonnes to sell, but 2 to buy, it cancels out. Usually it does not balance precisely, so within a few seconds each representative in the fixing room indicates if he is a seller, buyer or has no interest at that price. If no seller appears at the opening bid, the price will be moved up, perhaps by only 15 cents, but by as much as a dollar in a volatile market; if no buyer, it is moved down. Once both sellers and buyers appear, the chairman calls for 'figures please' and each member specifies how many good delivery bars he is offering or requiring. 'Mocatta, sixty bars' (that is, sixty bars of 400 ounces, making 24,000 ounces), 'Sharps, forty', 'Montagu, forty', and so forth. When the amounts match, the price is fixed. On occasion it may take twenty or thirty tries at different prices to balance perfectly, while many players tuned in to the fix may judge the way the tide is flowing before making their own move. And in a volatile market, fresh instructions may well materialize, justifying a little 'Flag up' showmanship while everyone is kept informed. The price may not be fixed when any flag is up.

Commission at the fix is by agreement, but is usually 20 cents; payment and delivery are made two working days later, with delivery at the member's vault unless otherwise agreed. The turnover is never revealed. Dealers brush aside such questions with a brisk 'a few tonnes'. In fact, it may range from zero to more than 20 tonnes. The continuing appeal of the London fixing is that it provides a benchmark twice a day on which deals can be done at a confirmed price. There is no argument about a sale or purchase on the fix, as there can be about other deals struck with a floating price, which can well be up or down a dollar or two within minutes of the chairman at Rothschilds saying, 'Fixed at three hundred and seventy-six dollars fifty.'

Just how strong is the role of the fix in a highly fluid global market? When I asked an experienced trader, who had been on the desk for several market-makers over the years, he said, 'It is still a benchmark for small consumers and producers, but larger sellers and buyers are sometimes worried now about its depth and it is sometimes short-circuited by the dealers. Let's say one Swiss bank needs to sell and another to buy; if they do it through the fix it costs them 20 cents, so they'll say let's do it directly for 15 cents. And if a central bank wants to do several tonnes a day, you'll see it on the fix, but if it's done outside you can conceal it.' Then a thought came to him and, with a gleam in his eye, he added, 'Of course, the fixing can take huge volumes, especially if you can push it at first by 50 cents.'

The fixing celebrates its seventy-fifth anniversary in 1994, the same year in which the Bank of England celebrates its three hundredth anniversary. Both are landmarks in the gold business, not forgetting Mocatta & Goldsmid, which notches up 325 years a couple of years later. By comparison, no other market has yet cut its teeth.

### Zürich: Number One for Physical Gold

Switzerland always strikes me as a user-friendly country for gold. No sooner are you off the plane than small gold bars and coins gleam seductively on the bank counter as you change money, while nearby discreet advertisements for this or that private bank remind you that they have been going strong for a couple of hundred years and usually accept the wisdom of a little gold in a portfolio. Take a Zürich tram (number 7, 11 or 13) down the Bahnhofstrasse to Paradplatz, and the solid edifices of Union Bank of Switzerland, Crédit Suisse and Swiss Bank Corporation pass by with gold nestling in their windows. In the lobby of Crédit Suisse you can sit at ease on comfortable sofas watching a giant revolving board tick up the prices before stepping over to the special gold sales window for a Swiss Vreneli coin, one of the designer small bars that Crédit Suisse pioneered, or even a glossy 1-kilo bar if you happen to have around $12,000 or 18,000 Swiss francs handy. Naturally the gold is tax-free; unwisely the Swiss authorities did levy a tax on physical gold a few years ago, but collected so little revenue, because everyone opened a tax-exempt metal account, or went to Luxembourg instead, that they soon cancelled it.

The respect for gold is shared by the Swiss National Bank, the central bank, which has 2,590 tonnes in its reserves, or 12.4 ounces for every man, woman and child in the country, easily the highest per capita holding in the world. The gold accounts for nearly 50 per cent of Switzerland's official reserves and by law must provide at least 40 per cent backing for the note issue. Nor must one forget that the Bank for International Settlements (BIS), the central bankers' bank, has made its home in Basel since it was founded in 1931. The BIS not only keeps its own nest-egg of gold, but very discreetly handles many central bank gold transactions, in which the Swiss banks on its doorstep can be useful counterparties; while the World Gold Council, promoter of the allure of gold on behalf of the mining industry, maintains its head office in Geneva. As a Swiss banker observed over lunch off the Bahnhofstrasse, 'Gold is part of our banking culture.'

Forget all those innovations of paper gold; this is the heart of the physical gold business, with the twin track of private investment and an unrivalled distribution network to the far corners of the world built up over two generations. When I first went on the gold trail in the 1960s to places like Dubai, Vientiane and Jakarta, it was the Swiss who were there first. They had a nice little operation going in the Oriental Store in the main street of Vientiane, which sold washing machines out front while the office safe at the back was full of kilo bars destined for Vietnam. Nothing has changed. What is the favourite bar in Vietnam in the 1990s? Swiss Bank Corporation's kilo bar with the logo of three crossed keys; the only change is that the gold is now routed via Singapore. Meanwhile, in the Middle East, virtually 80 per cent of the gold imports of Dubai are from Switzerland, and in Saudi Arabia this rises to over 90 per cent. A real asset for the Swiss in getting established in these regional markets was that they were acting as principals with their own substantial stocks of gold. They could afford, therefore, to hold large consignment stocks abroad, because they amounted to part of the bank's own reserves. Although much stricter accounting procedures, as well as security considerations in places like the Gulf, have made everyone more wary of placing big consignment stocks, they remain a useful way of keeping the Swiss foot in the door.

Sales are by no means all far flung. At home Swiss watch-makers require up to 30 tonnes (almost a million ounces) annually, while the neighbouring Italian jewellery industry takes upwards of 400 tonnes (12.9 million ounces) each year to fulfil its task as chain-maker to the world. The banks in Geneva have close links with the French, whose gold market was long controlled, while those in Basel have been handy not only for German investors, but also for the jewellery fabricators of Pforzheim. All told, Switzerland exports well over 1,000 tonnes (32 million ounces) a year, which is virtually half the world mine supply.

Moreover, this physical business runs counter-cyclical to private investment. When export business to Italy or the Middle East is booming because the gold price is low, portfolio managers in the private banks are rarely paying much attention to gold (they should, but that is another matter). The moment prices start to improve, however, the physical business dries up, but portfolio managers are scrambling to buy on the rising tide. Switzerland thus acts as a kind of sponge for gold, soaking it up in the private banks at one moment, but squeezing it out again around the globe at another. Curiously enough, by early 1993, after five years of a bear market in gold, it was almost squeezed dry. A Zürich dealer lamented to me that he could scarcely get gold to keep his refinery going to make kilo bars and 10-tola bars for export because the private banks had all sold out; the next week the price took off, exports slowed, but the Geneva private banks were running after gold again. His previous search for gold, however, brings us to the nub of the issue; Zürich became the world's premier physical gold market not just through the demand of the disparate customers it serviced, but because it latched on to the marketing of South African and Soviet output when those two countries accounted for almost 90 per cent of mine supply.

Although the main three Swiss banks all had experience in the gold business before World War II, initially through supplying the Swiss watch industry and then French hoarders in the 1930s, the foundations of their wholesale network were laid in the post-war years. The London gold market was closed, but they were free to deal in gold – often paying a good premium to get their hands on it (see Chapter 3). Once London reopened after the war in 1954, the Swiss were frustrated in getting gold at first hand, because South African and Soviet gold was all channelled there. They persevered, however, so that by 1968 they were consistently the largest physical buyers in London, often taking three-quarters of what was on offer. The closure of London for two weeks in 1968, after the collapse of the international gold pool, provided the window of opportunity to form a united front between the three banks and persuade South Africa to sell direct to them.

The Swiss grasp of the physical business meant they had no hesitation in bidding for South Africa's gold; they even committed themselves to take a substantial part of 1969 output at prices over $40 an ounce. A bold, even slightly rash, step because the market had a huge overhang of gold bought by the speculators, when they overwhelmed the pool in 1968, which took a while to digest. 'It's no secret,' a dealer admitted afterwards. 'We lost a great deal of money. It was a very difficult time for us and South Africa.' But it secured the Swiss the long-term dividend of marketing 80 per cent of South Africa's gold throughout the 1970s, and up to half of it thereafter.

The Swiss control of the physical business was further strengthened from 1972 when the Soviet Union emerged as a big seller again, for it, too, channelled the gold into Zürich. The Russians operated through Wozchod Handelsbank, just off the Bahnhofstrasse, where the convivial chairman of the bank greeted mid-morning visitors with a glass of vodka and sought their views on the prospects for gold. Counting on Swiss banking secrecy, the Russians would often start moving large amounts of gold into Zürich from about May each year, drip-feeding it into the market through the summer if a bad harvest was anticipated at home. Then, in October, came the public announcement that the harvest was a disaster. Pundits would look for Russian gold sales to pay for grain imports; the sales were already done. The Russians shifted just over 2,000 tonnes (almost 65 million ounces) into Zürich in the decade after 1972, with very heavy sales of up to 400 tonnes (12.9 million ounces) in 1976, 1977 and 1978, when they suffered serious deficits. Although Wozchod itself got into trouble in the early 1980s and sales became more diversified to Frankfurt, London, Tokyo and Singapore, the Bank for Foreign Economic Affairs of the USSR, which took on the Zürich operation, kept dealing gold there. And as the Soviet Union began to collapse and its gold reserves were shifted abroad to be swapped or sold, much of the gold came into Zürich. In the first half of 1990 alone over 200 tonnes was airfreighted into Switzerland.

Thus, for twenty-five years the Swiss banks have had at their disposal the mainstream of gold mine supply. The fountainhead of their activity is, of course, Zürich, from which most international business is done. Although the three major banks get most of the headlines, Bank Leu, Switzerland's oldest bank founded in 1755, was also an important gold trader and one of the world's largest coin dealers, until Crédit Suisse took a controlling interest and Leu's separate gold-dealing operations were suspended in 1992 – although its speciality in numismatic gold coins continues as a separate new company, Leu Numismatic AG. Julius Baer, however, just next to Bank Leu on the Bahnhofstrasse, remains an active gold trader on behalf of a wide range of investors and cantonal banks. Meanwhile, the big three, whose pool enabled them to secure South African supplies in 1968, also established their own brokers, Premex, in 1982, in which each has an equal share. 'Premex made us more of a market,' reflected a dealer, 'because it provided liquidity and brought in good counterparties from outside.' While Zürich focuses on international business, the big three also maintain customer desks in Basel, Chiasso and Geneva to concentrate on local business (the private banks in Geneva, for instance) or immediate cross-border requirements.

### Banking on Refineries

The unique asset all three banks possess, which does not apply to any other European or North American major market-maker, is that each has its own precious metal refinery. The oldest is Métaux Précieux SA Metalor at Neuchatel, which has its origins in a firm of gold smelters and watch case manufacturers, Martin de Pury & Cie, founded in 1852, and taken over by Swiss Bank Corporation in 1918 (Swiss Bank was a buyer in the first week of the London fixing in 1919, presumably for that refinery). Metalor also runs a small refining facility in Hong Kong, mainly for scrap, and has taken over Leach & Garner, the US refiner and semi-fabricator, securing London good delivery status for that refinery under the Metalor chop. While Metalor grew up serving Swiss watch-makers, the Argor refinery, set up in Chiasso in 1951, was on the doorstep of the Italian jewellery industry. Argor was taken over by Union Bank of Switzerland in 1973, which expanded its refining operations in 1986 in partnership with W. C. Heraeus from Germany to build a new refinery nearby at Medrisio (in which UBS has 75 per cent) with facilities for gold, silver, platinum and palladium. Crédit Suisse relies on Valcambi, founded at Balerna (adjoining Chiasso) in 1961 and a fully owned subsidiary since 1980. While producing the normal range of gold bars, Valcambi is also a leading manufacturer of gold watch cases and bracelets.

But the image of Crédit Suisse has been enhanced by its superb range of small bars, designed to capture a joint jewellery/investment audience. Its current range of 'Lingots d'or' embraces twenty-one different bars from 1 gram to 1 kilo, with additional variations in 1 tael (37.4175 grams) with Chinese markings for Southeast Asia and China, and 1, 5 and 10 tolas (1 tola is 11.6638 grams) for the Gulf and the Indian sub-continent. Alongside are 'Lingots de motifs', emblazoned with everything from a rose or an Arabian coffee pot to the Chinese dragon, available in sizes from 1 gram to 100 grams. The other Swiss refineries naturally compete with such exotica, but if you admire the gold displays in shops anywhere from Jeddah to Bahrain or Singapore to Taipei, the Crédit Suisse name tends to predominate.

Its real rival, however, is another refinery close to Chiasso, PAMP, which is short for Produits Artistiques de Métaux Précieux. PAMP was the creation of Mahmoud Shakarchi, the great Beirut exchange dealer and gold trader, who moved to Switzerland during the civil war in Lebanon (although he stuck it through the first few years virtually running the exchange business of Lebanon from his apartment with armed guards on the door). PAMP first set up shop in one room in Chiasso in 1977 and soon began turning out the Fortuna range of small ingots of 1 to 50 grams, depicting the Roman goddess of Fortune emerging from a conch shell. The Fortuna has since been marketed in diamond, oval and pear shapes, as well as the traditional ingot. The designs were an instant hit in the Middle East. In a record year from that small workshop in Chiasso, where it was quite hard to move around without tripping over long strips of gold or piles of tiny bars, PAMP produced over 27 tonnes (870,000 ounces), setting the seal on the small bar vogue. It graduated to a full refinery at Castel San Pietro in 1984, opened by Sheikh Yamani, then the Saudi Arabian oil minister, and soon won its London good delivery status. PAMP now produces a full range of bars that increasingly compete with the older-established Swiss refineries in the Middle East and Southeast Asia. Its latest innovation is a 1-ounce Fortuna gold coin which forms the face of a simple watch, which is marketed at only 20 per cent over the gold price. The concept is that if the watch ceases to function, the owner still has an ounce of gold.

On the trading front, too, PAMP's owner, MKS Finance SA in Geneva, has made a name for itself dealing not just in physical gold, but also in OTC and listed options and as a specialist in location swaps. It has been quite high profile in the market from time to time as a channel for Middle East clients. Indeed, much Middle East business that was once done in Beirut switched to Switzerland in the 1970s, as exchange dealers and bankers fled the civil war. Twenty years ago Beirut was the gold market for the Middle East, the turntable through which gold went to Turkey, Syria, Iraq, Jordan, Egypt and Saudi Arabia. Nowadays this business is mostly done, whether physical or trading, out of Zürich or Geneva. Admittedly, the enthusiasm of many Middle East players for gold waned over the years; there are fewer ready to buy or sell 300,000 ounces before the first London fix, just to get the market rolling, but it is often easier to get a clue to their mood through a couple of calls to Switzerland than by asking in Riyadh or Kuwait.

The enthusiasm for gold cooled everywhere in Switzerland after 1987 as price and volatility declined. Even when the dollar price sometimes rallied, the Swiss franc price drifted downwards. Portfolio managers in the big banks and investment committees in the private banks all crossed gold off their list of recommendations. Traditionally the Swiss had recommended that up to 10 per cent of a portfolio should be in gold; some of this might be in gold shares, but most was in kilo bars or coin and it was often held physically for the clients in allocated accounts, especially in the private banks. During the bull market of the late 1970s, for example, there was a substantial physical build-up as private banks squirrelled gold away; it happened again in 1986 when there was a build-up of 286 tonnes in Swiss stocks, as money managers turned more favourable to gold. By the late 1980s, it was a different story entirely; far from advising 10 per cent (even 15 per cent on occasion), there was, for the first time in my recollection, no recommendation to hold gold at all. 'We don't even discuss it at our monthly meeting any more,' a private banker in Geneva confided. At one of the big three banks, portfolio exposure to gold fell to scarcely 1 per cent by 1992. Between 1988 and 1991 there was an unprecedented shakeout of physical investment holdings. What little remained was often sold into any rally, such as that prompted by the Gulf War. One banker recalled that the rise then to over $400 was taken as an ideal chance by one Arab client to get rid of over 2 tonnes he had held for years; even a Swiss pension fund shed its last gold holding early in 1993. And in skiing resorts like St Moritz and Gstaad, where local banks had once done a brisk business in metal account or gold options for wealthy visitors each winter, the action was all in currency plays.

The shakeout had practical effects on gold-dealing desks; as the counterparties disappeared traders were often switched to foreign exchange with just a sideline brief to watch gold. The mood was summed up by a private banker, who was invited to speak on gold at a conference, but replied that he had not favoured gold for several years, so there really was nothing for him to say. An attitude reversed rather rapidly in 1993 when the price improved.

The Swiss preoccupation with physical gold did leave them slightly behind in the race for paper alternatives that began in the 1970s. They had nothing to match the magnet of futures on Comex in New York, which distracted many speculators who might otherwise have traded on metal account in Switzerland. 'The market has gone to New York,' conceded a dealer. In options, however, one of the first initiatives came from Valeurs White Weld in Geneva in 1976, on the inspiration of Robert Strebel, formerly head of gold and foreign exchange at UBS. Valeurs (later renamed Crédit Suisse First Boston Futures Trading) options were the forerunners of the over-the-counter (OTC) options that later became all the rage (see Chapter 14). Eventually, the big three banks joined in with their own OTC options books, but as late starters rather than pioneers. They have also gone worldwide with gold-dealing desks in branches abroad. Go to Bahrain, Hong Kong, London, Melbourne, New York, Sydney or Tokyo and at least one, if not all, the Swiss banks are trading gold or providing finance and marketing to the more diversified cast of international gold-mining companies.

The attention to mining finance is essential, because although the Swiss have huge capacity and muscle on the physical side, the natural supply from South Africa and the former Soviet Union, which has so long flowed their way, is often being diverted nowadays to regional gold markets. The markets of Asia, in particular, look increasingly to Australian or North American refineries for their gold. The ending of South African sanctions also means that part of her production is converted into kilo bars at the Rand Refinery in Johannesburg for dispatch to the Middle East and Southeast Asia, short-circuiting the Swiss refiners (although the bars may go on Swiss account). In the former Soviet Union gold production has declined and does not necessarily flow to Zürich. Here at least the Swiss can play the trump card of their refineries because, except for Russia herself, the other CIS republics like Uzbekistan and Kazakhstan which produce much of the gold, do not have their own refineries with good delivery status. The Swiss have hastened there to point out they can offer swap facilities, refining and marketing.

They have also been going after the output of new mines in Ghana and Saudi Arabia. Securing it is not easy; the strong Swiss franc and greater overheads make competitive prices tricky. 'We have higher costs in fabrication, insurance and transport,' admitted a Zürich dealer. That makes it tougher not just to match toll refining costs, but to deliver kilo bars into regional markets competitively. The Swiss would like to get at least $1.20 an ounce premium on kilo bars; their rivals sometimes quote less than $1.00, especially in markets where the special cachet of a Swiss brand image is less important because the bars go into the melting pot for jewellery-making, rather than hoarding. A different approach has become necessary, especially because the portfolio investment business in Switzerland has been less. 'We need a larger sales force,' said the dealer, 'going for mining finance, central banks and big institutions.' An admission that, after a generation as the world's turntable for physical gold, times are changing.

Not that all his Zürich colleagues are so pessimistic. Over coffee the next morning the head of a rival bullion department said confidently, 'The Zürich gold market is still stronger and more profitable than people assume.' Then he beamed and added, 'We've all three got global networks and all the product ranges.' He ticked them off on his fingers; 'You can deal large or small; spot, forward, options, refining, melting, finance – you get them all here. Who'll give you that in London?'

### Frankfurt: D is for Deutsche, Dresdner, Degussa

Frankfurt, the financial capital of Germany, may not instantly spring to mind as a major gold market, but do not under-estimate the sheer muscle of its banks. Who consistently hit the headlines in buying gold at the IMF and Treasury auctions in the 1970s? Dresdner Bank. Who made the Krugerrand bullion coin a best-seller and, more recently, headed the steering committee on Soviet debt which was partly secured by gold swaps? Deutsche Bank. Whose bars may you expect to find in Jeddah, Dubai or Singapore? Degussa, which has been a refiner in the frontier of gold technology since 1843. To this triumvirate of Ds, one should add H for Heraeus, also in gold refining since 1851, and now partnered, too, with Union Bank of Switzerland in a new Swiss refinery. While the Bundesbank, the central bank, just happens to be holding 3,701 tonnes (almost 120 million ounces), the world's second largest official reserve exceeded only by the United States.[7]

Those credentials give Frankfurt considerable clout in the gold market, even though it is not an international trading forum like London and New York. The Bundesbank, for instance, stands aside from the gold business, unlike the Bank of England's daily involvement with the London market. But the two main banks, Deutsche and Dresdner, are international market-makers with strong ties to central banks and major

---

7 This excludes just over 900 tonnes which the Bundesbank has with the European Monetary Co-operation fund, as part backing for the European Currency Unit (ECU).

mining houses.[7A] They enjoyed, too, long-standing links with the former Soviet Union, part of whose gold they were marketing in the 1980s. They had one discreet advantage in this regard in that goods coming into West Germany from East Germany were not recorded in import figures, providing a handy channel for moving some Russian gold.

Deutsche Bank's experience in precious metals dates back to the 1870s, when it was closely involved with the disposal of German silver stocks as the country went over to a gold standard. It was an early lesson in handling large disposals of precious metals. Gustavus Pietsch, the London manager of Deutsche at the time, told a British parliamentary committee on silver in 1876 that it had sold 26 million ounces and another 50 million ounces might be in prospect. 'The sales were never pressed,' he remarked. 'On the contrary, we lost many an opportunity to sell by holding out for prices which were above the market . . . sales will go on in the same way, with great moderation . . . it will be an operation which will go on gradually for a certain number of years until the whole operation is completed.'[8] These are words which have a real echo in the style of Deutsche's bullion department today and which will, one trusts, be pinned above every dealer's desk there should the Bundesbank ever contemplate selling its current gold stocks.

Dresdner Bank, on the other hand, really made its name in gold in the 1970s, as the major buyer at IMF and US Treasury gold sales (see Chapter 18). Time after time Dresdner's bullion department, under the flamboyant leadership in those days of Hans Joachim Schreiber, was bidding for 500,000 ounces at a clip. Who was the client? The gossip was that it was oil money from Kuwait and Saudi Arabia, but Herr Schreiber never volunteered a single clue. What he did do, though, was realize quickly that options offered an ideal way of hedging the huge positions he was acquiring at the auctions by selling calls, while also benefiting from the premium. Dresdner's granting of options helped considerably in making the fledgling Valeurs White Weld's option business in Geneva get off the ground by providing a much needed large-scale writer to give it counterparties on each side.

Both the German banks rode the mainstream of the gold market's expansion over the last twenty years, trading through their London, Hong Kong and New York offices, attracting business because they stood out as such strong players. And in the physical business, although neither owned refineries, they also had the back-up of Degussa, whose bars have become increasingly accepted in regional markets. Degussa itself has established a successful additional refinery in Singapore, to cater for the blossoming Southeast Asian market, feeding it from the

7A Deutsche enhanced its position in 1993 by taking over the London dealers Sharps Pixley from Kleinwort Benson and thus securing a seat at the 'fixing'.
8 Evidence of Gustavus Pietsch, House of Commons Select Committee upon the causes of the depreciation in the price of silver and the effects of such depreciation upon the exchange between India and England, 1876.

new gold mines just four hours' flight away in Western Australia.
Degussa has also been long established in Brazil, thus being on hand to
benefit from the gold-mining boom there. In all, it has three refineries
whose bars have London good delivery status. Its competitor, Heraeus,
also rates good delivery, but concentrates more on a worldwide network
of manufacturing facilities for jewellery alloys and specialist products in
the electronics, dental and decorative fields. Degussa and Heraeus have
been the pioneers not only in gold technology, but also in platinum,
putting Germany in the forefront of the industrial uses of these metals
(see Chapter 21).

Within Germany the domestic gold business in recent years has
been dictated by the tax regime. Prior to 1980 there was value added tax
on gold bars, but not on legal tender gold coins; from 1980 until 1992
the tax was extended to all gold coins; from 1 January 1993 it was taken
off everything. The story of the market is thus in three clear stages. The
Germans, of course, had good reason to have faith in gold. Two world
wars, the inflation of the early 1920s, and then the perceived threat from
the communists over the Berlin Wall in a divided nation: such a feeling
of insecurity in an environment that was nevertheless increasingly
prosperous, made West Germany, as it then was, a great market for gold
coins. Initially the favourite was the Austrian 100 Corona re-strike dated
1915, but that swiftly gave way in the mid-1970s to the new Krugerrand
bullion coin. As Deutsche Bank marketed the coin aggressively through
its 1,200 branches and Bayerrische Landesbank, also an authorized
distributor, filtered them into the network of *Sparkassen* or savings
banks, an annual demand of 2 million coins (over 60 tonnes) built up.
Germany, in fact, was taking two-thirds of all Krugerrands for a while.
Overnight the imposition of value added tax on the coins in 1980
virtually shut down the market. Only the professional interbank market
in Germany, including, besides Dresdner and Deutsche, such players as
Commerzbank, and DG Bank, was exempt. The investment business
simply went 'offshore' or rather just over the frontier to Luxembourg,
which obligingly did not impose any tax on gold. Commerzbank even
made its Luxembourg branch the main office for all gold business. This
diversion helped greatly in the establishment of Luxembourg as a gold
market in its own right, as we shall see in the following section. The
international market-making role of the big banks was not, of course,
affected, but the domestic market for physical investment shut down for
the duration; only a modest scatter of coins and small bars continued to
be sold over the counter within Germany. It was just much easier either
to buy a gold certificate in Germany confirming delivery in Luxembourg
or pop over there in person to buy.

Surprisingly, the arrival of the European Community's 'single market' for member countries from 1 January 1993 changed all this. The point is that within the single market citizens can move about freely and take whatever goods they wish 'for their own personal use' with them. For many this was seen as the chance to take home plenty of fine French wine, but it applies equally to gold. Since the gold market community in the EC could not agree to harmonize their value added taxes on gold, this left an unresolved anomaly of gold being liable for nil tax in Luxembourg, 1 per cent in Belgium, 14per cent in Germany, 17½ per cent in the United Kingdom and 30 per cent in Spain, yet with free movement between them. The German solution, diplomatically engineered by Deutsche Bank, was simply to get their tax 'harmonized' with Luxembourg's at zero. Tough on Luxembourg, which lost one of its best customers overnight, but a coup for Frankfurt which can now offer gold bars and coins to all EC citizens without tax The move, among other things, gives more meaning to the daily gold fixing held at 12 noon to set a DM price for 1-kilo and 12½-kilo bars in the local interbank market; this fixing continued during the tax years, because interbank dealing was exempt, but the volume was small.

Stopping over in Frankfurt a few weeks later, I found a new bustle. Bullion coin and kilo bar sales were brisk, while many investors were switching back home holdings that they had previously kept in Luxembourg or Switzerland. Since Germany has the highest savings rate of any EC country, local buying is expected to grow, given the uncertainties now facing much of Europe, especially if the Community decides to risk inflation in an effort to create jobs. The German initiative in going to zero rating on gold might just be overruled and some 'harmonization' of higher tax levels eventually agreed. In the meantime, Frankfurt is a more genuine market place for gold. That role will be enhanced by growing business with Eastern Europe now that the barriers are down. Initially, the banks got their hand in by discreetly selling 22 tonnes of gold that the newly united German government had inherited from the former German Democratic Republic. The benefit is likely to be felt not only by the banks, but also by the specialists like Degussa and Heraeus whose bars and jewellery alloys are already in demand in the east. On a visit to Prague, for example, a jewellery manufacturer told me that whereas under communism they got a minimal central allocation of gold each year to make simple wedding rings, they now bought up some local scrap, drove over to Pforzheim, the capital of German jewellery-making, and traded it against the new gold they required. 'The big advantage is our geographical location,' said Fritz Plass of Deutsche

Bank, 'and secondly that the currency mainly circulating in the East bloc is the DM so that avoids another exchange of money if people there want to go into gold.'

### Luxembourg: A Market of Convenience

Why did Luxembourg blossom as Europe's brightest new gold market in the 1980s? Answer: because Germany and Switzerland put a tax on gold and France abolished anonymous buying. Next question: what happens to the Luxembourg gold market in the 1990s now that these three policies have been reversed? Answer: not much, unless they are revised yet again, which is not entirely impossible. This may seem hard on the Grand Duchy, and it remains a thriving little nutshell of a financial centre in other respects, with its strict banking secrecy laws. It is also a pleasant place to visit, much more informal than most gold centres, with several of the banks quartered in handsome villas. There are a lot of them, which is another reason why gold flourished there almost overnight; they had only to add gold to the 'offshore' financial services already on offer. When Golddealers Luxembourg was founded in April 1983 to promote the market, it soon had ninety members, although some of these were abroad. But the slate of whom one ought to see was quite lengthy, and if you missed someone out they tended to hear you were in their small town and invite you over.

Luxembourg, then, was a gold market waiting to take off. West Germany and Switzerland slapped tax on gold in 1980. Luxembourg had a daily gold fixing for 1-kilo and good delivery bars going by March 1981. This was nice timing because the socialists won the election in France a couple of months later and there was a rush to get gold coins in there before all kinds of restrictions and the nationalization of banks were introduced, including cancelling the traditional anonymity of gold buying. That summer scores of students made a nice business going back and forth on the train between Luxembourg and Paris bearing gold coins for eager French hoarders. As it happens, that was the last great rush by the French to buy gold, but it got the Luxembourg banks off to a flying start with their French connections. And when the mood in France turned against gold some years later as the price languished, Luxembourg benefited from a nice reverse trade in dishoarded coins. The Swiss authorities, incidentally, having imposed their tax, got mighty suspicious of people arriving from this new tax haven. I arrived in Zürich one day on the little Crossair plane direct from Luxembourg and it was the only occasion in perhaps a hundred visits that the customs wanted to look in my briefcase. Anyway, the Swiss thought better of it before long and gave up their tax to compete equally with Luxembourg.

What both countries were really after was the German business.

The serious volume of physical and metal account business that Luxembourg developed over the years was with German investors, avoiding their own 14 per cent value added tax. This applied particularly to coins like the Krugerrand, which had been such a hit in Germany and later to Canada's Maple Leaf which rather took over as the preferred bullion coin of the 1980s, once sanctions on South Africa tightened. The main German banks offered gold certificates for bars or coins delivered *loco* their Luxembourg branches. Commerzbank even shifted all its gold operations to its Luxembourg office. Among the local banks, Banque International and Kredietbank became significant gold traders in a market that was handling upwards of a million ounces of physical bar gold and 250,000 bullion coins a year, much of it on allocated or unallocated accounts.

Golddealers Luxembourg also sought to educate its members about the wider world of gold and to explain itself to all comers in seminars and conferences, including the annual European Precious Metals Conference which it hosted for several years. All this effort, however, could not disguise the fact that it was walking on eggshells; not only were the policies that had initiated its start-up being reversed, but the European investor was rapidly falling out of love with gold by the early 1990s. The sales volumes were just not there and many of the banks cut back on their gold-trading desks. Golddealers Luxembourg merged with the local Forex association in 1992; the Precious Metals Conference was cancelled. The German agreement to 'harmonize' its tax on gold with that of Luxembourg – at zero – from 1 January 1993 really removed the last serious reason for Luxembourg to thrive as a regional centre. Naturally some gold business will remain in such an offshore financial centre, but it will be modest. That was the Luxembourg market, that was.

### Paris: the way we were
The French, one has to admit, run a very civilized gold market. Their gold fixing takes place in the basement of the Bourse at 12.30 p.m., so that as soon as it is over everyone can repair for lunch at a neighbouring restaurant (may I suggest A la Cloche des Halles, an authentic wine bistro, or Gérard Besson, which has two Michelin rosettes, for a grand blow-out). Over lunch, one can reminisce on the way it was in the Paris gold market a generation ago, when the French, encouraged by General de Gaulle, really were the world's greatest hoarders. In that famous summer of discontent in 1968, as the students took to the barricades, most other Frenchmen took to gold; they hoarded an astonishing 450

tonnes (14.5 million ounces) that year. The Paris fix really was the one
to watch in those days.

The trouble is that although for a brief period in 1968 France was
an open gold market, restrictions on the import and export of gold by
individuals were swiftly reimposed and lasted until 1987. This effectively
isolated France from the emerging global market, and made it merely a
domestic one increasingly concerned only with the constant recycling of
gold, particularly coins, within the country. The smugglers, *passeurs* the
French call them, did their bit, spiriting in kilo bars and coins, often in
specially adapted Citroen cars with cavities beneath the back seat that
could be revealed only if you did things like turn on the windscreen
wipers and push in the cigarette lighter in the right sequence. This kept
the market topped up and it was often quite an open affair. A *passeur* I
knew from Marseilles used to nip down to the post office every morning
to call up a bank in Switzerland to place an order; since French
telecommunications in those days were not too advanced, he had to
book the call and wait for a cabin to be free. One morning he had hardly
arrived and not yet ordered his call, when the girl behind the counter
piped up, 'I've already got Mr .... at ...... Bank on the line for you in
Cabin three!'

The French addiction to gold stemmed, of course, from two world
wars which swept across their country in a generation, leading to
repeated devaluations of the franc. Kilo bars and coins, especially the
20-franc Napoleon (first minted in 1803) and latterly US$20 Double
Eagle and Mexican 50-peso Centenario re-strikes, became the basic
form of savings. The total hoard in France is often estimated to have
reached between 5,000 and 6,000 tonnes, peaking in the early 1970s.
(Banque de France, of course, also has the national habit with a gold
stock of 3,182 tonnes.) Thereafter, political and economic stability
gradually weaned the French away from gold as their first line of savings,
until today a young generation that has no experience of the trials of war
and its aftermath is often concerned merely to sell the coins as they are
inherited. The French jewellery industry now virtually lives off the
supply of re-smelted coins. The only short-lived resurgence of the old
habit came when the socialists won the election in 1981 and declared
that gold buying could no longer be anonymous and was liable to 7 per
cent tax on resale. That initiated a flourishing *passeur* traffic between
Paris and the new Luxembourg gold market, as we saw in the previous
section. Anonymity was restored in 1986, however, and with full
relaxation of exchange controls the following year, the free import and
export of gold was permitted. But by then no one was really interested
in playing the international stage. Some of the French banks did talk of

getting more actively into gold with proposals for a Paris gold futures exchange, but nothing materialized. The big banks, such as Société Générale, have settled for including gold in the array of options they offer, while Banque Française du Commerce Extérieur (BFCE) found a nice line in supplying kilo bars to Vietnam, where gold is increasingly used as money (Chapter 17). The banks also took on board some swaps when the collapsing Soviet Union disposed of its reserves, but they do not carry the weight on the global gold scene of the big US, German or Swiss banks.

So, to savour the spirit of the French gold scene, it is still best to head for the basement of the Bourse a few minutes after noon to witness what is gold's only open-outcry fixing for physical gold. A little knot of spectators assembles outside the fixing room and is held back behind a low wooden barrier by a couple of policemen. The ceremony is presided over by Compagnie Parisienne de Rescompte (CPR) and there are nine other participants.[9] Jean-Claude Martini from CPR usually presides and he loves to whip up a little action when he has visitors at his side. Each firm has its own booth, where a couple of clerks crouch over phone lines to their offices. In the centre of the room the brokers themselves stand around a waist-high oval counter, clutching little slips of white paper with their buying and selling orders. Behind them the prices for bars and coins flash up on a large electronic board. The fixing starts by determining a price for the 12.5-kilo bar (the 400-ounce good delivery), then moves on to the kilo bar (*la savonnette*, or bar of soap, to the French) and then to coins. Surprisingly, the Mexican 50-peso Centenario is the most widely traded 'bullion coin' in France, because all are dated 1947, meaning they *could* have been imported in the short-lived open market of 1968, although they may have been smuggled in ten years later.

A broker who is selling will shout *'Je l'ai'*, while buyers call *'Je le prends'*. To the outsider it proceeds with bewildering speed; arms are waved, messengers from the booths dash up with new bids. Suddenly it's all over: the scoreboard reads, *'barre 995 − 67700 [francs], lingot 1kg − 67900, 50 pesos Mex − 2590'*. And so to lunch. At Gérard Besson, by the way, the specialities include *Homard et poissons de la baie d'Erquy*.

---

9 The others are: Banque Nationale de Paris, Banque de Paris et Pays Bas, Compagnie des Métaux Précieux (refiners and semi-fabricators), Comptoir Lyon-Allemand Louyot (also refiners and semi-fabricators), Crédit de la Bourse, Crédit Lyonnais, Crédit du Nord, Neuflize Schlumberger Mallet and Société Générale.

# CHAPTER 16

# North America

### New York: The Big League

A gold trader in New York has to get up early. The market opens at 8.20 a.m. The market, of course, is Comex, short for the New York Commodity Exchange, whose gold futures contract, launched around midnight on 31 December 1974, propelled New York into the big league in gold. The early morning start, too, is an acknowledgement of its worldwide clientele; originally it was 9.25 a.m., but the earlier kick-off suits the Europeans as they come back from lunch, the Middle East players as they return to their offices in the early evening and Hong Kong or Tokyo traders for a quick glimpse of the New York mood before they go to bed.

Comex put New York on the gold map and, almost twenty years on, remains the heart of the market. Yet nowadays when European dealers, for instance, say that 'the market has moved to New York', they are thinking not only of Comex as the great terminal market, but also of an increasing dimension of gold trading that is done outside Comex by big market-makers in spot, forward and over-the-counter options trading. Since Comex is located on the second floor of the towering World Trade Center, this other business is often known as 'upstairs'. 'The upstairs stuff is bigger and bigger,' says George Milling Stanley of Lehman Brothers. 'New York is becoming a genuine trading centre with much more done on a principal to principal basis outside the Exchange.' One element in this change, of course, is that North America itself is now a major gold producer, providing much more daily activity for big bullion houses in mining finance, marketing and exporting gold. Just to get a perspective: combined US and Canadian output in 1980 was a mere 82 tonnes (2.6 million ounces) for a continent where fabrication was 240 tonnes (7.7 million ounces); by 1992 output was 480 tonnes with fabrication still stuck at just over 240 tonnes. Thus, among other things, there is a substantial export trade in gold to Asia. The real volume, though, remains on the trading front, whether on or off the floor of Comex, and here it is worth just a glance at the expanded international cast of players on hand in New York to understand the modern muscle in the market.

### Expanding the Line-up

The original cast of gold in the United States in the days, not so long ago, when private holding and trading were forbidden, was limited. The US Treasury then granted licences to just a handful of banks and dealers to supply metal to the jewellery, electronics and dental industries, where each fabricator was also licensed. The mainstream then was Republic National Bank of New York[1], part of Edmond Safra's banking empire and Rhode Island Hospital Trust National Bank in Providence, Rhode Island, where much of the jewellery industry is located. And there was the refiner/semi-fabricator back-up of traditional firms like Engelhard, and Handy & Harman (whose daily quote for gold and silver was the benchmark for the US trade). They were joined by J. Aron & Co., the commodity traders who made their name with coffee before taking up gold (J. Aron is now a division of Goldman Sachs). Then came Mocatta Metals Corporation in an inspired link-up between Mocatta & Goldsmid, the oldest member of the London gold market and the Newhaven psychiatrist-turned-gold-trader, Dr Henry Jarecki. The squad was completed in those days by Philipp Brothers, a division of the commodity traders Phibro Corporation (but now part of Salomon Brothers). The four New York houses made the running after gold liberalization, particularly as the official distributors of the Krugerrand and other bullion coins. They also forged many of the links between the New York market (i.e. Comex) and Middle East speculators. Indeed, in the early 1980s meetings in Jeddah, Riyadh or Abu Dhabi were often like being in a revolving door, as representatives from these New York dealers were either just before or just after you. The US commission houses were at it, too; Merrill Lynch, Shearson, Conti Commodities, Prudential Bache and Drexel Burnham Lambert (before disaster struck) were all on the road around the world. I recall a dinner in Dubai with one of the local heroes of gold and silver speculation, to which the salesman of one of these houses came along almost as a kind of 'minder'.

---

1 In 1993 Republic entered into an agreement to buy Mase Westpac, the bullion bank, thus securing themselves a seat at the 'fixing' in London.

Our host hardly let him eat, sending him to the phone every few minutes to find out how the market was doing.

The fortunes of some of these players have declined over the years, but newcomers keep turning up. The latest powerhouse is AIG Trading Corporation (a member of the American International Corporation insurance empire), which has only been in gold since 1990, but is already a significant market-maker in New York, London and Hong Kong. But it took a while for the big names of US banking, J. P. Morgan, Citibank and Chase Manhattan, to become involved and then with mixed success. Citibank was all set to become an international force in gold in the early 1990s when its plans were abruptly aborted because of the bank's losses in real estate. Chase Manhattan, however, is active with spot, forwards and options in New York, is a market-maker in London and trades in Hong Kong and São Paulo. Above all, it is J. P. Morgan (otherwise known as Morgan Guaranty Trust Company of New York) that has become a really powerful trading force in the gold market since the early 1980s, active not just in New York, but in London (as a market-maker), Hong Kong and Singapore. Once the decision to go for gold was taken, Morgan went at it with absolute professionalism. It hired Guy Field, one of the most respected dealers in the London gold market of the last generation, to set it up and assemble a team of experienced traders. The bank's links not just with central banks, major investment institutions and producers, but with many of the world's wealthiest private investors, give a breadth to its business which few can rival. 'Morgan', conceded an admiring competitor, 'is the top of the tree.'

The ultimate seal of approval for New York is the line-up of international bullion houses which are in town, not just from London or Zurich, but from Frankfurt and Tokyo too. The full complement of gold traders in New York today may be judged from the fact that Comex has sixty-two clearing members.

### On the Comex floor

So, welcome to the floor of Comex at Four World Trade Center, where the floor traders are perched on the steps (a different step for each delivery month) of their respective pits, each 26 feet in diameter, ready to go at 8.20 in the morning. Each sports a green badge with a number so that his counterparty has only to jot that down when a trade is done (green is the colour code for gold and silver pits, blue is for aluminium and orange for copper). The pits for gold futures, gold options, silver futures and silver options nestle together. The opening price is flicking up on the electronic scoreboard: gold reads 3355 (that is to say, $335.50).

Banks of telephones around the pits are manned by runners getting instructions from their trading rooms to relay to the floor traders on little slips of white paper that are time-stamped to confirm to the client when they were accepted on the floor (the paper is shortly to be replaced by hand-held electronic cards).

The Comex futures contract is for 100 ounces of 995 fine gold for delivery in any one of six months: February, April, June, August, October and December. Originally, Comex contracts could be due for delivery up to 23 months ahead, but since 1990 the Exchange has listed gold for delivery as far out as five years (60 months) to accommodate long-term hedges being employed by producers. Trading is by open-outcry, non-stop from 8.20 a.m. to 2.30 p.m. So that, unlike the twice daily fixing in London, this is a rolling tide of battle with the price constantly in motion. Once Comex had a daily up or down limit of $25; this has been removed, although should the price move more than $75 in a session there is a mandatory fifteen-minute pause to take stock (and perhaps for floor traders to catch their breath). As a floor trader remarked to me the first time I went there some years ago, 'It's very, very physical . . . like playing football.'

Curiously enough, gold futures got off to a slow start in the mid-1970s and it was not until 1978 that, as Dr Henry Jarecki of Mocatta Metals once put it, 'They took off into the stratosphere.' The propulsion came from a combination of a weakening dollar, the second oil price shock, the hostage drama in Iran and the Soviet invasion of Afghanistan, which eventually pushed Comex to a peak of over 12 million futures contracts by 1982, which amounts to a turnover of 37,000 tonnes or one-third of all gold ever mined. Dr Jarecki called it 'the golding of America'. Thereafter, as the sparkle went out of the gold price for almost a decade (and options emerged as competition) volume slipped back to scarcely 6 million contracts in 1992. Yet it still takes only a second for some news, or rumour, to ignite the touchpaper and Comex bounced back swiftly in 1993 on rising prices.

On a somewhat lazy morning while gold still languished at $335, I was chatting to a floor trader named Mark, while his colleagues idly threw crunched up slips of paper at each other. He was lamenting the change – not just less action, but that there were now only a few heavyweight players in the market. 'Ten years ago', said Mark, 'there were individual speculators – doctors, lawyers; you could sense them and flush them out. Now it's the big commodity funds versus the big trading houses.' But for the occasion, one could still kick up a storm. 'Watch this', he went on. 'I need to get out of a short position.' He is on the top step of the pit, bouncing on his toes, waving his hand forward with five fingers extended to indicate he is selling five lots (contracts). 'At 20!' he shouts, meaning he is a seller at $335.20, with the aim of knocking the market down a trifle before covering his position. Suddenly everyone is standing, gesticulating and shouting. 'You're lying through your teeth!' a rival shouts at Mark, sensing what he is up to.

This is open-outcry at its best and, since few can make themselves heard over the racket, they use hand signals worthy of racecourse tic-tac men. The hand pushing forward, five fingers outstretched, means selling five lots of 100 ounces each. Beckoning indicates buying. Abbreviations abound. Instead of shouting 'I sell five December at $335.20', the floor trader bellows 'December at 20!' ('at' indicates he is a seller and everyone knows $335, while his five outstretched fingers indicate the number of contracts). 'Sell 2 August at market' means 'I sell two August lots at the current market price.' 'Sell 1 December $335' is interpreted as 'Sell the lot *if* the market falls to $335.' While, 'Sell 1 February 340 MIT' indicates 'Sell at market if touched', that is, 'sell *if* the price touches $340.'

Customers on Comex are not, of course, paying in full for their contracts; they buy on margin. That is the attraction and it gives them immense leverage. Once the initial deal is struck in the pit, the trading slips of the buyer's and seller's floor brokers are passed on by the brokerage or bullion houses to the clearing house, The Commodity Clearing Association, a separate corporation owned by the sixty-two clearing members, which then monitors every contract. Buyer and seller, through their brokers, post what is called initial or original margin of 5 to 20 per cent (according to their credit standing) with the clearing house. Thereafter every working day, as the price changes, the party who loses by that change must put up an additional variation margin. He may have to put up more margin one day if the price advances, but get some back the next if it retreats. This daily making to market means that buyers and sellers are not exposed to an increasing credit risk with their counterpart; they remain at the identical financial exposure to each other. Margin calls can also shake out weak players; if someone fails to put up fresh margin when called, the clearing house immediately liquidates the position.

Not that many players on Comex actually go for delivery. The speculator buys a contract not for gold, but for profit. Scarcely 1 per cent of the gold traded on Comex is delivered and paid for. Heavy liquidation of long positions often takes place just prior to delivery periods to avoid the embarrassing liability of having to accept gold or warehouse receipts. On the other hand, in the professional market, traders will often undertake an EFP (exchange for physicals) in which a

futures contract is switched ahead of time for physical or spot gold.
There is an active EFP market with dealers quoting bid and offer,
usually the Comex active month against *loco* London spot. This transaction
enables dealers to adjust their positions in different markets without
changing actual purchases or sales.

The Exchange itself also maintains stock against actual demands for
delivery and to avoid a squeeze if some big player suddenly calls for it (as
he is entirely entitled to do). But the stock is small (perhaps 20 per cent)
compared to the benchmark of 'open interest' on which professionals
keep a watchful eye, as the barometer of the market's mood. The open
interest is the daily statistic that indicates the number of contracts which
have not been fulfilled, but are still 'in play'. The level of open interest is
a key signpost, not just to how liquid the Exchange is, but how lively
the action may be just before the last trading day when all contracts must
be offset or liquidated. Increased open interest when the price is rising
signals new buyers joining in; conversely increased open interest in a
falling market indicates new sellers going short.[2]

### An option on Comex
Future contracts are only one side of Comex gold activity; the other is
options. Exchange options were first launched on Comex in October
1982 and caught on quickly. Volume hit 1 million contracts in 1984 and
peaked at over 2 million in 1987. The Comex option is for 100 ounces,
which provides the holder with the right to buy (call) or sell (put) a
Comex gold futures contract at the stated price on or before the
expiration date (see Chapter 14 for options background). The expiration
date is linked to the normal months for futures delivery. A $360
February gold call option, for example, gives the holder the right to buy
a February gold futures contract at a price of $360. As an exchange
option (as opposed to an OTC or over-the-counter option which is an
agreement between two principals) it has a value and can be traded on
the Exchange many times before it expires. But it is a much more
formally regulated instrument than the OTC options which individual
bullion banks tailor to the needs of each customer, particularly central
banks or mining houses. On Comex a list of thirteen strike prices is
listed for each put and call; they step up in increments of $10 for futures
prices below $500; $20 for prices between $500 and $1,000 and, perhaps
with some wishful thinking to the future, by $50 for futures prices over
$1,000 (at such an exhilarating level, strike prices would be staggered
£1,050, $1,100 and so on).

Although Comex options are used by the mining industry and
other professionals, they have become a speculator's favourite, accounting

---

2 See the author's *The Gold Companion*, for fuller cross-referenced definitions of the terminology of
Comex futures trading.

for perhaps 80 per cent of the turnover. Moreover, this exchange option, being a standard contract with a specific expiry date, will often influence the spot price on or near expiration day, particularly when options are just out-of-the-money, but a tweak of the price could bring them in. Let's say the strike price for a put is $385, but gold is trading at $381; an upward nudge through $385 can just do the trick. Although OTC options can have any expiration date, they are normally written with an eye on Comex expiration, so that quite often the market heaves one way or the other for a couple of days before, while exchange and OTC holders try a spot of juggling.

The complexity of options strategies has also meant some friendly rivalry between those hunkered down football players in the futures pit and the floor traders in the options pit next door. As a futures trader sniffed, 'Those options traders are college graduates with more mathematical skills – cerebral kids.' Although these wizards have enabled Comex to achieve serious options volume, the Exchange is somewhat overshadowed by the OTC market which has expanded through individual banks and trading houses outside the Exchange. 'We can't compete on the over-the-counter market,' admitted Donna Redel, the energetic chairman (as her card describes the title). But that has not stopped the New York Exchange coming up with new variations on the options theme, including short-term five-day options launched in 1991. But volume so far has been minimal – a mere 17,233 contracts in 1992.

### A shotgun marriage?

That may just be a symptom of the lack of volatility. What was missing in gold (and silver) between 1988 and 1992 was precisely that movement on which an exchange thrives. Even in 1990, helped by the flurries of Iraq's invasion of Kuwait, Comex did 9.7 million gold futures and 1.9 million options contracts; in 1992 it slumped to 6 million futures and 1.2 million options. 'The floor population needs volatility,' sighed Ms Redel. 'They need an order flow, but there's often very little activity.' The solution, it seemed, might be marriage. Comex went into a huddle with the Chicago Board of Trade (CBoT), the world's biggest futures exchange, although not in gold, early in 1993 with a view to an alliance. More bluntly the idea was that CBoT should buy Comex. But what was the marriage dowry to be? CBoT was reluctant to stump up the money. Meanwhile Comex floor traders, with a quiet market, turned their energy into opposing the deal. 'The offer is insulting,' snapped a trader, interviewed by the *Financial Times*. 'What is the Board of Trade bringing to the party?' So the party was postponed after an acrimonious meeting with the floor traders. Then the New York Mercantile Exchange

(Nymex), which offers a platinum contract but gave up on gold futures some years ago, stepped in to offer $10 million, and later raised it to $20 million. Comex remained reluctant, not least because the market had taken off with the renewed interest in gold. Comex's public relations chief Alan Hanson even told me he hoped volume might hit a record 15 million contracts in 1993. Marriage, however, still cannot be ruled out. 'It makes a lot of sense,' one leading Comex member admitted, 'because you can cut overheads and have a single clearing house. And there is mutual benefit because Nymex needs a new site and doesn't have one, but Comex does.'[3]

### Enter the funds

Alliance or not, the nature of Comex business has changed. A decade ago, the Exchange was a magnet not just for professionals in various aspects of precious metals, but for a host of small players who, through the commission houses, could trade a few contracts. Indeed, that is the long-standing essence of all futures trading in the United States, whether of gold, soya beans or pork bellies; a way to get a piece of the action without any worry about deliveries. Today, however, a powerful new force is at hand, hovering constantly like a great eagle over all the futures exchanges; it is the managed futures funds. They are said to have $25 billion at their disposal and they are into every aspect of futures and options, be they agricultural, financial or metal. 'Who are these guys?' you ask a banker, and he looks almost furtive, before he reels off names like Great Lakes, the Bacon Fund, Phoenix and Paul Tudor Jones. I wondered if I should discuss them under the heading of investment. 'No,' he said, 'they have nothing to do with investment in gold.' To which an analyst added, 'The funds have no love of gold; it's just one of many plays, but they can be a swing factor on Comex of up to 100 tonnes either way.' The investment angle should not be dismissed, because the funds' money comes from investors. And it is their track record of return that creates a snowball effect. 'They show a 25 per cent return in a year,' said another banker, 'and after a while if you are wealthy you think "I'll give them $10 million".' The approach to gold is no more emotional than it is to orange juice futures; their computer model signals it is time to get in or out, and they do so without a second's hesitation. 'The funds are almost like Jesuits, it's a true religion,' added a perceptive banker at J. P. Morgan. And based on the weight of money, one cannot discuss Comex in the early 1990s without considering the funds.

'In the past there were a lot of participants,' admitted Comex's Donna Redel. 'Now, it's a handful of funds and a smaller group of

---

3 In August 1993 the board of Comex agreed in principle to a $50 million takeover by Nymex.

dealers, so the behaviour of the floor population has been modified.' The volume is much more bunched together, as all the funds tend to come in or out in successive waves. 'One fund may come in at $351,' said Ms Redel, 'kicking up the price, so the next is in at $352; they run a trend in one direction.' They did this just a few weeks after our conversation, taking gold right up over $400. Their dimension is beyond any normal trader. 'Look at this, 8,000 contracts on only ten tickets,' said a trader going through the day's trading late one afternoon. Another was more blunt; 'The funds rule Comex,' he remarked.

At least the funds will stand up occasionally to explain themselves. At a New York seminar, organized by Goldman Sachs, three funds with around $1.3 billion at their combined disposal lifted the curtain slightly on their industry. First, they stressed its rapid growth. In 1979 the futures funds had only $500 million under management, by 1988 it was $10 billion and by 1992 it was approaching $25 billion. The funds spread this money widely; 'We trade forty-nine markets around the world,' said James McConnon of RXR group, which has $650 million to play with. 'Some markets', he added, 'are too small for us, we don't find the necessary liquidity.' The tactic is always multiple speeds. 'Sometimes we might trade a given market 35 times in a year, sometimes for one day, one week, one month,' said Mr McConnon. 'Our decisions are technically driven on mathematical models. It's not just red light or green light, but multiple speed entry and exit.' Besides futures, they were also 'heavy users of options'. As for gold itself, he said they had had a commitment to precious metals through 'thick and thin'. The aim, though, is always to ride with the market. 'Our desire is to get involved in a trend,' said Mark Fitzsimmons, of the Millburn Corporation, 'to identify it and become part of it.' He then confided, 'It's like driving a sports car: you need to feel the wheel when you're executing orders; you have to work very closely with the broker, be beside him in the pit and explain carefully what's to be done.' And he allowed that his firm has been less involved in gold because it was 'shallow and one-directional' and for the moment was more in currencies and financial futures. That raises the question of what happens to gold when the funds really do find a strong trend to ride. Their influence on the course of the price during the 1990s is likely to be substantial.

Comex itself is already limbering up to deal with them. With the approval of its regulator, the Commodity Futures Trading Commission (CFTC), Comex has removed its position limit of 6,000 contracts (i.e. 600,000 ounces), so that much larger positions can be run at the discretion of the Exchange.

While Comex braces itself, an increasing amount of trading is being done by dealers trading off the floor 'upstairs' in their own offices, hunched over computers and Reuters screens. 'Once the floor trader was perceived to have the edge because he could sense the mood down there,' explained Comex's Donna Redel; 'but now traders off the floor have the edge in detecting on their screens an over-bought or over-sold market, because their computers put in alarms at certain levels.' She turned to the screen by her own desk. 'Here it all is,' she said. 'CIBC [Canadian Imperial Bank of Commerce] is making the market, AIG is trading.' In short, a parallel market to Comex is growing upstairs or uptown. What remains to be seen, however, is whether this was more a symptom of quiet years, when there was not much to be done on the floor, so traders drummed up what other business they could in the office. But there is certainly no turning back in the use of OTC options and other derivatives outside the Exchange. What is really evolving out of this is a broader and deeper New York market.

Moreover, Comex has certainly beaten off all comers when it comes to gold contracts. No other US exchange even runs it close. Originally when gold trading was legalized, all the exchanges piled in. In Chicago the Board of Trade (CBoT), the International Monetary Market (IMM) and the Mid-America came up with a dazzle of contracts, while the New York Mercantile (Nymex) competed directly with its New York rival. Only the IMM came anywhere near Comex volume for a while, but faded out of gold in 1988, leaving only CBoT with its 100-ounce and 1-kilo contracts and Mid-America with 100 ounces, which between them clock up hardly 50,000 contracts annually. Nymex bowed out back in 1980. In gold, Comex is in a league of its own.

Indeed, outside New York the gold business as a whole is remarkably sparse, save for gold mining which is another story (Chapter 6). The jewellery manufacturers located mainly in New England and also around Los Angeles and Miami still get their supplies from Republic, Rhode Island (now part of Bank of Boston) and a tough new competitor Fleet National Bank, also located in Providence. They have the back-up too of getting gold directly from the refiners/semi-fabricators Engelhard, Handy & Harman, Metalor (formerly Leach & Garner) and Johnson Matthey, whose Salt Lake City refinery opened with perfect timing to catch the gold-mining boom in Nevada next door. All four of these refiners, incidentally, have London good delivery status and, as US exports increase, their bars do a brisk business in such places as Hong Kong and Taiwan.

However, unlike Germany or Switzerland, where the big banks can offer gold through hundreds of branches, the unit banking system in the United States means such networks just do not exist. One of the real difficulties in establishing the bullion coin or any kind of physical investment bar business in the United States is the virtual impossibility of distribution through such a diverse system of small banks in every state and town. The potential buyer often has to resort to small coins stores or a handful of dealers, such as Manfra Tordella & Brookes in New York (which, incidentally, markets China's Panda coin in the United States) or Monex in Newport Beach, California. That limitation in itself helps to fuel the futures business. It is much easier to call your broker and buy a couple of Comex gold futures contracts on margin, than risk going to some unknown coin store in the motel strip on the edge of town. This is the lesson of what makes a futures market work; local players give it the initial liquidity that gives it global appeal. As Donna Redel summed it up at a Comex annual dinner, 'Ounce for ounce, Comex is still the leading exchange in the world for precious metals.'

### Toronto: The Pioneers

Essentially the gold business in Canada dates from 1898, when the Canadian Imperial Bank of Commerce (CIBC) began buying up the gold from the Klondike gold rush through its office, little more than a log cabin, in Dawson City up in the Yukon Territory. Since the Klondike boom produced 75 tonnes (2.4 million ounces) in a little over three years and CIBC laid claim to quite a bit, that was not a bad beginning. The bank has been in gold ever since and not only in the marketing of local production. Both CIBC and the Bank of Nova Scotia, which are the two senior players, have been closely involved with the international market for many years, not least because the prohibition on gold that existed over the border in the United States from 1933 to 1974 did not apply in Canada. In the absence of any US gold trading or private buying, Toronto naturally fulfilled the role of market place for North America, giving the banks experience that none of their US colleagues could then enjoy.

While all was quiet on the US front, for example, Bank of Nova Scotia was busy as early as the 1950s, issuing gold certificates, along with Samuel Montagu in London and Deutsche Bank in Frankfurt. It also pulled off, together with Montagu, a famous coup in coin in 1963, when it persuaded the Uruguayan central bank to exchange a large collection of gold coins with promising premiums, which formed part of its official reserves, for good delivery bars. And when the Winnipeg Commodity Exchange pioneered gold futures for North America in 1972 with its 400-ounce contract, delivery was effected in certificates issued by Bank of Nova Scotia and CIBC. Although Winnipeg was eventually overshadowed by Comex in New York, the Exchange kept initiating new contracts to try to shake off the US challenge. Its response to the US opening was to launch its own 100-ounce contract in 1975, while four years later (well ahead of Comex) it came in with options. Although the volume was small, Winnipeg refused to give up until 1988 and must take the credit for signalling the way ahead in paper gold in North America.

An additional strength of the Canadian banks was their early links with central banks and other gold users throughout Latin America. If one was in Buenos Aires or Lima or Mexico City and wanted to find out who was who in gold, the local representatives of Bank of Nova Scotia, an engaging triumvirate who covered the continent and reminded me somewhat of the three musketeers, were sure to know. At home in Toronto, the gold department was presided over for a generation by a laconic fellow named Ernie Keith who, in those days, probably understood more about the byways of gold in North and South America than anyone else. Except, perhaps, his rival at CIBC, a diminutive woman named Elsie Raczkouski now also retired, who was equally knowledgeable on gold and opera.

Thus the Canadians had gold credentials long before the Americans and that got them clients. Toronto may have been a rather low profile market, nothing glamorous like the London fixing or the Zürich pool, but many wealthy people, including Greek ship owners, found it a discreet place to keep gold. At conferences of US *aficionados*, when the tide of gold investment was really running in the late 1970s, concerned gold bugs, who assumed some kind of financial apocalypse was nigh, would ask where the safest place was to keep their gold? Switzerland, which offered banking secrecy? Australia, which was a long way from anywhere? Usually the verdict went to Canada, just an easy drive over the border.

The real growth, of course, came with the gold-mining boom of the 1980s, which lifted Canadian output from 50 tonnes a year to an all-time record of 177 tonnes (5.7 million ounces) by 1991 (see Chapter 7). The need for mining finance, gold loans and marketing brought in a wider spectrum of Canadian banks, including Royal Bank of Canada and Toronto Dominion Bank. It also changed Canada's role in the international market because it became a substantial exporter to Asia. Previously Canadian gold had essentially been used at home for jewellery, for allocated or metal account stocks for international investors (the Canadians themselves are not great gold squirrels) and any surplus had easily been sold to US jewellery makers. The Maple Leaf bullion coin, launched in 1979, which became the best-seller on the international market once the South African Krugerrand fell foul of sanctions, also took up local gold (the Maple Leaf is another example of Canada front-running the United States, where the Eagle bullion coin did not arrive until 1986). Soaring production and falling demand for bullion coins, however, later outstripped domestic demand, so that by the 1990s, instead of Toronto gold being at a premium, as it always had been while North America as a whole was a net importer, it slipped to a discount. Canada had gold for sale. Hong Kong, Singapore, Taiwan and Tokyo took it; four Canadian refineries, including Johnson Matthey and the Royal Canadian Mint, have London good delivery status, so there was no problem with acceptance. On the contrary, Canadian bars were highly competitive. Building on this physical base, both Bank of Nova Scotia and CIBC have evolved as North American, indeed international, market-makers in spot, forwards and options.

The only jarring note in all this is the central bank, Bank of Canada. Since the early 1980s it has been bailing out of gold in a massive readjustment of its official reserves, in which gold used to account for 80 per cent. The Bank has sold close to 350 tonnes (11.2 million ounces) over a decade, but 94 tonnes of that in 1992 alone. The sales, much opposed by the mining industry, represent the most consistent sales programme yet undertaken by a central bank (Chapter 18). Gold lobbyists, mindful of the way in which Canada has led the United States in most aspects of gold trading, trust this does not foreshadow a similar programme by the US Treasury.

# CHAPTER 17

# Asia

*Dubai: the golden route to India*

The first time I came to Dubai, in the mid-1960s, it was on an old DC3 that made a leisurely journey down the Arabian Gulf from Bahrain to Doha to Abu Dhabi and finally came winging in over an isolated cluster of white-washed buildings huddled around a small creek that was surrounded by a limitless waste of sand. A long line of camels was strung out across the desert, which was unspoilt save for a few tracks where Landrovers had bustled off on unknown missions. Yet even in those days this little community on the shores of the Gulf was the third biggest buyer of gold on the London market. In 1966 it bought 124 tonnes (4 million ounces), exceeded only by France and Switzerland and, for good measure, was also the third largest supplier of silver to the London market, beaten only by the United States and the Soviet Union.[1]

Nowadays you can take your choice of two daily non-stop flights from London on Emirates Airlines or one non-stop on British Airways that bring you in across the coastline after dusk, almost level with the revolving restaurant atop the Hyatt Hotel, over a dazzling quilt of lights stretching far across the desert to land at the modern airport that is the hub of the Middle East. The taxi dashes into town to deposit you at the Sheraton or the Intercontinental; and there you pull back the curtains of your room. Below is the creek that made Dubai, its quay piled with boxes and bales labelled Al Mukalla or Bandar Abbas, or Karachi, waiting to be loaded on to the dhows moored alongside.

In the morning you walk amid that clutter to jump aboard the little

---

1 Timothy Green, *The World of Gold*, Michael Joseph, London, 1968; see Chapter 9 for an account of that journey.

wooden motor launches that ply across the creek and then down a maze of narrow alleys to the customs house. Sit sipping a glass of clear, sweet tea and enquire, 'How were the gold imports last year?' An all-time record, as it happens. Dubai imported 280.9 tonnes (9 million ounces) in 1992, which is over 12 per cent of world mine output. Silver, incidentally, was still good too at 1,660 tonnes (53 million ounces), but here there is a subtle change – Dubai now imports it from Europe, whereas before it exported it there, and sends it on to India.

India, of course, is what Dubai is all about. This little emirate, part of the United Arab Emirates (once known as the Trucial States), is the stepping stone to India and Pakistan, not just for gold and silver, but also for watches, pharmaceuticals and electronic goods. Those boats on the creek go to other places, too; Iran, Oman, Yemen, and on to Zanzibar, but the heart of Dubai's trade for thirty years or more has always been with the Indian sub-continent. Long ago Sheikh Rashid Bin Said Al Maktoum, who ruled Dubai for more than fifty years from 1938, realized that his sheikhdom with its 3-mile long creek offered the best harbour and haven within easy striking distance of India and Pakistan, where gold and silver could not be freely imported and duty on many other goods was exorbitant. Dubai became the smugglers' supermarket, although everything there was entirely legal. It is a free gold market and the only transgression occurred when the gold landed in India. On gold, it was a profitable exercise; the Bombay price was usually 30 per cent above the international price and even after expenses and the occasional 'accident' when Indian customs intercepted a gold-laden dhow, the profit margin was usually a steady 8 to 9 per cent. Over the years close to 3,000 tonnes of gold, mostly in the luscious canapé-size 10-tola bars (3.75 ounces), has passed along the golden route to India. Silver came out of India for nearly twenty years, lured by higher international prices, and also as one way of paying for gold; but as the silver price outside declined, so it became highly profitable to smuggle it back in again at a good margin of over 70 per cent. It was a highly professional, well-organized trade by a handful of syndicates, with excellent connections in India and Pakistan to ensure that the 'accidents' were not too frequent. The seizure rate was rarely more than 2–3 per cent on gold.

And then India changed the rules. First, in 1992, it permitted non-resident Indians (known as NRIs) returning home for a visit to bring in up to 5 kilos (160.75 ounces) of gold on payment of a modest duty of around 6 per cent and a year later extended this to permit up to 100 kilos of silver. The aim was to call the smugglers' bluff. Yet Dubai took this historic change in its stride, and notched up its all-time best in gold imports (the previous high was 254 tonnes in 1970), and started out

1993 in even grander style with another record of 106 tonnes in the first four months, although it then slowed down.

Through the years, though, there has been an important change. Originally the gold came mainly from London in 10-tola (t.t.) bars (often known as 'biscuits') with the Johnson Matthey chop; today the Swiss have the biggest share with t.t. bars from Credit Suisse, Swiss Bank Corporation, Union Bank of Switzerland and the newcomer, PAMP, vying for favourite brand. While the t.t. bar still accounts for 80 per cent of Dubai's trade, kilo bars are catching on, both for local jewellery manufacture and for re-export to Iran, which is making a comeback as a big market in the 1990s, and to Kuwait, where in the wake of the Gulf War Swiss banks are wary of leaving consignment stocks. The 'designer' small bars of Crédit Suisse and PAMP also fill the windows of the gold shops in the *souk*.

Nowadays, too, the half dozen biggest traders have their own offices with Reuters screens and telex; their dealers chatter all day to London, Zürich and New York, adjusting their positions and often booking t.t. bars three months in advance to be sure of enough supply. Locating these offices in the maze of the *souk* often remains a mystery for newcomers. 'Turn into the spice market, take a left down a dusty alley and opposite a shop with sacks of nutmegs and cloves, go up an unlit stairway and ring the bell at the first floor,' is the usual kind of direction from old hands. The traders themselves are normally families from India or Pakistan, who make up most of Dubai's commercial population. Nowadays it is often the sons who have taken over from the fathers I first knew in the 1960s.

The gold itself normally goes into consignment stocks held at Habib Bank AG Zürich, Standard Chartered Bank, Citibank, Middle East Bank or Bank of Oman, to be taken out by the traders as they need it. Dubai somehow manages to keep intact a house of cards known as 'unfixed' gold in which traders will take 500 or 1,000 t.t. bars, but often agree a price later (hopefully when it goes down) with their credit being assured by cash or securities held by the banks in Zürich and London. And the traders also pass on 'unfixed' gold down the pipeline to jewellers in the *souk* or clients bound for the wilder shores of India. This is not quite as dangerous as it sounds because the big syndicates, who have supplied India, have many investors whose risks are also spread over several journeys. An investor may have, say, 10,000 tolas constantly in play *en route* to India, but no more than 2,000 or 3,000 tolas on any single shipment. For the journey by sea or air, the t.t. bars were always packed into stout canvas jackets with rows of pockets, one for each bar. A 'jacket' could be fitted with 100 bars and a shipment was often described as ten or twenty 'jackets', rather than so much gold. Everyone knew a jacket meant 375 ounces (12 kilos). Packing them was an art in which there were several specialists. They were often critical of new brands if the corners were too sharp; an ideal 'biscuit' should have softly curving corners (not least because they must be comfortable if they are to be carried internally by smugglers, in the rectum or vagina). Late one evening some years ago, I was sitting in a small office when a customer climbed the creaky wooden staircase to buy thirty t.t. bars. The dealer, also a famous jacket packer, got out a stack of newly designed bars, taped around with adhesive, from his desk and counted them out. The man looked at them for a moment, felt them, and pushed them back. 'No', he said, 'I want Johnson Matthey bars.' Another taped pack of slightly more rounded, fatter bars was produced with the Johnson Matthey chop. The visitor paid up, stowed the bars carefully in a small leather bag and vanished downstairs. 'The Johnson bar is number one,' said the dealer with a broad grin.

The new regulations in India have, of course, changed the game. Now that NRIs can take in 5 kilos with them (though usually still as t.t. bars), the trick has become to find scores of potential travellers, offer them a cheap air ticket and perhaps a small fee to carry the gold. If an NRI can be provided with several names and passports, so much the better; he can return home often. The scheme has worked so well that within the first twelve months of liberalization, over half of the gold going into India went openly with the NRIs, while some continued to go by more traditional unofficial routes, though largely by air. The days of the gold-laden dhows were already in the past anyway, even before the rules changed, as a variety of subterfuges were used to get the gold on planes (often hidden inside machinery in containerized air cargo). Silver, being much clumsier to move in bulk, still went by sea. However, when the silver regulations were eased in 1993 so that NRIs could also take 100 kilos along, this posed a profitable new opportunity, but also some logistical problems. Fifty NRIs can reasonably check in at Dubai airport for each flight to India hand-carrying their legal 5 kilos of gold, but for each to stagger up with 100 kilos of silver in several suitcases was clearly not possible. The resourceful syndicates set about parcelling up three 1,000-ounce bars and chopped up bits of bars to make up the full 3,215 ounces permitted, wrapping them in hessian sacking and delivering them to a special baggage counter at the airport in the name of each NRI passenger, who thus has only to take the gold himself. On arrival in India, all he has to do at the airport is identify 'his' silver package in the customs hall before it is whisked off on a trolley along with all the other NRI silver, while he hands over the gold personally to someone waiting just outside.

Thus, most of the precious metal trade into India remains highly organized by the same syndicates who previously smuggled it. The relaxation, however, has meant that many people going home now take t.t. bars along on their own account. I sat in a box-like office of a small dealer one morning, sipping the customary glass of tea, and watched a succession of Indian customers proffer a thick wad of notes in return for a handful of t.t. bars which they wrapped up carefully in newspaper or plastic bags before departing. 'Every family is taking t.t. bars now,' said the dealer. 'They used to take jewellery, but now the bars are allowed and the making charges are less in India so they have the jewellery made there.'

The addiction to t.t. bars in both the organized and informal traffic continues, not just because they are more affordable and tradable items than the expensive kilo bar, but because unlike kilo bars, they are not numbered. Thus, a receipt for duty paid on even ten t.t. bars is a marketable piece of paper in an Indian bazaar, because it can be used to legitimize other bars that may have been smuggled, if awkward questions are ever asked.

The opening up of legal imports to India for the first time since 1947 has not been therefore the death-knell for Dubai that some predicted. On the contrary, it has simply provided the opportunity for many to take gold in for the first time, and since there is still a small premium, even when duty is paid, it is a profitable gambit. What might hit Dubai, however, are proposals by several European bullion dealers to put consignment stocks into Bombay itself, so that NRIs could buy gold, duty paid, before setting out, and be given a certificate entitling them to pick it up on arrival. That kind of competition might be hard to beat.

Yet even without all or part of the India trade, Dubai is still a uniquely placed crossroads for gold bars and jewellery. The jewellery factories in Dubai and in the neighbouring emirates of Sharjah have proliferated. Gold coin manufacture is a brisk, if little talked about, local talent. One wholesaler in the *souk* ticked off what he had ordered from the coin factory in a nearby alley just in 1992: 23,555 sovereigns, 14,974 half sovereigns, 25,058 quarter sovereigns, and an assortment of £5 George V coins and Mexican 50-peso Centenarios. The coin shop, in fact, has the dies to make almost anything you care to name. Gold jewellery from Singapore and Malaysia passes through *en route* for Saudi Arabia; alluvial gold dust from Tanzania comes through. Even the duty-free shop at the airport sells up to 3 tonnes of gold each year in small bars and jewellery to departing and transit passengers. Dubai now has its own refinery, Emirates Gold, taking in scrap and making t.t. bars and 18-

carat Italian-style jewellery. Thirty years' experience in the gold trade is not going to be lost just because India changes the rules.

### Singapore: top of the league

The founder of Singapore, Stamford Raffles, always predicted that one day this island at the southern tip of the Malay peninsula would be the emporium of the East. And latterly, Lee Kuan Yew, the presiding creator of modern Singapore since it became an independent city state in 1965, has carried that vision forward. One step on the way to making Singapore a financial as well as a commercial centre was to launch a physical gold market in April 1969 to serve her more populous neighbours, Indonesia, Malaysia, Thailand, Vietnam, Cambodia, Burma and, a little more distant, India and China. Within a circle of three hours' or so flying time from Singapore you are on the doorstep of close to 2.5 billion people; half the world's population. In that context it is less surprising that Singapore imported over 400 tonnes (13 million ounces) of gold in 1992, 20 per cent of world mine output; going into 1993 the flow actually accelerated to 150 tonnes in the first three months, although higher prices then slowed imports considerably. Gold was pouring in direct from Australia, Canada, South Africa, and the United States, as well as from the London and Zürich markets. What was going on to make Singapore the foremost regional market? All her neighbours were absorbing gold in prodigious quantities, encouraged by a cheap price of $330: 10-tola bars for India, kilo bars for Indonesia, Thailand and Cambodia, and high-carat jewellery, made here or over the border in Malaysia, for the Middle East and China. Singapore had become the junction of the gold business.

The beginning, back in 1969, was rather more humble. The market was fenced in with restrictions as 'a re-export market for non-residents only'. Gold could not be sold to local citizens nor to anyone with a British or British Commonwealth passport, which actually meant it was really only for passing foreigners who wished to smuggle it home, usually to Jakarta. Anyone buying gold at a local bank was required to leave Singapore on the first available plane or ship to his destination, and the bank was instructed to phone the customs authorities when it made the sale so that a customs officer could nip over to make sure the buyer indeed headed straight to the airport or docks. This led to hilarious episodes as three or four couriers, bound for Jakarta, would leave a bank by different exits to avoid the alert eye of authority, often having changed shirts in the bank for extra confusion. Despite such irritations, the market took off, especially for Indonesia, then in the throes of high inflation in the post-Sukarno era.

Restrictions were lifted, however, in 1973 making Singapore a free gold market open to all comers, local and overseas. Competition still came from the market at Vientiane in Laos, which conveniently serviced Thailand, just across the Mekong river, Burma and Vietnam until the communist takeover in the mid-1970s. India was also then very much in the province of Dubai. So Singapore cut its teeth in gold as the gateway to Indonesia, where high import duty made it profitable to spirit in kilo bars from Singapore at quite modest expense. The rule of thumb is that a 2 per cent premium over the Singapore price is required in Jakarta to make smuggling viable; and if the premium goes the other way, then gold will come out from Indonesia to Singapore. Thus, for many years, the Singapore gold market was really all about Indonesia, which even then had a population marching onwards from 150 million people (while Singapore is just over 2 million). The Indonesians were great speculators in the days of highly mobile gold prices in the early 1980s, and one would meet them for lunch with the dealers in Singapore, always eager for the latest gossip on what the price might do. The main Indonesian traders also always maintained positions in Singapore and Jakarta, to cut down the need for too much gold in transit. If the Jakarta premium was good, they could sell there and cover in Singapore. If it then reversed, they could buy back in Jakarta and sell from their Singapore position. Actual shipments were thus kept to a minimum. However, if the Jakarta premium was maintained for long, then Singapore's monthly imports would rapidly rise. If the 'Jakarta effect' kicked in, it was good for 5–8 tonnes a month extra imports of kilo bars into Singapore.

While Indonesia was the mainstay, the domestic jewellery manufacturing for machine-made chain and ornaments expanded, requiring up to 30 tonnes annually. And although some of the big manufacturers have since moved across the causeway to Johore Bahru in Malaysia or even set up in China, Singapore remains a significant manufacturing and wholesale jewellery centre. The facilities have been substantiated by the establishment of an official assay office for hallmarking jewellery, and by the setting up of a refinery by Degussa, the German precious metals group, which has London good delivery status.

In tandem, local gold investment grew, although it has never matched the speculative fervour of Hong Kong. The benchmark of Singapore's mood was judged for many years by the length of the queues outside Crédit Suisse on Shenton Way, where Singaporeans lined up for hours to buy or sell gold. The local banks, Overseas Chinese Banking Corporation (OCBC), Overseas Union Bank (OUB) and United Overseas Bank (UOB), joined in with various gold savings and gold passbook accounts, often accepting transactions as small as 5 grams. The roster of banks in gold is completed by Republic National Bank of New York and N. M. Rothschild.

The underlying enthusiasm for gold was maintained by the Monetary Authority of Singapore (MAS), which keeps a good part of its reserves in gold, although it has never revealed how much. A former managing director of MAS once asked me what the impact on the international gold market might be if Singapore revealed how much official gold it held. I replied that if he told me the total, I would hazard a guess at the impact. He laughed and I am none the wiser. But there is no doubt that Lee Kuan Yew, now in active retirement as senior minister, and Dr Goh Keng Swee, his cohort as finance minister, were deeply committed to gold as a bedrock holding for their city state. Among the private citizens, however, the fervour for gold has cooled considerably in recent years as it failed to perform – particularly in terms of a strong Singapore dollar. 'Singaporeans are totally discouraged by gold,' admitted a banker early in 1993. 'They prefer property and the stock market.' Yet as their interest waned, so the growth of other Southeast Asian markets caused Singapore's gold imports to accelerate. Instead of a modest level of around 150 tonnes (just under 5 million ounces) through much of the 1980s, imports rose to almost 300 tonnes by 1990 and then kept going.

Actually, the initial growth had much to do with a diversification of passages to India, where the classic Dubai to Bombay 'line' was varied to include Singapore to Madras and Dacca (in Bangladesh) from where it is an easy cross-border route to Calcutta. Singapore is normally a kilo bar market, but orders for 10-tola bars, the staple diet for the India trade, soon indicated what was going on. This switch was strengthened by the Iraqi invasion of Kuwait in 1990 and the subsequent Gulf War, which made Singapore a more secure entrepôt. Thereafter, India's relaxation on imports to permit non-resident Indians to bring in gold (see previous section) was very convenient for Indians living in Singapore, so that 20 per cent of the gold is now destined for the sub-continent.

Meanwhile, next door in Malaysia the jewellery manufacturing industry, which has lower labour costs than Singapore, has been expanding rapidly. Malaysia has a tradition of craftsmanship in gold fabrication, especially on the island of Penang and on the mainland opposite around Butterworth. This blossomed as factories, initially for electronics, but soon for jewellery, came to be established in the duty-free zone by Penang's little airport. Strong links were established first with Dubai and Saudi Arabia, with wholesalers positioning themselves in Singapore, dispatching gold to Penang for manufacture and bringing jewellery back to Singapore *en route* to the Gulf. Orders for China's burgeoning demand, however, soon dwarfed this business. 'Demand in China is really big just now,' said Mr Tham Yen Thim, president of the Malaysian Goldsmiths' Association. 'No one can cope with it.' Flights from Singapore to Penang are almost taken up with wholesalers shuttling back and forth with briefcases full of gold or jewellery, which they wheel on little trolleys in the planes. The 3.30 p.m. from Singapore is known as the 'gold flight'; they return on the 6.00 p.m. having swapped kilo bars for ornaments, and are still at Singapore's Changi airport in time for the last evening flight to Hong Kong, the doorway for China. The growth of this trade may be judged by the fact that as late as 1988 Malaysia took scarcely 10 tonnes of gold from Singapore, while in 1992 it was close to 90 tonnes; nearly one-quarter of Singapore's imports.

The other flourishing business is with Thailand, Vietnam and recently Cambodia, where various restrictions inhibit the free import of gold which is nevertheless in great demand for jewellery and even more for investment. Rapid growth in Thailand in the late 1980s created a requirement for well over 100 tonnes annually, which was supplied chiefly out of Singapore by cars going overland through Malaysia with upwards of 100 kilo bars a time hidden within. The offtake in the jewellery shops in the Chinese quarter of Bangkok could even be directly related to the success of rice harvests and prices; prosperous farmers went for gold.

Meanwhile in Vietnam and latterly Cambodia gold is used as money in many business transactions. The export of shrimps from Vietnam is paid for in gold kilo bars (those of Swiss Bank Corporation being the preferred brand), which then circulate within the country or are re-exported to Bangkok to pay for wholesale imports of motor-scooters or electronic goods. They are also melted into smaller, wafer-like bars to pay locally for rice, a scooter or even a house. This informal gold standard has also evolved in Cambodia, where the local currency, the riel, has little value. A small Cambodian bank, Canadia Gold and Trust Corporation, established in 1991, has been importing large amounts of gold from Singapore, both for the local economy and for onward movement to Bangkok, since the long Thai-Cambodia border presents few hurdles. The gold traffic has become practical because of the introduction of daily flights from Singapore to Phnom Penh. 'There are several couriers on every flight with 20–30 kilos,' said a Singapore trader. Ultimately some of this gold circulates onwards to Laos and Burma and thence into the southern provinces of China. The acceptance of gold as the basic means of exchange within this network of Southeast Asian countries as they struggle for development goes a long way to explain Singapore's exceptional transit trade in recent years.

That physical business, which has increasingly attracted fresh participants such as J. P. Morgan from New York, and Mocatta from London to the wholesale network, remains the essence of the Singapore market. Apart from some interbank business, Singapore has nothing to match Hong Kong's Gold and Silver Exchange as a trading forum, despite efforts to get a local futures market off the ground. Originally the Gold Exchange of Singapore was set up in 1978, with strong encouragement from the Monetary Authority of Singapore, but managed little turnover. So the Gold Exchange made an alliance in 1983 with the International Monetary Market (IMM) in Chicago to create the Singapore International Monetary Exchange (Simex). This is an open-outcry market with a 100-ounce futures contract quoted in US dollars, deliverable on even months in a one-year cycle. The contract is cash settled against the *loco* London morning fix on the last trading day of the contract. The volume, however, has remained small, because there is no natural local speculative fever to give it the liquidity that would woo a more international clientele. Singapore, like Dubai, is a hypermarket for physical gold.

### Hong Kong: doorway to China
Tap in HKGG on the Reuters Monitor Dealing Service and up comes the score card for the Hong Kong Gold and Silver Exchange Society (*Kam Ngan*). The mere prices on the screen, however, cannot possibly convey the animation, the sheer exuberance of what takes place on the floor of the Exchange when the market is volatile. The impression any visitor has of the *Kam Ngan* is that he has stumbled on a scene from a Bruce Lee movie. Even on the steps outside there is a jostling throng, elbowing their way through bootblacks and fresh fruit vendors, lured by the swelling roar of open-outcry trading from inside. The first time I went there some years ago, my guide had explained on the way that *kam* is the Chinese word for gold. He drew the Mandarin character: the symbol of a king crowned by the symbol of a man, implying he who has the gold makes the rules. Beside the main doorway is a coat of arms, depicting a golden key surrounded by four Chinese characters, meaning 'This is the key to a million sources of wealth.' An apt motto, as Hong Kong braces for integration in 1997 with China, which itself has emerged in the last year or two as the world's greatest consumer of gold.

The towering presence of China, however, should not overshadow the fact that Hong Kong is already Asia's most mature gold market. It is at once a multi-layered trading centre, integrated into the global network, and a major physical distribution centre for many years for much of Southeast Asia. While Hong Kong grew up as a modern gold market,

China was the sleeping giant next door. No inkling of the potential demand, despite the Chinese people's long love affair with gold, emerged until 1988 when Hong Kong's imports, normally around 100–150 tonnes annually, shot up to 460 tonnes (14.8 million ounces), with 433 tonnes the following year. Rapid economic growth, rising inflation and the political tensions that led to the uprising in Tiananmen Square in June 1989 almost overnight created a huge appetite for gold over the border. Shortly before the June uprising, one could sit in the banks in Hong Kong and watch groups of half a dozen young men come in to pick up 20–30 kilo bars each in briefcases or canvas jackets beneath their shirts, before departing by train, ferry or plane for mainland China. In the twelve months before the Tiananmen Massacre, at least 400 to 500 tonnes of gold went into China, much of it as bars for hoarding. Then the traffic stopped abruptly, and all went quiet for nearly two years, until the surge in economic growth by 1991 rekindled the demand for gold, although this time much more as a grass-roots desire in a prosperous China, for *chuk kam* (pure gold) jewellery. 'China', said *Gold 1993*, the annual report from Gold Fields Mineral Services, 'has become the world's largest jewellery consumer.' Most of that gold went through Hong Kong.

This role as a conduit to China, though, is really adding an extra dimension to a market that has many other credentials. And to understand the British colony's (until 1997) role in gold, it is necessary to look back at its evolution as a sophisticated market place. The original Chinese Gold and Silver Exchange Society was founded in 1910, and many of the modern generation of Hong Kong gold dealers fled from China after the communist takeover. The late Mr Woo Hon Fai, who was president of the Exchange for many years and did more than anyone else perhaps to introduce Hong Kong's gold market to a wider world, moved from Canton in 1950, to found Lee Cheong, one of the most prominent bullion houses. However, from 1939 until 1974 Hong Kong was officially a closed gold market; tael bars[2] could be traded on the Exchange, but direct gold imports into the colony were banned by the British rulers.

Local ingenuity got round that by arranging deliveries instead to the Portuguese colony of Macao, just across the Pearl river. For almost a generation gold bullion – usually 995 good delivery bars – was dispatched by air from London to Hong Kong, passing through in transit to Macao, originally aboard an ancient Catalina flying boat and later by hydrofoil. When the gold arrived in Macao it was whisked to the vaults of the Cambista Seng Heng and then apparently vanished. Or rather it was melted into tael bars, which were smuggled back to Hong Kong to be traded in the local market and then often smuggled onwards to other

2 1 tael = 1.20337 troy ounces or 37.429 grams.

Southeast Asian countries. This traffic was in the hands of a syndicate that paid the Macao authorities an import duty of $1.25 an ounce for the privilege and provided one of their main sources of revenue.

The restrictions were finally lifted in 1974, shortly after Singapore also took its market off the leash. Hong Kong was on its way. Daily volume on the Gold and Silver Exchange, which had previously been a mere 40,000 taels, took off to over 1 million taels in hectic periods. The Exchange has a unique contract. The basic contract is a lot of 100 taels, made up of twenty 5-tael bars, each 990 fine. The unique feature is that there is no time limit on settlement. The Exchange is, in effect, an undated futures market. Buyers can delay payment as long as they like; similarly, sellers can delay delivery. The pressure on either side to settle depends on what is known as the 'interest factor', which is really a premium or storage charge. The interest factor penalizes those who have a short position, but cannot deliver gold (when gold is in short supply), or those who have a long position but cannot pay (when gold is plentiful). As a Hong Kong trader once explained to me, 'There is nothing mystical about this — it approximates to the spot price adjusted for physical availability and carrying costs.' The 'interest factor' is fixed daily at 11.30 a.m. (10.30 a.m. on Saturdays). If the demand for physical gold exceeds supply, interest will be 'positive' because buyers who need gold will be paid interest by sellers unable to deliver. Likewise, negative interest is charged when the supply of physical gold is greater than demand. The actual degree of premium depends on volume either way.

The most powerful presence on the Exchange is Po Seng, an associate of Bank of China, which not only has a large speculative clientele through its network of Hong Kong branches, but actively represents the interests of Beijing. One can never be sure to what extent Po Seng's large trading book (often very influential when the daily 'interest factor' is fixed), represents a discreet conduit for mainland China to buy and sell gold. Bars with the chop of thirty-three members are accepted on the *Kam Ngan*, although in practice the majority of tael bars delivered are from Chow Sang Sang, King Fook, Lee Cheong and Po Seng.

The *Kam Ngan* is an open-outcry market where battle is joined from 9.30 a.m. until 12.30 and 2.30 to 4 p.m. six days a week (except on Saturday afternoons, when everyone gambles at the races instead). The floor traders wear white shirts, red waistcoats, slacks and trainers (the latter so the occasional Kung Fu kick is less lethal), as they wrestle beneath a huge mural of a tranquil Chinese lake. In quiet moments, which are rare, they may actually call 'buy in' or 'sell out' — the 'in' and 'out' being essential because the Cantonese pronunciation of the words 'buy' and 'sell' is very similar. Amid the usual racket, however, a trader raises his arm with his fingers extended if he is a buyer, and thrusts it down if he is a seller; the number of fingers extended indicates how many lots of 100 taels each he is trading. Buyers are called 'good pals' (*Kh'ung Tans* in Shanghai dialect) and sellers 'poor fellows' (*Dor Tans*).

When the Exchange really got into its stride in the mid-1970s as gold prices became more volatile, the huge volume attracted international bullion houses to establish a parallel market in *loco* London gold during Hong Kong's trading hours. This took advantage of arbitrage between a Hong Kong price quoted in Hong Kong dollars per tael and a London price in dollars per ounce. The pioneers were Mocatta & Goldsmid and N. M. Rothschild from London, but they were soon followed by everyone else from London, the three Swiss banks, Deutsche and Dresdner from Frankfurt, several US banks and, most recently, by AIG Trading from the United States. The international houses do not trade on the Exchange, but act more as wholesalers, dealing in lots of 2,000 to 4,000 ounces at a time. This alliance grafting local Chinese traders on to a wider world made Hong Kong a highly liquid market and the pacesetter of the early morning price for gold. Australian producers, Japanese trading houses, Thai and Indonesian speculators, all woke up with Hong Kong and an hour or two later Dubai and Saudi Arabian traders and speculators came in, usually dealing with the international firms as their counterparties. The volume did not match the Exchange, but on a brisk day up to 500,000 ounces of *loco* London gold was traded, together with several hundred thousand ounces of *loco* Comex contracts. Most dealers quote a Comex contract against the Hong Kong price, even outside Comex hours, which permits the unwinding of US positions during Hong Kong trading hours. With all these elements in play, the total turnover in Hong Kong on the hectic days of the early 1980s was often 2 million ounces.

Since then, things have calmed down somewhat. Lack of volatility and the long bear market in gold cut the volume here, just as in London and New York. A good day on the Exchange became 250,000 taels, rather than 1 million, although this picked up to over 300,000 taels a day in 1993 as the price improved. The players also thinned out dramatically in the parallel *loco* London market. 'During the peak period in Hong Kong there were twenty-three or twenty-four dealers active in the market,' said Robert Sitt of Mase Westpac; 'now it's down to seven or eight.'

The compensation is the China business. For the moment this is strictly physical, in tael bars and the pure gold, *chuk kam*, jewellery that everyone in China is scrambling to buy. The pressure on Hong Kong to deliver is immense. The famous jewellery firms, Chow Sang Sang, Chow Tai Fook, King Fook and Tse Sui Luen are at full stretch both in Hong Kong and at new factories inside China. New wholesalers open all the time, ordering up rings, bracelets and chain from Malaysia by the kilo. 'We cannot meet the demand,' said a friend of mine, who formerly marketed gold coin. 'I'm opening a factory in Hainan in China to do 10 kilos of ripple chain a day. Anyone, you and I, can set up a factory in China tomorrow.' Tael bars, ranging from the 1-tael that is shaped like a slipper bath, to flat, finger-length 5- and 10-tael ingots, are stuffed into the jackets of China-bound travellers.

Hong Kong's own bar imports have revived to a healthy 350 tonnes a year, almost all of it destined in one form or another for China (save sidelines in kilo bars to South Korea and Vietnam). Taiwan used to be the leading destination until it liberalized its imports policy, so gold can now enter directly instead of being smuggled from Hong Kong. Taiwan's imports are booming, too, not least because jewellery made there is going to China, while Taiwanese businessmen starting up in China often take kilo bars as their working capital. The immediate question for bullion banks in Hong Kong, ordering up kilo bars and good delivery bars from Australia, Canada and the United States (which was the largest supplier to Hong Kong in 1992), is just how large can the physical offtake in China become? According to Robert Sitt of Mase Westpac in Hong Kong, China took in at least 430 tonnes in 1992 and could consume 'a minimum of 900 tonnes yearly by the end of the decade'. That is just the physical metal. The next step will be trading. 'The Chinese instinct to trade gold could eventually lead to the official formation of gold trading exchanges on the mainland,' added Robert Sitt. 'Preliminary discussions have taken place between government officials in Shanghai and the Kam Ngan Gold and Silver Exchange in Hong Kong on the possibility of establishing a gold trading exchange in Shanghai.' China already has five futures exchanges for oil, coal, ferrous and non-ferrous metals; the pent-up potential for gold futures could be immense. Hong Kong has the expertise to tap it.

### Tokyo: Tocom finds its feet

Any discussion of the gold market in Japan has to begin with the price; strong yen, weak gold price is the story. The last time I arrived in the offices of Tanaka K.K., Japan's biggest precious metals dealers, the physical gold sales counter on the ground floor was deserted. The day's price posted above the counter was 1,300 yen per gram. That was the price in January 1974, but actually my visit was nineteen years later in 1993. Reflecting on this more closely with Tanaka's executives, we realized that the average yen price in Japan in 1992 of 1,446 yen per gram, was lower than the average for 1974 when it was 1,598 yen. In those days, of course, the yen/dollar ratio was around 300, but by 1993 was down to 116. Admittedly, the Japanese price did hit a high of 6,495 yen in January 1980, but it has been going downhill virtually ever since. So the Japanese are to be congratulated in getting a gold market off the ground at all when the price is *one-fifth* what it was in 1980. Japan has emerged as a substantial physical buyer of gold (fair enough, since the stuff keeps getting cheaper); as a force through its trading companies in the global market; and with its own futures exchange, Tocom, where turnover hit nearly 7 million contracts in 1990, equivalent to two-thirds of Comex in New York.

Over the last twenty years or so, the Japanese have eased themselves gradually into the world market. Originally their local market was tightly controlled by the Bank of Japan, which in the 1960s adopted the simple ploy of buying gold in London at $35 an ounce and selling it in Tokyo for $57 an ounce. This tactic was dropped in 1973, to permit precious metals dealers and the trading companies to import metal directly, but full liberalization allowing banks to trade in gold did not come until the early 1980s. The local market developed, therefore, very much around the traditional precious metal companies, all of whom have a long history. The oldest, Tokuriki Honten, was founded in 1727; then came Tanaka Kikinzoku in 1885 and, finally, Ishifuku Metal Industry was set up in 1929. These three houses, which all specialize as refiners and semi-fabricators (all have London good delivery status) also market their own kilo bars and small bars to wholesale and private investment clients. And Tanaka, which is the largest, runs its own gold savings or accumulation plans. This triumvirate remains the core of the precious metals business, also handling much of the platinum for which Japan is the world's biggest market.

Grouped around them are the major trading companies which, because of their international nature, provide a closer link between Japan and the global market. Thus Marubeni, Mitsui, Mitsubishi Corporation, Mitsubishi Materials Corporation, Nissho-Iwai Corporation and Sumitomo Corporation, have all become active market-makers in Tokyo, and also trade in New York and London (Mitsubishi Corporation, Mitsui, Nissho-Iwai and Sumitomo are all members of the London Bullion Market Association, while Mitsubishi Materials, Mitsui Mining and Sumitomo Metal Mining have refineries with London good delivery status). Since Japan has only one serious gold mine, Sumitomo Metal Mining's high-grade Hishikari, with just over 6 tonnes annually, the country is dependent on imports. The trading companies, especially

Mitsubishi Materials and Sumitomo, have become increasingly involved in securing mine production direct from the producers, be they Australian, Indonesian, or Russian. Australia has become Japan's largest supplier, often in 995 good delivery bars which are then upgraded to 999.9 in Japanese refineries. The competition between the trading companies is intense and, because of their traditional rivalry, they are often not very good at trading gold with each other. A trading house that is long would much prefer to sell to banks such as Crédit Suisse or Swiss Bank Corporation, which maintain gold desks in their Tokyo offices, than to a local rival. Japan's banks, incidentally, have stayed out of gold trading, except to offer customers gold savings accounts.

Since Japan is an end-user of gold for jewellery, electronics and other applications of at least 200 tonnes (6.4 million ounces) annually, quite apart from investment, the business is essentially one way. Re-export is limited, but when surpluses do build up in Tokyo through disinvestment, these can be laid off through *loco* London positions. Some dealers will also quote *loco* Tokyo prices. But unlike the other Asian markets, which are distribution centres, the real trick in Japan is to manage a balanced flow of gold for fabrication and investment (see Chapters 19, 20, 21). Not forgetting, of course, that Japan's Ministry of Finance did a very discreet job in picking up 323 tonnes (10.4 million ounces) at low prices in 1986 for special coins issues.

Besides this practical business, the establishment of a futures market in Tokyo created the opportunity both for professionals to hedge locally and for speculators to play the market. The fashionable word in Japan in the 1980s (though not now) was *zaiteku*, meaning financial technology, in exhibiting in personal money management the same skills that made Japan's industrial technology world famous. Gold futures provided the opportunity for a little *zaiteku*. The Tokyo Gold Exchange was originally launched in 1982, but was consolidated two years later with the rubber and textile exchanges to form the Tokyo Commodity Exchange (Tocom). Tocom also offers platinum, silver and palladium contracts. The gold contract is for 1 kilo at 999.9, priced in yen. If the contract is made in an odd-numbered month (January) delivery may be effected in any even-numbered month (February, April and so forth) during a twelve-month period or, if entered in an even month (February) may be delivered in an odd month (March). The price, however, does not float constantly during trading hours, so the exchange is relatively peaceful compared to Comex or Hong Kong's *Kam Ngan*. Instead, there are six daily price calls: 9.10 a.m., 10.30, 11.30, 1.10 p.m., 2.30 and 3.45. Initially, Tocom attracted only local business, because of the difficulties of foreign dealers becoming members and relatively high charges compared to Comex.

But once the Exchange notched up 2 million contracts in 1987, the increasing liquidity gave greater appeal to overseas players, who were then offered associate membership. In all, thirty-one overseas houses have since joined. Margin requirements were also reduced, so that by 1989, with the yen also rising for once, Tocom really took off, helped by speculators switching out of the stock market and from other commodities such as cotton on the Exchange itself. The peak was 6,873,304 contracts in 1990, aided by gold's volatility with Iraq's invasion of Kuwait. Thereafter, the onset of recession, the collapse of the stock market and the yen price of gold slipping relentlessly month after month, eroded the volume. Tocom did 4,193,775 contracts in 1992, down almost 40 per cent. *Zaiteku* is quite out of fashion: 'It has a bad connotation as a speculative bubble,' admitted one trader, who was full of praise for it a few years ago. However, that is a sign of the times; Tocom has held its ratio of doing two-thirds of Comex turnover, and on the world scene those two futures exchanges are in a league of their own. And a revival in the price, especially if it could improve in yen, would bring the speculators bouncing back. Tocom is a symbol of the stature that Japan has acquired in the gold market in the last twenty years, even if the local price has performed miserably.

# PART IV

# THE BUYERS

# CHAPTER 18

# Central Banks:
# The New Producers?

'And what about the new producers?' asked Eiichiro Tokumoto, the Reuter's commodity correspondent in Tokyo, adding with a grin, 'the central banks'. An apt description, for we had just finished discussing the declining output from the former Soviet Union and the end of the gold-mining boom and were looking for new developments in the 1990s. Central banks as sellers, even regular suppliers to the market, are a real prospect since 1992, when they sold more than in any single year since 1968 in that last misjudged fling to hold the gold price at \$35.

Embracing a policy of more active management of their reserves, more in a spirit of portfolio managers than central bankers, a number of them, notably in Europe, where gold often forms a high (40 per cent or more) proportion of their reserves, have started sales programmes, led by Belgium and then the Netherlands. And they really took the lead from Canada, which started disposing of its gold reserve in 1980, more judiciously at a high price. The key question is how strong is this trend? How long will it last? And how much might these 'new producers' really sell? As a leading Swiss gold dealer remarked, 'Are we seeing an overall central bank change in policy, or will the Belgian and Dutch sales be seen as an aberration?'

The other side of the equation is the extent to which other central banks, mainly in Asia, with large foreign exchange reserves but little gold, will take the opportunity to buy. In short, are we just witnessing the beginning of a redistribution of gold among central banks as it follows the new prosperity of the Asian Tigers, or is this the start of a fundamental disposal of central bank gold into the open market, as happened with silver precisely a century ago? Either way, any discussion of the gold market in the 1990s homes in on central banks. 'Central banks are the most powerful influence at work in the market today,' says Robert Guy of N. M. Rothschild; 'powerful because of the liquidity they inject into the market . . . powerful because they are perceived as regular net suppliers . . . and powerful tomorrow because of the anticipation that higher prices will only encourage further diversification out of gold into other reserve assets.'[1]

Amidst this hubbub, it is important to take a slightly broader perspective to see how this situation came about in the first place. A swift historical flashback reminds us that most nations went off the gold standard in the 1930s, but the United States set a new price of gold at $35 in 1934 and, crucially, stood ready to buy and sell gold to central banks at that price. This was the dollar exchange standard which, in the era of fixed exchange rates later conceived at Bretton Woods, underpinned the monetary system until 1971. Initially, it was one-way traffic into the US reserves, which ultimately amounted to over 22,000 tonnes or 75 per cent of all official gold by the late 1940s. But as European economies grew in the 1950s and 1960s, they constantly traded in dollars at the US Federal Reserve in New York for gold; US reserves dropped by over 11,000 tonnes. Central bankers were also the main buyers in the market, taking up 44 per cent of all on offer from 1948 to 1964. Thereafter, the weight of private buying made central banks sellers in their effort to hold gold at $35, until they gave up defeated in 1968 (see Chapter 3). The Washington Agreement that year created a two-tier market in which central banks were supposedly divorced from the hurly-burly of the market place, but could still turn in official dollars for gold at the Federal Reserve until President Nixon ordered that gold window closed in April 1971.

### Demonetization drive

The US Treasury, in concert with the International Monetary Fund (IMF), then launched an attempt to demonetize gold entirely. The IMF even altered its articles in 1978 to suspend gold as an ultimate means of settlement and as the international *numéraire*. These actions essentially froze, as if in a time capsule, the gold holdings of European central banks as they were in 1971. As the annual report of the Bank for International Settlements (BIS) observed a couple of years later, 'Gold remains in the vaults of central banks – unused but not unloved.' The world economy moved on, but the ebb and flow of gold holdings that had previously marked changes in the wealth of nations stopped. Admittedly there

---

1 Robert Guy, *Setting the Scene*, Financial Times World Gold Conference, Montreux, June 1992.

were sales, notably by the US Treasury and the IMF in the late 1970s, partly designed to check investment in gold to the detriment of the dollar. The IMF sold 777.6 tonnes (25 million ounces) over four years, for which it got an average of $246 and the US Treasury disposed of 530 tonnes (17 million ounces) at an average of $255. The gold price then took off to $850 which, as in 1968, showed you cannot take on the market. Sporadic buyers also appeared; oil producers had a little fling, as did Taiwan, but there was no clear sense of direction. The US Treasury also put pressure on possible buyers like the Bank of Japan to keep away. Thus, central bank gold holdings in the early 1990s were largely a snapshot of where they were twenty years earlier.

In that light, the actions of new, young, European central bank managers, who have inherited a high proportion of gold in their reserves, and feel they should now be indulging in active asset management, are entirely understandable. Had gold been moved around as it always used to be, the dilemma would not confront them.

Taking stock of the present position, central banks hold close to 29,000 tonnes (932 million ounces) on their own accounts, while another 6,000 tonnes (193 million ounces) is deposited with official institutions such as the IMF, which holds 3,217 tonnes, the European Monetary Co-operation Fund, and the Bank for International Settlements. It would also be prudent to add at least another 1,000 tonnes for central banks such as those in Iraq and Singapore, which do not declare their holdings, and for other discreet 'second books' or various government investment institutions ranging from the Abu Dhabi Investment Authority, to the Brunei Investment Agency and the Kuwait Investment Office. The total is thus close to 36,000 tonnes, which is about 30 per cent of all gold ever mined (a statistic often used to terrify when central bank sales are discussed, as if it might all come on the market next week). Valued at $350 an ounce, gold thus accounts for over a quarter of total international reserves, and is second only to the dollar as the most important reserve asset. This is ample evidence that, although its monetary role has changed radically, it remains a cornerstone of international liquidity; indeed, at the high price of $850 in 1980 gold reserves momentarily accounted for over 55 per cent of that liquidity. Central banks also often delight in extremely conservative valuation of their gold reserves to camouflage its real worth among their assets. The United States, Canada and Japan count their gold at less than 20 per cent of world prices, and while some Europeans do use market-related values, for the Group of Ten industrial nations as a whole the average national valuation was only 45 per cent of the market price at the end of 1991.[2]

2 T.R.G. Bingham, Bank for International Settlements, 'Gold in the international monetary system', *Central Banking*, Vol. III, 2, Autumn 1992, pp. 45–52.

### To Sell or not to sell?

The heart of the matter is that gold reserves are not evenly distributed and in a handful of nations account for an exceptionally high proportion of reserves. The leader is the United States, which still holds 8,144 tonnes (262 million ounces) or nearly one-quarter of all official gold, while Germany has 3,701 tonnes, France 3,182 tonnes, Italy 2,592 tonnes, Switzerland 2,590 tonnes, the Netherlands 1,308 tonnes (after selling 400 in 1992) and Belgium 974 tonnes (also after 329 tonnes sold in 1989 and 1992). This amounts to over 22,000 tonnes or 60 per cent of all monetary gold held by just seven countries. By comparison, the holding of some other leading nations seems derisory; Japan has 754 tonnes, the United Kingdom 724, Taiwan 421, China 398 and India 353 tonnes. Overall, it is a snapshot of the way we were in 1971.

The threat, as some would see it, comes from those large European holdings; in France gold accounted for 56 per cent of reserves at the end of 1992, in Italy 50 per cent, in Switzerland 46 per cent and in Germany 30 per cent. In the United States it was as high as 59 per cent. In the United Kingdom, by comparison, it was 18 per cent, in Japan just 10 per cent and in Taiwan (with huge reserves) a mere 5 per cent. To focus on the Europeans, the Swiss are on record as having no intention of selling and the Dutch have also said they will not sell any more. Moreover, no one is likely to go to zero gold. The Bank of England is probably as good a benchmark as any. The Bank makes no secret of the fact it can 'live with' 15–18 per cent and the governor, Eddie George, has said outright he will not sell gold. Since the Bank of England celebrates its three-hundredth anniversary in 1994 and, as a great ally of the London gold market is more experienced in gold than any other central bank, that is as good an indicator as one can get. Even if all those other Europeans gradually sold down to 15–18 per cent of their reserves in gold, it puts at risk 8,000 to 10,000 tonnes at the outside and in reality probably no more than 4,000 to 5,000 tonnes between now and the year 2000. That may not happen at all, or it might be handled largely in off-market sales to other central banks, as happened with Belgium's first sale in 1989 where most went to Spain, and with a large part of the Netherlands' sale in 1992.

The United States, of course, might also be perceived as a potential seller; it has the biggest stock, the highest proportion of gold in its reserves and a huge budget deficit. While further auctions by the US Treasury were ruled out by a special US Gold Commission in 1981, no doubt President Clinton, in his search for solutions to the deficit, might consider gold sales. But could he get it through Congress, where the gold miners' case is much stronger now that the United States is the world's second largest producer? And would such sales be detrimental to the dollar? It is the principal reserve currency and psychologically it makes sense for the world's number one currency to be backed by the number one stock of gold, even if the issue of the former is not directly tied to the latter. The chances of US sales, therefore, must not be ignored, but equally do not seem likely.

The message to the gold market is, do not panic. Yes, there are over 35,000 tonnes of gold in official hands, and perhaps 10–20 per cent of that may eventually be on offer over the next decade, but much of it will be taken up by other central banks, while an argument can be made that the market itself will be able to digest increasing amounts of official gold, given the broadening pattern of jewellery demand. Indeed, it is doing so already. Central banks have been net sellers of well over 2,500 tonnes since 1965, yet the dollar price is up ten-fold. That is without taking into account the gold absorbed by the market between 1989 and 1993 as the reserves of the collapsing Soviet Union were swapped and then sold off.

Significantly, such distress sales on a large scale are rare. The sales in prospect from Europe are not in this category and will be carefully planned to cause minimum disruption, if any, to the market. Experienced intermediaries such as the Bank for International Settlements (founded in 1930 as the central bankers' bank) and the Bank of England can, and have, scouted for potential buyers and sold gold discreetly. They take their time. The Netherlands central bank took the decision to sell its 400 tonnes in the autumn of 1991, delayed the programme because it heard Belgium was about to sell, and finally got going a year later, after the governor had forewarned fellow-European central bank governors. The gold was sold forward for delivery in February 1993, thus covering what was going on because no reserve figures changed in the International Financial Statistics until it was all over. Sales can be cloaked by central banks borrowing gold while the sales programme is underway.

The awareness of the market's sensitivity to potential sales brought some reassurance from Gavin Bingham of the Bank for International Settlements, who wrote, 'The very skewed pattern of gold holdings puts large and small official holders in rather different positions . . . small holders can manage their gold actively without disrupting the market. Large official holders have less scope for making radical and rapid changes . . . even a small change in their stocks would be large relative to supplies coming to the market.' And Mr Bingham added, 'Radical changes in aggregate official holdings of gold do not seem very likely in the foreseeable future. Central banks have a vital interest in the integrity of the monetary system and the stability of markets, including the gold market'.[3] In the rarefied atmosphere of central banks, which like to surround policies in secrecy and mystery, that is more than a crumb of comfort for gold bugs.

The Belgian central bank itself has also offered a word of explanation. Agnes Van den Berge, the head of foreign exchange, told a *Financial Times* conference, 'The recent gold sales of Belgium and the Netherlands have been executed with the intention to bring the share of their gold reserves . . . closer to the average of other European countries.' And she went on to state, 'Central banks will be very cautious when considering the possibility of selling gold. Their sense of responsibility will prevent them from disrupting the gold market, which would lead to a depreciation of their external reserves. Belgium, for example, has the clear intention to remain a gold-holding country . . . this is also the case for the Netherlands'.[4]

The reality, anyway, is that central banks have become an integral part of daily business in the market in terms of leasing, swaps, active trading and regular marketing of production. Indeed, those who tried to banish gold twenty years ago would be amazed to see how closely involved central banks are in many aspects of the market in the 1990s. The most immediate participation comes from those central banks in gold-producing countries which sell part or all of their output. That embraces not just South Africa as the largest producer, but as diverse a cast as Brazil, China, Colombia, Ecuador, the Philippines, Russia, Uzbekistan, Venezuela and Zimbabwe, which account in all for almost half of world output. They may prefer to stockpile the gold (the People's Bank of China lets very little go), but at least they get their hands on it and can sell, swap or save, as they choose. Although in the long run producing countries are almost bound to sell their output (just as oil producers market their oil), the central banks in all the above countries do withhold gold from the market often for months at a time, thus qualifying as buyers. The high level of sales in 1992 was partially offset by 'producer' central banks holding gold off a weak market.

### South Africa: mainstream market-maker

The central banks may also be substantial traders. Indeed, one of the major changes of recent years is that the South African Reserve Bank, to which all gold production in that country must be delivered (even if it is initially hedged elsewhere), has become active, not just in forwards and options, but in quite aggressive buying from time to time. Contrast this with the Reserve Bank's previous attitude that it was merely the conduit through which gold was sold. Indeed, when I first visited South Africa in 1967, the then governor of the Reserve Bank told me that there was

---

3 Ibid.
4 Agnes Van den Berge, *Central Bank Attitudes Towards Gold in the '90s*, Financial Times World Gold Conference, Istanbul, June 1993.

no point in its withholding gold, even for a few days. Today the Reserve Bank under Dr Chris Stals, the governor, and James Cross, the general manager for gold and foreign exchange, is highly market-orientated. 'The Bank occasionally intervenes by actively buying gold,' admits James Cross, 'without presuming to influence long-term price trends.' Actually, in the much thinner gold-trading market of the 1990s, James Cross often felt that he was the last line of defence when the market was hit by a wave of selling such as that from National Commercial Bank in Jeddah in 1990. In the volatile 1980s, there had always been players on a grand scale on either side, Cross observed to me, including not just big Middle East speculators, but also the Russians, to offer support. Now he alone had to plug the dyke. But the business can be two-way. Gossip also has it that the Reserve Bank has been a useful conduit for at least one large sale by another central bank, because the market sees it naturally as a regular seller, and so it can cloak what is really going on. In any event, if you sit in Cross's office, just off the trading room in the Bank's grand new offices in Pretoria, you sense at once you are right in the mainstream of the gold market, and not merely calling on a central bank that happens to sell some gold for mines. The Reserve Bank is also a substantial hedger on behalf of the mines, to which it offers a stabilized contango facility that attracts as much as 90 tonnes of output a year.

Inevitably South Africa is a special case, being the world's greatest producer for a century; how could it not be committed to gold? But it has also found in recent years that gold can be a real life-line for a nation swamped by debt and surrounded by sanctions. Faced with a debt crisis but denied normal access to IMF borrowing facilities, the Reserve Bank was able to swap almost 400 tonnes (12.8 million ounces) of its gold reserves for foreign exchange in the mid-1980s, later unwinding many of them and selling at least 250 tonnes into the market between 1988 and 1990, with little disruption and few people knowing. As the governor, Chris Stals, later candidly admitted, 'Pragmatism forced the Reserve Bank to hold its foreign reserves in a form that could be used without restriction, and without outside interference ... gold served South Africa well in its hour of distress.' And he revealed a catalogue of benefits South Africa had secured in the liberalized global markets. 'South Africa exploited these markets,' said Dr Stals, 'by selling its relatively large production regularly in the spot market and by making use of large amounts of gold swaps out of its reserves, by arranging pre-shipment advance payments against future sales, by operating in options and forward markets and by allowing individual South African gold producers to borrow against their future production.'[5]

5 Dr Chris Stals, *Issues in Reserve Management*, City of London Central Banking Conference, London, January 1993.

### Brazil: anyone for trading?

South Africa's experience is not unique. Brazil's central bank has been constantly in and out of the gold market over the last decade on the swings and roundabouts of its debt crisis, often with remarkable success. Initially the central bank had to sell almost its entire stock late in 1982, at an average of $436, but over the next three years quietly rebuilt the reserve, mainly from buying up local production and also by boldly going into the market for 25 tonnes at under $300 early in 1985. By late 1986 it had stockpiled over 100 tonnes, acquired at an average of $320. Encircled again by debt, it was forced to sell in 1987, but luckily at the top of the market, mostly between $460 and $490. The Brazilian bank's role is actually two-fold. It bids competitively for local production, which does not have to be sold to it and which can be held in reserves, swapped or sold abroad, and it intervenes in the domestic market to keep the difference between the official and unofficial rates for the dollar relatively close. Since high inflation in Brazil has resulted in large-scale gold investment both by private investors and by businesses, the central bank is always ready to sell gold into the local market if demand is strong, or buy back when investors may be selling. The bank is also a regular day trader in the international market, often running positions involving hundreds of thousands of ounces. The interplay of these activities not only makes it difficult to know precisely where Brazil's true gold reserves stand at any given moment, but has led to suggestions that it is acting for other central banks, which can hide behind the smokescreen of its operations. In fact, this is highly unlikely.

Brazil's policy, however, of bidding for domestic production with a price that always reflects the unofficial exchange rate for the dollar, has been copied elsewhere in Latin America. Central banks in both Ecuador and Venezuela have established gold-buying units to bid for local production, which they then swap or sell, but the quantities are smaller than in Brazil and they have not become involved in daily trading. Colombia's central bank has also long been taking up domestic production, often paying a slight premium in local pesos, which leads to gold being smuggled into the country from Panama or Venezuela to be passed off as 'local' output; the pesos thus secured can immediately be switched into dollars. While in the Philippines primary mine output (as opposed to by-product from copper-gold mines) has to be sold to the central bank, which also bids for unofficial alluvial production. The central bank even has its own refinery in Quezon City turning out 995 good delivery bars, which are usually dispatched to Hong Kong or Singapore, while the bank takes gold at the Bank of England in London through a location swap.

## Bank of England: centre stage

The Bank of England, of course, is both the depository and the turntable of central bank gold. While central banks often keep gold with the Federal Reserve in New York, which has substantial stocks of many nations quite distinct from the United States' own reserve, which is mainly at Fort Knox, or with the Bank for International Settlements in Basel, the Bank of England has increasingly become the nerve centre. It has the know-how that comes from daily involvement over three centuries with the London gold market and has an even-handed approach to all comers. For example, the Bank was the vital intermediary in the restitution to Iran in January 1981 of its gold, which had been frozen at the Federal Reserve in response to the seizing of the American hostages in 1979. Together with Algeria, the Bank presided over the complicated financial arrangements involved at the moment of the hostages' release. The Federal Reserve did not dispatch the Iranian gold to London, but credited the Bank of England with 50 tonnes held to its order (but not the actual Iranian bars), while the Bank transferred 50 tonnes from Britain's reserves in London to the account of the Algerian central bank for the disposal by Iran. Quite apart from demonstrating the Bank's reputation for political neutrality in sensitive episodes, this exercise is a simple lesson in the way much central bank business is done. Gold does not need to be flown around the world, but can be housed in a handful of internationally accepted depositories and switched by a computer transfer (listing in detail every bar number) from the account of one nation to another.

This is a cautionary tale, because central banks which have historically kept their gold at home or have bought it recently and flown all or part of it home (as Indonesia, Singapore and Taiwan did in the 1980s), then find it tricky to mobilize it as a collateral in moments of need. Word is sure to get out if the gold is shipped abroad, possibly creating panic that the country's finances are worse off than they are. Gold at the Bank of England can be quietly swapped. As the Bank's chief foreign exchange manager, Terry Smeeton, put it, 'The advice I invariably give to central banks which own gold . . . is the importance of holding their physical reserves in a major gold trading centre, rather than their own vaults. While it may be good for national pride to have gold within the country, from the point of view of using the reserves for the purpose for which they are intended, it is a definite obstacle. . . . We have seen the fears of adverse public reaction represent a deterrent to the movement of gold out of the country on more than one occasion recently. It is better held in London, Switzerland or New York'.[6] Most central banks take him at his word; with few exceptions all the major holders of gold keep some of it with the Bank of England.

6 T.R. Smeeton, *Gold in the UK Market*, The 5th Nikkei Gold Conference, Tokyo, September 1992.

The deterrent against moving gold abroad in an emergency is real. Undoubtedly the country Mr Smeeton had in mind was India, which got boxed in by a short-term foreign exchange crisis in 1991 and had to mobilize its gold. Initially, India used about 20 tonnes confiscated from smugglers which was technically not in the reserves, and it was able to swap that abroad in Switzerland without too much fuss. But under mounting pressure it had to ship 46 tonnes of its reserves from Bombay to the Bank of England to be used as collateral for a stand-by loan from the Bank of Japan. 'Even the elite in our society considered the movement of gold an act of national humiliation,' admitted S. Venkitaramanan, governor of the Reserve Bank of India, afterwards. In the event, it ended happily because the balance of payments rapidly improved and India was able to redeem its gold with its credit-worthiness restored. A good example of gold as a short-term life-line, but also an object lesson in where to keep it.

### Lending to the market
Crises apart, another good reason why central banks keep gold in major centres is to make money. Central bank deposits of gold with leading market-makers have become one of the fastest-growing activities since the late 1970s. At any given moment between 1,500 and 1,800 tonnes (58 million ounces) is estimated to be on deposit, providing the liquidity for forward sales, gold loans and the working inventory of fabricators. 'Central bank lending has become crucial to the liquidity of the market,' observed Urs Seiler of Union Bank of Switzerland. The gold is placed with market-makers for a set period, perhaps six months or one year, for a modest interest (usually paid in gold) of between 0.5 and 3 per cent. Considerable caution is now exercised in the addresses with which gold will be deposited, following the collapse in 1990 of Drexel Burnham Lambert, the New York investment house with which several central banks, including those of Portugal and Malaysia, had gold; the fate of the gold was still unclear three years later. While the facility is mainly used by smaller central banks, anxious to show a little return on a modest gold holding, regular depositors include the Austrian National Bank and the Bank of England. And the Bank of England also lends out on their behalf some gold it holds for other central banks. The availability of gold via the Bank makes London the leading centre for leasing.

The interest rate received fluctuates considerably, influenced both by central banks' willingness to lend and the market's immediate requirements. The current rate is posted on Reuters under GODFRA, Gold Deposit Forward Rate Agreement, and a jump may alert the market to something big afoot. For instance, in the autumn of 1992, it popped up, partly because one major institution withdrew about a million ounces that was on deposit (thinking it might sell it), while a couple of houses were borrowing gold to accommodate a new hedging agreement by a North American mining house, and yet others were borrowing to underpin the Netherlands central bank sale of 400 tonnes (sold forward for delivery in February 1993). This got the rate up in a matter of weeks (from 0.5 to 2 per cent), which seduced several fresh central banks to place deposits.

### Writing options

The other immediate way for central banks to make money on their gold is to write call options against their reserves. Indeed, central banks were among the first large-scale participants to take advantage of tailor-made over-the-counter (OTC) options. 'Central banks and government investment agencies are among the biggest speculators in options,' a New York market-maker confided to me in 1987. 'They have large reserves sitting idle and want to get some revenue . . . so they sell calls above the market and earn the premium.' Since then, central bank options writing has reached substantial proportions. David Pryde of J. P. Morgan told a US conference in 1992 that he estimated central banks might have calls outstanding for as much as 800 tonnes at any given moment. While Gold Fields Mineral Services, the London based research team, commented that 'although still the preserve of relatively few central banks, the number has grown . . . as has the volume transacted by major players'.[7] The Gold Fields report added that, 'most of the volume consists of passive writing of 'out-of-the-money' calls in order to earn premium income. A small minority of central banks, however, have developed more sophisticated trading strategies based on options. In all cases, maturities tend to be fairly short, with positions effectively being rolled over on a regular basis.' The subsequent 'delta' hedging of such options by market-makers can have an impact on the market. Gold Fields estimated, for example, that part of the 91 tonnes of extra 'supply' to the market through delta hedging in 1992 was on account of central bank programmes.

### Signs of pregnancy

A European bullion banker describes such temptations to earn a small return on gold as 'the first sign of pregnancy'; the birth, of course, is when they actually sell gold. He observes that central banks edge forward by such tactics as deposits, options and even issuing gold coins made with metal from their reserves (as did Belgium a year or so before its first sale), while they pluck up courage, square the finance minister

---

7 *Gold 1993*, Gold Fields Mineral Services, London, p. 34.

and settle any legal liabilities about the profit that comes from selling gold they bought long ago for $35 an ounce for ten times that amount. Austria has been displaying such signs of pregnancy for quite some time, being one of the first to lend to the market and then launching the highly successful Philharmoniker bullion coin in 1989. The bullion coin has done so well, being the best-seller in 1992, that Austria has actually 'sold' almost 40 tonnes of gold reserves by way of coin in four years.

No such direct link exists between Canada's disposal of much of its gold reserves since 1980 and the Maple Leaf bullion coin launched the previous year. The two operations are entirely independent. The official sales, sanctioned by Canada's Ministry of Finance and executed by the Bank of Canada, represent the longest-running programme of any central bank. When they began, Canada had over 650 tonnes of gold, which constituted 80 per cent of its reserves; by the end of 1992 it had 309 tonnes left. Usually the sales have been on a regular monthly basis, although in 1992 they were stepped up considerably, when Canada sold 94 tonnes. At that rate the gold will virtually all be gone by 1995, although the sales are expected to stop when the reserve is down to 155 tonnes (5 million ounces). The original decision to sell is entirely understandable; Canada had too little flexibility in the foreign exchange markets when most of its reserve was in gold. And by spreading the programme over fourteen or fifteen years, the sales have had little effect on the market (though Canada's mining lobby would argue otherwise). The Canadian approach, however, shows what might be anticipated over the next decade or two from European central banks; not an avalanche, but a regular snowfall.

### The Baltics back gold

The desire to dispose of gold, though, is by no means universal. On the contrary, there have been some touching examples of central bank faith in gold from the newly independent Baltic nations of Latvia, Lithuania and Estonia, which had determined to recover gold they had placed with the Bank for International Settlements and the Bank of France before their annexation by the Soviet Union in 1940. I have before me a photograph of Vilius Baldisis, president of the Lithuanian central bank, taking delivery of a neat little stack of 2.3 tonnes (74,000 ounces) in good delivery bars from the Bank of France, which had minded them for half a century (sending the gold to Africa during the war), while Jacques de Larosière, governor of the Bank of France, looks on with some pride. The Baltic countries also came calling for gold deposited with the Bank of England and the Riksbank in Sweden, only to find they had wavered, either transferring or selling the gold as part of agreements with the Soviet Union in the meantime. The obligation was, nevertheless, honoured by both central banks. Estonia regarded it as a matter of great prestige that it got back 11 tonnes of gold placed abroad. 'This has enabled Estonia to maintain a fully-backed currency board,' said Allan Karell of the Bank of Estonia.

## *Waiting for China?*

The market needs, of course, a few rather larger central bank devotees as buyers. All eyes are on the Far East – Brunei (with an investment portfolio of over $30 billion), China, Singapore, South Korea and Taiwan. The difficulty is that there is a legacy of what one might call 'bad experiences' in the region. Indonesia bought close to 80 tonnes (2.5 million ounces) in the early 1980s at prices around $580 and Taiwan bought 246 tonnes (nearly 8 million ounces) in 1987–8 at prices close to $450. Indeed, the price only stayed at that level while Taiwan was in the market and has never recovered to the same level since. The resultant loss of face by the governor of the central bank was such that although when prices declined below $350, bullion banks were pressing Taiwan to buy to average down, no one in the bank would listen.

China may be cannier. Although its official reserve is declared as 398 tonnes, it has stood at that level for many years, and makes no account of stockpiled local mine output. Its track record, however, is impeccable. China sold its sterling balances in 1967, just before sterling was devalued, and bought gold, then still pegged at $35, thus anticipating the price explosion. Although Bank of China, as the trading arm of the central bank, the People's Bank of China, has been an active trader, sales out of reserves have been rare. It sold in 1976 to finance damage from a major earthquake and in 1989/90 after the Tiananmen Square rebellion, when China's credit rating stalled and it had to make some gold swaps, which were sold out at the high of $420 early in 1990. China has shown signs, however, of wanting to get back that gold, sold in an emergency, at lower prices. The People's Bank will also have noted that when the Soviet Union fell apart, its gold reserves were revealed to be much less than analysts had calculated; they were probably never more than 1,000 tonnes, compared to the estimated 2,000 tonnes. Learning from that experience, China is certain to wish to maintain and even build a better reserve. So did it take 200 to 250 tonnes of the Netherlands sale of 400 tonnes? The price, down around $335, was certainly right. The gold was available for delivery at the Bank of England, where China already keeps gold. There was no problem of going into the market to buy it, where purchase on such a scale would almost surely be detected, if not identified. Anyway, the People's Bank simply does not have the in-house trading skills to tackle it. A neat package, however, offered by one central bank to another, which few would know about, may have been an offer not to be refused. And remember, the whole transfer is done by a computer reallocating just a few thousand good delivery bars from one account to another. The case is not yet proven, but the motive is.

### Shuffling the reserve pack

This may well be the way ahead. Central banks will redistribute, in part, the reserves among themselves to balance them out at a level more in tune with the world economy going into the twenty-first century. My own experience from talking to a wide selection of central banks and government investment institutions is that few are really averse to gold; they just do not want it to swamp their portfolio. The Bank of England, as I mentioned, is content with around 15 per cent of UK reserves in gold. In the oil-producing countries the 'fashionable' view when they were acquiring gold some years ago was to acquire gold as 7–10 per cent of a long-term strategic portfolio; in almost all cases they are now underweight even in that proportion. Taiwan's buying programme originally got the level up towards 10 per cent, although that has now also slipped back. Even to go to a 7 to 10 per cent holding in gold across the board of central banks and government investment institutions would accommodate a good slice of prospective central bank sales. The concept fits neatly into the multi-currency monetary system that is evolving. Once it was just gold, then the dollar, now 'baskets' brimming with dollars, Deutschmarks, yen, perhaps ultimately a new European currency, with a nice top-up of gold.

An added incentive for some nations is the anonymity of gold holdings which, if you have them at home, cannot be frozen in times of economic or political crisis. Iran's experience in having its assets, including gold, frozen during the hostage affair, has led since to other nations as diverse as Iraq, Libya and Peru acquiring and holding gold discreetly. Given the new world disorder, whether with the disintegrated Soviet Empire or the break-up of Yugoslavia, there will be small, new republics wishing to have a little gold against the day when the United Nations or someone else imposes sanctions.

### IMF: No Policy

There remain two other relevant questions. What happens to the IMF's gold? And what is the future of gold in the proposed European central bank? The International Monetary Fund, conceived in 1944 at the Bretton Woods conference on the future of the monetary system, and born in Washington DC in 1947, acquired its stock of gold because members were required to make deposits, or tranches, in gold, dollars and their own currencies against which they could borrow. At the peak, the IMF held 4,772 tonnes (153.4 million ounces), but by the 1970s was in the forefront of the move to demonetize gold. In competition, so to speak, it created its own credit units, called special drawing rights (SDRs), although initially these were defined as equivalent to 0.888671 grams of fine gold. The link to gold was later abandoned in favour of linking SDRs to a basket of leading trade currencies. Meanwhile, the IMF also ran down its stock to 3,217 tonnes (103 million ounces) by the triple track of holding forty-five auctions at which it sold 731.5 tonnes to all comers (bids were actually received for 2,199 tonnes); selling 46.6 tonnes in non-competitive bids from seventeen developing countries; and returning, or restituting, another 777.6 to its members. The declared aim was to raise cash for developing countries but it was also a tactic to undermine gold and, hopefully, help the SDR. Since then all is silence, apart from occasional suggestions that the IMF might auction some more gold for the benefit of developing countries, which has met little response (and the chance of getting auctions approved by a majority of members is remote).

So where does the IMF stand on gold? Nowhere. At a central banking conference in London in 1993, David Williams, the IMF treasurer, said in response to a question, 'The Fund has no policy on gold.' Actually, that is not strictly true, because he then admitted that the Fund still values its gold at $42 an ounce so that it is 'clearly an under-valued asset in the Fund's balance sheet and for that reason it helps the strength of the institution.' The Fund, incidentally, keeps its books in and thinks in SDRs, which is more or less unique. Just for the record, the dollar/SDR exchange rate varied from $1.30 to $1.42 in 1992. The IMF has issued or created 21.4 billion SDRs (though none since 1981), while it reckons that SDR 250 billion of international reserves is still held in gold. In the SDR v. gold stakes, it is easy to see which is most popular. Although future IMF gold sales cannot be entirely ruled out (Britain's former Chancellor of the Exchequer, Norman Lamont, brought up the topic at an IMF meeting in 1993), the chances of getting the necessary approval of 85 per cent of the IMF's members for such sales would prove difficult.

### Gold for Europe's central bank
The unresolved issue for the 1990s is the role that gold may play in the proposed European central bank or, more correctly, the European System of Central Banks (ESCB), conceived as a federal reserve set-up for the twelve members of the European community, which ought to

be in place by the turn of the century. The ESCB is crucial to the proposed monetary union in Europe. One step along this road already exists in the European Monetary Co-operation Fund, with which all EC countries deposit 20 per cent of their gold reserves in return for currency units, known as 'ecus', which count as a reserve asset. The Fund holds nearly 3,000 tonnes of gold and, in calculating the issue of ecus, values it at the full market price averaged over the preceding six months (unless the current day's price is lower, when it is adjusted downwards). Gold is thus already part of the basket determining the amount of ecus in the European system. Its role in the ESCB, however, has not been clearly defined. The draft statutes allow the bank to deal in and hold precious metals, and for participating central banks to pay their contributions to its capital in gold.[8] Beyond that, gold's function remains ambiguous. Indeed, the forerunner of the ESCB, the European Monetary Institute, is due to open in 1994 and its statutes approve only the holding and managing of foreign exchange; not a word is said about gold, so it will begin without it. As the Bank of England's Terry Smeeton has observed, 'I think it is in practice unlikely that any national central bank is going to pass over its gold reserves.'[9]

Actually, several European central banks have ambivalent attitudes to handing over gold to a federal institution. While it may provide a convenient opportunity for some large holders to divest themselves of gold without putting any pressure on the market, others may prove quite reluctant to hand over a substantial proportion of their gold, preferring to retain an asset which remains no one else's liability.

The latter argument remains the unique advantage of gold; in the multi-currency system that has evolved over the years, dollars, sterling, Deutschmarks and yen are someone else's liability. The Netherlands and Belgium learned that lesson the hard way back in 1931 when they had taken to holding part of their reserves in sterling, believing it was as good as gold; which it was, until Britain suddenly went off the gold standard without warning them. That is precisely why gold will remain an international reserve asset, but one less frozen, less sterile at the bottom of the stockpile. Central banks also want some return on their gold; they will swap, lend, write options and trade, treating it more as a currency. Gavin Bingham of the BIS has aptly reversed his bank's 1973 comment that gold was 'unused, but not unloved' to read, 'unloved, but not unused'.[10]

The last word, however, rests with the Bank of England, as it celebrates its tercentenary. The Bank's Terry Smeeton, who probably has a closer eye on the international ebb and flow than anyone else, remarked that, in his view, there have been three principal reasons for

8 Bingham, op. cit.
9 T.R. Smeeton, *Central Bank Attitudes to the Future of Gold*, Financial Times World Gold Conference, Montreux, June 1992.
10 Bingham, op. cit.

holding gold. 'These are', said Mr Smeeton, 'the war chest argument – that gold is the ultimate store of value in a volatile and uncertain world; secondly, that gold may be seen as a credit–risk–free alternative investment to holdings of currencies in reserves; and, thirdly, as security for loans.' And he concluded that these pragmatic motives will lead 'central banks to continue to wish to hold some gold in their reserves and may, in my view, lead to some of those newly wealthy countries which currently have little or no gold holdings to wish to take on or increase their exposure.'[11]

11 Smeeton, op. cit.

# CHAPTER 19

# The Investors: Profit or Protection?

'To invest', says the Oxford English Dictionary, is 'to employ [money] in the purchase of anything from which interest or profit is expected.' This is a definition which does not entirely do justice to the diverse galaxy of investors in gold, who may be seeking not profit, but protection, or even a mixture of both. Indeed, the historic reputation of gold is founded much more on the protection it offered. The perception of gold changed fundamentally, however, for many people with the ending of the fixed price in 1968. A metal that had been valued for the stability of its price, as insurance, even as bedrock when all around was in turmoil, suddenly had profit potential. And what profit! In the 1970s the compound annual rate of return on gold was 31.6 per cent against a mere 7.5 per cent for stocks or 6.4 per cent for bonds, as its price rose from $35 to $850 by January 1980. All good things come to an end; thereafter gold went into a thirteen-year bear market that brought it to $327 early in 1993. As a European banker observed with feeling, 'Not surprisingly . . . the investors' attitude to gold has become negative.' Curiously enough, so negative that when gold did turn around and make a nice run back up over $400 in a matter of weeks, many punters were taken by surprise. 'We missed it,' conceded a German bullion dealer. 'We were long, but sold at $360 and squared at $370. No one made full use of it.'

Actually, that is not quite correct, for one reason gold held just below $330 in the face of considerable central bank selling was precisely because investors throughout the Middle East, India and Southeast Asia knew a cheap gold price when they saw one in the local *souks* or markets, and took immediate advantage. Indeed, the demand was so great for physical gold that it soon became clear that the gold price had to rise to cool it. As a benchmark, for instance, one could take Jakarta in Indonesia, where the local price of gold went to a 'positive' premium once the international price slipped below $340 as investors took advantage of a unique opportunity; Indonesia imported virtually as much gold in the first three months of 1993 as in all of 1992.

The gold investor is a multi-faceted fellow. One may see a moment as time to get out, that another sees as the window of opportunity to get in. Profit is still not everyone's aim either. The classic hoarder, seeking insurance, is alive and well. Twenty-five years ago it was the French who had the greatest reputation for hoarding gold in the aftermath of two world wars sweeping across their country causing countless devaluations. Today, make that Brazil, Cambodia, China or Vietnam, where gold is bought as insurance against inflation and depreciation of local currencies. One legacy of the Gulf War in 1991 has been a return to physical gold investment not only in Kuwait, but in the other Gulf States and Saudi Arabia; everyone wants a little gold in case they have to run away. Wisely, some of this investment is in small bars and coin rather than expensive kilo bars, which are more practical for bribing a way through checkpoints. Kilo bars are often held as capital, though, because in an emergency it is no good running to the bank to draw out money, for the lesson of the Gulf War was that the Kuwait dinar was briefly worthless after Iraq's invasion and the banks soon ran out of dollars cash. Gold is also the capital of the jewellery business throughout the Middle East; a jeweller keeps his books in gold and assesses his worth as so many kilos. In the Grand Bazaar in Istanbul, the rent of the shops is even calculated in kilos of gold per year.

This broad spectrum of attitudes to gold remains one of the strengths of the market. Someone, somewhere, always has need to invest in gold. Nevertheless, its attraction has been changed by the pursuit of profit and by the range of paper gold derivatives in futures, options of every flavour, and warrants (see Chapters 14 and 16). 'Today's investors are concentrating on performance rather than holding gold as a long-term portfolio asset,' observed Ian MacDonald of Crédit Suisse in New York. 'The leverage effect of options opens up very attractive profit opportunities.'[1] Certainly, that is the view from New York and increasingly even from banks in Switzerland, which were previously renowned for keeping 5 to 10 per cent of portfolios in physical gold primarily as insurance (a percentage drastically reduced in recent years). At a lunch in Geneva in 1992, a partner at one private bank wondered if

1 Ian MacDonald, *Over-the-Counter Options and their Overall Impact on the Gold Market*, Financial Times World Gold Conference, Istanbul, June 1993.

it was the right moment to get back into gold with confidence of a 20 per cent return over three years. 'No', said the bank's chief foreign exchange and gold trader, also at the table. 'It isn't like that any more; you have to trade the market short term.'

This shift was immediately noticeable in the price rally of mid-1993. A Geneva banker told me that his clients had responded primarily through buying options and, significantly, gold shares.

Any analysis of gold investment today has to take account of the much greater market for gold shares in the 1990s. The total gold share market, now capitalized at roughly $50 billion according to Robert Weinberg of Société Générale Strauss Turnbull, has grown enormously in the last decade. 'Just look at the huge capitalisation of North American and Australian mining shares today,' Weinberg told me. 'In the 1970s there were only South African shares and a few small North American mines like Homestake, Dome, Campbell Red Lake or Lac.' For many investors the purchase of shares means they are 'in' gold and often that is the route they prefer rather than going for the metal itself. In the gold price rally of 1986–7, for example, the twenty-four listed US gold funds increased their assets by $2.6 billion, but scarcely $50 million of that was actually in gold. Again, in 1993 gold shares took the money first, signalling that investors anticipated a price rise. Among them, of course, was George Soros and his Quantum Fund with their highly publicized purchase of Newmont Mining shares from Sir James Goldsmith who, in turn, put his proceeds into gold options. Such actions lifted the *Financial Times* Gold Mines Index 240 per cent in a matter of months, as shares outperformed the metal. However, the diversion into gold shares, which undoubtedly dilutes the impact on the gold price, does not alter the fact that the gold market and the gold share market taken together are still minuscule when one considers the amount of money under management, let alone at investors' personal disposal, around the world. As Robert Weinberg points out, 'All of the world's gold mines together are not worth vastly more than British Telecom and substantially less than Exxon,' while the value of newly mined gold coming to the market each year is under $30 billion, with gold at $400. Compare that to the $300 billion dollars traded just on the currency market in London alone each day, or the $8 trillion under management in the United States on behalf of private and public investment funds, life and other insurance companies, mutual funds, security brokers and dealers, and foreign investors.

Only the subtlest shift in sentiment is required to direct a little of that money into the gold market with great effect. Caution, however, is essential. We have been here before in the early 1980s, when the same arguments were advanced to suggest a quantum leap in the gold price if only 1 or 2 per cent of the money under management even then in the United States alone was diverted into gold. The difference this time is not just even more money, but the leverage opportunities now available through the derivative market. As a leading New York bullion banker said to me, 'We have clients waiting to put $100 million into gold, but the leveraged effect of that is more like $500 million.'

Before getting carried away by that argument, a more general review of the whole field of gold investment, whether in the physical holding of coins, bars or even investment jewellery (that is, high carat jewellery bought on low mark-ups acquired as much for savings as adornment), metal accounts, in portfolio holdings or through paper derivatives, may give a more balanced perspective. This is essential because the 'mood of the *souks*', that is, the physical business in many regional markets, is usually contrary to the supposedly more sophisticated investor of Switzerland or New York. Time and again when *souk* business is brisk on low gold prices, the portfolio manager in Switzerland or the trader in New York has forsaken gold for the delights of the currency, equity or bond markets. When opinion reverses, as in the run-up in 1986–7 and again in 1993, *souk* business declines as western investors rush in. And if the price runs too high the *souks* will actually go into reverse and ship gold back to international centres, helping to defuse the price. Thus the ebb and flow of investor attitudes in differing corners of the globe is crucial in any assessment of price.

### Bullion coins

A straightforward signpost, however, to the grass-roots investor's mood on gold is the bullion coin. The concept of a legal tender bullion coin, sold on a small premium over the day's spot price, was the most imaginative initiative of the last twenty-five years in making gold more easily accessible to everyone. The bullion coin was intended to put gold within the means of the man or woman in the street. The pioneer was South Africa with the Krugerrand, which was the only serious contender in the 1970s until it fell foul of sanctions, but its success bred Canada's Maple Leaf in 1979, China's Panda (1982), the United States' Eagle (1986), Australia's Nugget and the United Kingdom's Britannia (1987), and Austria's Philharmoniker (1989). While Mexico was always in play with its Centenario 're-strike' dated 1947.

These coins, hopefully sold by the mints to wholesalers for a premium of 3 per cent over the spot price and available at retail outlets for between 4 and 7 per cent, caught the investors' imagination, especially in West Germany and the United States, during the inflationary 1970s.

Over 44 million Krugerrands alone were sold. In the 'vintage' years from 1974 to 1986, the bullion coins used almost 15 per cent of all gold supplies to the private sector. In the record years of 1978 and 1979 they took almost 290 tonnes (9.3 million ounces); in 1978 the Krugerrand alone took up over 193 tonnes (6.2 million ounces) or 27 per cent of South African mine output. Then, as the gold price slipped away in the late 1980s, so did the interest in coins. And with a market saturated with 60 million coins, premiums were hard to maintain. Krugerrands, in particular, could often be picked up at or even marginally below, the spot price.

By the early 1990s the new bullion coin sales were scarcely notching up 100 tonnes a year. The best show in 1992 came from Austria's Philharmoniker at 23.7 tonnes, with the Maple Leaf and Eagle fighting it out for second and third places at around 16 tonnes each, and the Nugget a handful of coins behind. The gold price rally of 1993, however, brought the first taste of renewed investor interest in bullion coins; sales were up 58 per cent on the same period the previous year and, in a novel promotion, seven mints joined with the World Gold Council in a $6 million promotion campaign to resuscitate investor interest through a slogan, 'Liquid Solid Gold'.

Such co-operation was unique, because the mints have previously spent much of their time coming up with new variations on the bullion coin theme to outdo their competitors. Originally, the Krugerrand paved the way as a legal tender coin at 916.7 fine (in line with such historic coins as the sovereign), containing exactly one ounce of fine gold, making its total weight 1.09 ounces (33.9 grams). The Royal Canadian Mint responded with the first 'four nines' bullion coin, the Maple Leaf, which, being essentially pure gold, did gleam rather more than the Krugerrand, which contains a reddish copper alloy. Thereafter, 999.9 fineness became customary for the bullion coins, except for the UK Britannia which stuck with the 916.6 formula in the sovereign tradition. The Maple Leaf's 'four nines' formula helped to make it the most popular bullion coin of the 1980s, although the playing field was not level because sanctions made circulation of the Krugerrand increasingly difficult; worldwide marketing of the Krugerrand ceased in 1984, although minting for the domestic market in South Africa continued. The dilemma for the South Africans, eager to relaunch the coin in the mid-1990s, is, do they stay with the 916.7 formula or redesign the Kruger as a 'four nines' coin?

Meanwhile, GoldCorp Australia, the marketing organization which operates the Western Australian Mint in Perth, has also moved the goal posts by having fresh designs on the Nugget each year. To begin with, as the name implied, the Nugget featured a series of famous nuggets on the reverse. A major design change in 1989, however, retained the name Nugget, but started an annual kangaroo series instead, tying in with the koala on the reverse of Australia's platinum bullion coin and the kookaburra on the silver coin. Thus, the 1989 'Nugget' starred the Red Kangaroo, followed by the Grey Kangaroo, the Common Walleroo and the Nailtailed Wallaby. The 1993 design, the fifth in the Kangaroo Nugget series, is of the Whiptail Wallaby. The animal series means they are collectors' as much as investment items. GoldCorp has also pioneered what the trade calls LBCs, which stands for large bullion coins, in denominations of 2 ounces, 10 ounces and 1 kilo; these Nuggets have always shown the red kangaroo. The concept of a 1-kilo coin was particularly aimed at some Asian investment markets, where there was a potential chance of avoiding tax on a legal tender coin that might apply to kilo bars. Just such a loophole materialized for a few months in Malaysia when the government suddenly put a 10 per cent duty on kilo bars, but overlooked legal tender coins. One-kilo Kangaroo Nuggets went into Malaysia by the tonne for a few weeks.

The real challenge in the 1990s has come from the Philharmoniker launched by the Austrian Mint as a 1-ounce 999.9 bullion coin with a face value of 2,000 schillings. The coin is named in honour of the Wiener Philharmoniker, the Vienna Philharmonic Orchestra, and bears the design of its instruments. The Philharmoniker is tax-free in Austria and, since the beginning of 1993, in Germany, so it has carved out a substantial niche with European investors, including those from Eastern Europe. The casualties from the bullion coins' success have not only been the more traditional coins such as the sovereign in the United Kingdom, and the Napoleon in France, but the 're-strikes', such as Austria's 100 Corona (Crown) and Mexico's Centenario. The Austrian 100 Corona was popular with European and American investors until the mid-1970s; the coin is 900 fine, weighs 0.9802 ounces (30.49 grams), and all were dated 1915. The Centenario at 900 fine was a hefty coin at 1.2 ounces (37.3 grams), dated 1947. Both these re-strikes had the disadvantage, not only of not being legal tender, which could affect their tax-free status, but of not weighing precisely 1 ounce, so that in the public mind their price did not instantly match with the gold price. The Centenario, however, has remained popular in France because of its date, 1947; since free gold imports into France were long forbidden, save for a window of a few months in 1968, the Centenarios could always be smuggled in because they *could* have come in during that period. There was no way of telling if a Centenario, dated 1947, was actually made in 1965 or 1975.

The consistent coin weathervane of investor attitudes to gold, however, has been the Swiss Vreneli. This 20-franc coin with a fine gold content of only 0.1867 ounces (5.8 grams) at 900 fine was minted between 1897 and 1949; in all, almost 60 million were struck. Today, it is traded primarily between a few Swiss banks and their customers. Because its circulation is limited (many have become worn and been melted) the attraction of the Vreneli is not only the gold price but its premium. This can fluctuate from as little as 3 or 4 per cent to 20 or 30 per cent (even to 60 per cent briefly in 1979) within a few months. A handful of shrewd investors, for instance, in 1985 noted that the Vreneli premium was bumping along at a mere 4 per cent, with the gold price also down towards $300; they switched out of Krugerrands and Maple Leafs into Vreneli. They then rode the double benefit of gold rising to nearly $500 and the premium to just over 30 per cent by 1987; the premium was back under 4 per cent a couple of years later, shot up to 30 per cent with Iraq's invasion of Kuwait, then slid away to 2 per cent early in 1993 when once again it was the time to buy. When the price picked up, the premium was at 5 per cent within days. 'It's still very cheap,' said a Zürich dealer. 'The next move will be to 15 per cent.'

### Mood of the souks

The same signal came, of course, from the investors in the *souks* of the Middle East and Asia; their buying was at an exceptional level. The theme of monitoring 'the mood of the *souks*', which I launched in an earlier book a few years ago, came quite simply from observation over a twenty-year period of what the Swiss banks used to call 'the traditional hoarding area'.[2] As the roller-coaster of the gold price evolved from 1970, it became apparent that on any major run-up in the gold price, the buyers of bars or high carat jewellery in markets as diverse as Saudi Arabia, the Gulf States, Indonesia or Hong Kong, stopped buying gold and after a while even traded it in at a profit, pushing their local gold prices to a discount to the international price and making it profitable even to ship metal back to London or Zürich. This first happened in a modest way on the run towards $200 in 1974, but more dramatically at $850 in January 1980. I was in Kuwait and Dubai that week; both *souks* were under seige from thousands of men and women laden with carrier bags, biscuit tins or simply bits of newspaper containing gold ornaments or small bars that they were trading in for cash at scores of gold shops, many of which did not have big enough credit lines at local banks and ran out of cash before noon each day. We watched ornaments being melted down into rough bars in nearby basements and then rushed to the airport to catch the next plane. Refineries in Europe were

2 'Mood of the *Souks*' was launched in *The Prospect for Gold*, Rosendale Press, London, 1987, pp. 138–40.

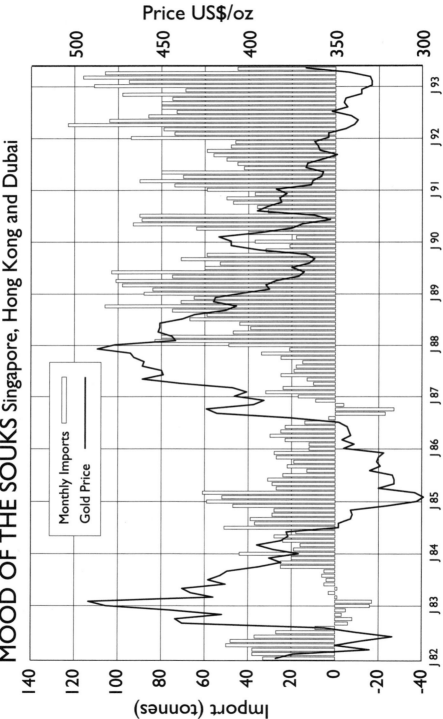

MOOD OF THE SOUKS Singapore, Hong Kong and Dubai

Price US$/oz

overwhelmed; much more gold would have been dishoarded that week if the refineries could have assayed more quickly, enabling them to confirm payment and keep the cash flow to the *souks* going. Even so, it was an object lesson in investor sentiment, or rather, profit-taking. Thereafter, in monitoring the key regional markets of Dubai, Singapore and Hong Kong on a monthly basis for more than a decade, it is possible to demonstrate these swings of mood. The *souks* are positive buyers on the low, but go into reverse very swiftly on any major price rise. As the chart shows, it happened again in 1983 and in 1986 when a price run towards $500 caused metal to be returned to Europe. Thereafter the building blocks of monthly imports became more solid through the long bear market, always with positive offtake, although always responding by a fall if a price rally occurred. This buying gave the floor to the gold price, when investors in Europe, North America and even Japan were long gone. And it is the interplay of these forces that moderates the price on highs and lows.

Make no mistake, however; these regional markets have always been large net buyers over the long haul. They may occasionally take profit and ship gold back, but it is a small amount when set against what they consistently absorb. Over the last twenty-five years more than 12,000 tonnes (396 million ounces) of gold, one-third of all new supplies to the market, has been hoarded, as bars or investment jewellery, in that great sweep of countries running from Morocco along the coast of North Africa, to Turkey, Saudi Arabia, the Gulf, the Indian subcontinent, and Southeast Asia. In all these regions gold remains closely involved with the social customs as a basic form of saving and often as a visible sign of wealth and status. For a woman in a Moslem country, her gold jewellery is her personal possession, her insurance (see Chapter 20). For a farmer in India it is the security against a bad harvest or sickness in his family; it is as good as cash in hand. While in the emerging economies of Vietnam, Cambodia and Laos it is the daily form of settlement of many business transactions. Although much of it is in jewellery form, sold on premiums of only 10–20 per cent over the gold price, investment in bars is also substantial. This trend has even been enhanced by the spread of Islamic banking which forbids not only the earning of interest, but also speculation in futures, options and other derivatives, whereas the spot purchase of gold, whose price may increase, is entirely permissible. Thus, in Saudi Arabia, the build-up of physical bar holding in the last twenty years is close to 300 tonnes (9.6 million ounces) and in Taiwan it is nearer 700 tonnes (22.5 million ounces). The Taiwanese treasure-chest (which is quite distinct from their central bank purchases) was largely acquired in the 1980s when restrictions on overseas investment gave them few other options at home and there was nervousness about the growing power and international recognition of mainland China. Liberalization has since widened their investment horizons abroad, but not only is the gold not sold back, but the Taiwanese remain positive new investors in gold in the 1990s.

### The China factor

China, however, is just beginning to reveal its investment potential. The first strong indications came in 1988 when rapid growth in the economic development zones of southern China created both significant purchasing power and inflationary pressures. Wealthy individuals and enterprises sought refuge in gold. This initial gold rush was entirely different from that more publicized growth of gold jewellery demand in the early 1990s; the demand was for kilo bars. The evidence was in Hong Kong's gold imports, which shot up from a customary level of just under 150 tonnes in 1987 to a record 460 tonnes (14.8 million ounces) the following year and 433 tonnes in 1989. Investors in China took up at least half that gold, although everyone kept rather quiet about it at the time, not wishing to draw attention to what was going on. But one could observe the reception areas of some Hong Kong banks filled with teams of young men with briefcases, all waiting to pick up 20 or 30 kilos of gold to take into China. The massacre at Tienanmen Square and the resulting clampdown stopped all that overnight. (Although in Hong Kong itself there was a brief investment rush, through fear of what was happening in China.) The kilo bar investment in China has never really come back, because the appetite for gold that has become so apparent in China is now with the mass of the population whose means are limited to small bars or jewellery – even though investment as much as adornment is the motive (see Chapter 20). Indeed, the declining value of the yuan in China in 1993 was accelerating the gold buying; as people chased gold, the price rose from 95 yuan per gram to 140 yuan per gram in a matter of months. Gold was the safe haven and, with few other options for investment among ordinary people, will remain so. Ultimately the growth of markets for stocks and real estate, along with the other diversions for consumers' money that already exist in western societies, will offer rival attractions to gold, but that will take many years. Meanwhile, gold will be one of the preferred investments for the Chinese. While annual demand will fluctuate considerably, the prospect of the Chinese taking up anything from 250 to 750 tonnes a year in bars and investment jewellery is entirely possible. But it will be sensitive to the gold price; consumption in 1993 slowed up considerably when the price rose to $400.

## *Japan: a fashion for accumulation*

Thus China is starting to fulfil the role in the gold market that Japan has assumed over the last ten or fifteen years. As the economic power of Japan grew and its gold market was liberalized, so investment blossomed. Japan stunned the world of gold in 1986 by absorbing 677 tonnes (21.8 million ounces), of which private investors alone picked up 376 tonnes (12 million ounces). This was exceptional, of course, because the investors snapped up 9 million of the special 20-gram coins minted to commemorate the sixtieth anniversary of Emperor Hirohito (and took a further 1 million the following year), but it showed the sheer financial muscle Japan could bring to gold. The more so because the Hirohito cost 100,000 yen, but only contained 40,000 yen worth of gold. The investors bought 180 tonnes of the coin, but paid for the equivalent of 450 tonnes of gold. This was most courageous, because the gold price in Japan has been in steady decline for many years because of the strong yen. The yen price in 1993 was less than one-fifth what it was in 1980. But through the 1980s, the Japanese set about acquiring gold with determination, buying up ever more as the price successively fell through the barriers from over 6,000 yen per gram to under 2,000 yen. The fashionable (but since discredited) phrase was *zaiteku*, financial technology; thus the Japanese have built up a private investment stock of over 1,200 tonnes (38.6 million ounces), excluding the Hirohito coin. This is mostly in kilo bars and 500 gram bars, paid for in cash over the counters of the bullion houses. Even senior executives of securities companies or of the bullion houses themselves invariably paid cash. The parallel growth of gold futures on Tocom (Chapter 17) did provide the opportunity for paper gold trading, but the exchange has been used primarily for hedging purposes by professionals; the Japanese investor prefers the real thing.

The consistent failure of the price to perform, however, has understandably brought disappointments. Great expectations were built up when it was announced that Japanese fire and marine insurance companies would be permitted to hold 3 per cent of their portfolios in gold, on the thesis that if a major earthquake struck Japan it might so damage local industry, in which the insurance companies are heavily invested, that it would be prudent to have some gold that could be sold to meet claims. The insurance companies, apparently, took little advantage of this ruling. Investment was also not helped by a 3 per cent sales tax introduced in 1989. Then recession and the collapse of the stock market took their toll of investment; investors often had to sell their gold at a loss to meet stock market obligations. 'The negative perception of investors now is huge,' admitted a Tokyo dealer early in 1993.

Yet, an undertow of fresh investment persisted. 'Sales of gold for investment have increased,' said Tadahiko Fukami of Tanaka K.K., Japan's largest precious metal dealers. 'But if we analyse this, it is due to accumulation plans.' Through these accumulation plans, offered by dealers like Tanaka, trading houses such as Mitsubishi Materials and major banks, such as Sanwa Bank, the investor signs a one-year contract to invest at least 3,000 yen (around $30), but more often 5,000 or 10,000 yen, each month in gold. This accumulates in his account and can later be sold or even taken out in the form of coin or bars or traded for gold jewellery purchases. The success of the plans, according to Moriki Aoyagi of Sumitomo Metal Mining, is that they cater to the Japanese preference for long-term saving, are relatively cheap to administer because of automatic bank transfers and involve a modest monthly commitment. 'The plans are gaining support among young women as a way to buy jewellery,' adds Tadahiko Fukami. 'Twenty-five per cent of our current subscriber base say it is for jewellery and the rest is for savings.'

The GAPs, as they are called, had 340,000 subscribers in 1992, accounting for over 25 tonnes of new purchases. With regional banks from Yokahama and Chiba joining, the prospect is over 400,000 accounts by the end of 1993 and perhaps 1 million by 1996. If that target could be reached, it would account for close to 80 tonnes (2.6 million ounces) annually. Although from the investor's standpoint the gold is unallocated (that is to say specific bars are not assigned to his account by number), the GAPs are usually fully backed by gold held in Tokyo, although as the schemes increase, some may be held *loco* London. Withdrawals, for all the talk of jewellery purchases, are rare; the dealers report that 90-95 per cent of the gold is kept and accounts are usually rolled over each year. The success of accumulation plans on such a scale is unique to Japan; variations on the theme of gold savings accounts with regular purchases have been tried elsewhere, notably in Singapore, but never consistently accounting for new business. Certainly the concept of putting perhaps $500 or $1,000 a year into gold does not seem likely to rock the market, unless you get a million people doing it, which Japan might just achieve.

### Portfolio players

Elsewhere the issue is usually the reverse; how much of an individual's or an institution's portfolio of $500 million is going to be put into gold? For many years the underlying philosophy of portfolio management in Switzerland, especially in the private banks, was that between 5 and 10 per cent of each portfolio should be in gold, usually a mix of kilo bars, coins and gold shares, and that this might be increased from 10 to 15 per cent at auspicious moments. I recall one bank going to over 40 per cent in 1980. Analysts liked to conjure up the calculation that if the twenty-four private banks in Switzerland had $100 billion under management between them, of which 10 per cent was in gold, this would call for nearly 800 tonnes with gold at $400. That was once upon a time. So far in the 1990s, the likely proportion has been zero per cent. The management committee of one Geneva private bank conceded the topic of gold did not even come up at their monthly strategy meetings (a policy hastily revised in 1993). The Swiss banks simply bailed out of gold between 1988 and 1990. From Basel, Geneva and Zürich, several hundred tonnes of gold were sold back into the market, actually making Switzerland for a while a net exporter. Even at the 'big three' banks, Crédit Suisse, Swiss Bank Corporation and Union Bank of Switzerland, total exposure to gold for money under management was scarcely 1 per cent. The final decision to desert gold at one of them was taken in February 1991 when the local Swiss franc price bottomed out at just over 14,000 Swiss francs per kilo. Any rally in the price thereafter was seen as an opportunity to sell long-standing positions. And by early 1993 it had got to a point where one Zurich banker was lamenting to me that he could no longer tap investors as a quick source of gold if he needed some for his refinery to make bars for export, because there was nothing left.

This was a measure not just of the Swiss mood, but rather of the global clientele who kept their money in Swiss banks. The Middle East investor was just as fed up as his fellow from South America; gold was not performing, currencies, bonds and equities were, so play them instead. As Marwan Shakarchi of MKS Finance in Geneva, which has many Middle East clients, told an international conference, 'Disappointed investors are not buying gold and are moving into alternative investments . . . gold has lost most of its monetary and security appeal.'[3]

The attitude was almost universal. In Paris the French were selling back their traditional hoard, making the local jewellery industry almost entirely self-sufficient from melted gold coins. Anything the French market could not digest went to Luxembourg, where the banks acted more as buyers of dishoarded gold than sellers to fresh customers. For gold to be so out of favour, so out of fashion, was rather bullish. In any shift in sentiment, buying had to start again from scratch. At no time in a generation has there been so little investment gold in hand. The genuine question, however, is will the days of 5 to 10 per cent of a portfolio in gold ever come back?

Certainly it is highly unlikely that the Geneva private banks will

3 Marwen Shakarchi, *The Gold Price – The Short and Medium-Term Output*, Financial Times World Gold Conference, Montreux, June 1992.

again fill their vaults with allocated kilo bars. But an intriguing new situation opened up in Europe in 1993 with the withdrawal of value added tax on gold in Germany. One of the growing inhibitions on physical gold investment in Europe in the last twenty years was the banning of imports of gold bullion coins to Britain in 1976, then the introduction of value added tax in Germany in 1980. Only Switzerland (which also tried tax but gave it up), Luxembourg and Austria offered tax-free gold. However, with the tax lifted in Germany to coincide with the European Community's single market, it became entirely legal for a citizen of the United Kingdom (VAT 17½ per cent), Italy (VAT 19 per cent), or Spain (VAT 30 per cent) to go to Luxembourg or Germany, buy gold bars or coins without tax and take them home, provided they are for his or her own savings, with no liability to duty. One German dealer, whose business in physical metal had already tripled in a matter of months, suggested boldly, 'If enough investors in Italy or Spain now realized they could do this, I think they might buy as much as China.' A trifle over-enthusiastic, perhaps, but the removal of tax in a major country like Germany, where there is some considerable tradition of investing in kilo bars and bullion coins, paves the way for more physical investment in Europe if either the price looks exciting or the future uncertain. When the *Financial Times* carries headlines like 'Dethronement of the D-Mark', is that the moment to hedge your DMs with a little gold?

Such physical business aside, the new investor, inevitably, will be more of a trader, in and out of the market with rapidity. He may trade on metal account, whose use became much more widespread in Switzerland in the 1980s, when tax on physical delivery was imposed for a while, but he will also go for options and warrants: simply the right, but not the obligation, to buy gold at a certain moment at a certain price. His gold position will be fluid and flexible; here today, gone tomorrow. Yet that can be the real factor in driving the price. This kind of serious investment money is the catalyst that gives a bull market momentum. The more 'bread-and-butter' physical offtake for jewellery and industry gives the price its floor and can even set up the scenario for a bull market. The investor then runs with it. Paper gold derivatives offer him greater leverage in the 1990s.

### Funds: the driving force

The single investor, however, is not the force to be reckoned with. The financial muscle today rests with the huge managed funds, which have come to dominate the US markets in particular. As we observed earlier (Chapter 16) the money at the disposal of the managed futures funds has risen from a mere $500 million in the last great bull market in gold in 1979–80, to over $25 billion, with 'leverage' value perhaps five times that. George Soros, very much the man of the moment with his bear raid on sterling in September 1992, his coup with Newmont Mining and later denunciations of the prospects for the DM, has over $4 billion under management in his Quantum Fund alone. And his entire group was reported to have lined up $10 billion for the attack on sterling. This kind of money, if committed to gold (and Soros initially went for gold shares, not the metal, but even so made an impact on the metal's price), could take the market into uncharted waters. As David Pryde, managing director of J. P. Morgan's bullion division in New York, remarked, 'We're seeing an explosive growth in derivatives, that could put a strain on the fabric of the market through the associated hedging.'

This is precisely where the gold market of the 1990s differs from that of twenty years ago. The real pace setter taking gold from $35 to $850 then was Middle East oil money. Today not only is that a spent force, but under strict application of Islamic banking, speculation and hedging in the derivatives markets is forbidden.

A real difficulty is that no one knows the true size of the market in gold options and the resulting 'delta hedging' to protect those options books. While some conservative estimates put the delta component at less than 100 tonnes, or at most a few hundred tonnes, some estimates have ranged as high as 1,000 to 1,500 tonnes. Already a rush of delta hedging to protect positions in a fast-moving market has sometimes greatly exaggerated a trend. The classic example was the night of the initial Allied attack on Iraq on 16 January 1990. 'The market ran up to $409 in a matter of a few hours, only to drop a couple of hours later by as much as $40 per ounce,' recalled Crédit Suisse's Ian MacDonald. 'The featured players that night in New York were not speculators rushing to buy gold, but options dealers rushing to buy gold and then having to sell it again as the market collapsed.'[4] More recently, MacDonald also noted, 'Large international financiers and investment portfolio managers have become active in the market . . . buying long-term out-of-the-money call options.' They could often obtain them very cheaply. In April 1993, while a bearish mood still prevailed, it was possible to buy a one-year $400 call for a premium of only $1.00 per ounce; $450 calls were even cheaper. Yet within weeks gold was nudging up towards $400, triggering massive delta hedging, which in turn helped that trend.

The potential pressure on the market has caused some New York dealers to consider 'melt down' if a combination of events got gold moving up very fast (as sometimes happened in the 1980s when $100 in a day was not unknown) and the hedging simply could not keep pace.

4 MacDonald, op. cit.

Cooler minds are confident the market can cope, but everyone would feel more confident if they knew the true size of the options market. Only its tip is measurable in the exchange options traded on Comex in New York or in Europe on the smaller European Options Exchange in Amsterdam; the over-the-counter options business written by individual banks and bullion houses may be five, six, seven times greater. No one knows. Moreover, since gold has been so out of favour with investors for some years, no one can be sure either what will happen when it does come back in fashion. Ian MacDonald, at least, is sure of one thing. 'The market always has a habit of going after volume. The largest volume in the option book has been the $400 and $450 strikes . . . [so] it is highly likely that at some point a move over $400 is to be expected because of the sheer volume of calls that have been written.' In short, the driving force in gold investment nowadays, is not kilo bars or coins under the bed as insurance, which it was scarcely twenty-five years ago, but the pursuit of profit.

## CHAPTER 20

# Jewellery:
# Today's Cornerstone

The original appeal of gold as it gleamed warmly in the rivers and streams of Africa, Asia and South America was its beauty. At the dawn of civilization, craftsmen found that it could be worked and fashioned with ease into magnificent ornaments and articles of adornment to enhance the human body. The basic techniques they perfected three and four thousand years ago, of drawing gold into wire to make into delicate filigree or foxtail chains, of casting it into a thousand shapes of flowers, birds and animals, that could also easily be engraved, have changed little. Nor has the basic fact that as we go towards the twenty-first century, gold jewellery remains the premier use of gold. Indeed, in 1992 the fabrication of carat gold jewellery worldwide exceeded the entire output of the mining industry for the first time. Jewellery is the cornerstone of the gold business. The real difference, though, is that what was virtually until this century the metal of the privileged and wealthy, is today within the means of millions. Gold jewellery has become a mass market consumer item anywhere from Birmingham (England or Alabama) to Berlin, Bahrain, Bombay, Bangkok and Beijing. Diamonds, so the catchphrase goes, are 'forever'; gold jewellery is for everyone, everywhere.

Three images come to mind. In Arezzo, Italy, watch the 400 chain machines at the factory of Uno a Erre unceasingly 'knitting' gold wire into miles of chain, the little automatic pincer heads turning and twisting the gold that glistens under a coating of oil as it spindles down into plastic buckets beneath each machine. Every time I see them chuntering away hour after hour, I cease to worry about the 'consumption of gold'.

There it is by the tonne; Italy makes about almost 200 tonnes (6.4 million ounces) of chain every year. Then one morning in Riyadh I was ushered into the vast pink-carpeted, pink-walled showroom of Othman Al Otair, one of Saudi Arabia's main wholesalers, to be confronted with row upon row of rails draped with necklaces, bangles, bracelets, rings, wedding belts (each 500 grams to 1 kilo in gold) and *giladas*, which drape a Saudi bride from neck to waist in a delicate frieze of light chains and discs. This Aladdin's cave supplies over 1,500 kilos a month in 21-carat ornaments to many of the 4,000 gold shops in the kingdom's *souks*. Or stroll down Wanfujing Street in the heart of Beijing to Huaxia Arts and Crafts, where red lanterns at the door beckon you in to a crush of men and women in multicoloured jackets, who are pressing their noses against counters and showcases filled with 24 and 18-carat charms, rings and chains (some of which weigh between 50 and 100 grams each). The manageress draws me the Chinese symbol for gold, explaining it means money or wealth. 'The future is very good for us,' she says. 'In Japan each lady has twenty-two pieces of jewellery; here each lady only two or three.' Trying hard to catch up, China became the world's largest consumer of carat gold jewellery in 1992, absorbing close to 400 tonnes (12.9 million ounces).

So the Italians are the biggest fabricators, the Saudis the biggest spenders (around $1,350 per capita, per year) and the Chinese, by virtue of population, the biggest market. It all added up globally to 2,270 tonnes (73 million ounces) of gold jewellery (excluding recycled scrap) in 1992 compared to 2,217 tonnes of new mine supply. Taking a longer view, in the twenty-five years from 1968, when serious market research began, carat gold jewellery has required almost 23,900 tonnes of gold out of a new supply of just over 36,900 tonnes; virtually 65 per cent of all gold over a quarter of a century.

### High or low carat

The designation carat (or karat, if you live in North America) gold jewellery is deliberate; although this does include carat gold watch cases, for which the Swiss are notably famous, it does not embrace gold-plated 'costume' jewellery, cigarette lighters, bath taps or other ornate trappings. It is jewellery whose purity is defined by the 'carat' scale. The word carat comes from the Italian *carato*, the Arabic *qirat* and the Greek *keration*, all meaning 'the fruit of the carob tree'. The horn-like pods of this tree contain seeds that were once used to balance the scales in Oriental bazaars. The word has been adopted to describe both the purity of gold and the weight of diamonds. Pure gold is 24-carat (or 1,000 fine). The proportion in jewellery varies considerably from country to country, and is preserved not only by custom, but often by law. The highest purity found in jewellery is sometimes labelled as 24-carat, both in the Middle East and Hong Kong, although in practice it will be, at best, 990 fine; the Chinese call this *chuk kam* (pure gold jewellery). More widespread in the *souks* or markets of the Middle East, India and Southeast Asia is 21 or 22-carat jewellery. In Portugal it must be 19.2-carat (800 fine), while in France, Italy, Spain and Sweden it must be 18-carat (750 fine). Belgium, Denmark, the Netherlands and Norway do not permit articles under 14-carat (585 fine) to be described as gold jewellery (although this is often skirted by calling them 'gold wares'). In the United States the lowest standard accepted is 10-carat (416.6 fine), in Britain 9-carat (325 fine) and in Germany 8-carat (333.3 fine). This does not mean that only 8 or 9-carat is sold; it is the lowest title accepted (and only this jewellery gets counted in the carat jewellery total). In the United States, for instance, most of the market is 14-carat; in Britain about 75 per cent is 9-carat, 12 per cent 18-carat and 13 per cent 22-carat (for the local Asian population). And some reshuffling of these definitions is taking place as part of the 'harmonization' of standards with the European Community's single market. The 8-carat standard is likely to disappear, with 9-carat being the lowest accepted as 'jewellery' in EC countries.

The advantage of lower caratage is that the hardness can be improved, while the colour can range through white, green, yellow and red hues, depending on the balance of other metals with which it is alloyed. White shades (often used in diamond jewellery) are achieved by alloying gold with silver and nickel or palladium; red alloys contain mainly copper and sometimes zinc; green tints are contrived by varying proportions of copper, silver, nickel, or palladium. A harder alloy is made by adding nickel or, in a recent development, a touch of titanium. The breakthrough with titanium has important implications because pure gold is too soft for most jewellery applications and that is why the best designers have always preferred 18-carat which does not wear or scratch so easily. The problem is conquered by '990 Gold' (23.76-carat), as it has been christened, which is 990 parts fine gold and 10 parts titanium. The technique was pioneered in Germany at the Precious Metals Research Institute in Schwabisch Gmund and by Degussa, the leading semi-fabricators, creating an alloy that is virtually indistinguishable from pure gold, but has the hardness and resistance to wear of an 18-carat alloy. '990 Gold is an unsung alloy,' argues Dr Friedrich Keller-Bauer of the German manufacturers Christian Bauer which has started test marketing it in wedding rings. The company has found the rings show no more scratching and abrasion than corresponding 14-carat (585 fine) rings over a five-year period.[1] Acceptance of this hard, high carat alloy by a conservative public in Germany schooled to think of 14-carat as the norm, has been slow, but it has immense potential worldwide in *chuk kam* jewellery for China or in the Middle East where ornaments often purport to be 24-carat, but rarely are.

### From hallmark to goldmark

The public perception of even quite low carat jewellery somehow being 'pure gold' is not helped by advertisements for '9-carat solid gold' articles, which are widespread, for example in Britain. All that means is that the articles are not hollow. The purity or 'title' of an ornament that is 9, 14, 18 or 21-carat is, however, normally guaranteed either by government enforced assaying or, more controversially, by self-regulation, while in countries such as India, there is not much regulation at all. In short, 9-carat jewellery in Britain, or 18-carat jewellery in France will be guaranteed by hallmark; in India, jewellery sold as 21-carat may be 18 or even 14-carat, and the motto is *caveat emptor*.

The concept of the hallmark originated in England in the thirteenth century and systematic hallmarking began in 1300. Shortly thereafter it came under the control of the Worshipful Company of Goldsmiths in London, which still operates one of four authorized assay offices hallmarking 9, 14, 18 and 22-carat jewellery weighing over 1 gram in Britain. Each has its distinctive mark: an uncrowned leopard's head for London, an anchor for Birmingham, a rose for Sheffield and a castle for Edinburgh. Strictly speaking, the word 'hallmark' means the mark of Goldsmiths' Hall in London, but the term has taken on a broader connotation to describe such stamping wherever it takes place. In France jewellery must be authenticated by the Bureau de la Garantie in Paris; similarly Finland, Ireland, the Netherlands and Sweden all have government assay offices. Elsewhere in Europe, the industry is left to police itself, although each manufacturer should stamp every article with both its gold content and an identifying mark for the company. The code ARI 750 inside a ring, for example, means it was made by Uno a Erre in Arezzo, Italy and is 750 fine (18-carat). The strict hallmarking system in Europe, however, is under threat following the introduction of the single market by the twelve members of the European Community from 1 January 1993. Already a European Hallmarking Convention states that an item hallmarked in, say, Portugal is accepted without further assaying in Britain. The acceptance of one EC country's mark, even if self-regulatory, by all the others is the likely outcome. But there is a movement in countries such as Germany and Italy, which are self-regulatory, to do away with hallmarking entirely, so that each

---

1 '990 gold', *Gold Technology*, No. 6, May 1992.

manufacturer simply stamps and stands by his own product. A strong rearguard defence is being mounted by the British, not anxious to see a system that has stood for 700 years swept aside. A compromise may emerge under the umbrella of the European Association of Jewellery Manufacturers (Emagold), launched in Italy in 1991, one of whose aims is to position itself as a recognized organization for pan-European quality control. Emagold has plans to introduce a voluntary caratage certification system acceptable in both hallmarking and self-regulatory countries, but pushing for certification of high caratage jewellery in 14, 18, 22 and 24 (990 fine) carats only.

Outside Europe, control often depends on colonial inheritance. The British and the French both introduced hallmarking offices to such countries as Morocco, Egypt, Lebanon and Kuwait (where the assay office was up and running again within a few weeks of the liberation from Iraq). More recently offices have opened in Bahrain, where hallmarking is compulsory, and in Singapore and Saudi Arabia, where it is voluntary. A global initiative on title guarantee has come from the World Gold Council, the mining industry's promotional arm, which has launched an international 'goldmark', like the well-established 'woolmark'.

The World Gold Council, established in 1986 to promote gold in jewellery, industry and investment, has forty-five gold-mining companies in nine countries as its members. Each should subscribe $2.50 annually for every ounce of production, providing the Council with income that fluctuates between $65 and $70 million, which is then supplemented by joint promotions with the trade. The concept of promoting gold, as De Beers has long done for diamonds and the platinum industry for platinum, is not new. The International Gold Corporation began this for jewellery and bullion coins in the early 1970s. But that was essentially a South African mining house effort, in the days when South Africa was in a league of its own as a producer. The World Gold Council more truly reflects the international mining community and the changed balance of output of recent years (even though it has a hard battle persuading some leading mining groups to sign up and there are notable absentees). Peter Munk, the ebullient chairman of American Barrick, who is an enthusiastic Council member, has challenged mining analysts to mark down the shares of companies that do not subscribe on the grounds that they are not helping to expand the market for their product. And Munk once told me he would happily subscribe $10 for every ounce his group produced – if everyone else would do so too.

The interesting thing is that since the Council came into being, jewellery fabrication has lifted off beyond anyone's expectations, actually doubling between 1986 and 1992. The $40 million that the Council is spending annually on jewellery promotion, backed up by close to $25 million more from the jewellery trade, certainly helped. And, one might add, not before time. De Beers has been patiently promoting diamonds since 1938. The gold-mining industry took much longer to realize where the real future for its product lay. As Julian Baring, the guru of gold share analysis, pointed out in the mid-1980s, the soap powder industry spent 6 per cent of its turnover on advertising, but the gold-mining industry scarcely 0.4 per cent. Actually, the ratio has not improved, but because gold production has risen so much in the years between, the budget is larger.

The pattern of World Gold Council offices also tells where the action is. Once they were concentrated in the industrial countries of Europe, North America and Japan; today they are also dispersed through the developing world in Dubai, China, Hong Kong, India, Indonesia, Saudi Arabia, Singapore, Taiwan, Thailand and Turkey. That reflects the growing significance of 'investment' jewellery which is high carat, but sold on low mark-ups, against 'adornment' jewellery, usually lower carat and higher mark-up, which is purchased essentially as a fashion item. The balance has shifted significantly in a decade; in 1981 worldwide adornment jewellery fabrication represented 60 per cent of the total; by 1992 the adornment share had fallen to 40 per cent. The pace setters are the Middle East, India, Southeast Asia and China, where rapid economic growth is bringing jewellery purchases within the means of hundreds of millions of new consumers who, because of social customs or insecurity, see it primarily as a basic form of saving. Whereas in Europe, the United States or Japan, jewellery is often purchased on a mark-up of anything from 250 to 400 per cent over its gold content, in the developing world the cost is normally only 10 to 20 per cent over the gold content, reflecting only the 'making charges'. Thus, even a modest rise in the gold price can return a profit.

### Italy, 'numero uno'

Yet, embarking on a global tour of the jewellery scene, there is one landmark that always stands out – Italy. Italian visual flair makes it the unchallenged design leader of adornment jewellery fabrication; over 460 tonnes (14.8 million ounces) of ornaments were made in 1992, accounting for 45 per cent of all adornment jewellery. The industry, over 6,000 workshops and 250 large factories employing over 30,000 people, is essentially gathered together in the four communities of Arezzo, Vicenza, Bassano del Grappa and Valenza. Since the 1950s they have become jewellery makers to the world. Buy a gold chain anywhere from Cairo to Caracas, London to Los Angeles, or Panama to Paris, and the chances are that it came from one of these towns. The Italians have shouldered aside all rivals in the mass production of jewellery and, above all, chain. They have proved the wizards not only with the designer's pencil, but also with the spanner in nursing the machines that make it. Their chain machines, which spew it out by the mile, are really a glorified version of a knitting machine. Many a mechanic who mastered managing a machine in one of the early chain factories in the 1960s, soon left to set up shop on his own. Often he installed a couple of machines in the kitchen or the garden shed, but before long had his own workshop and soon a factory. Since wholesalers would give him gold to work with and pay him only the making charges, he had little need of capital. This system of *conto lavorazione* or *conto lavoro*, working account, is the foundation of the Italian system. The gold is owned by wholesalers, not just in the main distribution centre of Milan, but throughout Europe, North America and the Middle East. They, in turn, will also usually borrow gold from a bullion bank, as it is usually cheaper to borrow gold rather than money.

The founding fathers of this ever-expanding network of chain-makers were Vittorio Gori and Antonio Zucchi, whose company Uno a Erre in the Tuscan hill town of Arezzo, just south of Florence, became the world's largest manufacturer, and Luigi and Mario Balestra at Bassano del Grappa in the hills between Venice and Verona. Ask any well known Italian chain-maker where he learned his trade and the answer is always with Gori and Zucchi or Balestra. The proliferation of chain-makers has been the prime reason Italy still manufactures so much gold. When I asked Vittorio Gori, the son of the founder, what he regarded as the most significant change of the last twenty-five years, he said, 'The growth of the chain specialist, because he can turn out 20 tonnes of 14-carat chain a year, particularly herring-bone chain, which is the number one item. He has few products, runs at full speed to be competitive, does big volume at a low price and relies on the US market for 70 per cent of his sales. But it's a gamble, you're in a tunnel.' Facing that challenge, Gori and Zucchi, once the champions of chain, have branched out more into fancy goods and higher mark-ups.

For all the tonnage in chain, the Italian industry thrives through the sheer originality of its designs and products. Glance through the pages of *l'orafo italiano* to see adornment jewellery at its best: a complex 18-carat interlinked bracelet of rings; chain adorned with granules from Primavera Preziosi; delicate earrings from Gold Engineering; bracelets in 18-carat yellow gold polished and mat from Orobase; an articulated mesh necklace in yellow gold or bracelets made with yellow and white gold spheres from Dieffeoro; a necklace in yellow, white and pink gold chain mail from Masella; a reversible necklace – yellow gold on one side, yellow, white and red gold on the other, with matching bracelet from Bottene; brooches in two- and three-coloured gold from Nicolis Cola; gold rings fringed with diamonds and lapis lazuli or mother of pearl centres from Form Preziosi.[2] No wonder the trade fair held at Vicenza each January and June is in every wholesaler's diary.

Where does it go? The Italians themselves appreciate their local industry, buying over 150 tonnes of gold jewellery a year, a domestic demand greater than the combined total of Germany, France and Spain. Even so, two-thirds of the jewellery is exported. 'The success of the Italian industry materialized in the '60s and '70s,' says Alberto Zenardo of Emagold, 'when, contrary to their European competitors, Italians started travelling from the Middle East to Latin America, seeking out even the most latent sales opportunities.' Thus, Italy rode the export wave first to the Middle East based on new-found oil wealth in the 1970s, then to the United States in the mid-1980s, when jewellery demand revived after the shock of the 1980 high gold price and many US wholesalers found it easier to buy Italian rather than home-made, and finally in the 1990s to a strong combination of US, European and Middle East demand.

The dominance of Italy is such that much of the rest of Europe nowadays simply looks there for its jewellery, as for the best pasta or olive oil, to the chagrin of local manufacturers. Italy alone accounts for 70 per cent of Europe's fabrication. Yet it would be negligent to pass on without also acknowledging the role of the small town of Pforzheim, just west of Stuttgart, that is home to over 400 jewellery firms who turn out most German production. Jewellery-making is the life-blood of this community, just as much as Arezzo or Vicenza, and much of the pioneering work on automatic chain manufacture was done here. Yet Pforzheim never really cut an image for well-designed, mass market jewellery in the way the Italians did; its jewellery is more Mercedes style; Italy's is Fiat.

### Turkey: the bridge to Asia

The city to watch out for today is Istanbul, astride the Bosphorus, where Europe meets Asia at the stepping-off point of the old Silk Road. For people who may never journey to the *souks* of Amman, Baghdad, Beirut, Cairo, Casablanca, Jeddah or Riyadh, Istanbul gives a true glimpse of the temptations of display. Whole streets of gold shops offer windows festooned with a shimmering cascade of bangles, chains, necklaces and belts, sold, if your bargaining powers are good, at no more than 20 per cent over the gold price of the day.

2 *l'orafo italiano nel mondo:*, Spring 1993.

Penetrating the maze of Istanbul's Grand Bazaar, up past the spice market and the carpet stores, you come suddenly upon a broad, covered avenue named Kuyumculuk, crammed with over 300 shops. The names are Ahmet Oguz, Erdal, Anadolu, Bektasi. Up behind the shops is a great courtyard, Cuhacilar Han, that dates back to the sixteenth century, where jewellery is made in hundreds of begrimed workshops, often by methods that have changed little since the Middle Ages. An estimated 4,600 of Turkey's 7,000 gold jewellery workshops are gathered together here in the Grand Bazaar. Each workshop employs perhaps four or five people. Each craftsman has his speciality. A master melter will hover over a small open furnace judging by eye when the metal is the right temperature. Next door a welder joins the strands of a twisted wire bracelet; down the corridor are inlayers, engravers, polishers. A few years ago much of what they made was 22-carat investment jewellery for local people. Today, Istanbul epitomizes the shift from investment to adornment jewellery in 14 and 18-carat, brought about both by Turkey's own economic growth, providing other investment options, and a booming tourist industry bringing in 10 million visitors a year. Here, in the Grand Bazaar, close to 60 per cent of the jewellery is now 14-carat as tourists from all over Western and Eastern Europe mingle with those from the southern republics of the former Soviet Union, just a step away across the Black Sea. In high summer they are joined by visitors from Saudi Arabia and the Gulf States, making Istanbul once again the real crossroads of the gold trade that it was, as Constantinople, a thousand years ago.

Besides the tourist purchases, formal jewellery export is growing. A dozen new factories, the largest employing 500 workers, are equipped with modern chain-making and casting machinery. Already jewellery fabrication from new gold (there is also considerable scrap recycling) is close to 100 tonnes (3.2 million ounces) annually, perhaps half of it for export. The new manufacturers, dispatching orders to the United States, Europe and all points in the Middle East, have a target – to overtake Italy. An ambitious goal, but Turkey has two advantages: low labour costs and a unique grasp of both the 22-carat investment jewellery and 14 and 18-carat adornment businesses; no one else really understands both camps so well. Turkey has also benefited from the inevitable decline of manufacturing in Beirut, due to the long years of civil war, which also affected Aleppo and Damascus, two traditional centres of craftsmanship. The industry has also been operating on a level playing field in terms of price since 1989, when the central bank liberalized gold imports, supplying the market with gold from consignment stock placed by international bullion houses. Previously Turkey had been a gold smugglers' paradise, but with the penalty of less competitive prices that a smuggling premium implied. The Turkish exporters pursue their Italian challenge seriously. Sit sipping little cups of tea or coffee with a wholesaler in Jeddah or Dubai in the evening and the chances are a Turkish jewellery wholesaler comes calling too.[3]

### Saudi Arabia: hey, big spender

Saudi Arabia has a population of around 12 million people, who manage to spend just over $1,350 a year each on carat gold jewellery according to a World Gold Council estimate (the Indians, who also have a considerable affinity for gold, spend a mere $16 per head). This statistic comes as no surprise to anyone who has whiled away an evening in the souks of Jeddah, Riyadh or Taif watching the endless congregation in the gold shops that are both emporiums and social centres. In a country where women are not permitted to work or even drive cars, they lack outlets for their energy and interests, so trading gold ornaments is almost a refuge. Many Saudi women keep in daily contact with two or three jewellers, often by telephone, to discuss new ornaments and the trading in of old ones. The cycle of new ornaments for 'old' is often as short as three months, although this may happen more rapidly if the price increases so that ornaments can be traded in at a profit or more slowly if the price falls. The quantity of ornaments in circulation is also enhanced by the custom that if a man takes a second wife, as he may under Moslem law, he must give his first wife an amount of gold ornaments equal to those which he bestows on his new bride; should he take a third wife, he has to give the first two similar amounts of gold. Thus in Saudi Arabia the social importance of exchanging gold at marriage and of it being the endowment of the bride to keep as her own property, which is common throughout the Moslem world from Morocco to the Gulf and beyond, is magnified both by restrictions on women and the wealth of the country. At a marriage ceremony a woman will wear at least 1 kilo of gold ornaments and that is merely the beginning of her collection.

The jewellery is mostly locally made, usually in 21-carat with a little 24-carat in the form of decorated small gold bars and a growing amount of 18-carat which is mainly gem-set. While the kingdom ought to be a natural market for ornaments from Italy, Turkey, Dubai and Southeast Asia, an import duty of 12 per cent imposed since the late 1980s has led to the rapid growth of a substantial domestic fabrication industry in both small workshops and factories. The largest factory, Saudi Gold in Riyadh, uses over 10 tonnes of gold a year. The factories use migrant labour from Pakistan or Indonesia, who come in on contracts of a year or more, usually living in the factory compound. The total

---

3 The information in these paragraphs draws on *Gold in Turkey*, Türk Ekonomi Bankasi, 1993.

manufacturing capacity by 1993 was estimated at well over 200 tonnes annually, which would rank Saudi Arabia third in the world after Italy and India; although this capacity is not fully used, Saudi still ranked fifth in world fabrication in 1992 with just over 150 tonnes (4.8 million ounces). This quantity, however, is augmented by the trade-in factor as old ornaments go into the melting pot to make new; at least one-third and sometimes as much as two-thirds of the gold used in ornaments comes from this scrap. The manager of the Hussein Saklou factory in Jeddah, which was originally set up in Penang, Malaysia, but moved back to Saudi Arabia once the duty was imposed, told me that of the 100 kilos he uses weekly, as much as 70 kilos came from scrap.

So what does the Saudi woman buy and how much does she pay? The most popular item is the 21-carat machine-made bangle weighing around 15 grams (but often much more) which is piled high in the gold shop windows and sells for a mark-up of about 3 rials ($0.83) per gram over the gold price of the day; that is to say, with gold at $380, a 15-gram bangle would sell for around $393. The bangle is the basic savings item that is draped by the dozen up the arms of many women. Equally popular are jewellery sets comprising a necklace, earrings, bracelet and ring. The necklace is a trifle more expensive; the making charges on a local hand-made necklace of around 20 grams are $11, but it would sell at retail for about $25 per ounce over the gold price; a machine-made necklace has making charges of only $4 to $5 and costs only $10 to $12 an ounce over the gold price (it is, of course, only 21-carat, so the mark-up is more than it immediately seems). The delicate gilada, like a cascade of golden autumn leaves with which a bride is decked, would attract a similar mark-up, but can weigh a kilo or more. At the Saudi Gold factory in Riyadh, I was once shown a spectacular gilada that contained 5 kilos of gold which would cost over $70,000. Totting it all up, one survey of the Saudi Arabian market estimated that in a single year consumption embraced 64 tonnes of jewellery sets, 61 tonnes of bangles, 25 tonnes of giladas, 24 tonnes of chain and 13 tonnes of rings and earrings sold through 4,000 shops.[4]

The buyers, of course, are not exclusively Saudi. Several million migrants from all parts of Asia and Africa work in the kingdom and take home jewellery and small bars; several million pilgrims also make the haj pilgrimage to the holy shrines of Mecca and Medina, providing a surge to souk buying for a few weeks of the year. The heart of the business, though, is the women on the telephone or on their evening expeditions to the souk (which in Jeddah does not close till 10 p.m.) for a little socializing and gold buying with their friends.

4 These are gross weights; with about 70 per cent at 21-carat and the rest mostly 18-carat, the fine gold content is closer to 150 tonnes.

## India: a social symbol

'Gold accompanies Indians from birth to death,' said an Indian friend of mine. 'It is the bringer of good fortune, the first thing to be seen on New Year's Day when you wake up, while marriage is symbolized by a holy chain and pendant in gold.' Somehow gold crops up in many casual conversations. One evening in Bombay I was accompanying Madhusudan Daga, the journalist who probably knows more about the gold business than anyone on the sub-continent, on his evening walk along Worli Seaface, when we met an acquaintance of his. Rather than pleasantries about the sea breeze bringing a welcome respite from the heat, or cricket or the calamitous state of Indian politics, we fell immediately into a discussion on gold, oblivious to the multitude of strollers or the vendors pressing us with fruit and trinkets. 'Every Indian woman, rich or poor, must have gold for security,' explained our fellow walker, 'and it is social prestige – the sale of family ornaments is a blot on the map.'

When I first came to India twenty-five years ago to investigate the gold trade, I recall an officer at the Reserve Bank of India lecturing me that banking was spreading fast into the rural areas and before long this custom of keeping one's life savings in gold would wither. On the contrary, as India has grown more prosperous over the last decade, the habit seems, if anything, to have been consolidated. Not least because of the repeal of the Gold Control Act in 1991, which had previously limited the quantity of ornaments each family might hold (not that anyone paid much attention) and denied entirely the right to hold coins and small bars, followed by the legalizing of imports the following year, largely ending over four decades of smuggling. Freed from these controls India forged on to a record manufacture of almost 220 tonnes (7.1 million ounces) of jewellery from new gold imports in 1992. The total was appreciably more if recycled ornaments are included, for although the trade-in cycle here is not so frequent as in Saudi Arabia, one heavy old ornament is often exchanged for two or three lighter new ones, or a forthcoming wedding may call for some recasting of the family jewels. The constant faith in gold was conceded by a senior economist at the Reserve Bank of India who admitted its hopes of change had not borne fruit. 'Gold is still the bastion,' he said. 'It is not just that it must be exchanged at marriage, it is the only way a villager in this country can get instant liquidity. He doesn't have a bank in his village and he doesn't buy government bonds, because they cannot be cashed instantly. Gold can.'

Every village in India has its goldsmith as the local banker. At least 3 million artisans are estimated to be working in gold and silver (also an important savings item) at the myriad villages of the sub-continent; they are supplied by a network of 25,000 minor dealers, in turn connected to 50 major dealers. Individual turnover is modest; a village goldsmith may handle 300 grams (under 10 ounces) a month, and a minor dealer only 3 to 4 kilos a month. Put together, though, it amounts to at least 300 tonnes annually (and possibly rather more if one includes recycling which is impossible to assess accurately), making India second only to China as the world's largest consumer of carat gold jewellery. Most of it, incidentally, is billed as 21 or 22-carat, but regulation is light and a good deal is under title. Given the population pressing on towards 900 million, however, the per capita expenditure is a mere $16 annually and surveys suggest less than 10 per cent of Indians buy gold jewellery each year – compared to over 90 per cent in Saudi Arabia.

Indian buying embraces the hiding of 'black' money, the ebb and flow of buying by farmers according to the harvest and, above all, ornaments for marriages. 'Gold continues to make gains because of very good offtake on account of the marriage season,' notes Madhusudan Daga in his latest letter to me. Five million marriages take place in India each year and the status of a family in its community is still judged by the gold exchanged as the bride's dowry. As Shantilal Sonawala, the former President of the Bombay Bullion Association, taught me long ago, between 2 and 5 tolas (23–58 grams) of gold are called for. 'The bride', said Mr Sonawala, 'must have two bangles, one pendant, one ring, earrings and perhaps a nose-pin.' Marriages, and thus gold demand, depend on auspicious astrological signs. One year Shantilal Sonawala warned me that marriages would be few because 'when Jupiter goes to Leo, which happens every twelve years, Hindus don't marry.' That occurred in 1980 (fortuitously a moment of very high gold prices) and 1992, but the way ahead now looks good until 2004.

However, the government has put temptation in the way of India's gold hoarders. It launched a gold bond in 1993 hoping to mobilize at least a little of the domestic stocks, estimated at around 7,000 tonnes, that have accumulated over the centuries. The bond, for which gold deposits of as little as 100 grams could be subscribed, was for five years with interest fixed at 40 rupees (about $1.25) per gram, but payable only at the end of five years; a return equivalent to around 2 per cent annually. The attraction was that no questions were asked about where the gold came from, nor the money to buy it. Several tonnes was indeed subscribed, but the word in the Bazaar was that it was a highly convenient way to launder 'black' money by simply buying a few kilos of the gold that could now be legally imported. Women seemed less impressed at the notion of handing over their jewellery. At a lunch in Bombay at the home of a leading dealer, the subject naturally came up. He looked across the table at his wife and laughed. 'I asked my wife, "will you give your jewellery?"' he said. 'Not one tola will she give.' And she concurred, 'Not a chance.'

### The magnet of China

To the east beyond India, the gold trade becomes the province of the Chinese. This is obvious in China, Hong Kong, Singapore or Taiwan, but it applies equally in Indonesia, Malaysia, Thailand and Vietnam, where the minority overseas Chinese community still dominates. Travelling from Singapore to Penang to Bangkok you will be passed along the family tree to brothers, uncles and cousins who have settled there. Often the tradition goes back generations. The oldest gold shop in Bangkok, Tang Toh Kang, was opened in the 1880s by the great-grandfather of the present owner. Not only do the Chinese control the business, but their own communities are the greatest hoarders. Catchphrases on gold, *kam* in Cantonese, *jin* in Mandarin, as a symbol of prosperity and happiness, abound. Gifts of gold jewellery begin at birth. 'Chinese babies are presented with amulets, chains or a golden animal symbolizing the year of the zodiac in which the child is born,' says Jonie Lai, the World Gold Council's Hong Kong manager. 'If the baby is lucky enough to be born into a wealthy family, he is said to be born, not with a silver spoon, but with golden chopsticks in his mouth.'

While China itself remained a closed door for a generation, the jewellery business thrived nevertheless in Southeast Asia, riding on the back of economic growth and, as in India, good harvests. A bumper rice crop in Thailand in 1989, for instance, created a record local demand for gold jewellery because the farmers had more disposable income.

The standard of craftsmanship, coupled with lower labour costs, has enabled Southeast Asia to challenge the Italians in the markets of the Middle East, Japan and the United States. An Indian friend of mine who runs one of the best jewellery shops in Abu Dhabi once made many ornaments in his own workshop; nowadays the chains, bracelets and necklaces all come from Singapore or Malaysia. And looking down a list of Saudi prices, I see 'necklaces, Singapore origin, without gems' slightly cheaper than 'Dubai origin' or 'Turkey origin'. The manufacturers use the latest Italian or German machinery. Even in Surabaya, which is the capital of Indonesian jewellery-making, I found a factory filled with excellently maintained chain machines; the owner himself had spent six years in Pforzheim, Germany learning the business and employed a German manager to ensure the machines performed perfectly in the tropical heat of Java.

Hong Kong, Malaysia, Singapore and Thailand have become serious challengers in the worldwide market for carat gold and gem-set jewellery. Hong Kong and Thailand concentrate on exports of gem-set while Malaysia and Singapore focus more on gold jewellery, for which Singapore has increasingly become the wholesaler and Malaysia the manufacturer because of lower labour costs. The centre is Penang, the little tropical island off the coast of Malaysia. Building on a long tradition of local craftsmanship, Penang's manufacturers work for Europe, the Middle East, the Philippines, and now are almost overwhelmed by China's demand. The first step came from a German wholesaler, who established a factory in Penang's duty-free zone in the 1970s; then came a Saudi wholesaler setting up with a local partner, followed by Singapore manufacturers, as their own labour costs rose. There were few big factories, mostly it was small workshops in and around Penang or just across the bridge on the mainland. Once I went to the village of Burkit Merah where I saw one whole street of small homes where chain machines had been installed everywhere from the kitchen to the bedroom. Thus Penang had the flexibility to respond when China became the magnet in the early 1990s, quite overwhelming the capacity of Hong Kong manufacturers. Suddenly, instead of Malaysia producing 20 tonnes a year, it was rocketing up towards 100 tonnes. How had they done it, I asked Mr Tham Yen Thim, the President of the Malaysian Goldsmiths' Association? 'By working seven days a week, twenty-four hours a day,' he said. 'Previously a small workshop might have orders for two or three days a week, now they work all the time.'

The speed of change in China itself is astonishing; in the mid-1980s gold jewellery demand was hardly measurable; by 1992 it was close to 400 tonnes, making China the world's largest market. Today on Wangfujing Street in Beijing jewellery shops virtually outnumber any others; the capital is said to have 200 of them. 'Solid investments – going for the gold' says a headline in *China Daily* over a story that 'Gold ornaments are acting as magnets on people's wallets.' 'Gold rush ends with $4.3 billion sales last year,' adds another headline, breathlessly reporting on Beijing's first jewellery fashion show. The paper also noted that per capita spending on jewellery had risen nine-fold in five years. Interviews with the buyers abounded. 'I believe in gold because it is permanent,' said a young man buying a ring. 'Usually I wouldn't care much about gold necklaces,' said a woman in the Marco Polo jewellery store, 'but when I heard that they are getting more expensive, I immediately felt the urge to buy one before it gets too dear for me.' Only two items, colour televisions and refrigerators, take priority over gold.

Such enthusiasm may stem from the television commercials which pepper programmes, especially in the southern provinces and enterprise zones close to Hong Kong, where economic prosperity took hold first. The major Hong Kong jewellery manufacturers Chow Sang Sang, Chow Tai Fook and King Fook, in joint ventures with the World Gold Council, have been targeting audiences with considerable success. In their first year of promotion, Chow Sang Sang sold 10 tonnes of *chuk kam* jewellery in Guangdong province, two and a half times its sales target. The constant flow of Chinese visitors to Hong Kong and 'overseas' Chinese bound for China is also wooed by commercials on the passenger ferries plying between. After China relaxed its currency regulations in March 1993 to permit mainlanders to take up to 6,000 yuan (about $100) out with them, shops in Hong Kong began accepting the Chinese notes against gold. 'The streets of Hong Kong's shopping areas are paved with mainlanders in search of gold,' reported Teresa Poole of *The Independent*, adding that they were responsible for taking 40 per cent of *chuk kam* and small bar sales in the colony's shops.

While much of this jewellery is made in Hong Kong and Malaysia, an increasing amount is made in China itself either with gold provided by the People's Bank of China (which requires to be paid in foreign exchange) or with gold sent across the border by Hong Kong and Singapore wholesalers, who have either opened their own factories or signed contracts with Chinese companies to benefit from low labour costs.

The range of ornaments now being made in China is astonishing. I called on Beijing Gold Jewellery, which put out a handsome catalogue with a golden dragon on the cover and the words 'Gold – the universal currency' in both English and Mandarin beneath. A young manager, named Zhang Ziaofeng, told me it is the largest jewellery maker in Beijing, and rank fifth in China; there are bigger manufacturers in the Shanghai and Guangzhou areas. Beijing Gold Jewellery uses around 3 tonnes of gold a year, and sells its jewellery through three of its own shops in Beijing, to other retailers and also to Hong Kong wholesalers. 'There are 200 gold shops in Beijing now,' said Zhang Xiaofeng, adding with a grin, 'The Chinese people got rich.' He started opening drawers in the showroom, pulling out great bundles of gold chain and bracelets, laying them on the table before us. 'An 18-inch chain weighing 30 grams [virtually an ounce] is the popular weight, and the bracelets are 25 grams,' he explained, 'but for a special person we have these.' He picked out a bunch of five *chuk kam* chains each weighing in at 70 grams. Really special persons might also fancy delicate cups, a coffee pot, a graceful horse or statues of wise men with long beards, all cast in pure gold, that adorned cabinets around the walls.

Such ostentation comes with a sense of release that the long drab years of uniformity are over. 'The Chinese like gold, it protects us, it brings us good luck,' said Harmony Wang, the bright eager young woman who acted as my guide, 'but the cultural revolution did not allow gold, so now we grow rich and feel proud of it. Many businessmen who are successful wear very heavy white gold rings, especially when they play Mah Jong, to show they are rich.'

This touching faith in precious metal in the new China naturally raises the question, just how much gold can the Chinese buy in the years ahead? For all the displays in the great cities of Beijing, Shanghai and Guangzhou, a real distribution network for jewellery throughout China does not exist. All told there are scarcely a thousand retail outlets; much of the distribution is simply through travellers to and from or within China taking gifts or buying for family and friends. The potential is enormous, but caution is needed. Much of what has happened in the early 1990s is due to sudden prosperity, that sense of release from long grey years with the added incentive of inflation and the falling value of the yuan. Any attempt by the government to cool the economy and slow growth will slow gold sales. The proposal, for instance, that government salaries for one month in 1993 be paid in government bonds rather than cash cut spending power. Eventually, too, people will have other options on how to spend their money. For the moment, the priorities are a colour television, a refrigerator and then gold jewellery. Ultimately, for a nation still largely on the bicycle it will be the motor scooter and the motor car and holidays abroad. However, that is years ahead. China has arrived as a major, even the major, consumer of gold; the stock within the country is starting from a very low base, and it has the world's largest population with a traditional affinity for gold. As the World Gold Council's Jonie Lai delights to remind audiences, 'The Chinese love gold. We eat it, wear it, flaunt it, heal with it, and hoard it. And there are over 1.14 billion of us.'

### Japan: land of the golden tea ceremony

All this excitement has rather eclipsed two substantial but more conventional markets for adornment jewellery – Japan and the United States. Their combined consumption is close to 350 tonnes annually, almost at par with China, and the United States alone was the world's premier consumer until China and India edged ahead in recent years. Moreover, while China still slept, it was Japan that really made the running in the 1980s as gold jewellery consumption there tripled from a modest 40 tonnes annually to almost 130 tonnes, giving it a slightly higher per capita offtake than the United States. The challenge for gold in Japan is also tougher because not only is it competing with aggressive diamond promotion from De Beers, but it is also the world's foremost market for platinum jewellery (indeed, one might almost say it is *the* market for platinum jewellery, for it consumes around 30 tonnes a year and it is hard to find anywhere else doing even 1 tonne). A strong alliance has built up between the diamond and platinum promoters on the concept that the former look good set in the latter.

The gold invasion of Japan really succeeded on two fronts, a huge swing to gold chain and some innovative gold jewellery stores. The *forte* in chain was a distinctive local variety of 18-carat curb chain known as *kihei,* which came to account for a third of all output by the late 1980s as an affordable fashion item around the necks and wrists of young Japanese women. The chain was virtually all home-made by forty companies, of which the biggest, Kawayama, can match output with Italy's best. Neither the Italians, nor anyone else have really cracked the Japanese market even for necklaces, rings and earrings; almost 85 per cent of the gold jewellery sold in Japan is made there.

To admire it, step into Japan's ultimate gold shop, Yamazaki, on Ginza. Pop music and a big TV screen featuring a fashion show of gold jewellery greet the customer. The day's prices for kilo bars, small bars, bullion coins and 22-carat jewellery flash up on an electronic screen, while a world map spotlights the latest gold price in key international markets. Yamazaki, which is part of the empire of Tanaka K.K., Japan's leading precious metal dealers, has four floors devoted to gold. The ground floor is given over to chain sold by weight. 'We offer 500 kinds of chain,' explained Tadahiko Fukami, the president of Tanaka, when he first took me round. 'In all, we have 20,000 kinds of jewellery, including rings, bracelets, and pendants.' On a good day, Yamazaki has 2,000 customers. The price of each item is quoted in gold and yen, so that customers can, if they wish, pay in gold. 'At this shop, you can use gold as money,' said Mr Fukami proudly. Tanaka was one of the pioneers of the gold accumulation savings scheme in Japan, so that customers who have an account with it can pay directly for their jewellery in gold (see Chapter 19 for gold accumulation accounts). A buy-back price is also quoted, so that jewellery can be traded in.

Yamazaki also features an immense display of the corporate gifts that Japanese companies present to favoured customers, such as 24-carat teapots and vases, weighing a kilo or more, along with saki cups and chopsticks. Even more elaborate items can be made on request. A hot springs resort outside Tokyo features a famous phoenix-shaped tub fashioned from 143 kilos (4,580 ounces) of pure gold, in which a dip is supposed to prolong life. Since the water is close to 40 degrees C the ordeal of getting in and out gracefully while stark naked may actually shorten it; certainly I came out resembling a boiled lobster rather than someone discovering the fountain of youth. A more soothing attraction is the golden tea ceremony room at the Moa Art Museum at Atami in Shizuoka prefecture, where 50 kilos of gold were employed. The pillars and beams of the room are covered with rolled gold, the walls are papered in gold leaf. The teapots and cups are, naturally, 24-carat gold.

The recession in Japan during the early 1990s not only took some of the shine off such exotica, but even sales of the humble *kihei* chain took a tumble. A noticeable shift in consumer attitudes was apparent. Previously people were ready to buy an ornament on a high mark-up for status because it cost over, say, 100,000 yen (around $850); suddenly everyone wanted to pay under 100,000 yen and less than 50,000 if possible. 'The consumer wants value for money,' said a Tokyo analyst. 'If you want *kihei* chain now, you find it in the discount stores.' The place to go for bargains is a store with the unlikely name of Big Camera. The shake-out from high mark-up to bargain basement, however, meant that actual consumption fell only marginally despite the long recession. And it may result in the more cost-conscious Japanese jewellery buyer being able to afford more ornaments when things get better.

### United States: lunch-time shopping

The Americans, of course, always want bargains. If you venture down New York's *souk*, otherwise known as West 47th Street, between Fifth and Sixth Avenues, or the *souk* in the Seebold building of downtown Miami, the 'special offers', 'low mark-ups', and 'clearance sales' abound. While the average price paid for adornment gold jewellery in the industrial countries is a modest $175 (and 60 per cent of sales are for under $500), in the United States it is a mere $88. The best-sellers are necklaces, at an average of $119, and earrings at $42. 'It's a lunch-hour purchase,' said David Enloe of the World Gold Council's New York office. 'Twenty or thirty years ago it was a more substantial piece, but now it's lightweight chain and electro-form earrings. There's less gold in each piece, but more is moving.'

Americans buy almost 100 million gold baubles, bangles and beads annually, most in 14-carat, at a cost of around $8.5 billion. Although 60 per cent of that is home-made, chiefly in the towns of Attleboro, Massachusetts and Providence, Rhode Island, or the environs of Los Angeles and Miami, almost a third comes from Italy. Indeed, many of the large Italian manufacturers, such as Uno a Erre, as well as wholesalers, maintain US offices. Look at the code on any chain you buy in the United States and you may well find the stamp is AR1 for Uno a Erre or

522VI for Oromeccanica. The mainstream of US sales is still through independent 'Mom and Pop' stores, which account for just over half of the 44,667 'doors', as the trade calls retail outlets, but in the constant pursuit of bargains, the growth, as in Japan, is in the discount stores. This has knocked out some of the famous names like Zales, who once operated vast chains of stores.

Working women, according to the gold marketeers, are the driving force as consumers; 80 per cent of gold jewellery is for women and they buy 60 per cent of it for themselves. Earrings, apparently, are *de rigueur*. 'The American woman will not leave home without earrings,' said a hopeful salesman on 47th Street. 'It frames the face.' She is also the prime target in on-going rivalry between the gold and diamond promoters, who spend more in the United States than anywhere else. In this battle between 'plain gold' and 'stones', as the charts and graphs of tactics describe them, the current victor often depends whose field dispositions you last viewed. But there are signs that gold has gained market share from diamonds, especially during the recession of the early 1990s. The diamond, with a luxury image, is an easier casualty in such times; gold, as a more regular fashion item, survives.

The advertising slogans are reassuring; 'Nothing makes you feel as good as gold,' one purrs. The latest catchphrase is 'Gold Shivers', hinting that a woman feels a shiver of excitement when she puts on a new gold ornament for the first time. The ultimate place to catch the shivers may be in a new chain of 'Karat Gold' stores, being opened by Sterling Inc., which will sell only gold. Luckily, the first one is in West Palm Beach, so that even if you get the shivers, you can step outside into the Florida sun to warm up again.

# CHAPTER 21

# Industry:
# Nothing is as Good as Gold

In the British Museum in London there is an Egyptian funeral papyrus dating from the fourteenth century BC of a man named Neferronpet who was described as 'chief of the makers of thin gold'. Even in his day, the incredible malleability of gold which enables it to be beaten into wafer-thin leaf to adorn temples and statues was well recognized. Dentists in ancient Egypt also understood another of gold's unique properties, resistance to corrosion, for they were using gold wire to bind together molars before 2000 BC.

The realization that gold was not just a precious and beautiful metal, but also a versatile and useful one, goes back to the earliest civilizations. Modern technology, however, has found that its traditional virtues of malleability, ductility, reflectivity and resistance to corrosion are matched with unparalleled ability as a thermal and electrical conductor. Moreover, once you ally its resistance to corrosion with the facility to convey a tiny electrical current in temperatures varying from $-55$ to $+200$ degrees C, then you have one of the foundation stones of modern electronics. I always remember a scientist at Johnson Matthey, the precious metals specialists, saying many years ago, 'When people want something to be 500 per cent reliable for twenty years, we recommend gold.' But, mindful of advances in technology, I recently asked an American electronics expert what substitute might be in view. 'Gold is still better than anything else we have evaluated,' he replied. In short, the phrase 'nothing is as good as gold', often used to advertise jewellery, ought really to be the motto for its industrial and decorative uses.

Indeed, by-passing for a moment gold's more traditional applications in decoration and dentistry, one must acknowledge that our present age of high technology finds it indispensable in everything from pocket calculators to computers, telephones to television and missiles to spacecraft. The rocket engines of American space shuttles are lined with gold-brazing alloys to reflect heat, while much of the micro-circuitry aboard depends on gold-plated contacts and connectors conducting the subtlest of low voltages, or gold/palladium wires in thermocouples detecting the minutest variations in temperature. The eye of every visitor to the Smithsonian Institution's Air and Space Museum in Washington DC is caught by the glow of the gold-covered film acting as a radiation shield that shrouds the squat lunar module of the Apollo programme. The astronauts themselves were always tethered to their spacecraft by a gold-plated umbilical cord. And all the components of the Hubble space telescope's electronic camera are coated with gold to prevent heat build-up which could destroy its images from outer space. Even more mundane equipment employs gold. The ordinary touch-tone telephone contains thirty-three gold contact points, while Polaroid cameras are activated by gold-plated contacts. Printed circuits in gold even guide the sequence of washing machines and dishwashers.

Reliability and durability are the crucial factors; cost is often irrelevant. A communications satellite orbiting the earth must perform for years on end; an electrician cannot buzz up to replace a corroded antenna or connector. Silver as a replacement would not work. 'It might tarnish before the satellite was in orbit,' explained a scientist, 'but gold never oxidizes and will stay shining bright forever.'

A little gold also goes a long way. As micro-circuitry improves, the dash of gold used to coat a contact or the tiny pins of a connector is almost invisible to the naked eye. In 'thick-film technology', for instance, the circuit is printed onto a ceramic base using a paste of 'ink' containing gold. 'The thickness of the circuit is minimal,' explained an executive at Engelhard Industries, which is in the forefront of supplying the pastes, 'but the market size is colossal.' The trick nowadays is for a manufacturer to be able to show how less gold can be used in one circuit, but then actually sell more gold because the sheer volume of mini-circuits multiplies daily. Long gone are the days of $35 gold when it was sloshed around in electronics like butter on a piece of bread; now it is dispersed only where it is required. Plating thickness came down from 20 microns to 5 microns very quickly once the price rose in the 1980s; now 2 microns is thick and 1 micron or less is commonplace.

### Pioneers of gold technology

The gold potassium cyanide, normally shortened to GPC or PGC, used for electro-plating (and also employed for decorative uses on costume jewellery, watches or pens) accounts for nearly half of all industrial applications of gold. Its manufacture, along with such other specialist products as gold pastes for 'thick-film technology', wafer-thin alloys for bonding with other metals, bonding wire to link one circuit with another, or liquid gold for ceramics, is undertaken primarily by a handful of precious metal fabricators in Europe, Japan and the United States. Indeed, over 85 per cent of all fabrication for electronic, dental and decorative uses of gold takes place there; for electronics alone, 70 per cent of fabrication is in Japan, which is the leader, and the United States.

This select club of fabricators, almost all with over one hundred years' experience, has pioneered most gold, as well as silver and platinum, technology. Its worldwide distribution networks supply the needs, for instance, of the electronics industry throughout Southeast Asia, although increasingly it is establishing manufacturing facilities on the ground there in Hong Kong, Singapore and South Korea, while Degussa from Germany is also the chief fabricator of industrial products in Brazil. It was Degussa, along with Johnson Matthey in Britain, which set the pace in the nineteenth century. Johnson Matthey's worldwide metallurgical empire began in Hatton Garden, London in 1817 (although the Johnson family had been assayers of precious metal since the 1750s); Degussa was founded in 1843 by Friedrich Ernst Roessler. One of its early achievements was the commercial production of liquid or 'bright' gold for ceramic decorations, improving on a formula first tried out at the Royal Porcelain Factory at Meissen in Saxony. Degussa launched 'bright' gold in 1879 and permitted Johnson Matthey to manufacture from its formula two years later. Other early starters in precious metal technology were Comptoir Lyon-Alemand Louyot in France from 1800, W. C. Heraeus, which was founded in 1851 in Germany and remains Degussa's great rival there, and Métaux Précieux/Metalor in Neuchâtel, which began making special alloys for the Swiss watch industry in 1852, but now makes a wide range of industrial and dental gold products. In the United States, Parker D. Handy and John F. Harman set up Handy & Harman in 1867, which was followed rather later by Engelhard Industries, started by Charles Engelhard Sr in 1902.

The oldest fabricators also include Tokuriki Honten in Japan, founded in 1727, and Tanaka Kikinzoku Kogyo, started by Umekichi Tanaka in Tokyo in 1885. It was Tanaka which really began the production of industrial precious metal products in Japan. While today

Tanaka is also a major bullion trader, the focus of the company remains on industrial applications in both gold and platinum. Jun-ichiro Tanaka, one of the most admired figures in the world of precious metals of the last generation, who was president from 1963 until his death in 1989, regarded that as 'the backbone' of Tanaka K.K.'s business. 'It's our staple food,' he used to say. 'Like rice.' Tanaka is the world's foremost producer of bonding wire for electronics, accounting for 60 per cent of all output.

These nine semi-fabricators make between them most of the gold for electronics, dentistry and other industrial and decorative purposes; a record 282 tonnes (9 million ounces) for the western world in 1992, of which electronics took half. This is modest by the scale of jewellery demand, but still accounts for 15 per cent of western mine output. Moreover, the consumption, especially in electronics, has risen steadily over the last decade, despite fears that the high gold price in the early 1980s would force manufacturers to find an alternative or that they would apply less to smaller and smaller micro-circuitry units. They did, indeed, use it more sparingly, but the explosive growth of electronics has more than kept pace.

Such frugality did not apply in the former Soviet Union, whose industrial use is not included in the statistics above, as hard information is only now emerging. The Soviet Union, it appears, had a much higher allocation of gold for the military-industrial complex than anyone had guessed: around 110 tonnes (3.5 million ounces) annually throughout the 1980s. This was a centrally planned allocation not dictated by demand. The use of the gold in the military and space programme was immensely inefficient by western standards, but no one worried. Indeed, it appears that the Soviets often used gold when silver would have done, simply because the gold was available at home, whereas most silver had to be imported against hard currency. Book-keeping actually showed a higher internal price for silver than gold. 'The waste was astounding,' an analyst just back from Moscow told me. Nowadays there is good profit to be had in exporting Soviet electronic scrap unofficially to Europe for recycling, so rich are the gold coatings on switches and connectors.

### The perfect contact

Precisely the opposite now applies in western electronics; the gold is so thinly spread it is not worth recovering from most items, especially outdated consumer goods, so there is no haste to melt down your telephone or dishwasher. The serious amounts of gold in electronics anyway are in mainframe computers, telecommunications satellites and defence systems. The elements favouring it, of course, are the combination of its electrical conductivity, its ductility and its total freedom from corrosion or tarnishing at either high or low temperatures. Gold's almost perfect resistance to corrosion means it provides an atomically clean metal surface which has an electrical contact resistance close to zero, while its high thermal conductivity ensures rapid dissipation of heat when gold is used for contacts. The plating of contacts for switches, relays and connectors accounts for most of the gold used in electronics. The connectors include plugs and sockets for cable terminations, integrated circuit sockets, computer backplates and printed circuit board connectors. The quantities of gold, however, vary considerably. 'Two simple rules sum up the position,' noted Stewart Murray of Gold Fields Mineral Services, analysing the electronics demand. 'The more sophisticated the product, the greater the use of connectors, and the higher the need for reliability, the greater the use of gold in these connectors.'[1]

Thus a decline in sales of large mainframe computers in the early 1990s, while personal computer sales boomed, led to a slight fall in gold use. 'Mainframes make more intensive use of gold than PCs due to the greater complexity of their interconnections,' observed Stewart Murray. 'An increasing number of these [PCs] were of the lap-top variety, which has a high degree of integration and a correspondingly low chip count.'[2]

New challenges also face bonding wire, the other main use in electronics. Bonding wire, specially refined up to 'five nines' (999.99) and drawn to a diameter of one-hundredth of a millimetre (far thinner than a human hair), links parts of semi-conductors, such as transistors and integrated circuits, to ensure reliable connections between components. The ease with which gold can be bonded into position in tiny circuits by standard micro-welding techniques is an added bonus. While some bonding wire is made of aluminium or copper, over 90 per cent is gold. 'The versatility of wire bonding is likely to ensure that its use will continue and even grow for the foreseeable future,' argue Giles Humpstone and David Jacobson at GEC-Marconi's Hirst Research Centre in England.[3] These two researchers have been testing a new gold bonding wire to which a touch of titanium has been added to meet the demands of the semi-conductor industry for a yet finer, tougher wire. They believe that by adding 1 per cent titanium the strength of bonding wire can be increased three-fold, without upsetting its other electrical and bonding benefits. I asked Tadahiko Fukami, the president of Tanaka K.K., the number one makers of bonding wire, how he saw the outcome. He explained that he was a little worried at a new concept of semi-conductors being transformed into a wire-free 'package'. In any event the drive for finer, lighter wires would continue, but would be

1 Stewart Murray, *Gold 1990*, Gold Fields Mineral Services, London, 1990, p. 46.
2 Stewart Murray, *Gold 1993*, Gold Fields Mineral Services, London, 1993, p. 54.
3 G. Humpstone and D. Jacobson, 'A new high strength gold bond wire', *Gold Bulletin*, Vol. 25, No. 4, 1992, pp. 132–45.

offset by the volume required. 'Gold use in semi-conductors will be steady,' Mr Fukami forecast.

The real threat to consumption may come from declining gold use because of cutbacks in spending in all manner of military and defence uses for aircraft, missiles, satellites and space programmes. This, above all, has been the sector where performance and reliability counted more than the cost of gold (and not just in the former Soviet Union). The uses are not only in electronic systems, but in aerospace to reflect heat. A thin film of gold avoids the dead weight of asbestos insulation to disperse the intense heat of jet aircraft or rocket engines. The pilot of a fighter plane, for example, is sitting virtually on top of his engine, and the effectiveness of the heat shield is critical. Similarly, gold is used for all the external parts of rocket engines in the US space programme to provide thermal control and maintain the engines within safe operating temperatures while the spacecraft is boosted clear of the earth's atmosphere. Rolls Royce also found gold plating invaluable in its aircraft for the Anglo-French supersonic Concorde.

### Golden skyscrapers

Precisely the same benefit has led to the increasing use of gold in modern buildings, both to reflect the heat and to retain it. Glass coated with a thin film of gold (1 ounce will cover up to 1,000 square feet) not only reflects the sun in summer, but in winter can also bounce internal heat back into rooms, thus retaining warmth within the buildings. The Royal Bank of Canada building, which glows like a huge nugget over downtown Toronto, has 2,500 ounces (77.7 kilos) of gold in its 27,000 windows. 'Energy considerations were a primary concern in choosing gold reflective glass,' the architects explained.[4] Savings can be considerable. The use of gold glass in another Canadian building in Edmonton, Alberta not only cut capital costs by $37,000 because a smaller air-conditioning plant sufficed, but also reduced operating expenses for cooling and heating by 40 per cent.[5] Aside from economy, the subdued greenish light within can create a particular mood, especially in such places as the Garden Court of Coutts' banking house in London, which is roofed entirely with golden glass.

A thin film of transparent pure gold acts as an equally efficient heat shield on the visors of protective masks worn by firemen tackling air crashes or other intense fires. A similar film of gold deposited on the inner surfaces of laminated glass is also widely used as an electrical heating element to prevent windshields on everything from planes (including the Concorde) to Alpine trains from icing up or misting over.

Safety and saving energy are not, of course, the sole considerations.

4 Gold News, Vol. 2, No. 3, May 1977.
5 Gold News, Vol. 6, No. 1, January 1981.

Golden domes, roofs, ceilings or railings have an eye-catching glow, even if they lack the true splendour of the great Inca Temple of the Sun at Cuzco from which the Spanish conquistador Francisco Pizarro and his men ripped 700 plates of pure gold. Wafer-thin gold leaf, the traditional prestige decoration since Egyptian times for temples, cathedrals, the bindings of fine books, and picture frames, is also still widely applied. The ceiling of the Metropolitan Opera House, the 18-foot-tall statue of Prometheus presiding over the Rockefeller Center skating rink, and the Helmsley building astride Park Avenue in New York are all dressed in gold leaf. Politicians, too, seem to enjoy debating under an aura of gold; the state capitol in Denver, Colorado, and the Canadian Houses of Parliament in Ottawa have touched up their domes with gold leaf. Prestige is not the only reason. 'If you paint a capitol dome you're lucky if it lasts more than four or five years, but gold leaf will stay for twenty-five or thirty years,' says Matthew Swift, president of Swift & Sons, whose family firm has been beating it out in Hartford, Connecticut for a century.

The technique, now practised by only a handful of craftsmen, has changed little since antiquity, when it evolved because it required neither heat nor mechanical devices, merely muscle. The gold beater stands before a granite block set on a block of wood, the resilience of the wood base giving bounce and rhythm to his hammering. He then beats it endlessly with a series of progressively lighter hammers; about 82,000 blows are required to make it as thin as three-millionths of an inch. The gold is then so delicate that it can be cut only with a malacca reed shaped into a cutting tool or 'wagon', which is slid across the gold.[6]

Such versatility offers almost endless uses. For more than a thousand years gold has been applied in the binding and decoration of books and manuscripts. Originally a light pen or brush was used to embellish book covers, until craftsmen in Venice developed a new technique of hot gilding with gold leaf by means of a heated die stamped onto leather which has been treated with a 'fixer' of egg white and white vinegar whisked together. The technique of Damascene, originating in Damascus, Syria in the sixteenth century, involves the ornamentation of metalwork with inlaid gold, which is beaten into undercut grooves.

Enamelling, the technique of bonding enamel with gold, is also an ancient skill; among the earliest examples are Minoan and Mycenean jewellery from the late fifteenth century BC in which dark blue enamel was fused into depressions in gold sheet, a form known as repoussé. Modern jewellery designers still employ repoussé and two other refinements, *cloisonné* and *à jour*, especially for earrings and brooches.

Rather less esoteric is the process of gold fill or rolled gold (known

---

6 See Timothy Green and Deborah Russell, *The Gold Companion*, Rosendale Press, London, 1991, pp. 59–60, for a more detailed explanation.

as *plaque laminé* in France) in which a thin layer of carat gold alloy is bonded with base metal to make cigarette cases and lighters, cufflinks, pens, pencils, lipstick cartridges or optical frames. The precise description may vary from one country to another. In the United States gold fill can only describe an alloy of 10 carats or more which comprises at least one-twentieth by weight of the total metal content; if less than one-twentieth it must be labelled rolled gold plate or gold overlay.

Liquid gold, or liquid bright gold, which is widely used in the decoration of ceramics and glass, particularly perfume bottles, was first developed by the technical manager of the Royal Porcelain Factory at Meissen in Saxony in the early 1830s and then marketed commercially, as we noted earlier, by Degussa and Johnson Matthey. The Hanovia Liquid Gold Division of Engelhard Industries became the main supplier for the US market at the beginning of this century. These three companies still dominate production, which uses about 10 tonnes of fine gold annually. Liquid gold is a marvellous blend of gold granules dissolved with as many as forty ingredients including natural oils of lavender and balsam, natural resins and organic acids.[7] The cocktail is applied to ceramics or glass with a camel hair brush, by screen printing or by spraying. The object is then heated to burn off the organic components, leaving a thin 'bright' film of 22-carat gold. Liquid gold can also be applied to glazing tiles or bricks on the outside of buildings. The most notable is the Richfield building in Los Angeles, which has a ceramic veneer finished in liquid gold, which merely requires a good wash once in a while to remove the grime. Liquid gold is also used in space technology to reflect heat and infra-red radiation; in the US Apollo space programme reflective plastic film coated with liquid gold was wrapped around the lunar landing module and the moon buggy to protect sensitive parts from solar radiation.

### The politics of dental gold

The ease with which gold can be worked and its resistance to corrosion have led to its use in dentistry for over 2,000 years. Following the initial lead of the Egyptians, the Etruscans in the seventh century BC used gold bands to hold in place substitute teeth, usually from a cow or calf, when their own fell or were knocked out. And Roman law in the fifth century BC decreed that it was acceptable to burn or bury corpses 'with the gold with which the teeth may perchance be bound together'. The first printed book on dentistry in Leipzig in 1530 advises that cavities should be filled with gold leaf.[8] An alternative method was to melt an alloy of gold, lead, tin, bismuth and mercury and pour it directly into the cavity through a funnel. Modern dentistry, mercifully, is rather

7 Aram Papazian, 'Liquid Golds', *Gold Bulletin*, Vol. 15, No. 3, July 1982.
8 J.A. Donaldson, 'The use of gold in dentistry', *Gold Bulletin*, Vol. 13, No. 3, July 1980.

more sophisticated. The catch nowadays is cost. Dental gold is just too expensive for most people's pockets, unless they are fortunate enough to live in Germany or Japan, where social security picks up part of the bill. The impact on dental gold use, if the government pays, is quite remarkable. In Sweden and Germany dental gold consumption doubled for a while in the 1970s, when payments by the state were relaxed. But the high price of gold then cooled their generosity. Even so, consumption still reflects health insurance policy, more than consumer taste in gold teeth. Germany and Japan account for half of all dental gold fabrication of around 60 tonnes annually, thanks to their governments. And fabrication in the United States and Switzerland, the other main contenders, relies in part on exports of dental alloy to Germany. Degussa is the leading fabricator for Germany, although it has tough competition from Heraeus and two smaller local firms, Hafner and Weiland, in Pforzheim, the home town of German jewellery-making. In Japan the front-runners are Tokuriki Honten and Ishifuku Metal Industry, which are looking forward to even better business from 1993, because the government is raising the minimum title of gold alloys used in national health insurance programmes from 14 to 20 per cent. The US dental market is dominated by Jalenko, with Williams Gold and the ubiquitous Degussa hustling behind.

The real issue on dental gold is the balance between cost and gold content. The main application of gold in modern dentistry is in alloys which are a mixture of gold and the noble metals platinum, palladium or silver, plus copper and zinc. The aim is an alloy which the dentist can manipulate, but is strong, stiff, durable and resistant to the chemical attack of oral fluids. The gold content will usually vary from 620 to 900 fine, according to the precise application; a typical crown and bridge alloy will be 620 to 780 fine. However, the cost of gold has meant a proliferation of inferior alloys, with a gold content below 200 fine. Some palladium based alloys have 2 per cent (20 fine) gold. However, this can defeat the purpose of having gold work in the first place, for such low carat alloys can corrode and even start toxic reactions in the mouth. Hence the Japanese decision to require at least 200 fine alloys under national health insurance. Alternatively, gold alloys are being gradually replaced by a resin-bonding technique for bridges. The statistics on dental gold, incidentally, are far from complete, because they take no account of the fact that in many developing countries dentists make their own alloys, often from melted coins. The wafer-like Mexican 2½-peso coins, for instance, serve as the dentist's best friend in much of Latin America.

## The ultimate aphrodisiac

The unique properties of gold and the mystique surrounding it have naturally led quacks and alchemists through the ages to tout its medicinal properties. Pliny, in the first century BC, suggested gold 'is laid upon wounded men and little children to protect them against magic potions'. Alchemists devised recipes for potable gold for most ailments, though as one sceptical sixteenth century metallurgist rightly observed, gold gave warmth to the heart, 'particularly to those who have great sacks and chests full of it'. Modern medicine's most successful application is in the treatment of rheumatoid arthritis. A very mild solution of gold cyanide, at a concentration of only 0.5 ppm, is injected into the patient's muscles in slowly increased doses to a level of 25 milligrams per week. The gold solution inhibits the growth of the tubercle bacillus which causes the disease and considerable relief may be achieved after six months.[9] Gold also has a limited application in the treatment of cancer, in which 'seeds' of radioactive gold-198 are used.

A firm belief in more far-reaching medicinal benefits persists, however, in India, where gold still plays an important role in Ayurvedic medicine. The government's Gold Control Administration even authorized gold sales of nearly 75 kilos (2,400 ounces) annually to pharmaceutical manufacturers during the forty-five years to 1991 when gold use was tightly controlled there. Eager to learn the secret of the Ayurvedic cure, I once asked the Zandu Pharmaceutical Works in Bombay what they did with gold? After a while, Dr K. M. Parikh, the general manager, responded with a charming letter. Gold in Ayurvedic medicine, he explained, must be 'in a very pure form'. So, to begin with, the metal underwent *sodhan* or purification. 'This is mainly done by heating it and thereafter treating with various other articles like oil, whey, cow dung, kanjee and extracts of other herbs,' wrote Dr Parikh. 'After this *sodhan* it is powdered and mixed with sulphur and ground with lemon juice.' Other herbs or even metals might be mixed in according to the ailments involved. The gold preparations were then taken as powders or tablets washed down with water, milk or honey. They were recommended as 'heart and nerve tonic' and for increasing 'intelligence and memory'. Sclerosis, cirrhosis of the liver, melancholia and hardening of the arteries could all be relieved. Dr Parikh sent along a list of twenty-nine different preparations containing gold, variously named Chaturmukh Rasa, Jayamangal Rasa and Strenex Aphrodisiac. 'I marked items 9, 14, 17, 22, 23, 24, 27 and 29,' he added, 'which are very good and aphrodisiac.'

9 Gregory J. Higby, 'Gold in medicine', *Gold Bulletin*, Vol. 15, No. 4, October 1982; and Blaine M. Sutton, 'Gold compounds for rheumatoid arthritis', *Gold Bulletin*, Vol. 19, No. 1, January 1986.

# Conclusion:
# The Bull Market of 2000 AD

Coming up to the millennium gold looks in good shape. It has come through what could have been a traumatic transition from being principally a monetary metal to one principally used in jewellery, but with the added zest of continuing universal acceptance as a means of exchange and as a speculative or investment vehicle. It has bridged the tricky gap between being perceived as money or simply as a commodity much better than silver has done. The American professor Roy Jastram wrote books on the price performance of both metals, calling one *The Golden Constant* and the other *Silver – The Restless Metal*, which nicely judged the difference.[1] Historically these two metals ('the sun and moon', said Keynes) were locked in strict ratio over centuries; in Europe at 1:15 and rather narrower in the East at 1:12 or 1:13. Since silver lost its monetary role in the latter half of the nineteenth century the ratio has plummeted on occasion almost to 1:100. Silver sought a new role with more difficulty than gold. Its price actually declined for the last thirty years of the nineteenth century, until it was rescued by popular photography, which has sustained it as the main use through this century. Gold, by comparison, was hovering around $40 in 1971 when the US Federal Reserve closed its gold window, snapping the final link between a paper money and gold, and twenty years on not only is the price up ten-fold, but demand for jewellery alone is exceeding conventional mine supply. To be sure, there are huge above-ground stocks in private and central banks' hands, but experience shows that they are mobilized only in quantity on special occasions or at high

---

1 Roy W. Jastram, *The Golden Constant*, John Wiley & Sons, New York, 1977; and *Silver – The Restless Metal*, John Wiley & Sons, New York, 1983.

prices. The threat of those stocks to the market as an overhang is, largely, a red herring.

So what is the prospect for gold? Or, to put it more precisely, as everyone asks in every meeting, anywhere, 'What is the price going to do?' To which Brian Marber the technical chartist always gravely replies that it will go up and down. Quite so. And what will it do in the long term? Well, Keynes said that in the long term, 'we are all dead' and the analyst Robert Weinberg has observed that 'the long term is made up of lots of little short terms.' Much depends on the perspective. A trader worries about the next five minutes, a speculator about days or weeks, an investor may take a view of months or years – while a gold miner planning to develop a deep new mine in South Africa is thinking five to seven years out before he gets a return on a single ounce.

The message of this book, though, is that gold has come to terms with its new environment, it is as popular as ever (save with some central bankers and a few newspapers) and the broad canvas of supply-demand looks promising. The outlook certainly did not seem so good when I began work on this volume in the autumn of 1992; the fear of central bank sales hung over the market as a darkening cloud. Ten months later the market was basking in a price run-up towards $400. On reflection, that was no surprise. What I saw on the road through the Middle East, India, Southeast Asia and China in the early months of 1993 was a physical demand on a scale not equalled since the late 1960s for $35 gold. As the price hung stagnant around $330 an ounce, the offtake was accelerating. Physical gold demand, already a record 3,500 tonnes in 1992, would have pressed on towards 4,000 tonnes for 1993 had the price not risen to cool it. Set against mine supply of 2,200 tonnes, the gap to be filled was immense and would have required over 1,000 tonnes of net central bank sales to fill it, once recycling was taken into account. Since central banks were by then starting to signal that sales might actually slow down, the way ahead was easier. 'This time the rise is not inflation-driven,' said a German dealer, who had been sceptical for some time of gold's prospects. 'This is supply/demand-driven.'

Demand of course is price-sensitive; it eases off very rapidly. As a trigger, though, to bring a different kind of money, however speculative, into the market it worked. Such a spark was badly needed; the gold market was boring itself to death. Volatility put it back on the front pages, and got it discussed again on the cocktail party circuit in Scarsdale, New York (which a bullion banker I know regards as the test). This is not to predict a bull market on the scale of the late 1970s, when much of the rise was gold 'catching up' after being locked too long into $35. There will be 'lots of little short terms', when the news may not be so good. The price will go down. Yet underlying this is a worldwide depth of demand for gold that is growing and will continue to do so.

Two issues really face us. First, what will be the continuing role of gold as a reserve asset held by central banks? Will they become 'the new producers' by selling regularly? And secondly, will the gold mines keep up output?

Certainly central banks will be a prominent feature of the market, much more so than for much of the last twenty years. Some are still mobilizing their reserves into marketable form in international centres like London. There will be sales, but also purchases. The European central banks, which have caused most concern, are sending out those smoke signals, as for the election of a new pope, that they are not planning large-scale disposals. Sales may be more for central banks 'to extricate themselves from monetary potholes', as one analyst put it. But central banks are interested in doing business in the market. 'I can foresee six, seven or eight years from now, central banks selling on highs and buying when they perceive it is low,' Fritz Plass of Deutsche Bank told me.

No one expects a return to the gold standard, but the concept of gold as a useful reserve asset persists, especially when the alternatives, such as the dollar, are considered. What does one make of a headline in *The Economist* that the dollar's 'days as the world's most important reserve currency may be numbered'?[2] The article pondered alternatives to 'the ageing dollar', rather dismissing the Japanese yen because it is based on a smaller economy with a government reluctant to see it as a reserve currency, but seeing 'a stronger candidate . . . waiting in the wings' in the form of a single European currency. However, since then the road towards a single currency for Europe has turned decidedly rocky. One solution discussed by Hamish McRae, the thoughtful columnist of *The Independent* in London, is some kind of agreement towards a world currency, initially with an informal link between the dollar, DM and yen, which was actually instigated at the Louvre Agreement in Paris in 1987, but has largely fallen into abeyance. By letting those currencies move for a while within quite wide, but unpublished, bands, McRae argued that, 'by the end of the century a global system of loosely fixed, but adjustable exchange rates would be in place. . . . If the three biggest have a broad agreement that currency stability is a useful aim, then they can achieve it – if'.[3] In the meantime, to repeat what Charles de Gaulle said, 'Gold . . . universally accepted as the unalterable fiduciary value par excellence', will retain a reserve role.

Gold miners, meanwhile, are consolidating after a famous decade; rarely in history has output increased so dramatically. They have new

2 *The Economist*, 25 July 1992, p. 71.
3 Hamish McRae, *The Independent*, 5 January 1993, p. 19.

technology, new financing and new hedging techniques at their disposal, but they face tough new environmental controls. Despite promising new horizons in Africa, Latin America, China, the Pacific Rim and ultimately in the new CIS republics, miners' energies are going to be concerned primarily with replacing depleted production in South Africa, Canada and elsewhere. The goal will be to stay even. The time scale of mining is also important; the boom of the late 1980s came out of the high price of 1980. The weak prices of the early 1990s have made miners more cautious; several years of sustained higher prices and the prospect of the price increasing steadily in real terms would be needed to get a sharp growth in output. That will come, I suspect, after the year 2000, rather than before. Thus for the rest of the 1990s, the miners will not put pressure on the market in the way they have done in recent years. Rather they will observe how much, and at what price, it can absorb their product.

Which brings us to the crux – the buyers. When I first went to Switzerland in the 1960s to look at the gold market, I called on the Bank for International Settlements in Basel. I faced my first BIS banker with some trepidation, but instead of lecturing me about gold's monetary role, he gestured out of the window at the trams going by and said, 'Gold is cheap now in terms of work. Take a tram driver here; on his wages he can buy his wife a gold wedding ring and a gold bracelet once in a while.' Twenty-five years on, for Basel read Beijing. Gold has gone global, not just in markets, but in buyers. A genuine demand for it exists that can easily absorb mine production and is, at least at the price of the early 1990s, able to take up gold sold by disillusioned private investors and central banks. 'If the price stays where it is today,' observed Stewart Murray of Gold Fields Mineral Services early in 1993, 'then the demand side will almost certainly continue to grow faster than the supply side . . . if the official sector sells less in the coming years than we saw last year, then the only way the market can balance is by the price rising to a level at which additional supply is drawn in . . . and fabrication demand is depressed by the price-elastic effect.'[4]

The markets for gold jewellery also grow ever more numerous. China is just coming in, but wait for Eastern Europe and the former Soviet Union a few years down the road. Latin America is making a comeback as a jewellery buyer after almost a generation racked by inflation and distress sales of jewellery. That is without population growth. The world's population in 1950 was 2.5 billion; in 1993 it is around 5.5 billion and new estimates suggest it may be 8.5 billion by 2025. Millions today live below the poverty line; millions may then, but the trend has been for the living standards of many to edge upwards –

---

4 Stewart Murray, *Gold's Fundamentals – The Key to the Future?*, Australian Gold Conference, Kalgoorlie, March 1993.

witness India and China. Since gold has made the leap from being something afforded only by the wealthy, to something within the means of many wage-earners, the demand exists to provide the gold price with a realistic floor price.

Where is the ceiling? When the gold price lifted off in 1993 towards $400, the *Financial Times* in London smartly tracked down the Aden sisters, a charming couple of technical chartists living in San José, Costa Rica, who made a name for themselves by rightly calling $850 in 1980, but then rather lost it predicting $2,500 or more within a few years. Not much has been heard from them since, but the FT was curious to see if they now thought their prophecy might at last be coming true. They allowed only that it, 'could go to $380 or more'. Well, it did. What took it there, as we have seen in this book, was the combination of large funds using the derivatives markets, particularly options. The growth of derivatives, said one observer, has been 'supersonic'. And it takes gold, as in the late 1970s, into uncharted waters. The possible weight of money that could swing into gold is very great, while the associated delta hedging potential of covering options positions in a fast-rising market, *could* make anything the Aden sisters once said come true. 'It's a bit scary,' admitted Jeffery Nichols, the president of North American Precious Metal Advisers, an experienced gold market analyst who saw the 1980 flurry at close quarters. 'The funds are so unpredictable, you never know; one month they are interested in gold, and the next month they have no gold, but all currencies.' So I called Amy Gassman at Goldman Sachs and she dug out for me the information that over $8 trillion was under management in the United States alone. 'Would you believe it?' she said, in the accompanying fax. It is actually enough to buy all the gold ever mined five times over, assuming a price of $400. Only the slightest shift of sentiment has to move a tiny tranche of this into gold to give the price quite a jolt. The chances of it happening are remote, but the last few years have shown what happens when determined speculators take on a currency – and win. They also took on the central banks in the gold market in 1968 and the fixed price was surrendered in a week. This time central banks might be quite happy to profit from a runaway rise with a little selling, but they would not take on the market in defence of a specific price or ceiling.

A key factor, too, is that the physical gold market is adroit at going into reverse overnight; it does not merely stop buying, but sells back. The *souk* buyers, as we have seen, have always known when to take a profit at precisely the moment when 'sophisticated' speculators are getting in. This safety fuse helped in 1980 (even more dramatically in silver than gold) and could do so again. What it does not stop is the run-up, or down, of the price by $50 and $100 in a single day. That kind of roller-coaster is really what the arrival of the mega-funds in the gold market foreshadow. They will also cause the market to overreach on the highs and lows, because of the scramble for hedging cover.

The prospect for gold, therefore, is a lively market in which it may be wiser to go to bed at night with your position square. At least you can rest in the knowledge that there is a certain sense of security that the downside on gold is rather well protected by a large army of small buyers in every corner of the globe who know a bargain when they see one. They did in 1970, when gold was $35, and again in 1993 at $330: on the first occasion the peak took ten years to arrive. This time things may move a little faster. Gold looks set up to celebrate the millennium in fine style, and could go into the twenty-first century with a record bull market.

# Appendices

# Appendix I: Western World Gold Supply (tonnes)

| | Western World mine production | Net communist sales (purchases) | Net official sales (purchases) | Old gold scrap | Supply to private sector |
|---|---|---|---|---|---|
| 1950 | 755 | N/A | (288) | – | 467 |
| 1951 | 733 | N/A | (235) | – | 498 |
| 1952 | 755 | N/A | (205) | – | 550 |
| 1953 | 755 | 67 | (404) | – | 418 |
| 1954 | 795 | 67 | (595) | – | 267 |
| 1955 | 835 | 67 | (591) | – | 311 |
| 1956 | 871 | 133 | (435) | – | 569 |
| 1957 | 906 | 231 | (614) | – | 523 |
| 1958 | 933 | 196 | (605) | – | 524 |
| 1959 | 1000 | 266 | (671) | – | 595 |
| 1960 | 1049 | 177 | (262) | – | 964 |
| 1961 | 1080 | 266 | (538) | – | 808 |
| 1962 | 1155 | 178 | (329) | – | 1004 |
| 1963 | 1204 | 489 | (729) | – | 964 |
| 1964 | 1249 | 400 | (631) | – | 1018 |
| 1965 | 1280 | 355 | (196) | – | 1439 |
| 1966 | 1285 | (67) | 40 | – | 1258 |
| 1967 | 1250 | (5) | 1404 | – | 2649 |
| 1968 | 1245 | (29) | 620 | – | 1836 |
| 1969 | 1252 | (15) | (90) | – | 1147 |

| | | | | | |
|------|------|-------|-------|------|------|
| 1970 | 1273 | (3)   | (236) | –    | 1034 |
| 1971 | 1233 | 54    | 96    | –    | 1383 |
| 1972 | 1177 | 213   | (151) | –    | 1239 |
| 1973 | 1111 | 275   | 6     | –    | 1392 |
| 1974 | 996  | 220   | 20    | –    | 1236 |
| 1975 | 946  | 149   | 9     | –    | 1104 |
| 1976 | 964  | 412   | 58    | –    | 1434 |
| 1977 | 962  | 401   | 269   | –    | 1632 |
| 1978 | 972  | 410   | 362   | –    | 1744 |
| 1979 | 959  | 199   | 544   | –    | 1702 |
| 1980 | 962  | 90    | (230) | 492  | 1313 |
| 1981 | 985  | 280   | (276) | 242  | 1231 |
| 1982 | 1031 | 203   | (85)  | 2443 | 1392 |
| 1983 | 1121 | 93    | 142   | 296  | 1652 |
| 1984 | 1170 | 205   | 85    | 294  | 1754 |
| 1985 | 1239 | 210   | (132) | 319  | 1636 |
| 1986 | 1300 | 402   | (145) | 492  | 2049 |
| 1987 | 1387 | 303   | (72)  | 434  | 2052 |
| 1988 | 1552 | 263   | (285) | 353  | 1883 |
| 1989 | 1682 | 266   | 366   | 363  | 2677 |
| 1990 | 1746 | 412   | 7     | 493  | 2658 |
| 1991 | 1775 | 222   | 58    | 407  | 2462 |
| 1992 | 1841 | 66    | 599   | 435  | 2941 |

The definition of official sales was extended from 1974 to include the activities of government controlled investment and monetary agencies in addition to central bank operations. This category also includes IMF disposals.

Old gold scrap figures are only available from 1980.

Source: Gold Fields Mineral Services, *Gold 1993*.

# Appendix II: World Gold Mine Production (tonnes)

| | 1983 | 1984 | 1985 | 1986 | 1987 | 1988 | 1989 | 1990 | 1991 | 1992 |
|---|---|---|---|---|---|---|---|---|---|---|
| **Europe** | | | | | | | | | | |
| Western Europe | 14.1 | 15.1 | 16.5 | 15.3 | 16.9 | 18.6 | 24.9 | 28.1 | 28.7 | 23.5 |
| Eastern Europe | 5.3 | 5.3 | 5.2 | 5.4 | 5.6 | 5.1 | 5.3 | 5.5 | 4.4 | 4.6 |
| *Total Europe* | 19.4 | 20.4 | 21.7 | 20.7 | 22.5 | 23.7 | 30.2 | 33.6 | 33.1 | 28.1 |
| **North America** | | | | | | | | | | |
| United States | 62.6 | 66.0 | 79.5 | 118.3 | 154.9 | 201.0 | 265.5 | 294.2 | 293.5 | 322.2 |
| Canada | 73.0 | 86.0 | 90.0 | 105.7 | 116.5 | 134.8 | 159.5 | 167.0 | 176.6 | 157.4 |
| *Total North America* | 135.6 | 152.0 | 169.5 | 224.0 | 271.4 | 335.8 | 425.0 | 461.2 | 470.1 | 479.6 |
| **Latin America** | | | | | | | | | | |
| Brazil | 58.7 | 61.5 | 72.3 | 67.4 | 84.8 | 102.2 | 101.2 | 84.1 | 78.6 | 76.5 |
| Chile | 23.5 | 22.2 | 22.8 | 24.0 | 23.3 | 26.7 | 29.0 | 33.3 | 33.0 | 39.5 |
| Colombia | 17.7 | 21.2 | 26.4 | 27.1 | 32.5 | 33.4 | 31.7 | 32.5 | 30.7 | 29.9 |
| Peru | 9.9 | 10.5 | 10.9 | 10.9 | 10.8 | 10.0 | 12.6 | 14.6 | 15.1 | 15.6 |
| Venezuela | 6.0 | 9.5 | 12.0 | 15.0 | 16.0 | 20.0 | 17.1 | 14.2 | 13.2 | 11.7 |
| Mexico | 7.4 | 7.6 | 8.0 | 8.3 | 9.0 | 10.4 | 10.8 | 9.6 | 8.5 | 9.9 |
| Bolivia | 4.0 | 4.0 | 6.0 | 6.0 | 6.0 | 9.0 | 11.5 | 10.4 | 10.0 | 7.9 |
| Ecuador | 1.1 | 1.2 | 3.0 | 6.0 | 8.0 | 9.0 | 11.3 | 9.3 | 7.5 | 6.8 |
| Dominican Republic | 10.8 | 10.6 | 10.4 | 9.1 | 7.9 | 6.7 | 5.5 | 4.3 | 3.6 | 3.0 |
| Other | 5.6 | 6.0 | 6.7 | 7.2 | 7.3 | 7.3 | 6.4 | 7.4 | 8.0 | 8.9 |
| *Total Latin America* | 144.7 | 154.3 | 178.5 | 181.0 | 205.6 | 234.7 | 237.1 | 219.7 | 208.2 | 209.7 |
| **Asia** | | | | | | | | | | |
| Indonesia | 2.1 | 3.6 | 5.6 | 8.4 | 12.2 | 12.3 | 10.8 | 13.3 | 18.4 | 40.4 |
| Philippines | 33.3 | 34.3 | 36.9 | 38.7 | 39.5 | 39.2 | 38.0 | 37.2 | 30.5 | 27.2 |
| Japan | 3.1 | 3.2 | 5.3 | 10.3 | 8.6 | 7.3 | 6.1 | 7.3 | 8.3 | 8.9 |
| Malaysia | 1.2 | 2.6 | 2.6 | 2.6 | 2.6 | 3.2 | 3.0 | 2.9 | 2.8 | 3.5 |
| South Korea | 1.9 | 2.6 | 1.0 | 3.5 | 3.8 | 4.4 | 4.9 | 2.2 | 2.1 | 2.0 |
| Other | 2.3 | 2.4 | 2.1 | 2.5 | 1.7 | 3.5 | 5.6 | 7.9 | 8.9 | 9.9 |
| *Total Asia* | 43.9 | 48.7 | 53.5 | 66.0 | 68.4 | 69.9 | 68.4 | 70.8 | 71.0 | 91.9 |
| **Africa** | | | | | | | | | | |
| South Africa | 679.7 | 683.3 | 671.7 | 640.0 | 607.0 | 621.0 | 607.5 | 605.1 | 601.1 | 614.1 |
| Ghana | 11.8 | 11.6 | 12.0 | 11.5 | 11.7 | 12.1 | 15.3 | 17.3 | 27.3 | 34.0 |
| Zimbabwe | 14.1 | 14.5 | 14.7 | 14.9 | 14.7 | 14.8 | 16.0 | 16.9 | 17.8 | 18.5 |
| Zaire | 6.0 | 10.0 | 8.0 | 8.0 | 12.0 | 12.5 | 10.6 | 9.3 | 8.8 | 7.0 |
| Other | 15.0 | 15.0 | 17.0 | 18.2 | 25.0 | 27.5 | 25.2 | 25.0 | 30.2 | 33.2 |
| *Total Africa* | 726.6 | 734.4 | 723.4 | 692.6 | 670.4 | 687.9 | 674.6 | 673.6 | 685.2 | 706.8 |

**Oceania**

| | | | | | | | | | | |
|---|---|---|---|---|---|---|---|---|---|---|
| Australia | 30.6 | 39.1 | 58.5 | 75.1 | 110.7 | 157.0 | 203.6 | 243.1 | 236.1 | 240.0 |
| Papua New Guinea | 18.4 | 18.7 | 31.3 | 36.1 | 33.9 | 36.6 | 33.8 | 33.6 | 60.8 | 71.2 |
| New Zealand | 0.3 | 0.8 | 0.9 | 1.4 | 1.2 | 2.5 | 5.0 | 6.0 | 7.5 | 10.2 |
| Fiji | 1.2 | 1.6 | 1.9 | 2.7 | 2.8 | 4.1 | 4.4 | 4.1 | 2.8 | 3.0 |
| *Total Oceania* | 50.5 | 60.2 | 92.6 | 115.3 | 148.6 | 200.2 | 246.8 | 286.8 | 307.2 | 324.4 |

| | | | | | | | | | | |
|---|---|---|---|---|---|---|---|---|---|---|
| **Western world total** | 1120.7 | 1170.0 | 1239.2 | 1299.6 | 1386.9 | 1552.2 | 1682.1 | 1745.7 | 1774.8 | 1840.5 |

**Other countries**

| | | | | | | | | | | |
|---|---|---|---|---|---|---|---|---|---|---|
| Soviet Union | 267.0 | 269.0 | 271.0 | 275.0 | 277.0 | 280.0 | 285.0 | 270.0 | 252.0 | 237.0 |
| China | 58.0 | 59.0 | 59.0 | 65.0 | 72.0 | 78.0 | 86.0 | 95.0 | 110.0 | 118.0 |
| North Korea | – | – | – | – | – | – | 9.5 | 13.0 | 13.0 | 17.0 |
| Mongolia | – | – | – | – | – | – | – | 5.0 | 4.0 | 4.0 |
| *Total other countries* | 325.0 | 328.0 | 330.0 | 340.0 | 349.0 | 358.0 | 380.5 | 383.0 | 379.0 | 376.0 |

| | | | | | | | | | | |
|---|---|---|---|---|---|---|---|---|---|---|
| **World total** | 1445.7 | 1498.0 | 1569.2 | 1639.6 | 1735.9 | 1910.2 | 2062.6 | 2128.7 | 2153.8 | 2216.5 |

Source: Gold Fields Mineral Services, *Gold 1993.*

# Appendix III: Western World Gold Supply and Demand (tonnes)

| | 1983 | 1984 | 1985 | 1986 | 1987 | 1988 | 1989 | 1990 | 1991 | 1992 |
|---|---|---|---|---|---|---|---|---|---|---|
| **Supply** | | | | | | | | | | |
| Mine production | 1121 | 1170 | 1239 | 1300 | 1387 | 1552 | 1682 | 1746 | 1775 | 1841 |
| Net communist sales | 93 | 205 | 210 | 402 | 303 | 263 | 266 | 412 | 222 | 66 |
| Net official sales | 142 | 85 | – | – | – | – | 366 | 7 | 58 | 599 |
| Old gold scrap | 296 | 294 | 319 | 492 | 434 | 353 | 363 | 493 | 407 | 435 |
| Gold loans | – | 3 | 38 | 17 | 55 | 164 | 78 | 5 | – | – |
| Forward sales | 4 | 35 | 18 | 20 | 72 | 102 | 79 | 229 | 90 | 149 |
| Option hedging | – | – | 6 | 8 | 22 | 63 | – | 7 | 1 | 91 |
| Disinvestment | – | 58 | 164 | – | – | 186 | 19 | – | 299 | 2 |
| **Total Supply** | 1656 | 1849 | 1995 | 2238 | 2273 | 2683 | 2853 | 2898 | 2852 | 3182 |
| **Demand** | | | | | | | | | | |
| Fabrication: | | | | | | | | | | |
| Jewellery | 851 | 1101 | 1198 | 1177 | 1223 | 1542 | 1912 | 2046 | 2132 | 2461 |
| Electronics | 108 | 1332 | 116 | 124 | 126 | 135 | 139 | 149 | 152 | 141 |
| Other | 303 | 284 | 243 | 470 | 325 | 261 | 273 | 259 | 287 | 257 |
| Total fabrication | 1261 | 1517 | 1556 | 1771 | 1673 | 1837 | 2324 | 2454 | 2571 | 2859 |
| Net official purchases | – | – | 132 | 145 | 72 | 285 | – | – | – | – |
| Bar hoarding | 73 | 332 | 306 | 214 | 259 | 461 | 514 | 207 | 237 | 238 |
| Gold loans | – | – | – | – | – | – | – | – | 45 | 85 |
| Option hedging | – | – | – | – | – | – | 15 | – | – | – |
| Investment | 322 | – | – | 108 | 268 | – | – | 238 | – | – |
| **Total Demand** | 1656 | 1849 | 1995 | 2238 | 2273 | 2683 | 2853 | 2898 | 2852 | 3182 |
| Gold price (London PM, US$/oz) | 423.68 | 360.68 | 317.32 | 367.92 | 446.07 | 436.77 | 380.79 | 383.59 | 362.26 | 343.95 |

Source: Gold Fields Mineral Services, *Gold 1993*.

# Bibliography

**General Books**

W. J. Busschau, *Measure of Gold*, Central News Agency, Johannesburg, 1949.

Timothy Green, *The New World of Gold*, Weidenfeld & Nicholson, London, and Walker & Co., New York, 1985.

Timothy Green, *The Prospect for Gold: The View to the Year 2000*, Rosendale Press, London, 1987.

Timothy Green with Deborah Russell, *The Gold Companion: The A–Z of Mining, Marketing, Trading and Technology*, Rosendale Press, London, 1991.

Roy Jastram, *The Golden Constant*, John Wiley & Sons, New York, 1977.

Brian Kettle, *Gold*, Graham & Trotman, London, 1982.

Pierre Lassonde, *The Gold Book*, Penguin Books, Toronto, 1990.

C. H. V. Sutherland, *Gold: Its Beauty, Power and Allure*, Thames & Hudson, London, 1959.

**History**

Leslie Aitchison, *A History of Metals*, 2 vols, Macdonald & Evans, London, 1960.

R. S. Anderson, *Australian Goldfields*, D. S. Ford, Sydney, 1956.

Pierre Berton, *The Golden Trail*, Macmillan, Toronto, 1954.

Sir John Clapham, *The Bank of England: A History*, 2 vols., Cambridge University Press, Cambridge, 1994.

*Gold*, special number of *The Times*, London, 1933.

Timothy Green, *Precious Heritage: The Story of Mocatta & Goldsmid*,
  Rosendale Press, London, 1984.
J. S. Halliday, *The World Rushed In: The California Gold Rush Experience*,
  Gollancz, London, 1983.
W. P. Morrell, *The Gold Rushes*, A. & C. Black, London, 1940.
R. S. Sayers, *The Bank of England, 1891–1944*, Cambridge University
  Press, Cambridge, 1976.
Robert Skidelsky, *John Maynard Keynes, Hopes Betrayed, 1883–1920*,
  Macmillan, London, 1983.
Robert Skidelsky, *John Maynard Keynes, The Economist as Saviour, 1920–
  1937*, Macmillan, London, 1992.

**Mining**
T. E. Anin, *Gold in Ghana*, revised 3rd edition, Selwyn Publishers, Ilford
  and Accra, 1993.
A. P. Cartwright, *The Gold Miners*, Purnell & Sons, Cape Town, 1962.
W. H. Emmons, *Gold Deposits of the World*, McGraw-Hill, New York,
  1937.
J. D. Littlepage and Demaree Bess, *In Search of Soviet Gold*, Harcourt
  Brace & Co., New York, 1938.
E. H. MacDonald, *Alluvial Mining*, Chapman & Hall, London and New
  York, 1983.
Mase Westpac Ltd, *The Winning of Gold*, London, 1990.

**Markets and Trading**
Robert Beale, *Trading in Gold Futures*, Woodhead-Faulkner, Cambridge,
  1985.
Terry Mayer, *Commodity Options, A User's Guide to Speculating and
  Hedging*, New York Institute of Finance, New York, 1983.
Jeffery Nichols, *The Complete Book of Gold Investing*, Dow Jones-Irwin,
  New York, 1987.
Paul Sarnoff, *Trading in Gold*, Woodhead-Faulkner, Cambridge, 1989.

**Monetary Role**
W. J. Busschau, *Gold and International Liquidity*, South African Institute of
  International Affairs, Johannesburg, 1971.
Paul Einzig, *Primitive Money*, Eyre & Spottiswoode, London, 1948.
J. K. Galbraith, *Money*, André Deutsch, London, 1975.
Sir Roy Harrod, *Reforming the World's Money*, Macmillan, London, 1965.
R. G. Hawtrey, *The Gold Standard in Theory and Practice*, 5th edition,
  Longman Green, London, 1947.
E. W. Kemmerer, *Gold and the Gold Standard*, McGraw-Hill, New York,
  1944.

J. M. Keynes, *Treatise on Money*, Macmillan, London, 1930.
Robert Triffin, *Gold and the Dollar Crisis*, Yale University Press, New Haven, Conn., and London, 1961.

**Jewellery and Industry**
Guido Gregorietti, *Jewellery Through the Ages*, Hamlyn, London, 1979.
Graham Hughes, *The Art of Jewellery*, Peerage Books, London, 1972.
Edmund M. Wise, *Gold: Recovery, Properties and Applications*, D. Van Nostrand Inc., New York, 1964.

**Journals and Surveys**
*Central Banking*, quarterly, Central Banking Publications Ltd, London.
*Financial Times* World Gold Conferences, annual publication of speakers' papers, Financial Times Conference Division, London.
Gary O'Callaghan, *The structure and operation of the World Gold Market*, IMF Occasional Paper No. 105, Washington D.C., 1993
*Gold Bulletin* and *Gold Patent Digest*, World Gold Council, Geneva, Switzerland.
*Gold 1969–1988*, the annual surveys from Consolidated Gold Fields plc, London.
*Gold 1989–1993*, the annual surveys from Gold Fields Mineral Services Ltd, London.
*Gold Gazette*, published fortnightly, Resource Information Unit, Subiaco, Western Australia.
*Jewellery News Asia*, monthly, Hong Kong.
*L'orafo italiano*, quarterly, Milan, Italy.
*International Gold Mining Newsletter*, monthly, Mining Journal Ltd, London.
Papers, articles and speeches by RTZ staff, including papers on gold loans, options and hedging by Jessica Jacks, numbers 1–15, RTZ Corporation plc, London.
World Gold Council speakers' papers, annual meetings, Montreux 1992, Istanbul 1993.

# Index